THE MISSING LANDS

Also by this Author...

The Lost Art of Resurrection
Initiation, secret chambers and the quest for the Otherworld

First Templar Nation
How the Knights Templar created Europe's first nation-state

The Divine Blueprint
Temples, power places and the global plan to shape the human soul
(formerly Common Wealth)

Secrets In The Fields
The science and mysticism of crop circles

Chartres Cathedral
The missing or heretic guide

Book text and design© 2019 Freddy Silva

10 9 8 7 6 5 4 3 2 1

www.invisibletemple.com

to those who Watch

ACKNOWLEDGEMENTS

Teotokai Andrew, for the generous sharing of his people's hidden history. Peter Marsh for opening new doors in Polynesia. Jos and Chris at Castle Hill Station for access to the land. Mikeljon Winckel at eLocal Magazine for the images. My friends Irena Stenner, Marilee Marrinan and Wendy Craig for the valuable support. Miguel Angel Vergara for his friendship and invaluable knowledge of the Maya. Edgar Mijita, my excellent guide in the Andes. The librarians I overwork at Library of Congress and Portland Library. Alexander Turnbull Library, Wellington. Regina Meredith for the time. Gaia TV for the platform. And all you supporters out there. Thankx.

CONTENTS

1 THE CERTAINTY THAT THINGS ARE MUCH OLDER 15

Temples older than the flood; an ancient designed language; overturning the academic model; civilization suddenly and mysteriously appears.

2 LAST MINUTE ON EARTH 23

Great flood eyewitness accounts; why the Great Salt Lake is salty; forewarning by gods; Andean fear of comets; Fire Water and rocks that fall from the sky; rebuilding temples at high altitude; the value of myth; dating the great flood.

3 THE BIRTHPLACE OF GODS 35

New Zealand's hidden prehistory; Maori were not the first; red-haired giants; Urukehu gods travel between the Andes and New Zealand; where the gods first drew breath; Waitaha, the first people; the birthplace before 10,000 BC; the Tiwanaku-Easter Island-New Zealand antediluvian connection.

4 BUILT BEFORE THE FLOOD 57

The question of a pre-flood civilization; everything appears in 8000 BC; the Inka didn't build it; the true age of Tiwanaku and Puma Punku; four Andean building periods; Viracocha and his seven Shining Ones; white-skinned tall people; the city of Shining People; antediluvian projects interrupted by flood.

5 BEARDS 77

The Puquina recall Mu; the gods' distinctive beards; missing land of Kainga Nuinui; Easter Island's underwater quarry; bearded moai; arrival of seven sages; megaliths in the Marquesas; dating the moai; burying moai in New Zealand; Göbekli Tepe, hill of Osiris; the Orion-Giza-Göbekli Tepe correlation 10,450 BC; containers of knowledge on Pillar 43; the Enclosure of Anu; the H symbol, Orion and the ball courts of Yucatan; T-pillars and the Breath of God; temples inherited from antediluvian civilization.

6 POLYNESIAN BLONDES, ANDEAN REDHEADS 99

The Mandan of Dakota; Apkallu sages in the Pacific; Te Pitaka, the missing land of Anunaki; blonde and red-haired gods; Pacific island megaliths connected to the Andes and Egypt; underwater roads; Flores and Samoa megaliths built by tall ones; giants of Fiji, Togareva, Samoa, New Zealand and Solomon Islands; Egyptian language in Polynesia; Yasawa cave alignment 13,000 BC; red hair, fair skin people of New Zealand and Tahiti; white skin people of Ra; New Zealanders from the Middle East; Starwalkers and seafarers; redhead elongated skulls of Paracas and the Black Sea.

7 BUILT BEFORE THE FLOOD REDUX 119

Mystery of the Kaimanawa wall; geometric engravings in Java 500,000 BC; Gunung Padang temple, 22,000 BC; the 30,000-year old Oklahoma floor; Jericho c.9000 BC; Baalbek's 1800-ton monoliths; the Baalbek-Giza alignment.

8 MADE IN EGYPT BEFORE THE FLOOD 133

Osirion, a free-standing temple; Cygnus alignment 10,000 BC; Aku, ahu, Shining Ones and Easter Island; antediluvian culture reborn at Iwnw 10,400 BC; rebuilding the former world of the gods; sudden agricultural revolution on the Nile; Giza pyramids as pre-flood buildings; Saurid's vision of meteorites and the flood; pyramids in the time of Vega, 12,000 BC; Twt builds a vault for his books; true age of the Serapeum; locating the Serapeum after the flood; the Bent Pyramid, Angkor, Puma Punku and the 6:5 ratio.

9 THE ITZA, THE KAAN AND THE BALAM 155

Itzá arrive in Yucatan 9,600 BC; sunken Atitlán; founding of Utatlàn; Uxmal and the Architects of the Sky; the language of light at Tikal; new Atitlán on Flores island; Mayans validate Plato; civilizing gods Itzamma, K'uKuulKaan and Quetzcoatl; comparison to Izanami and Izanagi of Japan; the Olmec of Mu'ul; Chichen Itzá is older; underwater spirit roads; drowned caves and Mayan artefacts.

10 SUDDENLY SUBMERGED 171

Disappearing islands; when Egypt and Arabia were seas; menhirs 6000 ft below sea level; Maltese temples at 12,000 BC; Malta succumbs to tsunamis; Maltese art in Tiwanaku; reclusive culture of elongated heads; underwater pyramid in the Açores; Atlantic rocks exposed at 15,000 BC; temples built to mathematical world grid; Cuba's underwater city; Nan Madol and tall sorcerers; stones levitated by flying dragon; Taiwan as Tulan; sunken citadel of Yoganumi; Kumari Kandam and sunken antediluvian academies 16,000 BC.

11 SEVEN SAGES, TALL GODS AND OTHER IMMORTALS 197
Seven Rshis and other wisdom keepers; the island home of the Followers of Horus; 26,000 years of Egyptian kings; Sumerian, Japanese, Maya and Chinese dynasties before the flood; Japan's flying Sky-Rock boats; mysterious Kyushu island; Osaka megaliths; traditions of flying gods in Indochina; Visvakarma builds flying Vimanna vehicles; the brotherhoods of the Urshu, Watchers, Aku Shemsu Hor, Apkallu, and Lolos; Twt, Osiris, Viracocha and other scientist magicians.

12 PEOPLE OF THE SERPENT 213
Portugal's flood gods; the Kaanul of Yucatan; Quetzcoatl the Caucasian; serpent boats; K'uKuulKaan's companions; serpent cities; island of Snake People; Chinese dragons and divine bloodline; antediluvian serpent goddess Nu Kwa; snake venom and long life; Nagas of the east; Fiji's naga temple; Naga kings of Laos and Cambodia; Angkor, Draco's mirror in 10,500 BC; Nagas take on human form; homeland in the sea; Mesopotamia's serpent goddess; the Annunagi.

13 A MEETING WITH THE LORDS OF ANU 231
Anunaki on Easter Island; home of the Anu in Bahrain; the lost sailor and the serpent king; Anunaki and the People of the Serpent; Nommos of the Dogon as Watchers; Sumeria's older flood myth; records preserved for 150,000 years; Ua-annu and Apkallu created civilization before flood; Idris, Enoch and Twt were one; Enmed-uranna visits the gods; Jewish discrediting of the Watchers; Anunaki compound at Gar-sag; forty-nine Lords of Anu; the Watchers, the ones who are awake; why Shining Ones shone; Apkallu as white men; why some Watchers fell.

14 THE MECHANICS OF A COMET 253
Inland salt water lakes; Hopi in 8000 BC; comet impacts and the Younger Dryas; Earth's rotational shift and climate change; correlation to Shoemaker Levy comet; recurring conflagrations; comparing Solon, Plato, the Egyptians, Popol Vuh and Akkadian myth; Erra Epic and the Last Glacial Maximum; flipping poles and changes to planet orbit; ancient 360-day calendars.

15 MISSING COASTS 263

Crust displacement; when south was north; out-of-place maps; rivers in the Sahara; homelands of the primeval ones; Hor and Twt move to Egypt 10,400 BC; magic of the Builder Gods; Ta Neterw; Mogao caves and the map of a missing Pacific land; Muia of the Hopi, Mu'ul of the Maya; Era of Overturning.

16 STAR PEOPLE 277

Hopi worldview; antediluvian technological society; Massau'u and the Ant people; red Ant Men of Yucatan; Zuni Star People; Lookers and Watchers; katsina as pilots; flying shields; Three Mesas and Orion's Belt; Walpi, Place of the Watchers; Star People and Starwalkers; Lakota and space visitors; meeting the Watchers in Utah; thermal lances of the Tula and other technology.

17 THE TERRIBLE TAURIDS 297

November's day of the dead; associations with Pleiades; Hopi Wuwutcim ceremony; seven stars of death; Aboriginal Water Girls; fear of comets in China and Polynesia; Sumeria's great celestial inundation; Earth's orbit and path of debris 10,800 BC and 9700 BC; meteor impacts and nanodiamonds; the Carolina Bays and the 9700 BC impact; impact of Taurid meteor stream.

18 ORION THE UBIQUITOUS 307

How temples mirror Orion; non-terrestrial interpretation of the homeland of the gods; connection to Ur-annu and Anasazi; the True Shepherd of Anu; sky-ground relationship of Hopi mesas; Soyal ceremony; Masau'u the Watcher; Osiris, Orion and the katsina Sohu; the Pyramid Texts; ascent to Orion by metal throne; spiritual resurrection; Aboriginal Watchers arrive from Orion; Waitaha relationship with Orion's Belt; the Fish Trap of Outer Space, the Urukehu and the Followers of Horus; the belt of Orion as a doorway.

19 THIS UNSHELTERING SKY 319

Sótuknang's message to this World; Aztec postpone end of the world; gods leave evidence of their existence; the purpose of megaliths and long calendars; sacred sites and disconnected culture; Watchers and crop circles; Earth is missing in 2038; collision hazard with Taurids; the 19-mile asteroid; NASA's meteorite obsession; previous impacts and plasma events; Maya sixty-year window; reversal of poles 10,400 BC and 2030; altering the outcome; intention experiments; temples and consciousness; discovering the god within.

REFERENCES 337

CREDITS 359

INDEX 360

"Whispers tend to enlarge the unmet person."

— Paul Thereux

THE THREE MOST RECENT GLACIAL PERIODS ARE CALLED THE OLDEST, OLDER, AND YOUNGER DRYAS.

They are named for an eight-petal alpine wildflower. The Oldest Dryas began c.13,000 BC and ended with a brief warm spell until another freeze — the Older Dryas — began c.12,000 BC. It too ended with a warm spell.

The Younger Dryas began c.10,800 BC and ended c.9700 BC. Both markers occurred in a geological instant when large objects collided with the Earth. The last event generated a global flood whose waves reached the Himalaya.

During the Younger Dryas it is believed only primitive people populated the Earth. Yet around them existed someone else, a more advanced civilization whose deeds, traditions and monuments exist all around. After the flood, a select brotherhood appeared from the sea to assist humanity rebuild, then vanished...

...but not before leaving a warning.

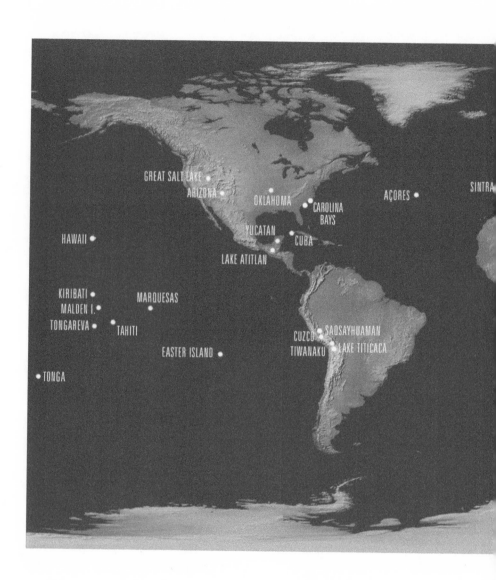

GREAT SALT LAKE
ARIZONA
OKLAHOMA
CAROLINA BAYS
AÇORES
SINTRA
HAWAII
YUCATAN
CUBA
LAKE ATITLAN
KIRIBATI
MARQUESAS
MALDEN I.
TONGAREVA
TAHITI
CUZCO
SAQSAYHUAMAN
TIWANAKU
LAKE TITICACA
EASTER ISLAND
TONGA

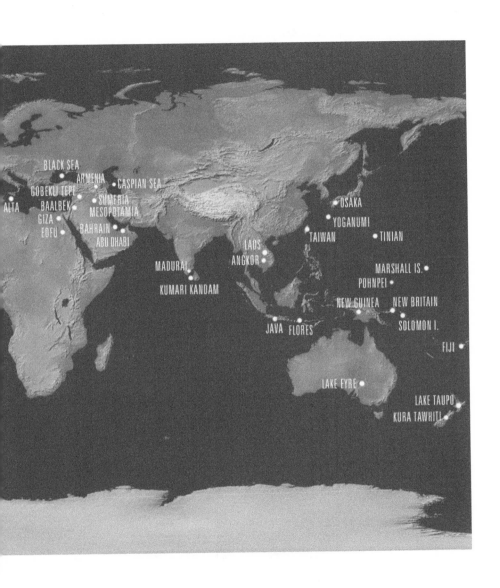

Where we are headed...

Saqsayhuaman, Peru. The Inka had no idea who built it either.

THE CERTAINTY THAT THINGS ARE MUCH OLDER

In 1914 the Dutch Department of Antiquities published a report of a temple made of columnar basalt, reached by five terraces on the slopes of a 3000-foot tall mountain in central Java. It would be another hundred years before exploration of the site using ground penetrating radar revealed something explosive: the temple was just one exposed section of a much larger site, and the Mountain of Light, as locals called it, turned out not to be a mountain at all but a large-scale engineering project, a series of step pyramids built over successive periods, complete with a sealed chamber. Traces of human activity date the colossal structure to around 22,000 BC.

At the other end of the Indonesian archipelago lies the island of Sumba, where villagers still use megaliths to build places of spiritual significance in the style of their forebears. No one remembers how long this tradition has been enacted, but local legends speak of unusual, giant people disembarking here after a global flood destroyed their homeland. These seafarers moved the original stones by means of some magical force from mountains on the other side of the island to where they stand today. One such monolith — a granite slab carved with perfectly squared, level and shallow steps — is identical in design to another at Saqsayhuaman, a megalithic metropolis 10,600 miles to the east, in Peru.

Another site in the Andes — on what used to be the ancient shore of Lake Titicaca before an earth-shattering cataclysm rearranged the region — is Puma Punku, one of the world's oldest temples, whose jumbled megaliths reveal an extraordinary level of finesse in the cutting and shaping of stone that modern masons are at pains to explain. How did primitive people achieve such results without metal tools or diamond drill technology?

The Bolivian altiplano is filled with oddities — such as the unsettling question of Aymara, a language some experts consider to be the oldest in the world. The computer scientist Ivan Guzman de Rojas demonstrated how Aymara is both skilfully designed and artificial — its syntax in particular, which, after careful analysis, was found to be rigidly structured and unambiguous, and seemingly developed from scratch, unlike standard language which evolves organically. Rojas proved how this ancient Andean tongue can be written concisely in the type of algebraic shorthand a computer can understand. Aymara is an algorithm with an ability to translate from one language to another, a bridge language, whereby the language of an original document can be translated into Aymara and then into any number of languages.[1]

And yet Aymara itself is derived from an earlier language, Puquina, a name likewise given to an Andean civilization whose remaining tribes-people still openly discuss their homeland, a landmass nicknamed Mu that once occupied a significant portion of the Pacific Ocean, from whence their predecessors fled after it sank during a global flood. It was they who assisted in setting up new temple cities on the shores of Lake Titicaca.[2]

At the northern end of the American continent, the Hopi maintain oral traditions recounting the destruction of the world on four separate occasions. The details of the second event appear to describe the onset of the Older Dryas glacial period some 14,000 years ago, but more to the point, they state how this climate change was induced by a violent alteration in the Earth's rotation and the reversal of its poles. In their words: "[the god] Sotuknang commanded the twins, Poqanhoya and Palongawhoya, to leave their posts at the north and south ends of the world's axis where they were stationed to keep the earth properly rotating. The twins had hardly abandoned their stations when the world, with no one to control it, teetered off balance, spun around crazily, then rolled over twice. Mountains plunged into the seas with a great splash, seas and lakes splashed over the land; and as the world spun through cold and lifeless space it froze into solid ice."[3]

Finally there is the case of Aotearoa, the island nation today called New Zealand, of which so little is ever mentioned and of whose prehistory even less is known. All this changed in 1994 when elders representing one of the nation's few remaining indigenous people, the Waitaha, published their oral traditions in which they describe their forebears — a race of gods called Urukehu — being overwhelmed by the gigantic waves of the great flood while traversing the Pacific, at a stroke placing their account some 11,000 years ago.

The Waitaha claim to have originated from Easter Island, one of the world's remotest islands, and yet they regularly set sail on large, ocean-going catamarans and undertook a 4000-mile adventure to New Zealand to pay tribute to the Birthplace of the Gods.[4] How did the Waitaha come to possess knowledge of such a distant land? From whom did they receive the coordinates to steer across a hostile and featureless ocean if not from master seafarers who'd already attempted the journey?

According to conventional thinking, everything described above ought not to have been possible during this prehistoric era. Wasn't this a time when humans were ignorant, barbaric and lived in caves like wild animals?

Speaking off the record, many historians and archaeologists now accept there is something deeply disturbing with the conventional paradigm of human evolution, one that imagines the slow but progressive linear rise of civilization. Faced with a mountain of new evidence presented by independent researchers and scholars alike, the mainstream theory of human prehistory becomes inadequate, the result of erroneous assumptions made two hundred years ago that were blindly regurgitated and subsequently accepted as valid facts. Yet when scrutinized, such assumptions disintegrate like piles of decaying bone.

Further complicating our understanding of what really took place during this antediluvian era is the fact that much, if not all prehistory has been written from a European, Anglo-Saxon point-of-view which, until recently, derided information from indigenous people as mere superstition or imaginative fabrication. Therefore what has generally been presented and taught about the origin of civilization is based on the assumptions of a tiny minority of the human race at the expense of the majority, particularly people whose ancestors knew better because they were closer to events and experiences that, in time, were immortalized in folklore and myth.

Recent discoveries are indeed undermining the accepted paradigm of human evolution. The birthplace of humanity is no longer seen as Ethiopia c.160,00 BC, but Morocco c.300,000 BC.[5] The earliest civilization, the

Sumerian, has been usurped by the Marrapan of the Indus Valley and the Scythian of the Carpathian region, who in turn are supplanted by an unknown people who built a factory and trading center in the Czech Republic 26,000 years ago.[6] As to language, the development of full human linguistics to infer information is now estimated to have developed at least 40,000 years ago,[7] while ancient art, believed to have begun with the Lascaux cave paintings around 17,000 BC, has been eclipsed by the discovery in a Siberian cave of a 40,000-year old finely carved green crystal bracelet, whose 0.3-inch diameter hole was created by the equivalent of a high-speed drill; latest research now puts the date closer to 70,000 BC.[8] And further, a female Venus figure from Berekhat Ram on the Golan Heights was found to have been carved more than 230,000 years ago.[9]

Then there's the problem of out-of-place temples and megalithic structures. Archaeologists tend to squeeze them into a socially-comfortable era beginning around 3500 BC, making the following monuments rather awkward: Stonehenge's original post holes 8000 BC, the Osirion of Abydos c.10,500 BC, Göbekli Tepe 10,200 BC, the Great Pyramids of Giza, 10,400 BC, Tiwanaku 15,000 BC, and Gunung Panang, our artificial mountain in Java, 22,000 BC.

It appears civilization has been a long, on-going experiment. And it emerged at not one but multiple locations across the Earth, far earlier than imagined and, rather than developing linearly, it has endured cycle upon cycle before succumbing to periodic convulsion and obliteration. Virtually every culture other than the Western accepts this as fact.

Mainstream historians find it perfectly acceptable that ancient civilizations such as the Olmec, Maya, Aymara, Egyptian and Sumerian sprang up complete, with fully-developed understanding of astronomy, geometry, mathematics, language, writing, complex mythology, megalithic construction technique, art, metallurgy, animal and crop domestication, and long-range ocean navigation — skills requiring tens of thousands of years of patient and gradual development. But in each case there was no development, such abilities materialized overnight. Cultures that should not have been in contact with each other, so we are told, arrive on the scene with elegantly conceived and identical creation pantheons — such as Creator Gods who travel between worlds on a boat along the Milky Way, a myth shared by ancient Egyptians, Polynesians and Central Americans alike.

All these anomalies are perfectly acceptable to academia.

The problem of humanity's recent and uneven development was the subject of a NASA-commissioned investigation that pointed to this disturbing trend in evolved civilizations 'suddenly' appearing completely developed, to technology and agriculture 'suddenly' appearing around 10,000 years ago, and to science, mathematics and astronomy 'suddenly' manifesting in hotspots like Mesopotamia, Egypt, Yucatan, Peru and China.[10] Was it all a huge coincidence? Did all humanity spontaneously experience collective inspiration?

Or did space brothers visit the Earth in their sky ships to teach Neanderthals the finer graces of civilization?

Or better still, was the knowledge pre-existent, the sum of previous civilizations who succumbed to periodic cataclysms and man-made folly, whose existence was wiped out and buried deep beneath silt and sea, evidence of its grandeur condensed to myth and anomalous megalithic structures?

The aforementioned NASA report was written in 1972. Recently, the renowned space agency has become infatuated with meteorites and

Summit of Gunung Padang, Java. The interior dates to 22,000 BC.

asteroids and debris whose path the Earth cyclically crosses, bringing with it unimaginable chaos. A recent study by Czech astronomers warns of an increasing risk of significant hazardous and continent-damaging asteroids embedded within a specific meteor stream whose orbital path the Earth predictably intrudes every October and November, and again in June. This concentric ring of debris is so wide it takes the Earth two weeks to cross.[11]

Is the recurring encounter with this field of rubble responsible for wiping out a previous high civilization? Because it does not take a genius to realize that our ancestors were obsessed with the sky. Stone circle after stone circle, temple after temple, megalith after megalith tracks the Sun, Moon and stars, reference specific constellations, even mark stupendous lengths of time, and yet for all the hard work involved in their calculation and construction, anyone armed with a bundle of sticks could achieve the same on their front lawn. It is not necessary to move megaliths weighing up to 1600 tons — which today only one crane on Earth is capable of lifting — so that future generations could tell the time, unless there was a need to provide them with foreknowledge of looming events.

Geologists have so far pin-pointed fifty impact craters so massive they left impressions greater than 600 miles in diameter.[12] Yet despite such setbacks, life on Earth was defiant, it persevered. The mere fact you are reading this proves someone survived on a near-barren planet and told their offspring a tale of such proportion it would never be forgotten. We are told that since the close of the Younger Dryas 11,000 years ago, the present geologic period has been relatively stable, allowing humanity unprecedented upward mobility — some for better, some for worse — and yet this theory is misleading, for the Earth has succumbed to a dozen known catastrophes during this period. One of the most recent c.1600 BC shaped the rise and fall and regeneration of countless centers of civilization from Europe to the Middle East.

The truth is, we rebuild, adapt, become complacent, fall, and the cycle repeats *ad nauseam*. Ancient Chinese astronomers were well aware of far more important calendrical systems than those governing solar and lunar cycles. One of them tracks the Earth's 25,920-year axial rotation. During this great cycle, stargazers describe a cosmic mechanism winding itself up and unravelling in a great convulsion of nature, when "the sea is carried out of its bed, mountains spring out of the ground, rivers change their course, humans beings and everything are ruined, and the ancient traces effaced."[13]

If entire landmasses were obliterated, memory of such a disaster can take the extreme psychological form of collective amnesia. If entire civilizations fell, they took with them the learned and the literate, their homes and monuments pounded into oblivion and laid beneath thousands of years of mud and debris, evidence of their deeds buried deep beneath our feet, our cars and skyscrapers.

But indigenous traditions adamantly state that people *did* survive the great flood at the close of the Younger Dryas, individuals of unusual stature, whose advanced knowledge of astronomy, mathematics, architecture, and control of the mechanics of nature had them compared to gods. Their know-how became the catalyst for raising the human race from the state of barbarity to which it reverted. Myths were created. Legends spoke of global upheaval as a consequence of humanity falling out of sync with nature — storytelling mechanisms designed to engage audiences of the future with an unbroken narrative lest the events and lessons be forgotten. Because the events *were* real and, like a boomerang, liable to return.

It is probably for this reason why a network of temples was erected across the face of the Earth using stone of a size beyond what is both practical and necessary for the singular purpose of marking days for sowing and harvest. And how it all comes around, with astronomers and space agencies of late becoming obsessed with the sky and Earth-destroying projectiles, with hardly a week going by without a press release on the subject.

It seems we've been here before. And that's the point of this adventure.

If we invert the conventional European model and examine the narrative from the perspective of the oldest cultures on Earth, we receive a different version of ancient events, for virtually every one of them recalls an advanced antediluvian world civilization whose messengers survived an unimaginable catastrophe and disembarked at strategic locations after the Younger Dryas to build technologically advanced temples and establish laws which led to the sudden flourishing of human civilization. These gods were described as humanoid yet unusual of appearance and physique, magicians whose island homes succumbed to titanic forces.

So what happened 11,000 years ago? Who were these gods, where did they come from and what did they want with us?

The Great Salt Lake, Utah. The salt was introduced by a tidal wave of seawater that swept North America around 10,000 years ago.

LAST MINUTE ON EARTH

"There have been and there will be many and diverse destructions of mankind, of which the greatest are by fire and water, and lesser ones by countless other means. For in truth the story that is told in your country...has the fashion of a legend, but the truth of it lies in the occurrence of a shifting of the bodies in the heavens which move around the earth, and a destruction of the things on the earth by fierce fire, which recurs over long intervals."

— Egyptian priest to Solon [1]

Had you been living on Earth 11,700 years ago, today would be particularly challenging, shocking, potentially fatal and, if you survived, indelibly memorable.

The Wichita of Oklahoma describe their experience: "There came to the people some signs which showed that there was something in the north that looked like clouds. And the fowls of the air came, and the animals of the plains and woods were seen. The clouds... were a deluge. The deluge was all over the face of the earth."[2] Fortunately one wise man was forewarned, by shamanic dream or godly intervention, to prepare for the impending flood by selecting seeds and animals which were to be housed in a protective vessel. After the waters subsided he and his wife descended from a mountain, discovered domesticated corn, and together repopulated the Earth.

In another corner of North America, the Chocktaw faced the same plight: "The earth was plunged in darkness for a long time... a bright light finally appeared in the north... but it was mountain-high waves, rapidly coming nearer."[3]

As the oceans consumed the Earth, the Chiglit of Canada saw their dwellings blown away by terrific winds, and as they lashed their boats together, gale-driven waves traversed the Rocky Mountains, followed by intense heat, killing most people; the Sun and Moon disappeared, like all the land, and the few survivors faced a prolonged and bitterly cold climate. The Shokomish people made ropes of cedar limbs to fasten their canoes to the hills, all to no avail, because the flood waters rose higher and higher into the Olympic Mountains — to the west of today's Seattle — snapping ropes and casting the canoes adrift. Neighboring tribes in Oregon were luckier, their canoes came to rest upon the summit of Mt. Jefferson, 10,000 feet above sea level.[4]

A righteous man of the Yakima tribe was warned of such events in a vision which he shared with others: "I have heard from the Land Above, the land of the spirits, that a big water is coming that will cover all the land. Make a boat for the good people, let the bad people be killed by the water... The Earth will be destroyed."[5]

To the south, the Ute describe the sSun shivering into a thousand fragments that fell to Earth. One supernatural being caught in the conflagration ran from the blazing Earth, and as his own body began to burn, tears gushed forth creating a flood that engulfed the planet and put out the fires.

One factor corroborating such accounts is the Great Salt Lake that covers a goodly part of the high plains of northern Utah, allegedly the remnant of a massive body of freshwater created by glacial melt that once stretched into neighboring Idaho and Nevada. Evidence shows people once fished around its shores. It is claimed in geological circles that its saltiness was acquired from tiny amounts of mineral salts accumulating over time from streams feeding into the lake. The problem is, the salt in the Great Salt Lake is composed of sea salt, and the change occurred some 10,000 years ago — around the time tsunamis from the great flood are supposed to have overrun North America.

Traveling south along the American continent, the predecessors of the Maya recorded the event in great detail: "It was ruin and destruction... the sea was piled up... it was a great inundation.... People drowned in a sticky substance raining from the sky.... The face of the earth grew dark and the gloomy rain endured days and nights.... And then there was a great din of fire above their heads."[6] Survivors, which were few, describe the falling debris as a black viscous residue similar to bitumen, "much hail, black rain and mist, and indescribable cold."[7] Finally, as calm began to return, the K'iche' migrated inland after crossing a sea enveloped in a somber fog.[8]

The conflagration was not restricted to the Atlantic coastline of Central America, both coasts were simultaneously transgressed, "the sea, breaking out of its bounds following a terrifying shock, began to rise on the Pacific coast. But as the sea rose, filling up valleys and the plains around, the mountain of Ancasmarca rose too, like a ship on the waves. During the five days that this cataclysm lasted, the sun did not show its face and the Earth remained in darkness." [9]

More worryingly, the Maya describe the Sun rising only partially above the horizon and standing still for days, while the Moon also stood uncharacteristically motionless in the sky,[10] as though the Earth, hit by some stupendous cosmic impact, stopped rotating on its axis. Maya recordkeeping describes this era as the destruction of the Fourth Sun, a time when the world was plunged in darkness, literally and metaphorically, for twenty-five years. Amid this profound obscurity, ten years elapsed before the appearance of the Fifth Sun, the period marking the regeneration of humanity.[11]

Meanwhile in northern Mongolia, the Buryat were experiencing a particularly bad-hair day. A heavenly source forewarned a fellow named Shitkut to go into the forest to build a great ship into which he was to deposit specimens of all animals. Only one refused because it deemed itself so large that no flood could kill it. Alas, the flood that followed was so overwhelming that even this largest of creatures — the mammoth — became extinct.

Their neighbours to the west, the Tartars of central Siberia, add that a man called Nama built a ship with eight cables, each eighty fathoms long. Over the course of seven days the waters rose 480 feet, the cables reached their structural limit, snapped, and the ship floated free. All that could be seen from aboard were the tops of mountains. To the north, the Ugrians and Ostiaks describe how the few survivors were saved on their rafts or by clinging on to logs, settling in different parts of the Earth when the waters receded, and for this reason, different languages developed over time across the world.

By no means was the great flood restricted to a wall of mountain-high water, the event was accompanied by hurricane-force winds. As the Middle East was being ravaged, the flood — Arabs call it *tufan* (deluge) — was chaperoned by a mighty strong west wind, the *tyfoon*. Samoan islanders describe an accompanying acrid smell which "became smoke, which again became clouds... The sea too arose, and in a stupendous catastrophe of nature the land sank into the sea... new earth arose out of the womb of the last Earth" — referring to the islands of Tonga, Samoa, Rotuma, Fiji, and Uvea and Fotuma that subsequently rose out of the Pacific Ocean.[12]

The account from the Polynesian island of Takaofo describes how "the sky was low, then the winds and waterspouts and the hurricanes came, and carried up the sky to its present height." [13]

Over in Mesopotamia a man named Utnapishtim was minding his business when a god named Enki warned him to construct a giant boat with a height of one acre, in which he was to house his family, various craftsmen, animals and seeds, and prepare for a tumultuous ride. As he was about to close the hatch Utnapishtim saw what appeared to be a massive black cloud rising along the horizon to the south, which turned out to be a wall of mud-laden water. A great flash of light was followed by twelve days of darkness and hurricane-force winds, while the waters rose and overwhelmed the distant mountains. The land, he said, was smashed like a cup: "On the first day the tempest blew swiftly and brought the flood... No man could see his fellow. Nor could people be distinguished from the sky."

For six days the wind blew while torrent, tempest and flood raged at one another like sparring hosts overrunning the Earth. Utnapishtim's boat finally ran aground on the hills of Nisir, and for seven days he looked out and saw water everywhere. When land re-appeared it was flattened like a terrace, with destruction evident everywhere: "Desolation... stretched to heaven, all that was bright was turned into darkness... the hurricane, deluge, and tempest continued sweeping the land... and all human back to its clay was returned." [14]

Utnapishtim's experience is almost identical to that of his Sumerian neighbor Zin-Suddu, king of Shuruppak prior to the flood, who may have served as the model for Noah that future Israelites would borrow during their captivity in Babylon. The figure of a gargantuan eroded hull still lies on the slope of Mt. Ararat, deposited, strangely enough, along the same latitude as Mount Tomaros in Greece, landing place of Deucalion, the hero of the Greek flood narrative.

Somewhere in the Middle East another righteous man by the name of Enoch was forewarned of this impending catastrophe some two hundred years ahead of the event. He describes being admitted into the company of seven beings who led this scribe "to a mountain, the point of whose summit reached to heaven. And I saw the places of the luminaries and the treasuries of the stars... and beings came forth from heaven who were like white men, and four went forth from that place and three went with them. And those three... grasped me by the hand and took me up, away from the generations of the earth, and raised me up to a lofty place, and showed me a tower raised high above the earth... And one said to me, 'Remain here till you see everything that befalls.'" [15]

Enoch was subsequently shown the impending impact of a disintegrating comet, "seven stars like great burning mountains... a star fell from heaven... I saw many stars descend and cast themselves down from heaven... I saw how the earth was swallowed up in a great abyss, and mountains were suspended on mountains, and hills sank down on hills, and high trees were rent from their stems and hurled down and sunk into the abyss.... And the sea... is driven forward and disperses amid all the mountains.... And water gushed forth from above, rushing like a copious watercourse towards the northwest." [16]

One of the beings explains to Enoch how such meteorites "transgressed the commandments of the Lord in the beginning of their rising," essentially telling the flabbergasted scribe how these space rocks periodically become dislodged from their regular course, with the Earth in the wrong place at the wrong time. Enoch watched the futuristic vision of a wall of water swallowing animals and trees, sweeping across a desert to the east and reaching the mountains.

He was not alone. Somewhere in the region of the Indus Valley a man named Manu was washing himself when a similar god — this time disguised as a fish — warns him of an impending deluge that would sweep away all creatures. To save himself, Manu was instructed to build a boat, which he did, and when the floodwaters began to rise Manu fastened a rope to the fish's horn and the boat was steered over the Mountain of the North.

So strong is the memory of this event that it survived as an oral tradition for thousands of years in the high Andes. A herdsman saw his llamas staring in the direction of the Sun. Protecting his eyes with his hand, he looked up and saw a cluster of large objects between the Sun and Moon. The animals told him this was a sign that the world was about to be destroyed by a great deluge, so the herdsman gathered his family and animals and took refuge on the summit of a high mountain just as the waves rose and swamped the land. Many days passed before the waters receded, and in all this time the Sun was hidden by a great darkness.[17]

Two brothers and their families were similarly advised to take five days' worth of food and climb to the summit of the high mountain Huillcacoto, where they found a number of animals already ensconced in the safety of its caves. They moved their flocks and soon the rain began. It poured and poured. As predicted, all mountains were covered by water except the summit of Huillcacoto. Looking down into the valleys they heard the cries of dying humans overwhelmed by the waters. Miraculously, the mountain grew taller and taller as the waters rose. Even so, water lapped at the door of the cave, but still the mountain grew. For the next five days the Sun was said to have died and it remained night for five days.[18]

Those living on the edge of Lake Titicaca, 12,500 feet up on the altiplano of Bolivia, had to contend with the consequences of brusque tectonic shifts resulting from impact shockwaves generated by incoming aerial projectiles, for they witnessed the breaking of bulwarks on the lakes situated at greater altitude to the north, causing the release of a second unstoppable wall of water that overwhelmed the temple city of Tiwanaku, tossing its megaliths like matchsticks, crushing and jumbling its inhabitants along with fish, marine life, mammals, utensils, jewels, tools, pottery and shells into one confusing heap.[19]

When the story was transmitted to the Inka many thousands of years later, villagers were still paralyzed by the fear of a change in the appearance of the Sun because, they said, it foretold doom. A Spanish chronicler in 1555 described their trepidation: "[when] there is an eclipse of the Sun or the Moon the Indians cry and groan in great perturbation, thinking that the time has come in which the Earth will perish." [20]

Had these people found themselves in a bar with the ancient Chinese, the latter would have nodded in agreement with the accuracy of the story: "When the sky becomes hostile to living things and wishes to destroy them, it burns them; the Sun and the Moon lose their form and are eclipsed; the five planets leave their paths; the four seasons encroach one upon another; daylight is obscured; glowing mountains collapse; rivers are dried up; it thunders in winter, hoarfrost falls in summer; the atmosphere is thick and human beings choked; the state perishes; the aspect and the order of the sky are altered; the customs of the age are disturbed." [21] The Chinese recorded their most ancient knowledge in the *Yih King*, a book that is at least 5000 years old and whose origin is as mysterious as pyramids, yet at its core there are uncannily similar stories, for China has its own flood hero, Fu Hsi, who escaped the rising waters along with his wife and three sons and daughters to found Chinese civilization.

What kind of sky phenomena causes such a conflagration? The Voguls speak of a Creator God who sent a sea of fire upon the Earth in order to destroy the wickedness that had befallen the human race, referring to the event as Fire-Water.[22] It was a shared experience because the people of the East Indies speak of *snegle-das* (water of fire) that rained down from the sky and killed everyone.[23] In what seems to be a description of a comet, the Voguls describe it as a recurring conflagration appearing in the eastern sky, accompanied by a tail stretching from one corner to the other and the sound of a fearful thunder.

Manu leading Seven Sages during the flood. Identical groups of learned people are found throughout most indigenous flood stories.

Given the vast expanse of the Australian continent, Aboriginal tribes saw the event from slightly different perspectives yet all agree on the same outcome. The Bundaba tell of a mighty noise coming from a cloud in the north that grew bigger and bigger until it covered the entire sky. Gradually a great sound like rolling thunder arrived, accompanied by hurricane-force winds and the pouring of the sea from the mountains in the north, covering the entire land for days. Two people survived on a raft and were guided to the safety of Mt Broome. The culprit was Yunggalya (Running Star) from which several pieces fell to Earth and made holes in the ground.

But by far the most disturbing image comes from the Himalaya, the highest mountain range on Earth, hundreds of miles from the ocean. One would assume it was spared the ravages of monstrous waves, yet even this apparent safe haven of highlands was encroached by tidal waves claimed by Tibetans to have been generated by comets that regularly create upheaval on Earth.[24]

Such events are recorded in dramatic fashion in the *Kalevala* of the Finns. Once in a while Ukko, the highest of deities, relinquishes support of the heavens, and hailstones of iron rain down on Earth, resulting in a generation of darkness. As a consequence the seasons do not return to their established order. The Icelandic tradition adds that a never-ending winter followed the last conflagration, with only a pair of humans surviving to reseed the Earth.[25]

It seems that no matter who you were or where — the Chewong in Malaysia, the Karen in Burma, the Mechoacanesec in Central America, the Chibca in Colombia, the Canaria in Ecuador, the Tupinamba in Brazil, the Araucnaia in Chile, or the Luiseno, Sioux and Chickasaw in North America — the shockwaves of this catastrophe were permanently engraved upon every culture.

According to orthodox historians, humans did not get about much 11,000 yeas ago, so how did indigenous people on opposite corners of the globe come to own traditions sharing near identical details? The forewarning, the heat, gale force winds, the blotting out of the sky, Earth pausing on its axis, and so on. Most accounts agree that the wall of seawater rose as high as mountain summits, and in some cases actually surpassed them. The annals of Emperor Yao describe the waters reaching deep into the center of the Chinese mainland, "overtopping the great heights, threatening the heavens with their floods." The *Vedas* of the Tamil describe the highest mountains being "ground to powder and destroyed,"[26] while in the Andes the ocean left the shore before submerging South America with a terrible dim, and the Sun failed to appear for five days and nights.[27] Aboriginal cultures refer to this period as "the time of darkness," when sufficient debris ejected into the atmosphere would have been capable of inducing solar radiation for up to a thousand years.

THE MEMORABLE POWER OF MYTH

Whereas the modern world equates myth with imaginative invention, ancient cultures used it as an instrument for recording important facts and events so they would be memorized and recalled generation after generation. Such stories may seem alien and abstract to us because their social point of reference and literary construct differ from ours, and yet events were observed, then poeticized to give them artistic color, intrigue and conflict, before finally being mythologized to imbue the scene with imagery so unforgettable it would be branded upon the listener's imagination. Thus myth became the memory stick of earlier ages, a mnemonic device for transferring knowledge, particularly during times of illiteracy. For example, the telling of a sea voyage by a group of men to retrieve an important object was not enough, the story had to be embellished into Jason and the Argonauts, later rewritten for another audience as Arthur and the Grail. When dissected, such myths reveal multiple layers of information: mathematics, astronomy, astrology, history, even a road map to self-awareness and transcendence. Myth is a method of making connections at a level beyond the obvious and the superficial, an efficient technique for encoding a complex series of facts, so much so that its storytellers were highly prized because they were, in effect, wisdom keepers.

Folklore works in the same manner, recording events that indigenous cultures refer to as "time immemorial." For example, an archaeological excavation on the Heiltsuk peoples' reservation in British Columbia confirms their oral history of settlement at the site during the Younger Dryas. "It was a place that never froze during the ice age and it was a place where our ancestors flocked to for survival," said William Housty, a member of the Heiltsuk Nation. Subsequent dating of unearthed artefacts indeed places the tribe at this location in 12,000 BC, when much of North America was one massive ice sheet.[28]

In many flood myths and traditions the Sun is described as behaving abnormally. It is absent in Central America for five days, while in Persia and the Indus region — on the same latitude on the opposite side of the world — the Sun *remained* in the sky between five and ten days, suggesting the Earth's rotation did slow considerably or stopped altogether. The same phenomenon was observed much later in China c.2200 BC during the time of Emperor Yao, and evidence suggests another meteorite impacted the Earth c.2345 BC.[29]

Ancient accounts also describe a combustible fluid accompanying the global flood. It has been suggested this may have been the debris of a comet's tail, composed as it is of carbon and hydrogen — the components of petroleum that, when interacting with oxygen in the atmosphere, become highly combustible. The effects were predictably devastating: "For seven winters and summers the fire has raged... it has burnt up the earth."[30] Hailstones of iron descended from the sky, so say the myths of the Finns, making the Sun and Moon disappear, and the heavens replaced by new celestial bodies.[31]

It would be nine thousand years before the philosopher Philo learned of such stories during his tenure at Alexandria's fabled library. He succinctly summarized how, over the course of long periods of time, the Earth is subjected to "fire [that] pours out from above and spreads over many places and overruns great regions of the inhabited earth," [32] what astronomers today refer to as a mass coronal ejection, an eruption of plasma from the Sun. Before him, Plato compiled similar accounts handed down from those great students of the stars, the Chaldeans, who were under no illusion that the orbits and velocities of planets were in any way absolute, but instead are subject to change and variation.[33] They forewarned future citizens of the chaos such changes visit upon the Earth, one of them being the obliteration of all traces of former civilizations. Such observations became the foundation of Plato's accounts of the final destruction of Atlantis, which the philosopher elegantly wove into a dialogue between two statesmen, using the mechanism of creative storytelling to impart vital knowledge to future generations. Since modern historians fail to understand the importance of such a mechanism, his work is dismissed by them as fiction, despite his dating of the great flood aligning to within one hundred years of the latest supporting geological evidence.

Perhaps the most important thing about the flood stories — for that is what they are, real-life observations — is that they were transmitted by survivors and passed along orally from generation to generation, eventually recorded for posterity on paper, papyrus, vellum and stone. The *Vedas* of the Indian subcontinent provide a highly descriptive, if sometimes baffling narrative of events that took place in prehistoric times, one of them being the *pralayas* (cataclysms) which occasionally overrun the Earth, destroying everything, and how certain Rshis (wise men) survived such events to "repromulgate, at the beginning of the new age, the knowledge inherited by them as a sacred trust from their forefathers in the preceding age... Each *manvantara* or age thus has a Veda of its own which differs only in expression and not in sense from the antediluvian Veda." [34] Rather than haphazard, these catastrophes are claimed by many cultures to be predictable, typically associated with the close of a cycle, and seemingly in response to, or as a consequence of, humans transgressing the laws of nature — rebelling against the high gods, as the metaphor goes. Since what happens in terrestrial life is believed to be mirrored in the sky, a degeneration of society was reflected in the disturbance of heavenly order, when planets alter their habitual motions and meteorites fall from the sky.

Which brings us to the date of the great flood that brought the Younger Dryas to a close. In 2008 a team of Danish geologists conducting an extensive examination of ice cores in Greenland were startled by a thick layer of soot in the ice which pointed to a cataclysmic world event. "The climate shift was so sudden that it is as if a button was pressed," they remarked. The samples yielded a date of 9703 BC. [35]

What is fascinating about these traditions is how they all feature unusual people coming out of nowhere to forewarn specific humans of impending global doom and afterwards assist them with the rebuilding process.

Who were those people?

The image of Marotini, tutelary goddess of Kura Tawhiti, once shaped by human hands. It gazes over the Birthplace of the Gods. a site that is potentially 16,000 years old. New Zealand

THE BIRTHPLACE
OF THE GODS

Even as a child I had an irrational yearning to visit New Zealand, possibly because it lay on the opposite side of the world to where I was born and was therefore mysterious and unattainable, or because some latent generic impulse motivated me. During my early teens I also developed a passion for volcanology but never followed it as a career because I couldn't figure out how the study of **3** erupting magma could possibly lead to dating girls, at least the type who interested me. This was, after all, the early 1970s and it would be another three decades before geeks became fashionable.

But patience has its reward. The opportunity to travel to that faraway land finally presented itself in 2005 after I became a best-selling author, and this newly found status afforded a four-week tour. I found New Zealand — Aotearoa in the native tongue — to be a natural paradise. Ironically if one were to insert a long needle into the Earth at my place of birth it would re-emerge at Aotearoa's North Island and beside the sacred mountain Taranaki, a majestic volcano bearing a passing resemblance to Fuji-yama. This is how the gods get their kicks with mortals. Naturally I climbed the magnificent cone and I have been smitten with the landscape ever since.

I was also in New Zealand to conduct research. I took an interest in the history of its earliest settlers, little of which is known to most Kiwis let alone the outside world — myself included, until I was presented with a book by one of my hosts.

What little is known about pre-European settlement in New Zealand comes to us via the Maori who sailed to its shores some time around the twelth century after migrating from Polynesia. Upon arrival they displaced people already living on the North Island,[1] among them the peaceful Waitaha who inevitably retreated to the even more isolated South Island, where their numbers dwindled to what they are today, an estimated 10,000. I couldn't help but draw a comparison with the Hopi — similarly peaceful, similarly displaced by migrating foreigners, and whose numbers nowadays barely scrape beyond 13,000. Both cultures possess folklores describing events before, during and after the flood.

In the early 1990s a local historian by the name of Barry Brailsford was approached by the reclusive Waitaha elders and given permission to publish their oral traditions, finally setting the record straight concerning the true prehistory of New Zealand and, much like the recently-published Hopi prophesies, to warn humanity of the consequences of living out of harmony with the land and sky. Predictably, like other independent scholars presenting facts that overturn histories written by the victorious and promoted by the complacent, Brailsford endured praise and hate in equal proportion.

There are complex politics at play here: by highlighting the Maori as non-indigenous to New Zealand risks, in the eyes of their recent tribal council, losing favourable treaty rights awarded by the British after they, ironically, displaced the Maori; not to mention Maori indigenous rights at the United Nation. There's also the unquestionable matter of pride at stake. And yet it is a matter of record in Maori history that its early migrants found people already settled in New Zealand.[2] Maori elders of previous generations acknowledge the existence of Kiri-puwheru (red-skinned Stonebuilders) prior to their arrival. Traditions describe giants living on the North Island, one being a celebrated hero by the name Kiharoa who lived in Tokanui Pa, still referred to this day as a giant's grave. A giant by the name of Matau lived on a hill above the Wairaka River and by all accounts stood eleven feet tall.[3] The discovery in 1875 of another giant buried seven feet below the sand on a spit in Timaru led one reporter to reopen the investigation in 1999.[4] And no wonder, the individual was reportedly twenty-four feet tall and belonged to a local tribe of giants called Te Kahui Tipua, who were still in existence in the eighteenth century. Hundreds of their remains have been unearthed, all have mysteriously vanished — along with said reporter's job after he contacted a local resident who'd kept one huge lower jaw as both evidence and souvenir.[5]

A similar fate befell the remains of giants found in caves along the curving neck of New Zealand's northwestern shore, specifically at Port Waikato and Raglan. Residents there have been reporting finds since at least the 1920s, and each time, the bones were taken away by authorities and never heard of again. Except in one case where diggers came across a giant skeleton and were instructed to blow it up. Dumbfounded by such a drastic measure, they saved the jawbone and gave it to the museum in Kao Kao.[6] In a similar situation near Raglan, in the vicinity of Mount Karioi (literally Mountain of the Red-haired Giants), a human skull the size of a large pumpkin was unearthed during road works. The find was removed and never heard of since. Meanwhile a nearby cave that yielded dozens of giant skeletons, some with red hair still attached, was ordered dynamited, the bones handed to the Maori council and reportedly ground to dust.[7]

As if the prehistory of New Zealand couldn't get any more peculiar, a number of archaeological accounts validate a human presence far earlier than historians are prepared to accept, resulting in official paperwork going missing, books expunged from libraries, even public documents declared classified and made inaccessible to the public for seventy-five years. And no wonder: in 1874 workers fitting a sewer in Auckland dug fourteen feet down through layers of clay, sand and two lava flows before finding a charred stump of a large manuka tree, alongside which lay an adse, a type of ancient axe. The engineer who made drawings of the find noted how the remaining branches showed clear signs of chopping by the stone implement. The veracity of the report was acknowledged by the Inspector of Surveys. After dating the various

Tree chopped some 30,000 years before the Maori arrived in New Zealand.

sedimentary layers it was concluded that a person had been busy chopping a tree on this hill around 30,000 BC.[8]

Research carried out by a UK forensic pathologist on skeletal remains from former Waitaha sites in the region, at the request of Noel Hilliam, the late curator of the Dargaville Museum, traced its DNA to Wales c.2500 BC.[9] As with the adse and the tree stump, the results were explosive, and explains why Hilliam requested the tests be conducted in secret from the New Zealand government and the cabal of academics who have carried out a relentless whitewash of the country's pre-Maori history, including the discrediting of anyone whose evidence contradicts their sanitized view of events.

Speaking with independent ancient history researchers in New Zealand, I was told the topic wasn't always so controversial. A couple of decades ago it was still possible to speak freely with Maori elders

Maori never worked with stone, so who carved these spirals (top) and why are they identical to those in Tiwanaku and Malta?

concerning the prehistoric peoples of Aotearoa. The subject was hardly taboo. Nowadays such talk is met with denial and derision by a younger tribal council, as David Rankin, chief of the Ngapuhi Maori tribe illustrates: "Maori are not the indigenous people of Aotearoa. There were many other races already living here long before Kupe [first Maori leader] arrived. I am his direct descendant and I know from our oral history passed down 44 generations. I believe this needs to be investigated further because every Maori community talks about Waitaha, Turehu and Patupaiarehe. This goes hand-in-hand with the other research... In 2002 I went to the Austronesian Leaders Conference in Taiwan and we discussed similarities with Taiwanese Aborigines. We traced our origins and the Maori and Polynesian connection to

China. All the leaders such as myself and Matiu Rei, Aborigines, Solomon islanders, Rapa Nui and Hawaiians were all interested in early settlement theories. There is a lot of writing about the whole ancestral link." [10]

And to quote Rankin again: "Who were these red-headed, fair-skinned people who greeted our wakas [canoes]? You can't deny your oral history. If we try to as Maori we're actually denying our history." [11]

So Hilliam had cause to act without consultation, and in the end was vindicated by the DNA results. A similar independent study by immunologist Jean Dausset on the genetic origins of Easter islanders also found their DNA a close match to Welsh people, along with Native Americans, and the Basques of northern Spain, a people with a mysterious origin of their own. [12]

The Welsh connection brings up an interesting observation regarding the beautiful art of Maori tattooing, whose spiral patterns some Maori artists claim are not indigenous to their Polynesian homelands at all, but developed only after migrating to New Zealand. For this to have occurred, the early tatooists must have been exposed to another culture already practicing such art, one that is clearly and unequivocally Celtic. Additionally, dual spirals have been discovered cut in relief on rocks in and around the Oahi Caves southeast of Mount Taranaki, bearing more resemblance to those carved at Tiwanaku than to any known Maori art. As the historian W.J. Phillipps observed, "only on the South American continent is there found an ordered series of spirals which can be compared with those of the Maori." [13] The style of these spirals is also common to the temple of Tarxien in Malta, so the question is, since the older Maori never worked with stone, who exactly carved the petroglyphs?

That's the back-story.

THE LONG MEMORY OF THE WAITAHA

What excited me most about the hitherto undiscussed Waitaha is how they retain the memory of events pre-dating the great flood. Their history begins on the world's most isolated island Waitangi Ki Roto (Island of the Weeping Waters), or as it was named by European seafarers who only found it in the late 18th century, Easter Island.

The ancestors of the Waitaha are said to have "walked with the gods and touched the distant stars." [14] These people appear to have been composed of several groups with specific functions. There were Kiritea (Stone People) who came from Asian lands. And then there were Urukehu (Starwalkers), people skilled in reading the geometry of the stars and navigating the oceans who would eventually instruct people in the Pacific how to locate Aotearoa. The Urukehu's light-colored hair and skin set them apart from Polynesian people. The historian Mākereti Papakura believed this light-skinned strain dates back to their traditional place of origin, Havai'iki, although the word literally means 'homeland' and does not refer to a place; certainly it is not related to Hawaii.[15]

Every year on Easter Island the Waitaha welcomed "the appearance of the *waka* of the gods," the massive double-hull canoe of the Urukehu, and with each encounter another layer of wisdom was added to the *kete* (basket) of knowledge held by the Waitaha's wisdom keepers. But one year the canoe failed to return when "angry stars gathered close to the Moon to give birth to the Tides of Chaos, the dreaded Deluge. And a terrible tragedy unfolded before them. Far beyond the veiled horizon, seas began to climb to terrible heights before rolling out to attack all in their path. Dark storm winds shredded the clouds, swept birds from the sky, sucked fish out of water and smashed them into the sail. Cold hands struggled to lower it before the waka capsized... Huge waves crashed over the washboards, fierce winds bent the tall mast, and the hull... was forced beneath the waves. It survived but wallowed deep within. Then the winds gained new strength from the gathered stars to push the waka relentlessly across the wild waters." [16]

The story describes how the commander of the *waka*, watching half his canoe crippled and breached, made the sensible decision to cut loose the bindings of the two hulls and allow one to avoid capsizing.

Could the formidable Tongan double hull canoe be a legacy of the wakas once used by the Urukehu 11,000 years ago?

Thirteen days passed. The *waka* was driven further and further south, pushed by fierce winds until it finally reached the shores of an island to which was given the name of the surviving canoe, Aotea Roa, the traditional name of New Zealand's South Island but today applied to the nation as a whole.

The Waitaha narrative picks up some time after the world was "turned by water," when the *children* of the gods appear. Sailing from a land in the east and following the star Sirius, a man named Kiwa arrives on Easter Island. From this base he makes numerous voyages across the Pacific, charting its remaining lands, many of which had become islands following the catastrophic rise in sea level. As the Waitaha accurately recall, some of those islands are no more.[17]

At this point in the narrative a second hero survivor appears, a female leader from the west by the name of Hotu Matu'a, commander of a fleet of double hulled *wakas* to whose captains she instructs, "go forth and find the Sacred Birthing Cord of the World,"[18] the nickname by which Easter Island was known, and from which derives its oldest name Te Pito O Te Henua (Navel of the World). That's quite the panegyric for such a small dot in the middle of the Pacific, the meeting point of two ancient currents stretching horizontally across this ocean, suggesting Easter Island once served as a kind of focal point.

Like Kiwa, Hotu Matu'a was an accomplished seafarer, and for her mapping of many islands she became known as the Net of the World. She was described as tall and dark with black hair and brown eyes. Kiwa, on the other hand, couldn't be more different: fair-skinned, blue-eyed, golden or red-haired, features defining him as a genetic link to the Urukehu gods. In time the two heroes are wed and their ten children follow in their footsteps, mapping more of the restructured Pacific Ocean, but primarily visiting Aotea Roa, and returning to Easter Island on multiple occasions.

But it is their grandson Māui who is of importance to our quest. During his formative years Māui was schooled by his grandmothers, memorizing the oral traditions dating from a time "long ago when the stars shone in a different sky and a different pattern," [19] an indication of the remote period from which the tribe's knowledge is drawn and remembered. Māui was taught to respect the seven gods, each representing an aspect of nature. He learned about the two great oceans that made up the world, how to navigate the great currents, and the stars that guide seafarers across vast and truculent seas. Not surprisingly this instilled in the young lad a respect for the wisdom handed down from the antediluvian gods, so much so that he hoped one day to navigate the dangerous currents of the central Pacific himself and locate a distant land said to be protected by the old tides: the Birthplace of the Gods.

The opportunity presented itself soon enough. Sailing his great *waka* westwards along the north current, Māui and his crew survive mountainous seas, connect with the southern current and arrive at the mist-covered North Island of New Zealand. After stocking up with provisions, the crew set sail down the east coast and the short hop to Aotea Roa. Māui must have had foreknowledge of the exact location of "where the gods first drew breath" because he searches for specific features along the coast — a considerable feat given 1200 nautical miles of coastline to choose from — before the *waka* finally beaches at a wide estuary opposite a place called the Mast of Aotea Roa, today known as the eroded volcanic peninsula of Onawe, to the east of the present city of Christchurch.

Māui then instructs his most able runners to mark a trail leading to a specific location deep in the mountainous center of the island. For two days and nights the runners follow the winding, snow-fed waters of the Waimakariri River, returning to describe the magic of the land and waters they found. Emboldened, Māui assembles a party of twelve men and twelve

The Sacred Nest, as seen from Kura Tawhiti.

women to walk the river to the Pukenga hills, crossing majestic tussock grasslands, beech forests and a mountain pass before finding themselves in an alpine basin of great mystery and power. "He stood in awe of a *wairua* [spirit] that filled the air with forces that stretched his being to another plane. His triumphant *karakia* [prayer] echoed strongly from the soaring towers of stone that marked forever the Birth Place of the Gods." [20]

Song of the Waitaha — the collective name of the oral traditions — is highly descriptive of Māui's exuberance as he stood in this, the Crucible of the World. It is clear the sacred site induced in the ancient navigator a reaction that was nothing short of spiritual, and having experienced the site myself on five occasions I can attest to the accuracy of what this adventurer must have felt. Kura Tawhiti, as the main site is called — Castle Hill in anglicised form — is both breathtaking and exhilarating, it is proof that when a sacred place remains continuously unadulterated by human folly its power is palpable to even the most cynical of visitors. Even now it is difficult to find the superlatives to describe the feel of this place. I, for one, empathise with how Māui must have felt when gazing upon the Birthplace of the Gods for the first time — as did another pilgrim who journeyed to the site in 2002, the Dalai Lama, who described it as one of the great spiritual centers of the universe.

The natural alpine basin in which Kura Tawhiti stands was once part of a shallow seabed, since thrust three thousand feet closer to the stars, leaving the limestone exposed to the elements to create two groups of freestanding megaliths. The first resembles a labyrinth of curiously shaped stones that seem somehow animated, while the second stands individually apart along the backbone of a nearby ridge, in a certain light resembling the outstretched fingertips of a buried giant.

Two adjacent sites complete the Birthplace of the Gods: Flock Hill, and Prebble Hill, which the Waitaha refer to as the Sacred Nest, undoubtedly the focal point, a place that keeps its mysteries very close to its chest. Visually it is an awesome lunar-shaped escarpment, similarly composed of scores of limestone monoliths, its concave basin appearing as though molded by the curved underside of a massive spaceship. Around the time of the Younger Dryas it would have been surrounded by deep, turquoise waters fed by nearby glaciers, making the Sacred Nest resemble an island in a primordial lake.

Kura Tawhiti translates as 'School Distant', it is a vast outdoor academy whose stones are said to contain the wisdom and cosmology of the Urukehu gods and, later, the Waitaha who followed in their footsteps. Each monolith — whether natural or deliberately placed — was selected to impart a specific teaching of the Mysteries to visiting initiates, in the same tradition as the stone circles of western Europe. The metaphor behind 'distant school' refers to how the knowledge placed here not only came originally from the stars, but its combined and applied wisdom serves to reconnect the initiate *with* those distant points of light — a relationship any ancient Egyptian or Chaldean would find familiar; its secondary meaning accurately describes its reclusive location on the globe. The ancients always worked with multiple layers of interpretation in every name or symbol.

The reward for hiking the long trail to the summit of Kura Tawhiti is an enigmatic fifty-foot tall monolith named for the tutelary goddess of the site, Marotini. The combined forces of thousands of years of veneration, plus the action of water percolating through the limestone bedrock — the bi-product of which is the creation of a natural electrical charge — produces an immediate and palpable energy of place. This point of high wisdom, literally and metaphorically, may also have once been a place of shamanic travel, a portal that by its very geology alone connects one to the stars.

Long before I'd read the traditions of this landscape temple, as transmitted by the Waitaha, I experienced its power first-hand, hearing the voices of the ancestors that later became a framework for this book. As is the case at most sacred sites, information is revealed layer by layer, visit upon visit, the understanding building like a play in many acts. On one occasion I had a chance to meditate beside the Marotini stone, which even to the casual observer resembles the eroded face of a kind of lioness. The stone was trying to confirm something that had occupied my mind during the uphill trek: how the eroded monoliths, even the tall outcrops forming the labyrinth in the lower section, seemed to portray faces and forms deliberately carved into the limestone but long since eroded. Of course the average geologist would explain — and correctly — how the action of rain and weather over time on exposed rock does give the impression of features familiar to the eye — faces of people and animals, a phenomenon known as *simulacra*, particularly common in waterborne rock such as sandstone and limestone. And yet I found this valid scientific explanation wanting. There was something different about these stones, they really did appear to be a picture gallery of faint faces worn by thousands of rainy seasons.

It was much later, sitting in the comfort of the main library in Wellington, the capital, when I finally spent quality time pouring over the Waitaha narrative. Much to my amazement it contains references to the creation of monuments at Te Kohanga, the collective title for the Birthplace of the Gods, of which Kura Tawhiti is but one component. The story goes back to the days following the Deluge — after the gods stopped visiting Easter Island, but before the time of the great navigator Máui — when a group of people called Tu Mata Kokiri (Keepers of Stone) appear from the west Pacific. Nothing else is mentioned until several generations after the Deluge, when the Waitaha on Easter Island welcome another canoe, whose passengers are described as pale-skinned with hazel eyes and red or fair hair, not dissimilar to some inhabitants already living on the island by then, but with a difference: the visitors arriving from somewhere to the northwest, from a land even by then lost to memory, are described as having eyes with a half-closed appearance. These voyagers are referred to as *kanohi karapa*, and since they carried knowledge of "shaping stone without breaking its spirit" they were named Tu Takap (Stone People).[21] The Waitaha recorded their story thus: "We are and we are born to stone... hidden in the hugeness of stone built so tall, other eyes failed to see our monuments... Huge are the sacred monuments we carved at Te Kohanga." [22]

I had my answer. The faces in the stones hadn't been a figment of imagination. The monoliths had been shaped using "hammer stones" by the Tu Takap, who also carved the image of Marotini and other figures related to ancient mythology: "A towering column of the purest stone was shaped to place Marotini in the land... we asked so much of the Stone Shapers when they carved her to stand against the stars. Tall timbers and thick ropes lifted them high above the land to carve Marotini. Ever higher they climbed to cut away the curving charcoal lines to reveal the beauty of our *tupuna* [ancestor]. And when the last blow was struck, and the inner stone stood true, we made *kumara* [sweet potato] to place at her feet." [23]

Interestingly, the related word *tunupa* (mill-bearer) is the Andean nickname for the Creator God Pachacamac, upon whose shoulders the mill of the heavens churns. His effigy is carved onto the vertical mountainside overlooking the temple city of Ollantaytambo.

It wasn't just heroes who were commemorated in stone at the Birthplace of the Gods. As I mentioned earlier, this was a great seat of learning, an ancient academy. The Waitaha narrative implies that the Urukehu with whom they'd interacted were great navigators as well as astronomers. In one account it is stated how these Starwalkers went to Kura Tawhiti to record the movement of the stars on a monolith called the rock of ages. I've climbed to the site on five separate occasions but have yet to locate this calendar stone, hardly surprising given the thousands of years of weathering, it may no longer be obvious to the eye, however, another quote clearly states there were other monoliths used for the same purpose: "Many were the wondrous shapes worked in the stone of Te Kohanga, and none was more sacred than the Tai Atea, the stone set in place to hold the central star of Matua Tonga [Southern Cross]." [24]

A 16,000-YEAR OLD CALENDAR STONE?

In 2018 I switched my attention to Flock Hill, the third site, because so little of it has been explored. Like Kura Tawhiti it features the same type of limestone monoliths, lots of them, and from its escarpment one is treated to a dramatic side view of the Sacred Nest. Not a whisper could be heard on the hill or the entire plain below, a total absence of sound. A falcon landed on an unusual monolith nearby, whose top appeared to have been artificially shaped into a large, flattened disc. Taking this as a beckoning call, I wandered over. A raised relief stood on the surface of the disc, much like a sundial. Unlike a sundial, the relief was two-thirds along the diameter of the disc, enabling an observer on the ground to line up the relief with the top of the disc.

Since the disc was also inclined at approximately 30° it was possible to look at the relief face-on and make out what appeared to be an elongated face; I shifted my position to observe it from the side and the effect was still obvious. Whether or not it was merely a trick of the light, of greater importance was that the relief had a long axis, thus it cou;d be used to reference an object in the sky. If this stone was the one used to mark the Southern Cross, a few days playing with a program called Stellarium would reveal if ever the two lined up.

The problem was, where to start? The two most important calendar events used by ancient people were the spring equinox and the winter solstice, so I decided to work with these around 8000 BC, well after the great flood. Nothing. The Southern Cross was way off the mark by then. 11,000 BC, still nothing. But around 14,000 BC the constellation began to rise in alignment with the relief, yet still below the mountain range in the background. Then on the spring equinox c.14,800 BC, magic. An observer would have seen

Flock Hill calendar stone, with Kura Tawhiti and Marotini in the distance.

the Southern Cross rising above the disc for the first time, carried along a vertically inclined Milky Way as though the celestial river was oozing from the monolith itself. The effect must have been dramatic.

The exact same alignment repeated on the winter solstice.

But was this what the Urukehu had had in mind? Another pivotal constellation in their world — and later the Waitaha's — was Orion, so I took the opportunity to examine its relationship with the calendar stone. In 14,800 BC Orion was 17° off the mark, but around 12,400 BC its belt stars could finally be seen rising above the disc on the winter solstice. As the program rolled forward in time to 10,400 BC, Orion's belt remained aligned above the disc but now with most of the constellation above the horizon. As we shall see later, this date has enormous implications in our quest.

I walked around the Flock Hill calendar stone and found an adjacent monolith with a convenient alcove to sit on and write down my observations.

When I got up and looked back at the stone in which I'd been sitting, I was amazed to find it too had every appearance of having been carved by

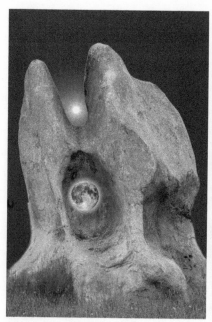

*Left: Sun and Moon positions as observed from the alcove stone c.10,400 BC
(front of stone shown for clarity).
Right: Southern Cross as observed above calendar stone c.14,800 BC.*

*Orion's Belt above calendar stone c.12,400 BC,
and the full constellation c.10,400 BC*

Marotini (shwn face-on for clarity), would have looked at the Southern Cross rising into a natural hollow between two peaks across the valley on the spring equinox c.10,400 BC.

human hands. The oval alcove resembled an upright bowl into which the light of an object is meant to shine; above the alcove, and slightly offset from its axis, the stone has been shaped into two horns, as though carved to mark the trajectory of an object in the sky. Turning to Stellarium, the only object that aligns with the narrow gap between the horns is the rising winter solstice Sun c.10,400 BC; the other is the Moon, whose Minor Standstill is precisely marked by the stone's alcove; just like the stone, both objects' trajectories are slight offset to each other.

It was turning out to be a very productive day. I returned to take a fresh look at the calendar stone. From the rear it resembled a boat, in fact the southern end of the entire monolith looks as thought it was carved like a figurehead at the bow of an old ship. Again, this could all be *simulacra*, and yet the head was precisely aligned to the south celestial pole. I positioned myself behind it. The head was clearly looking through the gap between two large boulders and right across the valley to another gap in the distant mountains. An observer sitting in the same position on the winter solstice in 10,400 BC would have seen Sirius, a major navigational star throughout the Pacific, rising into this natural cup.

I returned to Kura Tawhiti — another two hours of climbing — to see if another alignment presented itself. Its most obvious landmark is the Marotini stone on the summit. Due to long-term erosion, the monolith's axis isn't absolute, but it does point to a prominent dip between two peaks on the opposite mountain range, a convenient bowl. The spread of 90-98° means we could be looking for anything in the eastern sky along this arc. Using 10,400 BC as a marker, the only object of note that rises out of this bowl is the Southern Cross, once again, on the spring equinox.

It appears there are two potential dates being commemorated at the Birthplace of the Gods, with the location and its monuments carefully selected to take advantage of the background of mountains that the Urukehu would have used to frame the sky and reference significant stellar objects and dates.

The same technique was employed on the other side of the Pacific, at a site strategically founded by another group of flood gods at another kind of birthplace, Cuzco Cara Urumi (Uncovered Navel Stone). Seen from its original Qorikancha temple, the passage of the Milky Way establishes an intercardinal horizon against the foreground of mountains, creating a cosmic axis as it arcs through the night sky. This was recreated and marked on the ground using *huacas* (sacred sites). As any ancient seafarer knows, by understanding the position of the stars it is possible to predict the behavior of the oceans, even when doing so a hundred miles inland, making long sea voyages possible and assuring the safe passage of ships.

DISTANT EVENTS ETCHED IN MEMORY

Despite living on a near-paradisal land, life wasn't all wine and roses for the Waitaha. Like many people whose existence covers great spans of time, they too record disasters that have befallen the Earth over the course of 11,000 years besides the great flood. One account describes how stars fell, "long showers of flame rained down, fiery darts falling out of the sky, a fiery waka descending out of the sky... burning rocks crashed to earth. And a frightful humming was heard. And a great burning ball plunged down." Everything burned, a massive fire destroyed much of the eastern side of the South Island, followed by a change in climate. First came floods and heavy winds, then droughts that sparked more fires. No date is set for the event, but given the story's place in the narrative it seems to coincide with a comet and mass coronal ejections in 3150 BC and 2345 BC,[25] both events causing havoc on a global scale, the latter recorded by Chinese astronomers.

Another fire of unknown origin c.1200 BC — quite likely another mass coronal ejection — destroyed practically every urban civilization in the eastern Mediterranean between Anatolia and Palestine and brought about the sudden collapse of the Bronze Age. The terror of "the Star Fires" — the Waitaha term describing meteoric or solar induced events — forced people to seek protection in deep caves, much in the same way they'd done on Easter Island under similar circumstances.[26]

Another dramatic event imprinted in Waitaha memory is the creation of Lake Taupo, which covers a substantial portion of the North Island. According to mainstream geologists the lake is a caldera formed by the eruption of a supervolcano c. 24,500 BC whose magnitude ranks as one of the greatest eruptions of all time. It is suggested that the debris ejected into the atmosphere may have been responsible for starting the Great Ice Age. However, the Waitaha beg to differ and, like their aboriginal neighbours in Australia who recall events proven to have taken place deep in prehistoric times,[27] they too have eyewitness accounts to tell. According to the Waitaha, "Tohunga [wisdom keepers] hold within their *kete* [basket] a most sacred *karakia* [prayer] that travels the sky trails in the dawn. Its words reach out to the thirty-six houses in the heavens to awaken Auahi Tu Roa [Firebird] who carries messages across the darkened skies for the Sky Father. If the *mana* [spiritual integrity or magic] of the Tohunga is great enough he frees that shooting star to fly just as the last stars disappear." Unfortunately the wisdom keeper got the prayer wrong on this occasion, allowing the passing comet to break away from its typical trajectory and crash to Earth. The impact was so strong it reversed the Earth's rotation: "the days went backwards and the night became the day, and the day became the night." Fire engulfed the land. Survivors hid in caves before rains finally quelled the flames and the earthquakes stopped. Re-emerging, the people predictably found a land completely altered, with Lake Taupo created when part of this "Earth Shaker" crashed. "It did not fly from a volcano to crash to Earth but came out of the heavens along the track of the Moon and Sun," they said, causing "fires that fell from the skies." Hence why the name originally given to the lake was Tauponui Atea, which roughly translates as 'big lake created from space'. [28]

THE THREAD TO SOUTH AMERICA

Let's now rejoin the narrative after Māui reached Kura Tawhiti.

He continued his journey throughout the South Island, marking other power places and connecting them to specific stars — the ancient practice of astro-archaeology that underlies the design of virtually every ancient temple on Earth[29] — and locating nearby islands that in time became part of New Zealand's mainland due to the ever shifting tectonic forces of this region. Finally, he asked a group of families to stay behind and establish a home before setting sail back to Easter Island. But before he could return, his *waka* vanished somewhere in the Pacific Ocean.[30]

The importance of Waitaha history is two-fold: first, it marks, with absolute precision, the antediluvian Birthplace of the Gods, or at least one of them; and two, it depicts events before, during, and after the flood. The earliest point of the narrative places the Urukehu sailing the Pacific as the flood is taking place. If Māui was their grandson, it stands to reason he and

The ridge of Kura Tawhiti. Marotini is along the top, left of center.

his crew were present in New Zealand within two generations, ostensibly around 9600 BC. A second time-frame is provided by the Waitaha grandmother elders in the second narrative *Whispers of the Waitaha*, in which they declare that the sacred teachings were carefully maintained, orally transmitted and applied for 10,000 years until 1743 — about 25 years prior to Captain James Cook's arrival in New Zealand — when the elders were instructed to hide the knowledge until more appropriate times. If so, the compilation of teachings began about 1443 years after flood.[31]

This leaves a discrepancy of 1343 years between the flood and the arrival of Māui, meaning that each generation of the Urukehu lived for seven hundred years! As absurd as it may seem, one characteristic of antediluvian gods in India, Mesopotamia and Egypt is their superhuman life span, as we shall see later.

All this changes everything and what little we have known about the prehistory of this part of the Pacific, and provides one point of origin for the antediluvian gods.

But there's one more aspect to be learned from the seafaring traditions of the Waitaha. They describe the manner in which the great ocean currents behave between New Zealand and Easter Island, and how the return journey required sailing *past* Easter Island to "a great land in the East before returning." [32] There are two possibilities here: either there used to be a landmass beyond Easter Island, now submerged, or the "great land" referred to is South America. The Waitaha narrative provides a clue. When visiting this land it was customary to take along a totem: "two birds, titi and kaka, went with them, and their names are joined in the most sacred waters of that distant homeland of the ancestors." [33] Obviously this refers to Lake Titicaca, whose shore was once home to a great civilization who built the temple cities of Puma Punku and Tiwanaku. Given how the megaliths marking Tiwanaku's immense rectangular plaza align with stellar events along the horizon in 15,000 BC,[34] the Waitaha of Aotearoa invariably give shape to a lost civilization in prehistoric times who sailed great distances as effortlessly as driving to the supermarket.

How or why did three disparate points on the face of the Earth become so intrinsically linked? Part of the answer is mathematical: measure the distance from Tiwanaku to the Birthplace of the Gods via Easter Island, divide one section into the other and Easter Island marks *phi*, nature's mathematical proportion. The discrepancy is a mere 0.02, far too close to be mere coincidence.

It appears that a remote outpost 12,000 feet up on the Bolivian altiplano might have been another home of the gods.

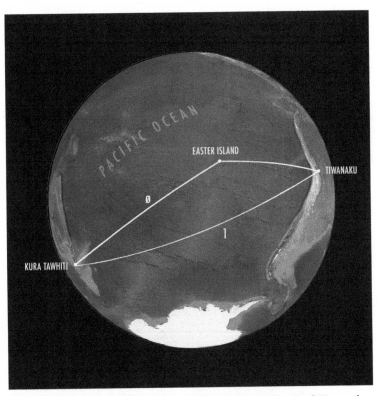

The locations of the gods — Easter Island, Kura Tawhiti and Tiwanaku — are related to each other by phi.

Sun Door of the Kalasasaya and its complex astronomical detail. Tiwanaku, Bolivia.

BUILT BEFORE
THE FLOOD

"Now, I don't believe an industrial civilization existed on Earth before our own — I don't think there was a dinosaur civilization... but the question of what one would look like if it did is important. How do you know there hasn't been one? The whole point of science is to ask a question and see where it leads." [1]

4

The statement is by Adam Frank, astrophysicist at the University of Rochester in New York who co-authored a paper with Gavin Schmidt, director of NASA's Goddard Institute for Space Studies, hypothesizing that advanced civilizations may have once populated the Earth.

Their point is this: If complex life has existed on Earth for a period of 400 million years and an industrial civilization has only occupied a mere 300 years of it, surely somewhere along such a vast expanse of time other industrial civilizations might have flourished and fallen? In context of a 13.8 billion-year old universe, it is feasible that even extraterrestrial civilizations might have risen and expired.

The problem is finding their traces. After a prolonged amount of time, artefacts of civilization are buried beneath rubble, dirt, volcanic ash, rising seas, creeping vegetation and encroaching urbanization. Even remnants of recent civilizations such as the Roman are hard to find on the surface; statues and pottery and tools are often discovered by blind luck or abrupt erosion. And if we were to rely solely on fossil evidence, it ought to be remembered that only a tiny fraction of fauna and flora become fossilized because the process requires a number of geologic and atmospheric conditions. Since most physical reminders of planetary civilizations may be erased by now, Frank and Schmidt proposed looking for subtle evidence of earlier industrial civilizations in sedimentary anomalies and chemical balances in the geological record, something that would indicate an alteration of the Earth's habitat through human intervention, such as pollution. Certainly that's one way to look at it.

Another is to examine myth and folklore; and of course, to look at anomalous megalithic structures, things that look entirely out of place relative to their culture and level of sophistication, at least to our eyes. Curiously, the co-authors raised the possibility that the end of one civilization could sow the seeds for another, which brings up an anomaly that happened across the Earth around 8000 BC, the period when humans suddenly and collectively discovered agriculture, domestication of animals, astronomy, mathematics, and so on.

An accident? A global impulse? Or did we inherit seeds sown by an earlier, advanced civilization whose roots were erased by cataclysm?

THE ENIGMA OF TIWANAKU

One of the greatest anomalies lies hidden in plain view in the Andes.

The Inka ruling class rose to prominence in the 15th century. Barely a century-and-a-half later it was all but wiped out, conquered by a small band of Spanish glory hounds that the Peruvians mistook for returning gods. In this blink of a historical eye we are meant to believe the Inka took the art of advanced stone masonry to the highest levels of any civilization, living or dead, achieving it without knowledge of alloys and the specialist tools required for complex stone cutting and shaping. And to make it easier for themselves, they allegedly built hundreds of megalithic citadels such as Saqsayhuaman, Tiwanaku, Puma Punku, Pisac, Cuzco and Machu Picchu while simultaneously dealing with a civil war.

Exquisite masonry robbed for a local home.

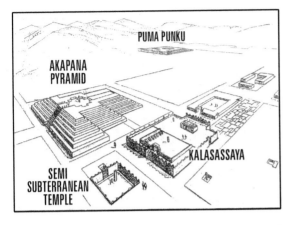

Anyone who's traveled extensively through the Andes is dumbstruck by the stratospheric architectural mastery of Saqsayhuaman. Or the razorblade precision of the Sun temple porphyry wall above the town of Ollantaytambo. Or the high-tech H-blocks of Puma Punku, originally slotted together like Neolithic Lego. Surely projects of such magnitude, of such unique vision and endeavor, would have been recorded and loudly proclaimed by their architects? Yet no claim exists. Inka literature mentions such places casually as though already familiar and accepted, because the truth is they *were* in existence long before the Inka. The compiler Pedro Cieza de Léon describes his encounter with the Aymara living around Lake Titicaca who, when asked about the Inka having built Tiwanaku, laughed at his question, asserting that everything seen in this temple complex was built long before the Inka,[2] assembled by magic in a single night when "the stones came down of their own accord, or at the sound of a trumpet, from the mountain quarries and took up their proper positions at the site." [3]

Tiwanaku's temple complex covers 2000 acres, and the latest aerial surveillance locates dozens of additional buildings still waiting excavation. Six known rectangular enclosures border a stepped mound called Akapana, whose megaliths have been heavily looted over the centuries, first by the Spanish looking for accessible building material for the capital La Paz, then by robber barons who literally robbed what remained to build the Bolivian railroads. The locals joined in, helping themselves to the fine masonry scattered about the place to build the homes and streets of the little town of Tiwanaku itself; one adobe house that once stood within the archaeological site employed large stone blocks carved with reliefs taken from the Akapana for a doorway. No doubt its humble owner was inspired by the actions of the zealous local Spanish priest Pedro de Castillo who destroyed a noteworthy third site in the 17th century, from which he built a disproportionately huge church in the center of this otherwise unremarkable town; his acolyte, the Andean chief Paxi-pati, behaved no better. Still, his actions helped me understand there once existed a relationship between the Akapana, Puma Punku, and a third, lost temple now beneath the church, for the three sites form a perfect equilateral triangle. In the ancient world it was standard practice to link sites sharing common functions using perfect triangles.[4] It is also well known that the Spanish followed an official policy of building churches over pre-existing temples.

Despite such travesties, enough masonry remained buried in 1904 for the Austrian archaeologist and engineer Arthur Posnansky to dedicate forty-eight years of his life to documenting Tiwanaku and its equally impressive satellite temple Puma Punku. He published five copious volumes detailing the impressive nature of the site, its stupendous scale, and the means by which it met an ugly fate 11,000 years ago.

Posnansky was well aware that, like so many of its kind, Tiwanaku would have referenced the position of objects in the sky during the epoch in which it was built. He used as his main subject the relatively well-preserved quadrangle of standing stones called Kalasasaya (the name means 'standing stones' in Aymara). In his day the stones were still mostly freestanding, with just a low boundary wall connecting them; ignorant but well-meaning latter-day restorers have filled the spaces in-between with poorly fitted stones to form an enclosed courtyard. Posnansky reasoned that the monoliths mark celestial objects along the eastern horizon, when seen from an observation platform to the rear of the quadrangle. He took the corner megaliths to mark the position of the solstices, but the alignment missed the mark by 18 angular minutes.[5] This is because the *present* position of the Earth relative to its celestial meridian has shifted over time, causing a relative shift in the marked position of the Sun.

Celestial mechanics work like this: the Earth rotates with a kind of

PRECESIONAL CYCLE
(wobble of the Pole)
25,920 years

AXIAL TILT
one cycle = 21,600 years

wobble at the poles which completes a full cycle over the course of 25,920 years, a phenomenon known as the *precession of the equinoxes*, meaning that celestial objects observed from the ground will be seen to shift in the sky, imperceptibly so. While this is taking place the Earth's axis tilts about 4° over the course of 21,600 years, an action called the *obliquity of the ecliptic*.

Taking these two elements into account, Posnansky refined the date and got an exact match for the Kalasasaya. The row of megaliths referenced the solstices in 15,000 BC.[6] In Posnansky's words: "The calculations of the age of Tiwanaku are based solely and exclusively on the difference in the obliquity of the ecliptic of the period in which that great temple was built and that which it has today... the calculations were only possible by means of a building located exactly on the meridian and the length and width of which conformed to the maximum angle of solar declination between the two solstices." [7]

His work was peer-reviewed for three years and the calculations were proven to be sound.[8]

The Kalasasaya's earliest name by the Puquina, Oka-uru-ymata, means Measure-Day-Observed. It is a massive courtyard calendar measuring 421 feet long by 389 feet wide, almost twice the size of an average football field, and yet the simple design belies its complexity — its length-to-width ratio of 1:1.08 is the difference between solar and lunar calendars.

TIWANAKU AND THE FLOOD

Prior to 11,000 BC the agricultural conditions around Tiwanaku and the altiplano of Bolivia in general were excellent. There is even evidence of introduced agricultural experiments, such as raised soil tables. But within 5,000 years Tiwanaku was to face its biggest desecration, a disaster that marked the region with slow and irrecoverable decline. Tremendous seismic movements forced the waters of Lake Titicaca to overflow. Other lakes to the north broke bulwarks, their waters emptying into Titicaca to form a wall of water that overwhelmed everything and everyone in its rampage. Archaeological digs reveal a jumble of human remains tangled with those of fish, pottery and utensils. Stones were mixed with jewels, tools and shells, and megaliths weighing hundreds of tons were tossed around like matchsticks.

One of the surviving artefacts is an impressive 440-ton monolithic block of andesite carved into a doorway. Along the top, a set of beautiful reliefs depict the Creator God Pachacamac holding two serpents, each representing the alternating electric and magnetic currents that give life to the universe. The nineteen rays around his head cleverly reflect the Metonic Cycle, the calibration of solar and lunar calendars every 18.6 years. Along the periphery, bird-like creatures depict, in stylized form, information relating to the cycles of Venus, Sirius as well as eclipses. This calendrical masterpiece is the work of an inspired artist-astronomer, carved for posterity on one single, massive block of stone whose height and width also conform to the ratio between solar and lunar calendars.[9]

But more revealing on this doorway are the forty-six reliefs of toxodons, a type of rhino made extinct by the flood 11,000 years ago. Since the stone masons would have borrowed from observation or memory, the doorway must have been carved when the creatures were still roaming the altiplano, and still relevant to people of the period.

Posnansky adds the following remark on the condition of this calendar stone: "The Door of the Sun which was found lying on its face on the ground, has been preserved in wonderful condition with all its inscriptions; but its back, and especially the end exposed to the adverse atmospheric conditions, shows an enormous wearing away. It should be pointed out that the block from which this notable monument was carved is composed of andesitic hornblende, vitreous and very hard lava, which, if polished as it was in that period, required several thousands of years to wear away in the form in which we see it today." [10] By implication it is likely that the quadrangle in which it was placed was originally built before the flood.

As I walked around the ramparts of Tiwanaku I appreciated Posnansky's passion to bring some sense of order to the site. His discoveries, together with meticulous measurements and reconstruction drawings by Alfons Stüdel and Friedrich Max Uhle in the 1890s, paint a vivid picture of a complex, well-designed city complete with polished megalithic floors, and piers capable of accommodating thirty ocean-going vessels. This would have been when the water level of Lake Titicaca was up to one hundred feet higher and the edge of the temple city lay at its shore.[11] Tiwanaku was essentially one large man-made island. Indeed by following the contours of the lake before the flood one discovers how temples around its periphery,

The Kalasasaya viewed from the Akapana Pyramid in 1890. Note the disproportionate size of the church (top left) for such a small, remote village.

The Kalasasaya buried in a deep sediment layer. Only possible through thousands of years of pluvial climate and exposure to higher water levels from Lake Titicaca.

When Lake Titicaca's level was higher (white) its temples were connected along the shore. Right: the Tiwanaku triangle.

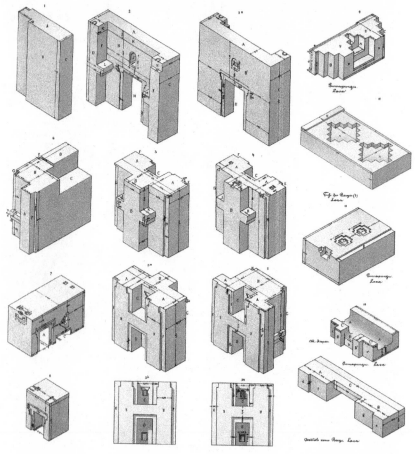

Prehistoric Lego, anyone? Puma Punku's H-blocks and a small selection of other stones, as surveyed in the 1890s. More the work of a machine than man.

such as Amaru Muru, Cutimbo and Silustani, were once connected to this massive inland sea and accessed by boat — not dissimilar to temples along the Nile.

HIGH TECH AT PUMA PUNKU

For me, it is the haunting beauty of nearby Puma Punku and its jumble of intricately carved andesite platforms and monoliths that captures the imagination. Its scattered, enigmatic H-blocks made from greenish lava, quarried fifty-five miles north of Titicaca, resemble building blocks made for giants, designed to interlock and form impressive walls, sections of which still existed in the late 1800s. They possess the aura of an intricate computer schematic or engine room. The blocks appear identical, as though poured from a mold, yet close inspection shows each one to have been individually made.

The same applies to the mortise and tenon method with which large masonry blocks have been cut to slot perfectly into each other, a time-consuming enterprise requiring the removal of large amounts of stone, although the result offers great structural integrity against earthquakes. The blocks were further strengthened by I-grooves cut between adjoining slabs, a feature common to megalithic sites throughout the Pacific, Cambodia and Sumeria; identical grooves can been at the temple of Kom Ombu in Egypt. It is claimed that copper was poured into each I-groove to create a connecting strap between the stones. However, this ignores the fact that the resulting profile of the straps would be concave, and yet examples recovered from the site show they are convex. Furthermore, poured copper would have molded itself to the imperfections in the stone, but the items in the local museum show they are not; rather, they were individually manufactured for the purpose. Copper is a soft metal, it would snap when the heavy stones shifted during an earthquake; using iron would have been more sensible, and it is abundant throughout the region. The only viable explanation is that copper served as a conductor.

What remains at Puma Punku gives an idea of what Tiwanaku would have looked like in its prime. One massive, recumbent stone resembles a kind of architrave, beautifully polished, without a hint of tooling, featuring parabolic curves which would tax any modern mason or machine. An identical stone exists at the Sun temple at Ollantaytambo, and again among a field of stones still waiting to be catalogued at Saqqara in Egypt! Either the stonemason responsible must have been present at all three sites, or three separate ancient architects performed the same work, in the same era, using the same manual.

It has been noted how the blocks dispersed around Puma Punku feature tiny drilled holes, 0.15" in diameter, into which were inserted gold nails to fasten large sheets of gold with bas reliefs of the stone carvings beneath. Some of the nails were still in existence in 1930 because the local boys in charge of the museum found it impossible to remove them without damaging the stone.[12]

While the Akapana and Kallasasya are essentially solar based, Puma Punku was the companion temple, a lunar site under the symbolic protection of the Puma, an animal believed to represent the watery associations of the Moon. Just as Kallasasaya had its Door of the Sun so Puma Punku had its lunar counterpart. By the time Posnansky managed to analyze it, all that remained of this "most sublime and significant monument of the Americans" were fragments, albeit beautifully crafted ones.[13] This impressive monolithic door also deviated from the Door of the Sun in that the carvings were no longer of birds but of fish.

Puma Punku's T-shape foundation incorporates an obscure mathematical ratio. The mound's proportion of 6:5 commemorates the Earth's precessional cycle of 25,920 years divided by its axial tilt of 21,600 years. The ratio is unique to this planet, so to incorporate it in a building project implies the architects possessed knowledge of obscure celestial mechanics observed over a vast period of time, the implication being that whoever built Puma Punku must have been around for at least that long, or they inherited the information from an even older civilization. Either way we are dealing with a staggering span of time. If this fails to impress, consider how the same ratio is created when taking the two fundamental building blocks behind all molecular structures, namely the sphere and tetrahedron. When the latter is placed inside the former, with the points of the tetrahedron touching the inner surface of the sphere, the ratio of the two surface areas is 6:5.[14] This ratio also forms the earliest depiction of the ubiquitous Andean stepladder motif, the *chakana* or Andean cross, examples of which still existed on site a decade ago before they were stolen.

There is no doubt we are dealing with a technological and sophisticated culture in the high Andes that spanned every Dryas period, one that was clearly a cut above standard Neanderthal education.

THE MISALIGNMENT OF TIWANAKU

But there is a bigger riddle at Tiwanaku that has escaped attention. Ancient designers were masters of proportion and relationship. Countless examples around the world attest to the work of a people obsessed with placing temples in perfect relationship to each other and their natural surroundings, what later became the art of *Feng Shui*. And yet the Kalasa-saya enclosure has been awkwardly placed beside the tallest structure of the complex, the Akapana mound, as though the two sites are linked yet herald from two different ages.

Perhaps so. The Kalasasaya's alignment reflects its relationship to the meridian in 15,000 BC, as do the temples to the west and north. They form a unit. However, the same is not true for the Akapana, nor a small enclosure immediately to the north called the semi-subterranean temple — nor Puma Punku half-a-mile to the southwest; these three are misaligned by 2º 50' to the rest of the site.[15] They not only belong together, they belong to an even more remote period when they were aligned to a very different sky.

Is this possible? It is worth bearing in mind that the semi-subterranean temple was once a free-standing quadrangle of standing stones, since surrounded and buried by silt. It now sits some twelve feet *below* the level upon which the standing stones of the adjacent Kalasasaya rest. It stands to reason that it must far older than 15,000 BC, and by implication so must the Akapana and Puma Punku. Posnansky was of the same opinion when he noted how Tiwanaku shows signs of three distinct building periods. He too groups the three above temples into the first period, noting how the Akapana itself belonged to a remote age and was subsequently repaired and improved. In Posnansky's words: "With regard to the first, or prehistoric, period of Tiwanaku, as we have decided to call it, this is much more remote and we do not have, because of the present state of science, any basis for the establishing astronomical calculations; rather, we can only use a geological basis for the determination of the period in which it was built."[16]

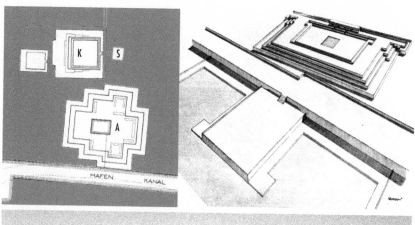

Top: The misalignment of Akapana and semi-subterranean temple relative to Kalasasaya; the same is true of Puma Punku (right). Middle: semi-subterranean temple, well below the level of the Kalasasaya behind it. Below: machined andesite at Puma Punku, and how its H-blocks might have fitted together.

The second period belongs to the Kalasasaya, which, he correctly maintained, was aligned to a different horizon, even showed signs of having been repaired after a catastrophic event hit the region. The third period is marked by refinements inside the Kalasasaya, such as an inner court, which again differs in orientation relative to its predecessor.

I have to agree with Posnasky's assessment because it plays out in other temples throughout the Andes sharing the same mythology as Tiwanaku. I have made the journey from Lake Titicaca to Cuzco on several occasions and each time is like walking slow motion into a revealing riddle. If one pays attention to the masonry of the sites it quickly becomes obvious that Andean temples experienced four distinctive building periods. Using central Cuzco, Saqsayhuaman, Pisac and Machu Picchu as examples, even the casual observer will note how the top portions of buildings are made from the most inferior and smallest sized stones. They're also joined together with mortar, rendering every reconstruction pointless in the face of the devastating earthquakes that terrorize this region. This style represents both Spanish handiwork and recent attempts at restoration. Below comes Inka standard, where the stones are larger than colonial efforts, less mortar is used, and in some cases an attempt has been made to imitate the older layer below, with the caveat that Inka stonework lacks the same precision, and tool marks are evident to the eye.

Comparing the Inka layer to the third layer is like comparing a stagecoach to a Bugatti. The stones are impractically large, fitted without mortar, the edges are clean, sharp and precise, and the absence of tool marks makes them look as though they were polished to perfection. Clearly there has been a huge technological leap forward, except we are now traveling back in time. The Peruvian researcher Alfredo Gamarra believes there were certainly three different building periods, which he classifies as Ukin Pacha, the Inka period of tool marks and mortar and imprecision; Uran Pacha, a more technical and sophisticated earlier craftsmanship; and Hanan Pacha, first world megaliths of natural stone shaped as though softened through the application of an intense heat.[18] It's this lower layer that is the most fascinating. Megaliths as tall as forty feet and weighing 500 tons, their faces curved like pillows, with edges no longer linear but rounded and slightly recessed, as though a potter's hand caressed a lump of clay. They are also cut into individual shapes, with anywhere between four to sixteen corners and as many angles per stone. No two are alike, and so precisely fitted that even an alpaca hair cannot be inserted between them. They interlock like an upright jigsaw puzzle, making them not only artistic wonders but also earthquake proof.

And, it seems, instructional as well. In 2014 Dr. Derek Cunningham discovered that the way in which the Saqsayhuaman stones have been cut are not just functional and artistic, they deliberately encode information, because their angular values correlate to known astronomical data. "Each astronomical value (there are 9 standard values in total) was chosen by ancient astronomers to aid the prediction of eclipses. These astronomical terms are a mixture of values astronomers use to measure time (the 27.32-day sidereal month) and values to determine when the moon, earth and sun align at nodes. This includes the use of the 18.6-year nodal cycle of the moon, the 6.511 draconic month period between eclipse seasons, and also the 5.1-degree angle of inclination of the moon's orbit. The remaining values typically are either half-values of various lunar terms, or values connected to the 11-day difference between the lunar and solar years." [18]

To demonstrate this he measured the lowest, and oldest, tier of stones and discovered the walls of Saqsayhuaman are, literally, a library in stone.

HIGH HEAT AT SAQSAYHUAMAN

Now it gets *really* interesting. These stones are high-density limestone bearing the remains of small marine organisms and shells. However, something happened between the time the blocks were removed from the quarry, and shaped and placed upright to form the walls of the citadel. An intense thermal effect was applied that left "no obvious fossils and

organic remains... but only clearly visible fine-grained structure." [19] The conclusion is that the blocks were subjected to an intense heating process of as much as 1500° Celsius that re-crystallized the "biogenic siliceous limestone into microcrystalline siliceous limestone. In normal conditions this process is absolutely

Megalithic architects' fastidiousness with detail; 2-inch keystone. Cuzco.

*The megalithic layer (A) has been patched by less precise Inka work (B).
Spanish and later work (C) gets sloppier and sloppier. Cuzco.*

impossible."[20] Close observation of the stones shows they are also covered with a thin glassy glaze around the joints, as though indeed subjected to intense heat. A similar example can be seen on the stone masonry along Cuzco's Loretto Street, site of the original Qorikancha temple.

Who possessed the knowledge to work stone like this? The Inka knew nothing of it nor did they have memory of such unparalleled architectural achievements, let alone the understanding of moving enormous blocks of stone from one hill to another. The chronicler Garcilaso de la Vega recounts in his *Royal Commentaries of the Incas* how one Inka king tried to emulate the efforts of the ancients by having a monolith brought to Ollantaytambo from the quarry several miles across the valley, to help *rebuild* the temple: "This boulder was hauled across the mountain by more than 20,000 Indians, going up and down very steep hills... At a certain spot, it fell from their hands and over a precipice killing more than 3000 men." [21]

Twenty thousand men to shift a single stone? Given the amount of masonry used to build thousands of temples, who was left to tend to the fields, to fight a civil war, to attend to procreation and lovemaking? The chroniclers of the period offer only shrugs: everything to be seen throughout the Andes had been made long, long ago by magicians using some unknown force.[22]

The question is, who? Garcilaso recorded the traditions of the founding of Cuzco following the great flood, a period when the survivors fell into a lowly, uncivilized state, living without clothing in caves. A god then sent "one of his sons and one of his daughters from heaven to earth" to bring civilization to the people. Bearing a golden rod, this couple was instructed to plunge it into the earth at certain points along the Andes, and wherever the rod disappeared into the soil they were to establish temple cities, one being Cuzco Cara Urumi, the 'uncovered navel stone'.[23]

This story is not unique to Andean gods, because it mirrors the actions of the Zoroastrian flood hero Yim. The opening section of the *Zend Avesta* describes this antediluvian figure as the first human and founder of civilization, who is presented with a golden ring and knife by the god Ahura Mazda, which "he pressed into the earth and bore it with the poniard." [24] For his services Yim was forewarned of the flood and prepared accordingly.[25]

The Cuzco valley is unique for its *huacas* (sacred sites), hundreds of them fashioned into steps, seats, alcoves, and other various geometric shapes from outcrops of living stone. Their creators are known to the indigenous people as Ñaupaq Machula (Wise Old Ones), gods from an era long ago. Many *huacas* exhibit signs of considerable water erosion in a region that last experienced a prolonged wet climate over five thousand years ago. In some cases there are signs that the worked stone has been

One of many large buttes carved with stairs leading nowhere, alcoves with astronomical functions, and upside down staircases depicting creation myths.

The standing stones of the Kalasasaya, since infilled with broken masonry.

marked by glaciers, a sign of profound antiquity.[26] This places Cuzco's *huacas* close to the Younger Dryas era, not a far-fetched idea given that the giant mound of Huaca Prieta, on Peru's northern coast, shows evidence of human involvement in 11,700 BC.[27]

Andean traditions refer to the megalithic monument builders by the nickname *huari*, a race of white-skinned, bearded, red-haired tall people led by a god named Viracocha, who appeared after the flood on a boat on Lake Titicaca together with seven *Hayhuaypanti* — Shining Ones — one of whom was his wife and sister.

Did these *huari* move the stones through the air and build megalithic sites to the sound of a trumpet? Polynesian people might agree, because in their culture a *oaro* is actually a type of trumpet.

HOME OF THE SHINING PEOPLE

From these morsels of information we can now connect the events in the Andes to the narrative so elegantly told by the Waitaha. If these Shining Ones were white-skinned and red-haired tall people, they are most likely the Urukehu gods who voyaged between New Zealand, Easter Island and South America, taking with them the two totem birds *titi* and *caca*. If so it explains why a group of strangers magically appear at Tiwanaku, on a remote altiplano 12,500 feet above sea level. They had prior knowledge of its existence, they had been there before. If so, I feel confident in proposing the following scenario: the Urukehu returned to Lake Titicaca after the flood to assess the damage. They most likely *rebuilt* Tiwanaku, just as Posnansky speculated. Certainly the site was already long established and was geodetically important, as evidenced by its Aymara nickname *taypikala* (stone at the center). Like Kura Tawhiti, Easter Island and Cuzco, Tiwanaku was a navel of the earth, a birthplace of gods.[28] Its original name *tiwa naku* comes from the Tongareva dialect of the Cook Islands and means My People.[29] Or more accurately, My Shining People, since the syllable *aku* is Egyptian for Shining Being. Tiwanaku was the home of the Shining Ones.

We now have a potential link between the antediluvian gods of Easter Island, Polynesia, New Zealand, Egypt and the Andes.

Once Tiwanaku was up and running again, this brotherhood set out to create other cult centers and promulgate the ideals of civilization throughout the Andes, exactly as local traditions recall,[30] establishing and re-establishing temples stretching in a line from Lake Titicaca to Cuzco, as evidenced by the two oldest layers of megalithic masonry mentioned earlier which, to many eyes, provide clear evidence of an antediluvian cultural project interrupted by a major catastrophe. Both styles of construction share obvious common elements yet differ drastically in terms of style, the oldest being fluid and organic, while the successive is sharp, linear and urbane, yet loses none of the craftsmanship of the former. They are clearly linked and yet disconnected by a period of time.

The mechanical precision of second generation masonry. Qorikancha, Cuzco.

One piece of circumstantial evidence lies near the quarry used to build Ollantaytambo, where beautiful recumbent monoliths mark the path leading down to the river plain and up to the temple itself. These massive works appear to have been abruptly dropped en route as though work was curtailed due to some other, more pressing matter. When you've just extracted and shaped a 300-ton rock, nothing could be more pressing than an impending meteorite and tsunami!

So, what else can we find out about these ancient architects? One answer lies in a seemingly trivial detail: beards.

A typical corner of Saqsayhuaman reveals the superlative craftsmaship in curving the stone. Obviously aesthetics were of great importance.

Made of red volcanic scoria, Tukuturi features large eye sockets, long ears and, uncommon for Easter Island, a beard. Similar statues around Lake Titicaca depict Viracocha.

BEARDS

Men cannot grow facial hair in the Andes. You need to travel across the Pacific to Asia, India and the Middle East to find such physiognomy. And yet my good friend and guide, Edgar, has a beard. But then he's Aymara, a very ancient people with mysterious roots, the pun on hair notwithstanding.

I made this seemingly innocuous observation while driving through Puno, a city on the shore of Lake Titicaca, and it led to a lively discussion about the remote origins of the people living around the lake's periphery, particularly that most famous of local personalities, the god-man Viracocha, who "wore a thick beard, whereas the Indians are clean shaven, and his robe came down to the ground, while that of the Incas came only to their knees; this is why the Peruvian people called the Spanish 'Viracochas' the minute they saw them."[1] On the southern end of Lake Titicaca, an anthropomorphic pillar was found buried in deep silt inside the semi-subterranean temple at Tiwanaku, roughly at the level where the lakeshore used to be 11,000 years ago. Carved from red volcanic scoria, it depicts the bearded Viracocha. It is not an isolated idol. Traditions state that one of the first acts performed by the Viracochas was the raising of many such effigies throughout the region. Some exist on the Mocachi peninsula facing Tiwanaku to the north, an area of scattered megaliths as tall as 8 feet, marking a rectangle much like the Kalasasaya, and appear to belong to the earlier Tiwanaku building period. One red statue representing a bearded Viracocha is surrounded by the snake symbol, just as it is at Tiwanaku. This will of great importance later.

When Spanish missionaries arrived in Cuzco they found a similar statue still standing inside the Qorikancha, depicting a man looking remarkably like an itinerant monk, tall and lean and wearing a long robe and sandals, his pale face fully bearded — a Caucasian. No wonder Pizzaro and his band of barbarians were mistaken for the progeny of the gods, handing thirty conquistadores a major psychological advantage with which to subdue half a continent despite being vastly outnumbered. It is not by accident that the same fate befell the Cholulans of Mexico when they too mistook Cortez and his bearded pirates for another returning, light-skinned, bearded god, Quetzalcoatl.

Edgar, who is also a shaman, impressed me with how the Aymara are themselves the progeny of the Puquina, who fled to the Andes when the flood sank their home in the Pacific, an island continent they call Lupakije, better known by its nicknames Mu and Lemuria. They still talk openly about it as a matter of pride even thought the event occurred 11,000 years ago; even a false door, carved on the face of a hill beside Lake Titcaca, was named Amaru Muru — Old Bearded Man From Mu.[2] Legends of Viracocha's arrival in Tiwanaku and his eventual departure across the Pacific were handed down from them.

The Puquina's tradition neatly overlaps that of the Waitaha, whose

A bearded and girdled Viracocha from the semi-subterranean temple at Tiwanaku, and right, in Mocachi, with recurring serpent symbolism.

predecessors, the Urukehu, frequently sailed between Tiwanaku, Easter Island and New Zealand, a nautical triangle covering over 14,000 miles. The adventurer Thor Heyerdahl proved such long distance travel across the Pacific was possible when he reached French Polynesia from South America on his famous Kon-Tiki voyage of 1947; sixty-eight years later a second Kon-Tiki expedition reached Easter Island itself. A text acquired by Heyerdahl on Easter Island mentions the existence of an ancient land named Kainga Nuinui (Enormous Land) and how, after it sank in the flood, Hotu Matu'a — one of the heroes of the Waitaha narrative — sent seven scouts to Easter Island on a reconnaissance mission before bringing survivors with her to the island.[3]

EASTER ISLAND'S NAVEL

Two thousand miles separate the temple cities of Tiwanaku, Pisac, Cuzco and Machu Picchu from the monuments of Easter Island, yet you'd think they belong to the same culture. For one thing, the shared attributes of the Urukehu and Viracocha's Shining Ones — light-skinned, red-haired and bearded — suggest they were one and the same brotherhood. And for another, all the locations associated with the flood gods are defined as navels of the earth.

Over one hundred *ahu* (ceremonial platforms) are spread over the island. The oldest — Ahu Tahiri, Ahu Mata and Ahu Vinapu — are also the best constructed. If one were to take the stones of Ahu Vinapu and replace them for those in Cuzco no one would notice the cunning swap, right down to tiny, three-inch keystones; another *ahu* by the name Hanaunakou contains impressively large megaliths that appear to show carved faces, now heavily weathered due to their antiquity.[4] Such *ahu* differ from newer platforms in that they are built from basalt, which is not found on the island, so where did it come from? When marine explorer Jacques Cousteau explored the island, he and his team came across rectangular cavities in basalt layers on ledges *below* sea level, thus the basalt must have been extracted when the quarry was still accessible 12,000 years ago, prior to the dramatic rise in sea level, when Easter Island was considerably larger and part of an archipelago stretching several hundred miles.[5] Folklore adds that when the island was a substantial landmass, it was criss-crossed by roads so long that no one was able to determine where they began or ended, and indeed there are still traces of these tracks leading to the edge of the sea, into which they disappear.[6]

Whoever built the original *ahu* was most likely responsible for the sites in the high Andes, and not just because the methods of construction are identical, but for the manner in which the stones were moved. The masons of Easter Island are said to have focused their *mana* (magical power)[7] around a special spherical stone called Te-Pito-Kura (the golden navel stone),[8] enabling the stones to be lifted and making them appear as though walking through the air to their locations during the course of a single night, much as they did at Tiwanaku and Cuzco. The Swiss ethnologist Alfred Metreux made extensive studies of Easter Island and wrote down oral traditions involving levitation: "When Easter Islanders of today are asked about means by which the statues were transported, they only say: 'King Tiikoihu, the great magician, used to move them with the words of his mouth... the idea of flying statues did not seem strange to the natives... C.E. Fox reports such a concept from San Cristobal in the Solomons: "Levitation is described as common both in the case of sacred stones and of priests, some of whom were levitated large distances through the air.""" [9]

Easter Island's flood myth features an antediluvian supernatural being called Uoke "who traveled around the Pacific with a gigantic lever with which he pried up whole islands and tossed them into the sea where they

Ahu Vinapu, Easter Island. Identical to megalithic stonework in the Andes.

vanished forever under the waves. After destroying many islands he came at length to the coast of Te-Pito-O-Te-Henua, then a much larger land that it is today. He began to lever up parts of it and cast them into the sea. Eventually he reached a place called Puko Pihipuhi... in the vicinity of Hanga Hoonu [site of the navel stone]. Here the rocks of the island were too sturdy for Uoke's lever, and it was broken against them. He was unable to dispose of the last fragment, and this remained as the island we know today." [10] Uoke's actions appear oddly similar to those of the Finnish god Ukko.

The first survivors to reach Easter Island after the flood are said to have come from a massive Pacific island called Hiva which "submerged under the sea" due to "the mischief of Uoke's lever." [11] These were the 300 people picked up by Hotu Matu'a and her Seven Sages, "all initiated men," whose first task upon arriving was the construction of *ahu*. [12] As to where Hiva might have been remains a mystery. There are two islands in the Marquesas bearing the name Hiva Oa and Nuku Hiva, although the names may be in homage to the original homeland. They lie to the northwest of Easter Island and feature their own extensive collection of *ahu*, along with unusual goggle-eyed statues not dissimilar to those in Easter Island and Tiwanaku. Before the flood, the Marquesas also had a substantially larger footprint and ostensibly formed one massive island.

BEARDED MOAI

But back to beards. Easter Island's most celebrated inhabitants are made of stone and stare longingly at the sky. At least the oldest do. Over a thousand of these *moai* (statue) dot the island, some erected on *ahu*, others along the slopes of Rano Raraku volcano, covered up to their necks in deep sediment. Excavation of one statue revealed the head to be attached to a long torso, making the *moai* just over 40 feet tall. [13]

The *moai* tend to be lumped together as a single event but they were definitely carved by different people over different epochs following a similar recipe. The younger are shaped from the readily available volcanic tuft and tend to lack the finesse and attention to aesthetic detail of the older *moai*, whose style and facial features differ significantly, are carved from the tougher basalt, and are found at deeper stratigraphic levels, or beneath newer *moai* and their *ahu*; some have been recycled to shore up damaged structures.[14]

Like the question of megalithic masonry in the Andes, the skill of the stone masons on Easter Island began at an exceptionally high level and degraded over time, the complete opposite of what civilization is supposed to induce. This brings up an uncomfortable issue for historians who claim all the *moai* were carved by Polynesians arriving up to 1500 years ago, who allegedly conducted this labor-intensive symbolic project while conducting a civil war on a sixty square-mile speck of rock in the Pacific. The problem with this theory is, stone cannot be dated, only undisturbed organic matter found under it, and to date no one has bothered to conduct a thorough radiocarbon test to determine the age of the sediment upon which the statues stand, probably because thirty feet of soil covering a *moai* is incompatible with a few centuries of erosion. Such a depth is more likely the result of *thousands* of years of accumulation, an opinion shared by the noted Harvard geologist Robert Schoch.[15] Expectations were raised early in 2018 when UCLA archaeologist Jo Anne Van Tilburg and assistants dug to the base of another *moai* and were finally in a position to secure organic material. I was in communication with her at this time and was told that by November of that year we should see a paper published with the results. November came and went, no paper emerged, and upon expressing my surprise, her response was that "several papers will be published... none of them carbon date the moai but present associated dates." [16]

Sensing a whitewash-in-the-making, I turned to the Waitaha narrative — which covers at least 10,000 years of oral history [17] — to enlighten us on this affair, but it does not mention the original carving of *moai*, despite the Waitaha's predecessors originating from Easter Island. As with the Inka and the megalithic structures of the Andes, the few references appear matter-of-fact, suggesting the statues were already established on the island in this time. There are only two notable mentions in their narrative: one, during a journey back from New Zealand the seafearers are described as "eager to stand beneath the great monuments carved by the Stone People. Everyone stood in awe of the Mokai, the towering stone figures shaped by those ancestors to keep the God of Earthquakes quiet in his lair." [18] It is for this reason that the oldest *moai* face inland, toward the volcano.

The Stone People arrived from the direction of Asia after the flood and during the period when the island was densely forested. This implies a more remote age than the one proposed by academics, who claim the island was already sparsely forested and subsequently depleted as a result of carving *moai*, the consequence of which was famine and civil war. The Waitaha claim the Stone People were conscionable, they knew how "to shape stone without breaking its spirit," just as they held a particular sensitivity towards the environment. Only lunatics would deplete an already meager infrastructure by embarking on a vanity project that exacerbates soil erosion on an overcrowded island. There is also the issue of the island's indigenous palm trees. Historians claim the trunks were used to move the statues, however, the bulk of this type of palm is too pulpy to carry such heavy loads, the trunks would easily crush, rendering the argument of transportation and deforestation null and void.

The second notable mention is when the Waitaha returned to New Zealand with six small *moai* totems to be deliberately buried at strategic locations throughout three islands, where they remain safely concealed to this day.[19]

Aside from their enigmatic gaze at the sky, the older *moai* along the slopes of Rano Raraku feature unusually elongated chins. Unlike the typical human face where the distance from mouth to chin is twice the distance from mouth to nose, the sculptuors of the *moai* extended the face much lower to represent a bearded chin. Smaller, wooden carvings of the *moai* are depicted with goatees, along with extended earlobes, another trait common to the gods; the historians Albert Metreux and Eve Routledge have even pointed out that four of the *moai* inside Rano Raraku show the same form of goatee. Although the statues have been subjected to much erosion, a close look at the Rano Raraku group does reveal worn vertical lines along the chin indicating stylized beards, while Moai 002-077 features a pattern of curved incisions depicting hair on its neck, along with traces of red pigment.[20] One unusual kneeling statue called Tukuturi shows a bearded giant with elongated ears, carved from the same red volcanic scoria as the statues of the bearded Viracocha in and around Tiwanaku. According to the wisdom keeper of Tongareva — whose ancestors once lived on Easter Island — the bearded effigies represent the visiting Starwalkers, the Urukehu. It is the later *moai* who represent the chiefs of the island.[21]

Bearded men are not indigenous to this remote Pacific region, but then Easter Island has an unusual history of unusual people, including the closest descendent of its last king, a man with high cheekbones and forehead, inset eyes and a beard, features consistent with Caucasians. There were other out-of-place people still living on the island in the 18th century. When the first Europeans arrived, an entry in the ship's log describes how a boat came to greet them, steered by a giant of a man: "With truth, I might say that these savages are all of more than gigantic size. The men are tall and broad in proportion, averaging twelve feet in height. Surprising as it may appear, the tallest men on board of our ship could pass between the legs of these children of Goliath without bending the head. The women cannot compare in stature with the men, as they are commonly not above 10 feet high." [22] These giants were referred to as Long Ears, compared with run-of-the-mill humans, the Short Ears.

It's not difficult to experience affection for the *moai*. Their elongated ears, their pouting expression carved so eloquently on enormous blocks of stone, their arms reaching around a protruding belly to hands with slender, outstretched fingers spread around a navel. An arresting image. With so much focus on that navel, and of course the umbilical connotation, the statues' inherent symbolism commemorates Easter Island as a fundamental place of creation, a birthplace.

If the Waitaha narrative is correct, and Hotu Matu'a — "a child of the gods" — appeared after the flood from the west to "find the Sacred Birthing Cord of the World," [23] the logical assumption is that the island was already a strategic location before the flood, much like Tiwanaku. The earliest *moai* may have been raised after the flood to re-establish the connection, "to keep the God of Earthquakes quiet in his lair," as the narrative says. After the tectonic convulsions

Moai with exaggerated, bearded chins.

of 9700 BC, the statues may have served a symbolic as well as a practical, even magical function, after all, these gods are described as having the ability to imbue physical substances with life as well as possessing a degree of control over the laws of nature.

There's another location where outstretched fingers point to navels, and it too is considered a Navel of the Earth. It lies a world away in Anatolia.

GÖBEKLI TEPE, HILL OF OSIRIS

Beards are not out of place in the Middle East. But belts are, particularly if they come with distinctive H and U symbols and attached to slender, anthropomorphic pillars near the summit of a hill in Anatolia by the name of Göbekli Tepe.

The naming of places, people and objects in the ancient world was a serious affair, particularly in regard to places of sanctity. A given name enshrined the purpose for which the site was intended, or reflected a truth about its history. Thus by understanding the original name of Göbekli Tepe we find the single greatest clue as to why people of a forgotten era created a monument that is both out of place and out of time. The latest ground-penetrating radar reveals a collection of between sixteen to fifty large oval stone circles consisting of elaborately carved pillars up to nineteen feet tall, deliberately interred and made to resemble a natural hill. This staggering project was built during an epoch when humans were supposed to have been nothing more than primitive hunter-gatherers.

Its ancient Armenian, and probably oldest name is Portasar, and it breaks down into two syllables: *port* (navel or umbilical cord) identifies the site as a Navel of the Earth, a seeding place where the knowledge of the gods was first deposited — where kingship was lowered from heaven, to coin the Mesopotamian phrase. Wherever such epicenters were created, wisdom spread across the land like ripples, touching the uncivilized and the brute and elevating the potential

H and U symbols on the pillar's girdle.

of humankind. This alone confers onto Portasar enormous significance.

But there's more. The second syllable *asar* is revelatory, for it is none other than the original name of Osiris, primary Egyptian deity and lord of the Otherworld (Osiris is a later Greek transliteration). It can be said, then, that Göbekli Tepe is the Umbilical Cord of Osiris, who, as it turns out, was a bearded god.

The site was rediscovered in the 1960s by a team of surveyors from Istanbul and Chicago, yet no great importance was given because, to the naked eye, the few artifacts scattered upon the parched surface were deemed to belong to a recent civilization. It was not old enough to be of value, and so its true antiqueness and uniqueness were left unrecognized for over three decades until a German archaeological team led by the late Klaus Schmidt realized the enormity of what might be concealed below the surface, based on his earlier excavations of a nearby site, Nevali Cori, shown by radiocarbon dating to have been inhabited by 10,000 BC.

Dating sites of extreme antiquity poses enormous challenges. For decades, radiocarbon dating has been deemed a reliable method for providing objective age estimates for carbon-based materials originating from living organisms. The method works by comparing the decay rate of

Göbekli Tepe.

three different carbon isotopes. Over time, one of the isotopes, Carbon-14, decays to nitrogen. Most C-14 is produced in the upper atmosphere where neutrons produced by cosmic rays react with atoms. It then oxidises to create carbon dioxide, which is dispersed through the atmosphere. This CO_2 is used in photosynthesis by plants, and from there is passed through the food chain.

There are two issues when using C-14 to date temples. First, few if any organic material is ever taken from *beneath* megaliths, which would at least identify the date when the stones were placed. The main problem is that the vast majority of temples were predominantly erected on virgin bedrock. Instead, samples are generally taken from the lowest habitation level where soil has accumulated and trapped organic material.

Bear in mind that any sacred space, much like one's own home, would have been maintained in a state of cleanliness rather than allowed to fill with dirt and debris, or food scraps and broken pottery. Therefore what C-14 dating will indicate is a period long *after* the site has fallen into disuse; the site itself could be hundreds, even thousands of years older. Second, mainstream science has assumed the radioactive decay rate remains constant under all conditions. It doesn't. In August 2008 physicists Jere Jenkins and Ephraim Fischback published a paper claiming that decay rates are not constant, they fluctuate in correlation to solar flares as well as the changing distance between the Earth and Sun.[24] Naturally this threatened to overturn scientific conventions. Sixty years of established science was proven flawed, calling into question the time frame of prehistory, including the age when megalithic structures were erected. Not surprisingly the Purdue University's physicists have been given the academic cold shoulder.[25]

With this in mind let us examine Göbekli Tepe. The lower habitation layer in the three primary stone circles, or enclosures, yielded the following dates: Enclosure D, 9990-9600 BC, Enclosure C, c.9700 BC, and the youngest, Enclosure A, 9559-8880 BC. Beyond this point the site was no longer used.[26]

The date range is impressively old. However, virtually all testing came from the fill material dumped into the enclosures after each was carefully packed with debris. Since the enclosures and their pillars were built upon virgin bedrock, all the C-14 dates tell us is when the enclosures began to be decommissioned.[27]

The archaeological team decided that a more reliable method was to date the mortar used in the rough stone walls erected around each enclosure prior to their interment. Using Enclosure D as an example, the average age returned was 9984 BC — before the flood. Again impressive, except the stone walls and the mortar were not integral to the original site. The masonry is crude compared to the elegance of the pillars, and the fact that the walls cover important reliefs on the surface of the pillars proves they were added much later, at the end of the site's useful life. With these parameters in mind the scientists preliminarily concluded that Enclosure D may be the oldest, with a construction date c.10,500 BC, placing part of Göbekli Tepe firmly within the Younger Dryas.[28]

Why should these enclosures, with their dignified T-shape pillars, have been deliberately buried? Two possibilities come to mind. One, in temple tradition, the sites are designed to mirror specific heavenly bodies, what is referred to as sky-ground dualism. The Waitaha narrative elegantly describes this purpose, with understatement: "Only when star and stone are held together in one hand is the mind truly at one with the beginning and the end of the Tai Atea [Cosmos]. Only then do we know the oneness of the Universe and walk the deep trails of wisdom where everything is possible. For the Mind Song is without end; it joins with the ancestors to know the completeness of the circle of the dream."[29] After the passage of two to four thousand years, however, the Earth's axial rotation — its precession — has changed the planet's position relative to the background stars to which the temple was originally aligned. When this sky-ground relationship is broken, the temple ceases to mirror the sky and becomes nothing more than a beautiful enterprise, even if its sanctity remains forever. With its life span complete, the temple is either sealed, or adjusted and expanded to allow for a fresh astronomical alignment. The temple of Luxor in Egypt, with its two distinct axes, is a perfect example.

A second possibility is that the site was buried to prevent its destruction. Dating Enclosure D to the mid 10th millennium suggests people were present at Göbekli Tepe three hundred years after the first encounter with a fragmented meteorite that triggered the Younger Dryas. By the same token, the C-14 dating of mortar and the lower layer of debris to 9990-9600 BC places the activity one hundred years either side of the second strike that generated the great flood and brought about the end of the Younger Dryas.

It would appear people came to this hill in Anatolia to construct what appears to be a library in stone, then carefully packed up the site and left prior to the calamity about to unfold. For this to happen they must have had foreknowledge of the event, and if they were expert astronomers — the site is astronomically significant — they certainly would have been aware of the cycles that affect and afflict the Earth, and acted prudently to preserve the knowledge therein.

A look at the astro-archaeology of Enclosure D, the best preserved so far, ought to shed more light. It features thirteen T-shaped pillars, each erected on 8-inch-tall plinths carved in relief on the bedrock, an astonishing engineering achievement in itself considering how an area of 600 square feet would first need to be leveled, then much of it shaved away to leave the raised plinths and the slots into which the pillars are inserted. Each pillar features a plethora of animals and symbols carved in relief, many bearing astronomical connotations.

It has been suggested that the pillars of Enclosure D were aligned to reference the setting of the constellation Cygnus.[30] It is an elegant theory except it omits one glaring obstacle: the stone circle is not on the summit of the hill but sits approximately thirty feet below the horizon line, making it

Vega and the passage of the sky on the winter solstice c.10,400 BC.
Cygnus is obscured by the hill and rises briefly to the right before dawn.
(angle of Enclosure D shown for illustration only)

very difficult to observe and mark descending or ascending objects with any accuracy in the northern sky. Additionally, ancient people typically commemorated the *rising* of astral objects or their mid-heaven position, not their setting. However, there is some merit. A viewer standing on the south perimeter of the circle would have used Pillar 43 to mark Cygnus' brief appearance and descent after sunset, and just before sunrise, used Pillar 30 to mark its brief rise before the light of the rising Sun erased the effect.

Perhaps a re-examination is in order. After the winter solstice sunset in the epoch c.10,400 BC, a person standing between the two massive central T-pillars and looking north would have seen Vega, the star then closest to the celestial pole, glistening like a jewel at 352°, the angle of the central T-pillars 31 and 18. Vega's position is actually marked by Pillar 43 along the northern perimeter, while its 20° elliptical rotation around the celestial pole from sunset to sunrise is framed within the field of vision of the central T-pillars. Most importantly, Vega's altitude at the time made it wholly visible above the summit during the course of the night.

Vega's light is of such magnitude that it features prominently in the lore of ancient cultures, and not surprisingly it was used as a navigational beacon, particularly throughout the Pacific Ocean. Its name derives from the Arabic *waqi* (falling, swooping), referring to a time when the rotation of its host constellation Lyra was seen as a swooping vulture,[31] the motion being especially obvious during the epoch c.10,400 BC. This might explain why the heavily decorated pillar 43 features a prominent relief of a vulture

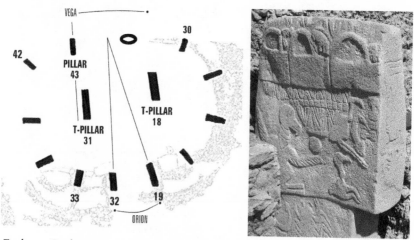

Enclosure D alignments, with Vega the vulture on Pillar 43 circling the celestial pole.

with outstretched wings, one of which touches a circle; two smaller, less mature vultures stand either side. Seen together the birds appear to mimic the circling of Vega around the celestial pole, each bird representing the star's diminishing brightness as it completes its nightly circumpolar journey around an imaginary circle in the sky.

The siting of Enclosure D below the summit suggests the northern sky was perhaps not the primary aim of the monument. Turning to face south while Vega is prominent in the north, the belt of Orion can be seen rising briefly above the horizon, the narrow arc framed by pillars 19 and 33, with Pillar 32 marking its highest ascension in that era.

By comparison, the epoch of 9600 BC — the late C-14 date for Enclosure D — sees Vega rising 10 degrees further to the west and well outside the alignment of the central pillars, certainly out of alignment with Pillar 43, while Orion has shifted a few degrees to the southeast but remains acceptably within the pillars' frame of reference.

So, what are we to make of this combined reference to the pole star and the ascent of Orion's Belt c.10,400 BC? For one thing it marks a significant period when Orion reaches its lowest meridian transit during the Earth's 25,920-year precession cycle.[32] Taking the hill's original name Portasar — the Umbilical Cord of Asar — Osiris is himself associated with Orion, his primary dwelling place being Giza, the limestone plateau identified in Egyptian texts as Rostau, a gateway to the Otherworld. The researchers Robert Bauval and Adrian Gilbert have convincingly argued that the three main Giza pyramids form the pattern of Orion's belt as it appeared relative to the celestial pole on the spring equinox in the epoch c,10,400 BC as though some cosmic architect wished to memorialize this date in time. According to Bauval and Gilbert, "What now emerges from the visual picture of the southern sky at the epoch c.10,400 BC is this: The pattern of Orion's Belt seen on the 'west' of the Milky Way matches, with uncanny precision, the pattern and alignments of the three Giza pyramids!" [33]

Could Göbekli Tepe be an Armenian Giza Plateau, an extension of the house of Osiris? Certainly there exists a geodetic relationship between the two locations. Stretching a cord through the corner of the pyramids of Menkaure and Khufu and continuing 700 miles along the surface of the Earth, one arrives at Göbekli Tepe. The margin of error is 1.5°, a miniscule discrepancy given ten thousand years of plate tectonics. With each site referencing Orion's Belt on the spring equinox and winter solstice respectively, together they mark the opening and closing of a long-established nine-month ritual cycle.

But Göbekli Tepe's siting *below* the summit and deliberate southeastern exposure isn't just referencing the sky. On a clear day, if one finesses the eye through pillars 32 and 19 it is possible to see in the distance the ancient observation tower of Harran, far taller back in the day, unmistakable as a lone landmark.

Harran lies in what used to be northwestern Mesopotamia. Archaeological artifacts date human activity in the region to c.8000 BC. Its earliest name was Harranu, the nearest translation being Path of the Anu. It was once a major center for astronomy and home to the Sabeans, a group of sages who were among the ancient world's keenest observers of the stars,[34] whose name derives from the Egyptian *Sba* (star).[35] Their temple city, featuring the aforementioned astronomical tower, was dedicated to the lunar god Su-En (contracted to Sin). The Sabeans were described as "people of the book" of Twt — the antediluvian magician god whom the Greeks call Thoth — and were still consulting it in the 11th century, by which time the Greeks had translated it and titled it Hermetica. The book was concealed for an unspecified period before being discovered by Leonardo de Pistoia, an agent of Cosimo de Medici, while journeying through the Near East in the 14th century.[36]

Harranu is said to have been named in honor of the son of Noah, the Hebrew flood hero.[37] Later, Noah's great-grandson Cainan discovered antediluvian inscriptions carved on standing stones preserving the science of astrology and the secrets of the stars, an art taught by antediluvian gods who went by the names Anu and Watchers, who once lived in this region.[38] The *Sefer ha-Yashar*, a Hebrew *midrash*, also records this story.

Could Cainan's carved standing stones be the same

Enclosure D looking south to Orion's Belt.

Giza pyramids ley to Göbekli Tepe.

pillars so carefully buried at Göbekli Tepe? Because the site appears to have been the focal point of an astronomical cult already in existence prior to the flood, whose practitioners may have returned to the region to continue the tradition. The Sabeans themselves were known to be following an older tradition, and were still undertaking regular pilgrimage to Giza as late as the 14th century BC.[39]

Many of the two hundred limestone pillars so far uncovered are shaped smooth and feature reliefs of birds, bears, snakes, salamanders and other creatures. The central T-pillars are the tallest: 18 feet high, 4 feet wide and a slender 8 inches thick.[40] One of them — again in Enclosure D — hums when brushed with the palm of the hand.[41] They are anthropomorphic, carved on either side with long arms that reach around the corners to hands with slender fingers pointing directly at a navel. Where have we seen this motif? The statues of Tiwanaku and Easter Island, in fact the hands and fingers on a similar pillar uncovered by Klaus Schmidt at Göbekli Tepe's sister site, Nevali Cori, are near identical in style to those of the *moai*.

The same is true of the relief animal carvings on Göbekli Tepe's pillars, who find their twins in Tiwanaku and nearby Silustani and Cutimbo.

This still leaves the question of our earlier observation, the belt with distinct H and U motifs worn by Göbekli Tepe's anthropomorphic figures. While sitting outside the dusty old train station at Tiwanaku I caught up with notes and observations from my journeys. Since so many antediluvian gods around the world are associated with Orion, could the H be a stylized representation of this constellation, like a graphic logo, a symbol of office?

And the U, could it refer to the antediluvian god of Mesopotamia, a figure depicted with fish scales and a beard, just like Viracocha's — a god-man by the name U-annu who is regularly depicted holding a strange container?

CONTAINERS OF KNOWLEDGE

A derivative of Portasar is Gandzasar (Mountain of Treasure), however, in old times treasure didn't infer jewels or loot, but knowledge. The oldest known iteration of the word is the Greek *thesauros* (a storehouse, treasure), the root of *thesaurus*, in essence a treasure of wisdom contained in words. The Waitaha refer to such treasure in spiritual terms as *taonga*.

At Göbekli Tepe we find not words but symbols, a storehouse of them, all carved in relief on enigmatic T-shape pillars. The builders could have saved themselves a colossal amount of time by simply fashioning raw stone into straight shapes, so the extra effort that went into the T-shape implies purpose, perhaps a symbolic meaning. And nothing in temple design is superfluous or by accident.

The T is a culturally shared symbol known in Yucatan and Guatemalan temple culture as the Breath of God,[43] just as in the ancient Japanese and Chinese spiritual traditions it is called Shu-gen-do and Tayi respectively, the supreme knowledge of the gods.[44] The Hopi, Zuni and Anasazi applied this symbol and the teaching it represents in their sacred dwellings, one example being the large T-shape window in the great kiva of Chaco Canyon.

The supreme knowledge of the Cosmos consists of the balance between light and dark forces. Thus the T represents one aspect, and a second T its mirrored opposite. Joining the two and turning the composite image sideways reveals H, the symbol on the belts of the anthropomorphic pillars of Göbekli Tepe. It follows that the individuals represented by these totems — much like the *moai* — must have been people who personified the knowledge, perhaps the gods who brought the civilizing arts to humanity following the devastation by the flood.

Might this also explain the idea behind the curious H-blocks scattered about Puma Punku? Was the Breath of God literally and symbolically bestowed onto the walls of this temple?

The H-symbol also forms the underlying design of Mayan ball courts, where initiates were taught the secrets of the Cosmos in the ultimate game of life, death and rebirth, also referred to as the Game of the Gods. Never were the ball courts intended for blood sports, as any respected Mayan elder will inform.[45] The reference to death is metaphoric, it alludes to the symbolic death of the initiate leading to the resurrection of the spiritual

T symbol at Göbekli Tepe, Chichen Itzá ball court, and windows at Palenque.

self. This is why ball courts — the most exceptional example being Chichen Itzá— are lined with friezes depicting the motions of the planets, the Tree of Knowledge, the creation of the world, and other sacred teachings. They also incorporate some of the best sonics known to architecture, along with angles synonymous with the motions of the Earth. Such details are obviously at odds with the theory erroneously expounded by western academics.[46]

Which brings us to a striking carving in Enclosure D at Göbekli Tepe, what appear to be three containers in a row along the top of cryptic Pillar 43. It has been a mystery up until now as to what these might represent. The Waitaha narrative provides working proof of the function of these unusual receptacles. Called *kete* (basket), they represent the container into which all tribal knowledge is deposited; the word is still used by Maori wisdom keepers. Therefore an individual who holds the *kete* is a wisdom keeper, and this truth aligns perfectly with images of wisdom keepers from Sumeria to Mesoamerica who are pictured holding the exact same vessel.

One of the most fabulous archaeological discoveries in the Olmec world concerns a unique stela of what ancient alien theorists adamantly believe to be an astronaut riding a space capsule, except the capsule is in fact a rattlesnake. But that's not the real riddle here, for in his hand this 'astronaut' — who incidentally appears to be wearing either a beard or a stylized snake helmet or both — holds exactly the same container. A close look at the rattlesnake's head reveals a feathered crown, a feature also depicted on the head of Sumerian zoomorphic, falcon-headed figures called *Apkallu* (sages), the title given to a group of seven antediluvian emissaries entrusted with bringing the civilizing arts to humanity following the flood.

Hardly surprising, then, that the *Apkallu* are regularly depicted standing beside the Tree of Life and the Tree of Knowledge, picking fruit with one hand and holding a *banduddû* in the other — the same container held by our Olmec astral-naut, and carved on Pillar 43 at Göbekli Tepe.

Bearded kings such as Ashunarsipal are shown on Sumerian panels standing beside the Tree of Knowledge, *banduddû* in one hand, while the other points directly at the Creator God Ahura Mazda inside his winged disc. Obviously anyone holding the container of knowledge was awarded a privileged position since the object marks its owner as an individual who has gained access to transcendental information possessed and revealed by the gods. Mesopotamian friezes and clay seals depict the first *Apkallu* — the aforementioned bearded fish-man U-annu (later transliterated to Ou-anna and Oannes) — holding the *banduddû* in one hand and a scroll bearing godly information in the other.

It stands to reason that the *kete* carved on Pillar 43 at Göbekli Tepe not only identifies the site as a location where the gods deposited the same knowledge — for which it was elevated to the status of Navel of the Earth, umbilical cord of Osiris — it also represents the oldest expression of this symbol, one that has been promulgated from the Middle East to Central America for over 12,000 years.

EVIDENCE LIES SIDEWAYS

Besides demonstrating the existence of an antediluvian culture with links around the world, the beauty of Göbekli Tepe is how effortlessly it inverts the accepted academic model concerning the ascent of humanity

Long, slim fingers and navels: pillar, Nevali Çori; Göbekli Tepe; a moai.

Containers of wisdom: Pillar 43; Apkallu sage; Quetzcoatl stela, La Venta.

from rudimentary experimentation to highly complex civilization, because on this remote mountaintop in Anatolia these oldest of structures appear fully developed, complex and megalithic, without development or precedent, before devolving over time. By way of analogy, it is like a group of scientists developing space rockets only to end up with fireworks.

The answer to anomalous places such as this, to paraphrase the late Egyptologist John Anthony West, is simple: such civilizations were not developments but legacies.

But there is one further mystery at Göbekli Tepe and it literally lies on the other side of the hill, where the stones were quarried and fashioned from the bedrock. There is something eerie about a 20-foot T-pillar lying on the ground, still partly attached to the bedrock, waiting to be fully detached, polished and transported. It is as though something interrupted the work in-progress and destiny took a different course.

The reason I find it unsettling is because the situation is repeated far too often at key megalithic sites — such as the string of abandoned monoliths meant for Ollantaytambo; or gargantuan rectangular monoliths left idly in a quarry in Lebanon, meant for the temple of Baalbek. Like an abandoned *moai*, there's a certain melancholy looking at these recumbent stones because it seems their journey was abruptly curtailed by some uninvited astral event.

Blonde and green-eyed, and still lovely as a grandmother. Monika Matamua of the Ngati Hotu of New Zealand — and Egypt and the Middle East.

POLYNESIAN BLONDES AND ANDEAN REDHEADS

One wonders how the early Waitaha felt when coming face-to-face with people so different to themselves — flood heroes such as Kiwa, offspring of the Urukehu, with their light skin, golden or red hair and blue or green eyes? Probably much the same as early Europeans did when first exploring North America, perplexed by the rich traditions and myriad languages they discovered as they made contact **6** with what they'd been led to believe were savages. After all, wasn't this supposed to be the uninhabited New World?

What fascinated them most was a tribe of indigenous people who looked positively Caucasian. In 1738 the French Canadian trader Sieur de la Verendrye, traveling along the Missouri River in the Dakotas, sent back reports of the Mandan tribe, whom he described as fair skinned with red or blonde hair and blue or grey eyes. The women in particular were distinctly Nordic in appearance, and aside from clothing, they were indistinguishable.

Within fifty years of contact the tribe was decimated by smallpox. When the explorers Lewis and Clark visited the Mandan in 1804 they were again described as "half-white, peaceful, civilized, courteous, and polite." The pictorial historian George Catlin spent several months drawing and painting the Mandan in 1832. He too was struck by their Europeaness and how they were more advanced compared to neighboring tribes: "They are a very interesting and pleasing people in their personal appearance and manners, differing in many respects, both in looks and customs, from all the other tribes I have seen. So forcibly have I been struck with the peculiar ease and elegance of these people, together with their diversity of complexions, the various colors of their hair and eyes; the singularity of their language, and their peculiar and unaccountable customs, that I am fully convinced that they have sprung from some other origin than that of the other North American Tribes, or that they are an amalgam of natives with some civilized race." [1]

The Mandan's tribal myth is particularly enlightening given how they lived in the high plains, far from major bodies of open water, yet claimed in no uncertain terms to be descended from a strange white man who appeared aboard a canoe in ancient times after an enormous flood wiped out everything in sight. He taught them agriculture, domestication of animals and all the civilizing arts. [2]

Mandan was the name given to Verendrye by his guides, a simplification of Mayadana, however, the tribespeople collectively referred to themselves as Numakaki (People by the River). I couldn't help ruminating on this name and how it sounds like a corruption of Anunaki, People of Anu, antediluvian gods of Mesopotamia said to have descended from heaven and maintained a lineage of divine kings and queens long after the flood.

Numakaki shares no obvious linguistic connection with Anunaki, but Mayadana does, since it incorporates the syllable *ana*, a recognized variant of *anu*. Since each group existed on opposite sides of the world I wasn't sure what to make of the relationship, if one exists at all, until I was introduced to a gentleman from an island few outside the central Pacific have heard of, which was to remind me of how western preconceptions of ancient civilizations are often incorrect.

THE ANU OF TONGAREVA

Tongareva is an atoll with a circumference of forty-eight miles enclosing an azure lagoon. Nine degrees south of the equator and two hundred miles from its nearest neighbor in the Cook Islands group, it is literally in the middle of the Pacific Ocean and sits atop the highest submarine volcano, 16,000 feet from the ocean floor. The name means 'island floating in space', and seen from space it looks exactly like the name implies.

There are 213 people living in Tongareva today. Teokotai Andrew is a descendent of one of the oldest families and has been given responsibility for safeguarding his ancestors' genealogies and oral traditions. He is quite possibly the tribes' sole surviving wisdom keeper. "We have links with Teiwanaku and Te titi o Motu taiko i titikaka," he said, referring to Tiwanaku and Lake Titicaca. "Peru is the homeland of my ancestors, my people come from a lady called Punaruku who is from Puno." [3]

Puno to Tongareva is a six thousand-mile excursion. Not surprisingly I was keen to hear what else Teokotai had to share regarding Tongaveran tradition, handed down from generation to generation. As curious researchers find, if you ask politely and demonstrate good intentions, people in Teokotai's position are generous with their time and accumulated knowledge, and the stories inevitably paint a picture that diverges dramatically from the one promoted by academics, especially as they were directly experienced by people who lived thousands of years closer to the events. For that reason alone I view such accounts as more reliable.

During our conversations Teokotai informed me about "an island disappearing in the sea, we call it Motu Taiko [the land that disappears and re-appears], it used to exist in the vicinity of the Cook Islands. My ancestors left Motu Taiko after the flood covered the island, in search of a very similar landscape with water around it. One tribe who arrived in Tongareva from Motu Taiko were called *Titi* or *Maori*, they had blonde and red hair, fair-skinned, blue eyes and green eyes. In our language *maori* means 'fair skinned voyager'." [4] Many Tongarevans still bear such physiognomy.

The Mandan or Mayadana.

I thought for one excited second that the story of the disappearing island referred to the great deluge, but it turns out this particular event took place in the ancient past rather than the remote past, and climatic data shows a notable sea level rise of twenty-six feet occurred between 3200-2500 BC, enough to drown many of the Pacific's low-lying islands. This is the epoch described in the tradition. Naturally it caused a migration to Tongareva, as Teokotai explains: "They were called the people of Tupenaki or Tupenake, also known as Anunaki or Anunake, they came from Saupewa [Mesopotamia]. The Titi/Maori people from Motu Taiko and the Tupenake all met in Tongareva, intermarried, and together became Hare Vananga [House of Knowledge]." [5]

This was quite a revelation. The Anunaki are believed to have been singularly involved in Mesopotamia, if one accepts the conventional argument, and their association with the great flood places them in the same region much earlier, in the period of the Younger Dryas. The Tongareva tradition demonstrates the lineage continued for another 6000 years, and whereas the Anunaki have always been described as gods, Tongarevans bring them down to earth. According to Teokotai, "most historical facts about the Tupenaki/Anunake are exaggerated. The are not gods but normal people, great sages, star navigators and intelligent human beings." [6]

Of course it all depends on one's definition of a god. In ancient times the term applied to any individual capable of understanding and bending the laws of nature. But the bigger questions on my mind were, what would have driven a group of sages in the Middle East to travel all the way to a remote island in the middle of the Pacific? And how could the Anunaki still be living some six thousand years after the flood?

The first thing to examine is their possible reason for migrating. The Pacific was not the only place affected by rising seas 5000 years ago, Mesopotamia too was subjected to a significant incursion of the ocean, validating the Tongareva narrative; an earlier incursion of the sea c.8600 BC led to the creation of the Persian Gulf. Still, if I were living in Mesopotamia in 2600 BC my natural impulse would have been to move inland, not take off to the middle of the ocean. Clearly something possessed the Anunaki to undertake a 9000-mile sea voyage, and the most rational explanation is they already had an established presence in such a remote region going back to prehistoric times.

I wondered if there might be a connection between the Anunaki and the red haired Urukehu who once arrived in Easter Island from the direction of Tiwanaku. This is where Teokotai dropped another bombshell: "The flood is recorded in my ancestor's chants, stories and tradition. My remote ancestors came from Te Pitaka, a circular island with water around it, which was situated in Te Piupiu o Nahari Kiokura [Arabian Peninsula]. This was around the time of the flood, but that land today bears no resemblance to what it looked like then, there is virtually no trace of it. They came via Teiwanaku, well after the flood. We have proof in our stories and chants as well as ancestral genealogical names from those areas. Te Pitaka was also the ancient name of Tongareva, so that the people remembered their original homeland." [7]

A missing land of the gods in the vicinity of the Arabian Peninsula? This is a revolutionary upturning of history, to say the least.

The Tongavera tradition not only places the Anunaki in the central Pacific c.3000 BC, it also claims the link extends back to the great flood, when they lived on an island somewhere in the region of what is today a vast desert. If they also journeyed westerly from Tiwanaku, ostensibly the Anunaki may be the same people as Viracocha and his seven white-skinned, red-haired Shining Ones, least of all because the same description of the Anunaki is given in post-flood Mesopotamia: seven sages (*apkallu*) led by a charismatic leader appear from the sea, depicted as half-human half-fish and nicknamed Shining Ones. Both groups were tall and bearded. We could just as well be describing the Urukehu, in fact it looks as though these once disparate groups of gods now appear to be one and the same people.

There exists a monument in the hills of Abu Dhabi that may provide the link in this Andean-Pacific-Mesopotamian connection. It is said to be a burial site from c.3000 BC, but the basis for the date is purely speculative. Sited in the town of Al Ayin, it is a round structure, 36-feet in diameter by 14-feet in height, buried in dirt until 1967, after which it was faithfully restored; the thickness and slope angle of the walls suggest it may have once

Al Ayin chamber masonry identical to Easter Island ahu, and Andean chullpas.

been much taller, perhaps a tower. If visitors from Tiwanaku were taken here blindfolded they would assume they'd never left the Andes, because the design and method of construction are identical to the flood-era megalithic temples around Lake Titicaca, in fact it bears a resemblance to the *chullpas*, the round towers at Silustani and Cutimbo. Both the Al Ayin enclosure and the *chullpas* feature the same tiny entrance aligned to the equinox, and both have been mistaken for tombs (the *chullpas* were shown in my book *The Lost Art of Resurrection* to have been originally used for a restricted initiation ritual).[8]

It would seem the same culture built the same monuments, in the same style, in the same era on two separate continents. And if you throw in the numerous *ahu* of Easter Island, Tahiti, Tinian, Tonga and Fiji we are left with an unbroken megalithic fingerprint stretching in a band from the high Andes, across the Pacific to the Middle East.

BUILDER GODS IN THE PACIFIC

When European explorers first ventured into the Pacific they were often astonished at the sight of megalithic structures on uninhabited islands, some accounts describing the stone platforms on Malden Island or Kiribati as indistinguishable from those in South America. The Marquesas — Hiva Oa, in particular — were once filled with colossal *ahu*. The novelist Herman Melvile described them while marooned there: "One day in returning from this spring by a circuitous path, I came upon a scene which reminded me of Stonehenge... a series of vast terraces of stone rises, step by step, for a considerable distance up the hillside. These terraces cannot be less than one hundred yards in length and twenty in width. Their magnitude, however, is less striking than the immense size of the blocks composing them. Some of the stones, of an oblong shape, are from ten to fifteen feet in length, and five or six feet thick. Their sides are quite smooth, but though square, and of pretty regular formation, they bear no mark of the chisel. They are laid together without cement.... Kory-Kory, who was my authority in all matters of scientific research, gave me to understand that they were coeval with the creation of the world; that the great gods themselves were the builders." [9]

On Tonga's main island, Tongatapu, there are three-tiered platforms called *langi*, made of megalithic slabs of limestone, with older sections made of basalt, closely fitted, with the type of L-shaped elbow design common to Saqsayhuaman and Egypt's Valley Temple. Basalt is found nowhere near Tongatapu. Myth states such stone was moved by magic from the volcanic island of Uvea some six hundred miles away. There is also a massive, dolmen-style structure called Ha'amonga a Maui, made of eight-feet thick, fifteen-feet tall coral slabs, said to have been brought to the island by the god Maui on a giant canoe after raising the islands from below the ocean. Could this be the same Māui, grandson of the flood heroes in the Waitaha narrative?

Coincidentally, *mawi* is an Egyptian word meaning 'navigator or guide', while the related word *haawi* in the Hopi language means 'to descend'.

Tonga's ancient capital itself, Mu'a, is said to memorialize the name of the land from where such gods lived before it was destroyed by a global flood. To the west in New Guinea — along with New Hanover, New Britain and New Ireland — tribespeople speak of megaliths, pyramids, basalt obelisks, and petroglyphs left by "men belong time before," unusual people of whom they speak with great respect, who were culturally superior and appeared out of nowhere on large canoes, hiding many artefacts on the sacred mountain called The Mother before disappearing back into the sea. James Sheridan, a government malaria expert traveling to the region in the 1950s, saw the obelisks himself, carved with lines, fish and bird-like heads facing the rising sun. These wandering gods also shaped rocks as large as a double garage and covered them with petroglyphs of unusual

L-shape allows great structural integrity but is labor-intensive, requiring extensive removal of stone.

figures. One plantation owner recalls how the megaliths reminded him of ones back in his native Germany, in fact he was adamant they were linked to the same type of megalithic constructions found in Egypt and the Andes.

A man by the name of Jack West, who lived in New Guinea in the 1920s, recalls finding massive carved boulders near the town of Wewak. He located others on nearby islands, along with an obelisk some eight feet high, all facing the rising Sun; surrounding it was a group of smaller stones with petroglyphs, by then half buried. Larger megaliths were discov-

From the top: Step pyramid, Tahiti: standing stones in Fiji; ahu on Malden Island; Tonga is packed with one megalithic curiosity after another.

Obviously built on a human scale. One side of the three megaliths forming Ha'amonga 'a Maui. Below: one of the smaller ahu on Tonga.

ered in New Guinea by a planter named Peter Murray, who found a stone circle "like Stonehenge" on Unea, the main island in the Vitu group. "The stones are rectangular, each about eleven feet long, and carved with circles and squiggly lines like hieroglyphs. Two old men, Uva and Umbelevi, guided me to where they're positioned on top of a 2500-foot peak known as Kambu. The stones are not volcanic; obviously they have been quarried elsewhere and taken up the mountain by some means. They are so ancient that the natives do not even have legends about them." [10]

On the western side of Tahiti there's a fine example of a step pyramid, 267 feet long by 87 feet wide, featuring nine tiers. The megalithic architecture is made with stones as much as 8 feet in length, shaped and close-fitted without mortar. Such step pyramids reach their acme in size and complexity on the Caroline Islands, while the deserted Malden Island features megaliths, and roads built with close-fitting basalt slabs that continue under the sea.

But are these monuments the remnants of a destroyed civilization or were they built from scratch after the flood? Or both, an overlap, a refurbishment, much like the two oldest layers of megalithic architecture in the Andes, comparative yet separate? When myth becomes a reliable memory of past events it completes the picture that archaeology cannot. In Samoan mythology, the outlying Manu'a archipelago is said to be the first island of creation, a navel of the earth, while the island of Savai'i is claimed to be a remnant of Havai'iki, the original homeland of the antediluvian gods and birthplace of Polynesian culture. Certainly it features the largest mounds in all Polynesia, and what else may exist now lies beneath thick lava flows from the islands' dozen or so volcanoes, which sit atop the biggest shield volcano in the Pacific.

The Indonesian island of Flores is another place with its own share of enigmas, out-of-place artifacts, and stories of unusual people doing unusual things. The Nages who live in the center of the island recall the story of the forefather of the tribe, Dooy, and how he was saved from the great flood by a ship. His grave lies beneath a large stone platform in the public square of the tribal capital Boa Wai. A harvest festival honoring this great ancestor still takes place to this day, when the presiding chief is adorned with a gold model of a ship with seven masts, in memory of the fortunate survival of their ancestor.[11]

In the main public space of the village of Bena stands a group of menhirs and dolmens that are used as instruments of communication with people in the Otherworld — much like the megalithic traditions of Europe, except the root of this Flores tradition arises from the ancestors of the region who arrived after a great flood around 12,000 years ago, on a ship propelled by an engine, no less! Their descendents laid out the entire village in the shape of the ship, with a large megalithic chamber marking the place where the engine house would have been. The megaliths themselves were moved to the village from the slopes of a mountain twelve miles away by the use of special powers possessed by these ancestors, one of whom is described as a giant by the name of Dhake.[12]

THEY MIGHT BE GIANTS

It's funny how the topic of giants keeps rearing its head here and there, and although I originally had no intention to pursue this topic, it is so intrinsic to the understanding of the missing antediluvian civilization that it shouldn't be overlooked. In most flood myths the outsiders are described as very tall, but whether their height was relative to indigenous people, or they were truly gigantesque, is not always clear. Being a six-foot five-inch tall white Caucasian I might be looked upon as a giant in the Andes, whereas in Central Europe I would merely be tall; in Norway I am actually normal. Too bad I no longer have the blonde hair I had as a child because, with my green eyes, I too might have been mistaken for Viracocha!

But seriously, I want to return to my conversations with Teokotai the wisdom keeper, whose stories are never short on illumination.

He states there are numerous accounts on Tongareva of tall ancestors with red hair, but, to confuse matters, they are twenty-two feet tall, fair skinned, with blue or green eyes. One of their graves was exhumed in 1969 by anthropologists from the University of Osaka under the auspices of the United Nations. They unearthed bones of a twenty-two-foot long humanoid skeleton, beneath which they found urns. As they attempted to remove the items a booming voice emerged from the lagoon warning them, in no uncertain terms, they'd seen enough and to put back the artefacts. Shaken, the anthropologists left and never returned.[13] I contacted the university to solicit an opinion but no one wished to revisit the topic.

An individual of similar stature washed up on a beach near the northwestern tip of New Zealand in the 1950s, found by a young girl whose mother called the authorities, who hauled the remains onto a flat bed truck, drove off, and the case was never brought up again. Residents of the densely forested island of Isatabu in the Solomon Islands come face-to-face with such giants on a regular basis. Even during the Second World War, Japanese and American troops stationed there witnessed the giants, to the point where the thought of being attacked by them gave the soldiers plenty of sleepless nights. As one former Air Force officer said, "The people of the Solomon Islands have shared their islands with a race of hominoids previously undiscovered to the modern world for millennia right to this present day. The larger and more commonly seen are over 10 foot tall, but I have come across numerous islander accounts with evidence that supports that they do grow much taller than that." [14]

The giants are said to inhabit the island's vast tunnel system which is composed of a type of self-illuminating stone. This invites a comparison with a description of the Hebrew flood narrative and its hero Noah, whose "ark was illuminated by a precious stone, the light of which was more brilliant by night than by day, so enabling Noah to distinguish between day and night." [15] Noah's Zoroastrian counterpart Yima had the same assistance inside the *Vara* he was instructed to build, illumination for which was provided by means of a "window, self-shining from within." [16] As the god Ahura Mazda explained to Yima, "there are uncreated lights and created lights."[17] The first account clearly specifies a stone; the second, however, seems more like technology.

Incidentally, Isatabu literally means Sacred Abode of Isis. In the Pacific one is never far from an Egyptian word or two.

North of the Fijian group lies an isolated, nine mile-long island called Rotuma. For such a small place it is filled with mysteries of ages long gone. Its inhabitants are noted for their significantly lighter skin color as though representing a different race altogether.[18] During the Second World War, coast watchers were building a viewing station on the summit of Mt. Sororoa when they unearthed shin bones over 3 feet long, making the person to whom it belonged 12 feet tall. The summit was an ancient cemetery, as were nearby caves. While searching for places to hide in the event of a Japanese invasion, the locals found the caves filled with giant human skeletons.

Graveyards are also aplenty in the village of Itu'mut. The small size of the island leaves inhabitants little choice but to stack the graves above ground and recycle them every twenty years or so. The thing is, the modern graves are placed on top of megalithic platforms built by people from a forgotten era. Looking at them one could be mistaken for being in Saqsayhuaman, so precise and similar is the masonry. Adjacent to this plot are graves of a different kind, marked with stones of enormous size, beneath which lay the remains of 12-foot tall people. A road built in 1927 accidentally uncovered graves of identical skeletons but, due to superstition, the bones were quickly reburied and the road re-routed.[19]

Despite having little land above water nowadays, Fiji enjoys a disproportionate number of megalithic sites — at least twenty-nine —as though the island is a fragment of a once larger landmass. Many archaeological sites feature rock art with concentric rings and dots in a style identical to that used in Europe to mark stars and other astronomical data; near Vuna, a pair of menhirs are carved with circular cup-and-ring marks, the kind thought to have been unique to western Scotland.

One massive dolmen is of the type commonly seen in Korea and western Siberia; the council meeting place of Na Ututu resembles a scaled-down version of a Guatemalan pyramid: and the sacred hill Takiveleyawa, which is said to be a portal to the Otherworld, resembles the kind of hills in Yucatan once mistaken as natural but later proven to be man-made structures. When did this civilization exist in Fiji?

Many sites are now partly submerged, indicating their extreme antiquity, places like Sawailau, a sacred cave and abode of an ancient god by the name of Ulutini. It lies to the northwest of Fiji on the island of Yasawa. A diver with excellent lungs can reach this air pocket and gaze at a series of beautifully etched pictograms on the cave wall. The mouth of the cave was last above sea level 5000 years ago, so the carvings must be significantly older. The most recognizable is a horizontal lozenge shape of the type used by early Neolithic people to mark the extreme positions of the Sun at the solstices. Because the angle of the rising Sun changes relative to one's latitude, the lozenge changes shape accordingly — the closer to the equator the more horizontal, the closer to the pole the more vertical.

The Yasawa lozenge has a horizontal aspect and precisely matches the Sun's position at the latitude of the cave. But there's an appendage like a bow attached to the right of the design as though marking some other object rising in the east. Just below, a line of three fist-size circular protrusions are carved in relief, with one of the circles offset from the other two. The combination bears a remarkable resemblance to the three stars of Orion's Belt. Perhaps the 'bow' above this relief refers to Orion's shield. Let's see.

As we have already seen, the Orion constellation was of prime importance to ancient cultures — something we'll examine in detail later — particularly its heliacal rising on the winter solstice and spring equinox. If we roll back the night sky as though we are sitting at the mouth of Sawailau cave when it was still above sea level, two prominent occasions appear on the horizon. The first is 13,000 BC when Orion's Belt aligns with the horizon on the spring equinox. The second is when the *entire* constellation appears for the first time above the horizon, the epoch of 9500 BC. Is it possible people marked this alignment to commemorate the onset of the Oldest Dryas, then returned to this marker two hundred years after the Younger Dryas? Were they referencing the new sky, like navigators charting missing lands in this drastically rearranged landscape? I could not help but be reminded of the Waitaha narrative after the world was "turned by water," when Kiwa arrives on Easter Island, from which he makes numerous voyages across the Pacific, charting its remaining lands, many of which had

become islands following the dramatic rise in sea level.[20] Coulde this cave have been a point of reference?

Fiji is not the only archipelago with connections to a post-diluvial race. On the small atoll of Lae in the Marshall Islands there is the legend of a huge cylinder made of timber that came ashore filled with giants, weak from drifting across the ocean. The fearful villagers overpowered and killed them, but upon discovering that one

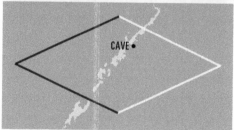

Orion's Belt inside Yasawa cave. Note lozenge with appendage. Below: shape formed by the solstices at this latutude.

was a princess they were filled with remorse, and to this day the islanders toss a food offering into the sea to ask forgiveness whenever they pass by the islet where she is buried.

But from which missing land did these people drift? Legends of Samoa claim that a tribe of giants, the Hiti, lived there before a great flood, while Aborigines of the Northern Territories claim the area near the Brimmy Valley was once Burrangie, the secret place of the giant people from the Dreamtime. Or maybe they came from the island of Tinian in the Marianas archipelago, home to a most unusual set of megaliths collectively known as the House of Taga. Sometime in prehistory a ten-foot tall chief named Taga erected two parallel rows of monoliths, fifteen feet in height, topped with enormous hemispherical caps hollowed into cups. Of the twelve upright stones sketched by explorer George Anson in 1742, only one remains upright due to earthquakes. The House of Taga was just one of eighteen such structures on Tinian, all out of place and time.[21]

RETURNING TO BLONDES AND REDHEADS

Teokotai Andrew's narrative of fair-skinned, red or blonde-haired voyagers arriving from the Middle East via the Andes is corroborated by

Orion's shield.

another indigenous group of New Zealand, the Ngati Hotu. Historians such as J.M. McEwen researched the tribe for nearly two decades based on the writings of Maori elders Raniera Te Ahiko and Paramena Te Naonao. A quote from one elder about the Ngati Hotu makes some startling claims: "Generally speaking, Ngati Hotu were of medium height and of light colouring. In the majority of cases they had reddish hair... and were spoken of as Te Whanau a Rangi [Children of Heaven] because of their fair skin. There were two distinct types. One had *kiri wherowhero* or reddish skin, a round face, small eyes and thick protruding eyebrows. The other was fair-skinned, much smaller in stature, with larger and very handsome features. The latter were the true *urukehu* and Te Whanau a Rangi. In some cases not only did they have reddish hair, but also light coloured eyes."[22]

Fair skin, light color eyes, children of heaven? What's going on here?

When Captain Wallis arrived in Tahiti from England on an exploratory voyage in 1767 he was astonished to find over ten per cent of Tahitians were white-skinned and blonde, with the greatest concentration living on the island of Ra-Iatea — literally 'White-skinned People of Ra'. Local traditions claim that most ancient Maori tribes intermarried both blonde, blue-eyed people and red-haired green-eyed people who'd migrated from afar.[23] The historian J.M. Brown noted similar Caucasian features still prevalent in many Easter Islanders during his visit to the island in 1920: "There is a general consensus of the European-like features and colour of many of the natives of Easter Island. And the faces of the images confirm this Caucasoid impression; they are oval, straight-nosed, large-eyed, thin-lipped and short in the upper lip, the features that distinguish or are supposed to distinguish the highest ideal of beauty of the north-west of Europe." [24]

Thor Heyerdahl himself was persuaded that the red volcanic tufa cylinders found atop many *moai*, like crowns, are representative of the Urukehu's red hair, after all it would have been far easier to carve these additions as one piece with the statues, an observation made earlier by the archaeologist Henry Balfour. For one thing,

House of Taga as it appeared in 1742.

Polynesians used to dye their black hair red to simulate the gods.[25]

Despite the Ngati Hotu's near-extinction at the hands of invading Maori tribes in the 14th century, a fair number still exist today in New Zealand. They are described not simply as manifesting the Urukehu strain, but as *direct* ancestors of the Urukehu themselves.[26] Their oral traditions unequivocally state they are of Middle Eastern origin, specifically from Persia and Egypt, forced out of the region long ago by war with dark skin people, compelling their ancient predecessors to sail to Madagascar, around Africa, across the Atlantic, settling for a time in Yucatan and Central America. Later they migrated south to the Andes, contributing to the culture around Lake Titicaca before finally sailing westwards to Easter Island and New Zealand. Based on the evidence presented so far, it appears they were following in the footsteps of the Anunaki, merely taking the long route.

Fed up of having her tribe's traditions brushed under the carpet by historians and government officials alike, an elder of the Ngati Hotu by the name of Monica Matamua — who is blonde and blue eyed — submitted a sample of her DNA to the National Geographic Society DNA Register. The results validated her claim: the Ngati Hotu's origins were to be found in the Middle East, the Steppes, Egypt, Madagascar and Central America, with the most recent concentrations around Lake Titicaca and Easter Island.[27]

All in all, fifteen New Zealand tribes feature fair skin, red hair and green eyes, or blonde hair and blue eyes, and most of them claim a part in the nation's prehistory, the one academics and latter-day Maori claim does not exist.

THE ART OF LONG OCEAN TRAVEL

Monica's DNA aside, there is an artefact that may corroborate the Ngati Hotu's presence in the Andes. A large stone bowl unearthed by a farmer in 1958 near Lake Titicaca is inscribed with a fertility figure and inscriptions in two languages, one Puqara, the other proto-Sumerian from c.3000 BC.[28] It has been a mystery as to how a proto-Sumerian bowl of such antiquity could have appeared in the Bolivian altiplano five thousand years ago. Now it appears to have been taken there by the ancestors of at least two peoples from the Middle East.

Virtually every flood myth of god-men who come out of nowhere to rebuild human civilization connects them with the sea in some way, they always arrive on boats or double-hull canoes, leading to the conclusion they were master seafarers with long-term experience of navigating the open ocean as well as a proficiency in astronomy that moved them efficiently from A to B. They were intimate with the Earth's topography and clearly knew where they were headed, setting down a precedent for later people to follow.

One of the anomalies surrounding these long distance navigators centers around two massive cedarwood boats concealed in deep pits at the foot of the pyramids of Giza. The Egyptians of the historical period were not known for their seafaring skills, allegedly opting to become masters of chariots and calm navigation up and down the Nile. The boats contravene this theory. The largest of the two is 141 feet long, with a high prow than would have made it not only an extraordinarily stable sea-going vessel but would have out-performed even the formidable Viking *knarr* and sixteenth century European galleys, products of expert shipbuilding from people with a long, solid tradition of sailing the open seas.[29] Therefore, either ancient Egyptians were master seafarers, or a select group of foreign master seafarers arrived in Egypt from the eastern oceans and left behind a legacy of ocean travel. Could these people have made regular, long distance voyages from as far as South America? Given the influence of Egyptian language on islands throughout the Pacific, along with Thor Hyerdahl's famous Kon Tiki voyage, the answer is, highly probable.

RED HAIR AND LONGHEADS

In 1928 more than three hundred skeletal remains were found near Paracas by Peruvian archaeologist Julio Tello, all bearing the most extreme examples of elongated skulls ever found. Because of the dry climate, some still had hair attached — red hair, and the color was not a result of a change in pigment from burial in soil containing tannins or iron.

Nor was their elongation the product of deliberate cranial deformation. It is well known that Peruvian mothers bound the heads of infants so that in time their skulls would come to resemble those of the gods of old,

Andean longheads. Cranial volume is 25% larger than human skulls.

presumably to bestow higher social status upon their offspring. The practice was still popular in the Middle Ages in central and southern Europe, when high-ranking treaty brides from Romania and Bulgaria with deliberately induced elongated skulls were married off to nobles to cement political alliances.[30] However, at first impression, such skulls look really unnatural, ridiculous, cone headed.

The Paracas skulls, on the other hand, are simply unusual, and despite the deformation there's an air of grace to them. According to Brien Foerster, director of the Paracas History Museum, such skull elongation is caused by genetics, with some of the elongated skulls' cranial volume being up to 25 percent larger and 60 percent heavier than conventional human skulls. Thus they could not be deformed purposely through flattening or head binding, since the skull's shape can be changed by cranial deformation yet its volume and weight remain the same.

The Paracas skulls are also significantly different to *homo sapiens* in that they have highly pronounced cheek bones, larger eye sockets, and most importantly, no sagittal suture — the connective tissue joint between the two parietal bones of the skull. There is also the issue with the position of the *foramen magnum* — the opening at the base of the skull though which the spinal cord passes — which on the Paracas skulls is in a different location and cannot be the result of artificial binding. The difference is a purely genetic trait.[31]

And that wasn't the end of it. Hair sequencing determined these individuals to have come from a H2A genetic population group found in Eastern Europe, while bone powder tests revealed a T2B group which heralds from Mesopotamia.[32] Further DNA tests on the skulls revealed mitochondrial DNA with mutations unknown in any human, primate or animal known so far. In other words, we are dealing with a new human type that is very different to *Homo sapiens*, Denisovians or Neanderthals. Plus, the Paracas skulls share DNA with other elongated cranium people found between the Black Sea and the Caspian Sea,[31] a region that includes Armenia, and once was adjacent to Persia and Mesopotamia.

And thanks to a grandmother in New Zealand, we now have a clearer picture of just how far across the globe people from this region journeyed.

Big? Wait 'till you see the two blocks underneath. Baalbek.

BUILT BEFORE
THE FLOOD REDUX

With much evidence supporting the existence of a megalithic building culture throughout the Pacific before and after the flood, it is reasonable to ask if their handiwork exists in New Zealand.

In the middle of a forest to the east of Lake Taupo there is a cryptic structure called the Kaimanawa wall, consisting of rectangular blocks of volcanic stone — ignimbrite, according to a government geologist — each weighing four tons. With their smoothed faces and squared corners, the regular shape of the blocks is inconsistent with the action of weathering on ignimbrite.

7

The exposed portion of the wall reveals two levels of stacked blocks, and despite accumulated humus and tree roots the shape is suggestive of an *ahu* or perhaps the summit of a truncated pyramid. Like most pyramids, the structure is aligned to Grid North.

Prior to visiting the Kaimanawa wall, Waitaha elders approached the Tuwharetoa, the regional Maori tribe, who informed them the stones were of no significance to them, even fell outside accepted traditional Maori boundaries.[1]

I had the opportunity to visit the site with ancient history author Gary Cook and fellow enthusiasts under the cover of 'lost tourists', for reasons that will become apparent. Indeed the layered blocks have a symmetry about them and, for the most part, are fitted as well as any megalithic structure I have seen, despite long-term exposure to the elements. Standing on the top of the mound feels as though an electrical current runs up the spine, a feeling often encountered when standing near the magnetic hotspot of active sacred sites.

The removal of another six feet of soil revealed a third, lower layer composed of larger megaliths, meticulously cut and polished as though machined in a modern factory, with hardly, if any signs of weathering. The floor was cleared of soil to reveal a perfectly smooth and level stone platform extending at least six feet away from the wall. I jumped into the rectangular hole and my feet were met by a most unexpected sound: a booming echo from below as though the platform is in fact the ceiling of a large sealed chamber.

The highly volcanic nature of this region has covered the area with layer upon layer of ash over two hundred feet deep, yet this is hardly the reason preventing the anomalous structure from being excavated and analyzed. Once the lower course of stones was discovered, indicating an artefact of considerable importance, the Maori council changed its tune overnight and the site became culturally significant, allowing the council to issue an official order banning any further digging.[2] All this despite common knowledge that Maori never worked with stone, nor built sacred sites made of stone. To quote the New Zealand historian Elsdon Best: "The Maori never erected anything in the form of a temple. He made no attempt to add impressiveness to his ritual performances by means of any artificial erection, indeed he was strongly prejudiced against performing rites elsewhere than out in the open. So far as we are aware, the tapu houses in which tribal lore was taught were the only buildings in which important rites were ever performed. The Maori preferred to carry out such functions in the

Exposed blocks of the Kaimanawa wall.

open, not under a roof, and away from all artificial structures… Inasmuch as the tuahu, or tapu places whereat rites were performed by the native priests, were of such a simple or primitive form, it follows that there might

Fellow researcher and author Gary Cook examines the blocks. The concealed lower level revels a polished block and a platform over what sounds like an inner chamber.

well be a difficulty in recognising such places when seen. They were, in some cases, apparently not marked by anything, being merely a small open space... Some were marked by one or more unworked stones, or a small wooden post. Occasionally a small, rough wooden platform, elevated on stakes, termed a tiepa, was erected, on which offerings were placed... It is a peculiar and interesting fact that the Maori has never constructed in New Zealand the marae or stone pyramids of his former home in eastern Polynesia. We might think that those erections are of comparatively modern date, erected since the ancestors of the Maori left those parts, but the late Colonel Gudgeon has recorded the fact that some knowledge of them has been preserved by the Maori. An old native informed him that those marae or stepped, truncated pyramids, were places where religious rites were performed... If the Maori constructed, at great expense of labour, the great stone pyramids of Tahiti, why and how did he acquire in New Zealand such a strong distaste for anything like an elaborate altar?" [3]

Geologists, in comical contradiction to the Maori, claimed the perfectly rectangular stone blocks were produced by the natural fracturing of hot ignimbrite when it cools — despite the fact that no similar example can be produced because the unconsolidated nature of ignimbrite does not allow it to form perfectly smooth and symmetrical slabs with corners that turn at ninety degrees. To their further embarrassment, when a sample of the wall was analyzed at a laboratory in Auckland it was found to be not ignimbrite but another type of volcanic stone, rhyolite, which only occurs naturally ten

A mountain that is a step pyramid. The summit temples of Gunung Padang.

miles to the *west* of Lake Taupo, meaning that the raw material for the wall had to have been physically transported to the site.[4]

Antediluvian or post-diluvial? Department of Conservation archaeologists simply debunked the site so as not to contravene the politically acceptable paradigm that no culture existed in New Zealand before the arrival of Maori in 1200 AD, despite the Kaimanawa wall being covered by debris from the 232 AD eruption of a vent in Lake Taupo which dumped a six-foot layer of ash over the region.[5]

As for the Waitaha, they claim it isn't theirs either, it precedes their culture.

THE ENLIGHTENING MOUNTAIN OF JAVA

Before sea levels rose dramatically at the end of the Younger Dryas, the archipelago that is Indonesia was joined to southeast Asia and formed a formidable piece of land referred to by geologists as Sundaland. After the flood, Indonesia lost more habitable land than anywhere on Earth, making the search for a lost civilization in this part of the world that more enticing and, paradoxically, more difficult.[6] Geometric engravings "indicative of modern cognition and behavior" have been found on Java, one of the largest islands, and dated to half a million years ago — that's over a quarter of a million years before the alleged appearance of anatomically modern humans.[7]

The Javanese have been climbing to the summit of the Mountain of Enlightenment since remote times. In 1914 it was the turn of a group of archaeologists. There, they found dense undergrowth and trees sprouting out of a man-made rectangular court composed of large pieces of columnar basalt, hundreds of them. Eventually it was realized that no less than five terraces were covered with structures that local people regularly used for meditation. Despite saying so, the villagers failed to persuade the scientists that the *entire* hill was a man-made step pyramid.

It would be nearly one hundred years before another archaeologist by the name of Danny Hilman Natawidjaja took an interest in the site and assembled a team to conduct a geophysical survey using ground penetrating radar, electrical resistivity and seismic tomography. Up to this point the Indonesian scientific community had arbitrarily assigned a date of 1000

BC to the rectangular court on the summit. The assessment was based on pure guesswork. When Natawidjaja conducted the first radiocarbon tests on organic matter beneath the megaliths, the results indeed clustered around 500 to 1500 BC, so no surprises there.

This all changed when the team expanded their investigation into the interior of the hill using tubular drills. The extracted core samples contained fragments of worked columnar basalt, indicating that far below the summit there lay older, man-made megalithic structures. At this point the accompanying organic matter began to yield radiocarbon dates that were about to make the rest of the scientific community very uneasy: at a depth of 90 feet the dates quickly climbed from 3000 BC to 9600 BC, 11,000 BC, culminating at an uncomfortable 22,000 BC. Natawidjaja's team had successfully proved this step pyramid spanned all three Dryas periods and then some. His conclusions were affirmed by Robert Schoch — the geologist best known for dating the sphynx enclosure in Egypt to the end of the Younger Dryas — who concurs Gunung Padang may have been in use for as much as 24,000 years. Layer Three of the excavation was particularly interesting because of the extensive damage to the man-made structures at the radiocarbon date of c.9600 BC, the general period of the great flood.[8] Subsequent layers indicate that people survived the event and added to the structure over millennia, just as they did at sites in Egypt, Peru, Yucatan, and Göbekli Tepe.

Indeed mainstream archaeologists didn't like any of this one bit. A very public campaign was quickly undertaken to discredit Natawidjaja, insisting he was disturbing an archaeological site without following scientific protocol (he'd strictly adhered to protocol), and undertaking illegal digs without government permission (he'd been granted permission from the President himself). Finally in a desperate attempt to stop further excavation (and limit any potential embarrassment), they petitioned the President with the argument that the date for the site had already been professionally established at 1000 BC so there was no further need to explore and disturb the site. So much for the open-mindedness of science.

Obviously the President saw through the rouse because, shortly after, Danny and his team resumed excavations. The results were impressive and added to what is already an explosive piece of evidence in support of an antediluvian civilization in Indonesia. The presence of a pyramidal structure covered by centuries of debris is unmistakable, and buried beneath twenty feet of soil lies a large open chamber in the middle of the monument.[9]

There is additional circumstantial support for the 9600 BC date at the site. To the southwest of Gunung Padang lies the coastal town of Pelabuhan Ratu (Harbor of the Queen), dedicated to a mythical Queen of the Southern Ocean, a goddess who ruled over a now submerged city.[10] More tellingly on Sunda — an island across the Java Sea — traditions describe the great flood as submerging all mountains except Gunung Padang.[11]

FLOORED IN OKLAHOMA

On a typical hot June day a team of construction workers was busy digging the foundation for a new warehouse on the Broadway Extension of 122nd Street between Edmond and Oklahoma City. The year was 1969. As they dug deeper into the rock shelf they finally reached the ancient limestone seabed, whereupon they noticed something out of character: an ancient mosaic floor covering several thousand square feet and containing perfectly round post-holes. Given the depth of sediment under which it was found, the artefact could have been tens of thousands of years old.

Predictably the story generated a heated debate among experts. "I am

Mosaic floor near Oklahoma City, potentially 30,000 years old.

sure this was man-made because the stones are placed in perfect sets of parallel lines which intersect to form a diamond shape, all pointing to the east," stated Durwood Pate, an Oklahoma City geologist who studied the site. "We found post holes which measure a perfect two rods from the other two. The top of the stone is very smooth, and if you lift one of them, you will find it is very jagged, which indicates wear on the surface. Everything is too well-placed to be a natural formation." [12]

The conclusion seemed reasonable. But Dr. Robert Bell, an archaeologist from the University of Oklahoma, was nonplussed. To him, the find was a natural formation because he could see no evidence of mortar — apparently ignorant of megaliths in Peru and Egypt, all of which were built with unmatched precision without a splash of mortar. Still, at the Oklahoma site a different type of mud was clearly distinguishable between each stone and the soil, leading a second geologist, Delbert Smith, to remark: "There is no question about it. It has been laid there, but I have no idea by whom."[13]

There was also the issue of the holes, which had been placed 16.5 feet apart or precisely 6 Megalithic Yards, the unit of choice used by megalithic temple-builders around the world.[14]

A few days later things became more complicated when *The Oklahoman* continued its coverage and reported archaeologists discovering what resembled an ancient stone hammer at the site. No further attempts on dating were made simply because they refused to accept anything this old

A human figure reveals the scale of the megalithic platform at Baalbek.

could exist in this part of the world. Construction resumed unabated, the site was cleared and covered over with a food processing plant. However, it would not be the only time that out-of-place artefacts were discovered in the region. An iron pot was found embedded inside a 300 million-year old lump of coal deep inside a mine in Wilburton. A miner came upon the solid chunk and, being too large to be of practical use, broke it with a sledgehammer whereupon the iron object fell from inside, revealing an impression in the coal. The incident was witnessed by a company employee.

LEVITATION IN THE LEVANT

The discoveries in Oklahoma represent the subtle presence of a remote and intelligent civilization in the central plains of North America. By contrast, what is seen throughout Palestine and the Near East can only be described as beyond overt.

Around 8000 BC humans were living in a primitive state throughout the Jordan valley, yet in the blink of a geological eye they turned the area into an agricultural oasis, domesticated cattle, and erected megalithic structures of preposterous scale. We are meant to believe it was done on a whim, without precedent or outside assistance, but clearly someone from elsewhere provided the necessary expertise that led to an evolutionary revolution at places like Jericho.

Arabic peoples refer to Jericho as the City of Giants.[15] Recent excavations to uncover the roots of this out-of-the-ordinary city exhumed the original megalithic foundation wall, 6.5 feet thick by 20 feet tall, 1200 feet in circumference, surrounded by sensational ditches cut from bedrock, which today would require heavy industrial equipment.

The radiocarbon dating of organic matter found at the lowest habitation level shows people already living in the general vicinity c.9000 BC, although it doesn't tell us when the stones were put there. The general consensus is that no evidence exists of solid structures at Jericho between 9070 to 8030 BC, that megalithic construction allegedly began in earnest two hundred years later, yet the dates were determined from habitation layers on top of the bedrock rather than uncontaminated organic matter taken from under or between the stones, which would give us a more accurate picture. What is certain is the city succumbed to a local inundation around 6540 BC.[16]

This immediately begs the question: if the region was only populated by hunter gatherers in 9000 BC, how did they come to possess the technology to move and place such extraordinary masonry and why should they have made work so difficult for themselves in the first place? The obvious explanation is, because the architects of Jericho were already technically proficient and comfortable working on a large scale, and if indeed a race of giants lived there — even the Bible categorically claims so — then assembling monoliths would have been as easy for them as stacking bricks would be to a human bricklayer.

With Göbekli Tepe barely four hundred miles to the northeast and already demonstrating the presence of an advanced astronomical-architectural culture by 10,000 BC, it is reasonable to speculate its architects also possessed the know-how to build Jericho.[17] So the more important question we ought to ask is, was Jericho already a work-in-progress when it was interrupted by the flood, and the city rebuilt by survivors? After all, the enclosures at Göbekli Tepe suggest they were sealed to protect the site from impending damage. The same architects may also have been responsible for the walls of the Hasmonean Tunnel, the one attached to the Wailing Wall in Jerusalem. Each stone block weighs around 500 tons and represents some of the oldest masonry supporting the modern-day city. Perhaps. And yet all of this cyclopean building effort was a mere warm-up for the people who erected a stone platform of supernatural proportions in the temple city of Baalbek, three hundred miles southwest of Göbekli Tepe.

The 17th century Patriarch of Lebanon claimed Baalbek was also originally peopled with giants, and looking at the scale of the foundation stones of its temple it is hard to disagree.[18] Nothing about this enterprise is on a human scale, and no written trace survives to explain its purpose, but what is clear is that it was built to last for eternity. Why else use such oversize and inconvenient building material?

The platform in question is made up of three courses of megalithic blocks of limestone totaling twenty feet in height. Resting above these along the northern perimeter is a row of nine huge monoliths neatly fitted without mortar, the gap between the stones barely perceptible; this is repeated along the south perimeter. Describing the west wall, however, requires a leap of imagination: Three stones have been raised twenty feet off the ground, each measuring 63 x 14 x 12 feet on average, and weighing an estimated 880 tons. They appear stacked as effortlessly as wooden pallets, and form a U-shaped enclosure with an opening facing east.

Dedicated to the Sun god Baal, the temple is a masterpiece of construction and aesthetics. Certainly it has acted as a magnet for a plethora of cultures who occupied the region over its long and tortured history, each adding their presence to the site. What is telling is how each successive course of masonry above the megalithic platform becomes progressively smaller, weaker and poorer in craftsmanship. Apparently it wasn't only Andean stonemasons who got sloppier as centuries passed. Parts of the wall have been repaired and patched, with stones looted from other parts of the temple and adjacent sites. Finally the Romans added their own flourish, a temple dedicated to Jupiter fitted inside the U-shaped enclosure; it too is impressive in scale, least of all the fifty-four towering columns, of which only six now survive — ironically due to earthquake damage, and yet the underlying platform remains as solid as the day it was constructed.

Regional traditions describe Baalbek as having been built in three stages: the original in antediluvian times; the second when Nimrod, great great grandson of Noah, sent giants to repair the walls damaged by the great flood; and the third when it was repaired again by King Solomon.[19] Certainly the contrasting construction methods are proof that different people from different eras repaired, extended and juxtaposed their ideas, needs and religious beliefs right up to the Roman era, when Baalbek was still known as an oracle featuring a "black stone which answered questions."[20]

All the above is mere foreplay for what follows.

Two stones were left behind at the quarry half a mile away. The first measures 71x14x14 feet and weighs 970 tons; the second measures 67x15x14 feet and weighs a slender 1242 tons. These were believed to be the largest pieces of worked masonry in the world until a German archaeological team digging around the second monolith in 2014 unearthed a third block buried beneath, revealing what is considered to be the single largest worked monolith in the world: 64x19x18 feet, clocking in at a puny 1650 tons.[21]

And just like in Göbekli Tepe, Easter Island and Ollantaytambo, something of grave importance forced the builders to abandon work.

Baalbek and Göbekli Tepe, along with Temple Mount and Giza, all share a number of common features: all are built on limestone bedrock; all are designated Navels of the Earth; all incorporate megalithic stonework.

They also share connections to Egyptian antediluvian gods: Giza and Göbekli Tepe are domains of Osiris, while Jerusalem's oldest known name is Gar-issa-lem, Issa being the oldest iteration of Isis. As for their divinely conceived son, the solar deity Horus, he may originally have been the tutelary god of Baalbek. The Canaanites who once populated the region are known

Corner alignment through pyramids of Khafre and Khufu.

to have undertaken regular pilgrimage to Giza in veneration of the sphynx, and even as late as 1543 BC they left votives with carvings inscribed with its original Egyptian name, Hor-em-Akhet — Horus of the Horizon — to which they added the Cannanite variant, Hurna and Hauron.[22] Being a traveling god, Horus' influence extended north of Giza. In Jordan, the main hill at Petra is dedicated to this falcon deity, and his cult in known to have been practiced in the port town of Ugarit, to the north of Baalbek.

Clay tablets portray Horus as a conjurer and magician,[23] he knew the medicine of plants and once cured a man of snakebite by distilling an antidote from a tree. As the resurrected form of Osiris, Horus represents the triumph of light, an attribute shared with Baal, from whom Baalbek takes its name. But did this antediluvian magician and his followers assist in the building of Baalbek, moving its stupendous stone blocks half a mile using some lost form of levitation, just like the legends from Tiwanaku and the Pacific? Ancient Egyptian literature describes the deeds of the magician Hor the Nubian who once "made a vault of stone 200 cubits [300 ft] long and 50 cubits [75ft] wide rise above the head of the pharaoh and his nobles... When the pharaoh looked up at the sky he opened his mouth in a great cry, together with the people who were in the court."[24]

Certainly there exists a link between Baalbek and Giza. A geodetic alignment of 45.1° through the corners of the two large pyramids of Khafre and Khufu extends 400 miles to Baalbek, with a margin of error of just 0.4°. The reference is all the more uncanny since the geodetic alignment through the third pyramid references Göbekli Tepe.

It would seem these three antediluvian locations share a unified plan, if not a common purpose, yet there is a twist with regard to Baalbek itself. The site has always been associated with the cult of the Sun; if ever there was a reference to a specific constellation or star, it is not know. Working with this basic assumption we can roll back the sky to when, say, the winter solstice might have aligned with the massive temple platform, which faces 75° east.

In the northern hemisphere the winter solstice marks the day when the light of rejuvenation begins to reclaim the longest nights of the year, hence the symbolic association with the triumph of light over dark, and the heroes who personified this quality, gods such as Hor and Baal. Due to the effects of precession the Sun now rises 45° to the south of the platform. To achieve a perfect alignment between the two, one needs to go back to the era of 20,000 BC. If so, how does this tie-in with Giza?

Baalbek aligns to the winter solstice sunrise 20,000 BC.

Labels within illustration: WALL OF SETI TEMPLE · TOMB OF OSIRIS · STAIRS TO WATER · VAULT OF OSIRIS · WATER OF STANDING WALL · GREAT HALL · STAIRS · CHAMBER OF MERENPTAH · PASSAGE · PETRIE'S PASSAGE

When news of its excavation reached the world in 1914, the Osirion at Abydos caused a major sensation. Equally exciting news came a century later when it was found to have once been a free-standing structure beside the Nile.

MADE IN EGYPT
BEFORE THE FLOOD

When it comes to discussing ancient Egypt, much of the attention falls upon its grandiose structures, such as pyramids, simply because their superhuman scale is candy to the eye and humans are so easily seduced by the scale of things. Yet as all Mysteries traditions teach, the eye is easily deceived by scale to the detriment of seemingly trivial things that ultimately lead to greater illumination.

That said, it would be a travesty to describe the temple of Seti I at Abydos as trivial, for it is a beautifully preserved jewel of a sacred space, and certainly ancient people treated the location with reverence, so much so that Abydos was already a thriving city by 5400 BC,[1] and two thousand years later pre-dynastic pharaohs were still building shrines, temples and mortuaries there.

8

Seti I added his own masterpiece during a reign that lasted barely more than a decade in the thirteenth century BC, an elegant temple featuring a series of interconnected halls and side chambers, covered from floor to ceiling in exquisite friezes, murals and hieroglyphs, with a play of shadow and light that penetrates the meticulous rows of reed columns inside a hypostyle hall. Still, people had long been coming here to witness another wonder.

Twelve thousand years ago the region bore no resemblance to the partly parched, partly cultivated strip of land it is today. The climate was wetter, it sustained a verdant and lush landscape as far as the eye could see, and to the west where now lies an endless desert, there existed an inland sea, much of which drained into the Atlantic when the events that generated the great flood overhauled the terrain. A small saltwater lake at Siwa is all that remains. Referring to an older source, Diodorus of Sicily describes how it "disappeared from sight in the course of an earthquake, when those parts of it which lay toward the ocean were torn asunder," leaving behind the Sahara.[2]

The course of the Nile was much different too, its shore was five miles closer to the town, its waters touching another kind of temple, one named for the Egyptian god of resurrection Osiris — the Osirion. When it was cleared of debris *The Times* of London described it as "a gigantic construction of about 100 feet in length and 60 in width, built with the most enormous stones that may be seen in Egypt."[3] In terms of construction and style, the temple bears no resemblance to Seti's. It is stark yet hauntingly beautiful, one of the finest examples of simplicity and economy of line, expressed with heavyset blocks of red granite, one of the hardest rocks on Earth, ferried from a quarry two hundred miles away. The construction logistics pose a conundrum for any modern engineer yet the Osirion belongs to a remote age. It was created with the sole intent of defying time.

The structure consists of two rows of columns connected by substantial architraves upon which once stood a voluminous stone roof. These are poised on a raised rectangular platform surrounded by a deep moat cut into the stone; two ascending staircases lead out of the water and onto the platform, where lie two sunken rectangular pools.

The surrounding courtyard itself is one massive and impenetrable wall made of 25-foot thick red sandstone, fitted without mortar, with corner stones cut and angled much like they are in Cuzco. Seventeen side chambers are meticulously cut into the wall and face the central platform.[4] The plan of the courtyard bears a passing resemblance to the head of Pachacamac carved above the Sun Door at Tiwanaku. It's a passing observation for sure, but the same cannot be said for the knobs carved in relief on sections of the courtyard wall, for they are an identical to those in Andean temples.

There are no inscriptions inside the Osirion, no dedications, no name to identify its creator, only a set of hieroglyphs carved into the wall adjoining Seti's temple and no doubt put there during the pharaoh's time.

Until recently the Osirion was believed to be a type of underground chamber fitted inside hollowed bedrock, an extension of Seti's temple. If so it represented a complete departure from standard temple design. However, a geologic appraisal contradicts this opinion. In ancient times the level of the Nile was fifty feet lower than today, its course seven miles closer to and beside the Osirion. When North Africa was subjected to major flooding between 10,500-8000 BC, layers of Nile silt gradually compacted and rose inch by inch until they surrounded and covered the Osirion, in other words, the temple was originally a freestanding feature on the floodplain.[5] Legend has it that people once reached the Osirion by boat and navigated its interior by boat, an opinion expressed by Henri Frankfort, one of the early archaeologists at Abydos,[6] but as the Nile crept ever more eastwards, it eventually became necessary to connect the Osirion to the river with a long canal.[7]

There is no doubt about river access. Twelve boats up to 72 feet long were found in the vicinity, buried in the sand, each designed with rounded, phallic tips, and enclosed in individual mud brick enclosures as though the ships were somehow special, something worth commemorating. Like the two boats found in deep pits beside the Giza pyramids, these were large and graceful ocean vessels capable of riding rough seas. The level of sophistication clearly points to people with long sea-faring experience. But why should they be 400 miles from the ocean at Abydos? The boats were dated to around 3000 BC, too late to match them to an antediluvian

A masterpiece in its own right. Seti I temple, Abydos.

race, yet wall paintings in the temples along the Nile depict the same boats c.4500 BC, so it is feasible that the seafaring tradition may date back further.

In this regard the Osirion has two counterparts downriver at Giza — the Sphynx Temple and the Valley Temple, all constructed with identical megalithic blocks of red granite (those of the Sphynx Temple were looted for building material), using the same clean, graphic layout, devoid of inscription. The Giza temples too were reached by boat when the waters of the Nile lapped at their respective entrances. The intermediate walls of the Valley Temple are made from massive blocks of limestone quarried from the sphinx enclosure next door and are clearly eroded by water, lots of water. Since it has been convincingly argued that the sphinx itself was carved to face its counterpart in the sky, the constellation Leo, on the spring equinox c.10,400 BC, ostensibly the two sites are contemporaries of each other.[8] Furthermore, the enclosure in which this lion sits was also weathered by extensive flooding and rainfall when a pluvial climate predominated northeast Africa, the epoch prior to 10,000 BC.[9] Thus by weathering and design alone all the above temples share the same period.

Returning to the Osirion, there is the question of why so many temples and shrines appear in its vicinity of yet none relate to it, as though it was no longer visible by pre-dynastic times, so when pharaohs came here to

Like the Osirion, the Valley Temple at Giza is freestanding and once bordered the Nile. Its top tier shows extensive water erosion, suggesting the area was submerged. The original limestone blocks were afterwards lined with granite during renovation.

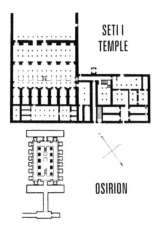

SETI I
TEMPLE

OSIRION

mark their devotion they were essentially honoring the *sanctity* of place. By the time Seti I came to build his temple— one of the last to be erected — he may have *rediscovered* the Osirion because his temple follows the same orientation, but stops short of the underground structure before resuming to the left and creating an L-shape, forcing the most holy of chapels to be placed sideways to the body of the temple, a complete violation of temple protocol.[10] The only rational explanation for such a drastic measure is that Seti's superimposed building broke through the chamber beneath during construction.

Could the enigmatic structure be a remnant of an antediluvian age? With its raised platform surrounded by a water channel, the Osirion can be regarded as a recreation of the primeval island of the gods in stone, an artificial representation of the original home from which the gods emerged. To determine exactly when it was built we must turn to astro-archaeology.

Time and again I have stood dumbstruck in the Osirion. Its orientation has puzzled me for years, for it does not face the solstices or equinox, nor does it relate to the pole star, nor any obvious object in the sky. Myth states this to be a resting place of Osiris, even if the association, as in so many cases in the ancient world, is metaphoric. Osiris is the classic depiction of the hero who is dismembered before ascending the Milky Way to reach the origin of souls — typically the Pole Star or the belt of Orion — and whilst in the Otherworld he is reconstituted by his consort Isis.

A look at the night sky at the time of Seti I produces absolutely no relationship to any stellar object, it seems the pharaoh broke yet another convention by ignoring the sky-ground dualism essential to the foundation of the temple and its function as a mirror image of the sky, as expressed in the maxim As Above So Below. Seti was an astute student of temple protocol, he wouldn't have made such an obvious mistake. Since his temple is aligned to the same axis at the Osirion, it follows that he may have may have attempted to revive the importance of its predecessor.

I turned my focus to Orion, the constellation with which Osiris is intimately associated. Perhaps this obvious clue would yield a sky-ground relationship, but no such relationship exists, not unless the Earth was upside down 14,000 years ago and even so it would be hard to prove.

Only in the epoch of 10,000 BC do connections finally emerge, when the constellation Cygnus appears in full upright ascent over the horizon in conjunction with the axis of the temple, the entrance framing its brightest star Deneb. As does the Milky Way, forming a vertical river for Cygnus to ride towards the vault of heaven. The correlation took place on the spring equinox c.10,500 BC, and again on the winter solstice.

No resemblance to the temple above it. Osirion, Abydos.

By way of validation the sky goddess Nut, who is identified with the Milky Way, is painted as a naked female spread across the sky on the ceiling of the Osirion's north-eastern chamber, her legs formed by the bifurcation at Deneb in Cygnus.[11] The symbol couldn't be more apt. Cygnus itself was regarded as both a swan and a kite hawk, and it is likely that Egyptian text references to the "kite of Osiris" may have had this constellation in mind. His bride Isis, who took on the form of a kite hawk when resurrecting souls, is depicted with outspread wings as a symbol of protection and to demonstrate her ability to fan the breath of immortality into those whom she oversaw, specifically her consort Osiris.

For this to occur, the soul of the hero must reside in the pole star, regarded by ancient cultures as the region of regeneration, a place in

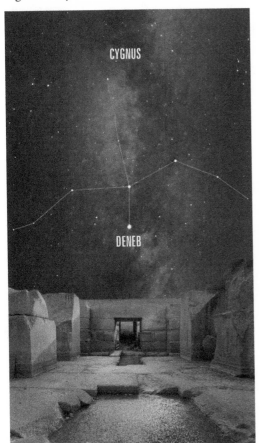

CYGNUS

DENEB

Cygnus rides the Milky Way, as viewed from the Osirion 10,500 BC. (Rear of site shown.)

the sky protected by seven great *akus* (souls), each represented by the seven circumpolar stars, Deneb being one.[12] Egyptologist Toby Wilkinson explains this in context of Egyptian ideology: "Circumpolar stars are a very good metaphor for the afterlife because when viewed, they never seem to set: they simply rotate around the pole star. They are the undying stars, or in Egyptian terminology, the Indestructibles, a perfect destination for the soul."[13] The Indestructibles or *ikhemu-sek* (the ones not knowing destruction) was a name created by Egyptian astronomers,

139

although the idea of these stars protecting a portal of regeneration is shared among indigenous cultures.[14] Interestingly Cygnus appears to occupy a region in space where such regeneration might occur. Research by NASA reveals this constellation to be a source of the most energetic and penetrating form of light — gamma rays. More to the point, it is one of our galaxy's richest-known stellar construction zones. In essence Cygnus is a star-forming region.[15] Perhaps it is for this reason that temples of the magnitude of the Osirion are referred to as places where an individual goes to be transformed into a god or into a bright star.

Indestructible? Portal of regeneration? What apt epiteths for a temple named for the god of rebirth and designed to outlast time!

Incidentally the derivative of *aku* is *akh* — a person filled with inner spiritual radiance, a Shining One — from which is derived *ahu,* the ceremonial stone platforms of Easter Island. We have already come across groups of seven Shining Ones in the form of the Urukehu, Viracocha and the Hayhuaypanti, and the Anunaki sages. Could any of these seafaring

gods have been responsible for the Osirion? Probably, based on a direct correlation between the Osirion and the position of Deneb c.10,500 BC, when this brightest of stars not only rose along the axis of the temple but, due to the effects of precession, it had by then also taken up its position as one of the Indestructibles.

The effective pole star during the course of the Younger Dryas was Vega.[16] In Arabic tradition Vega is *An-nasz-al-waki,* the falling eagle, named after its apparent swooping motion in the sky. Perhaps it is

The canal around the platform was drained in 1918, revealing the protruding knobs common to Andean temples.

Isis in her role as kite hawk.

more than ironic that a number of world traditions describe wise men being forewarned of the impending deluge by an eagle or a hawk. According to the Kamilaroi of Australia, for example, when the deluge was caused by the eagle-hawk Pundjel, two people survived by climbing a tree. The metaphor describes how the couple saved themselves through attachment to the World Tree representing the cosmic pole linking the three levels of creation, the knowledge of which guarantees their survival as seeds of a regenerated humanity. That's quite the symbol of rebirth.[17]

IWNW. ANTEDILUVIAN ABODE OF GODS

Surviving the suicidal tendencies of Cairo's drivers is one of life's great adventures, although it hardly compensates for the disappointment I felt when arriving unharmed at perhaps the most overlooked temple city in Egypt, Iwnw, because nowadays it is nothing more than an unremarkable, rubbish-strewn park hemmed in by an ever-encroaching suburb, its monuments long since scavenged for the building of medieval Cairo. Only a colossal carved head of Thutmosis II, recently dug out of the Nile silt, and a sixty-seven foot tall obelisk of Senusret I reveal a sliver of its former glory, for Iwnw was once the epicenter of Egypt's gods, the root of temple and priestly culture. It housed a fabulous library, thousands of years before Alexandria, and its grounds resembled a forest of obelisks. During the Ptolemaic era the Greeks renamed it Heliopolis.

I couldn't help but see the irony here. Senusret's father was the pessimistic pharaoh Amenemhet I. And well he should have been because when Amenemhet took control of Egypt in 1990 BC he inherited a wasteland decayed by civil war. Writing to an emergency council meeting, Ipuwer, a sage at Iwnw, laments the chaos and confusion spreading through the land: "Temples are defiled, texts are defaced, the districts of Egypt devastated and the treasury bankrupt." Ipuwer makes an impassioned plea for a leader of courage to step forward, someone with the kind of spiritual integrity as those from the Golden Era of the gods, to which he adds the astonishing remark, "that which the pyramid concealed has become empty."[18] Clearly there once existed something of supreme importance inside the Great Pyramid which by his time had been lost, looted or hidden. Still, part of Ipuwer's prayer was answered in the form of Senusret I, who rebuilt the by-then ruined temple academy.

How did Iwnw become the foundation of Egyptian history and when might this moment have occurred?

The Egyptian *Building Texts* describe the abode of the original primeval gods as *iw swht* (Island of the Egg), and every artificial focal point constructed thereafter was regarded as its equivalent, a mirror of the original domain. When an environmental catastrophe initiated the start of the Younger Dryas, it partly sank the Island of the Egg, forcing the gods to search for a suitable location where they could rebuild their civilization. They sailed to Egypt, found a mound surrounded by the Nile and called it *iw nw* (Island of Primordial Waters).[19]

As the effigy of the pregnant belly of creation, Iwnw — also transcribed as Annu and Awnu — was enclosed within a rectangular temple dedicated to the creator god Atum. Inside was placed an obelisk and the Temple of the Bennu, a phoenix-like heron who impregnates the mound with a life-giving essence called *hikê* or *heka*, the closest interpretation being 'magical power'; the final addition was a pyramidal stone, *benben*, whose root means 'seeding of a womb'. Taken together these symbols tell the story of how an antediluvian group of gods settled here and instigated a rebirth based on magic, which in ancient times was equated with the control and application of the laws of nature. It marked a moment in prehistory when civilization was reborn from the waters of chaos and divine order was reestablished following the devastation that marked the start of the Younger Dryas. Iwnw became the womb from which the whole Egyptian religious cult heralded, it was the central hub for initiates, for the study of the stars, symbolic architecture, and the sacred hieroglyphic writing unique to this region.

This navel of the earth was said to have been established at Zep Tepi (First Occasion). When might this moment have occurred?

Like the traveling Urukehu gods met by the Waitaha on Easter Island, the architects of Iwnw were expert astronomers and voyagers, and proof of their work appears in the manner in which subsequent temples were designed as terrestrial mirror images of stars and constellations.[20] In this respect, looking at the night sky above Iwnw it is possible to establish a founding date for this temple.

As already mentioned, Egyptian architects took a specific interest in Orion, specifically its belt stars which were considered the hearth of the universe. From Iwnw it was possible to see the ridge across the Nile where the pyramids might be. In the epoch c.10,400 BC the pattern of Orion's Belt seen on the 'west' of the Milky Way matches the pattern and alignments of the three Giza pyramids, and when this pattern is observed in the east as Sirius makes its heliacal ascent, a perfect match occurs on the ground with Iwnw, marking the time of its construction to that of the pyramids on the spring equinox.[21]

The implication is that a group of gods settled in Egypt within a few hundred years of the onset of the Younger Dryas to initiate the recreation of their former world, a substitute for a vanishing world with Iwnw as its nucleus.[22] This may explain why the region experienced an unexplainable Palaeolithic agricultural revolution around the same period, particularly the cultivation of barley, while ferocious floods and other natural disasters regularly swept down the Nile Valley, recurring periodically for another thousand years.[23]

However, this is hardly the end of the story. The *Building Texts* refer to another island of the gods, *iw titi* (Island of Trampling), a region occupied by some divine beings since primeval times.[24] Taking this at face value we can extrapolate that this island of *titi* lent its name to Lake Titicaca, amid which lies the Island of the Sun. According to the Andean creation myth this island represents the original mound emerging from the waters of chaos at the very beginning of time — much like the description of Iwnw. In one account this is the place from where Viracocha and his Shining Ones later emerged, at one stroke fusing Egyptian and Andean narratives. The name given to Titicaca, along with its attendant temple city Tiwanaku, was a way to symbolically link these places with the original island of creation, thereby maintaining a tradition to the beginning of creation itself. That *iw titi*, this island abode of the gods, was protected by a falcon deity may also be the reason why in the Togarevan tradition *titi-caca* is a compound name of two totem birds.

THE GIZA BLUEPRINT

An eight-mile ride southwest of Iwnw brings you to mosque Ibn Tulum, one of the oldest in Cairo, an unusual place insofar as it does not face Mecca, as mosques are generally designed to do, but misses said holy site by a full ten degrees. Ninth century Arab architects, mathematicians and astronomers were light years ahead of the competition, they would not have allowed such an error, unless the site on which the mosque stands is of older provenance. Orthodox Muslim historians are touchy when it comes to acknowledging archaeological places preceding Mohammed so, predictably, no information has been forthcoming on what might have previously stood on the site, although I predict that, in time, the location might come to be of enormous significance, because exactly eight miles to the east marks the middle of the three pyramids at Giza. Given ancient architects' disposition

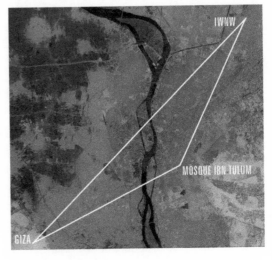

to arrange sacred sites in perfect triangles, the third point, Iwnw, creates a perfect isosceles triangle. We could be looking at the original geodetic blueprint mapped in this region by the gods 12,000 years ago.

Earlier I outlined the conclusion of the research by Bauval and Gilbert dating the Giza pyramids to 10,400 BC when their pattern matched Orion's Belt on that spring equinox. How might people of earlier times have interpreted such a proposition?

The general view that pharaohs Sneferu, Khafre and Menkaure were responsible for the buildings erected between Giza and Dashur is based entirely on circumstantial evidence, even graffiti, but most likely from taking the opinion of the Roman philosopher Pliny too literally — that pyramids were "the idle and vain ostentation of the wealth of kings" — and accepting his opinion as fact. The truth is, by the time early Greek travelers visited Egypt during the first millennium BC and wrote down whatever accounts they could gather, it is clear from the confusing and contradictory stories that no one by then had any reliable idea of when the monuments were built or by whom or for what purpose. From this mass amnesia one can deduce that the pyramids were erected not in historical times but during a prehistoric age, without discounting the possibility that the original structures were expanded upon at a later date.

Much to the consternation of Egyptologists, the closest anyone has come to dating the pyramids is Amenhotep II, who ruled around 1427 BC. If the star shaft theory proposed by Bauval and Gilbert is correct — that the internal shafts of the Great Pyramid align to Sirius, Ursa Minor, Thuban and Orion c.2450 BC, and thus provide an additional reference date for the building[25]— then it is extraordinary how within a relatively short span of 1100 years even this pharaoh did not attribute the pyramids to Khufu, Khafre or Menkaure. When Amenhotep built a small temple on the north

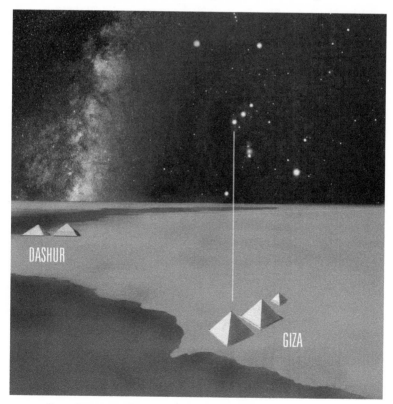

Giza-Orion correlation 10,400 BC (after Bauval and Gilbert).

side of the sphinx enclosure he placed in it a limestone stela bearing the inscription, "the Pyramids of Hor-em-akhet" (Horus of the Horizon) yet ignores their alleged architects; instead Amenhotep's poetic epithet refers only to the earliest name by which the sphinx and its environs were known,[26] implying that, by his time, the sphinx and the pyramids were accepted as an essential whole and shared the same time frame. Since the sphinx is dated to c.10,400 BC, by implication so too are the pyramids.

Support for this idea comes from the Inventory Stela rediscovered in the nineteenth century by archaeologist Auguste Mariette among the rubble of the Wadi Maghara. It was an explosive find, least of all because it strongly suggests the Great Pyramid, the sphinx and other structures in their orbit were already present long before pharaoh Khufu's reign c.2500 BC, with one pyramid being the abode of Isis. It states: "Khufu... found the house of Isis, Mistress of the Pyramid, beside the house of the Sphynx... on the northwest of the house of Osiris, Lord of Rostau. He built his pyramid *beside the temple of this goddess*, and he built a pyramid for the king's daughter."[27] The Inventory Stela appears to be a copy of an earlier original. It goes on to declare how Khufu found the temple of Isis in a ruinous state and "he built her temple again."[28] The same stela also states that the Valley Temple, attributed to Khafre, was built before his reign, in fact, it was considered extremely ancient even in the time of his predecessor, believed instead to have been the work of the gods during the First Occasion, when they arrived from afar to settle in this region. It was called the House of Osiris, Lord of Rostau, the ancient name given to the Giza Plateau.[29]

The Westcar Papyrus of c.1650 BC is likewise a replica of a far older document. It references an Inventory Building located in Iwnw where the wisdom of ages was maintained and promulgated. The papyrus mentions a chest of flint stored in a room containing "the number of secret chambers of the sanctuary of Thoth."[30] These documents were obviously of considerable importance because pharaoh Khufu spent considerable effort in the third millennium BC searching for them, possibly to assist him completing or restoring the pyramid to which his name has been attached and incorrectly so, because many remote sources claim the Giza building project was begun by someone else in prehistoric times. Ancient Egyptians and Arab historians such as Ibn Wasuff Shah and Ibn Abd Alhokm believed the pyramids were built by an antediluvian pharaoh by the name of Saurid ibn Salhouk following a prophetic vision in which the whole Earth was turned over, its inhabitants lying upon their faces as stars fell down, striking one another with a terrible din. He saw six massive chunks of rock falling to Earth, snatching up people and crushing them between two great mountains whose debris blotted out the sky. Awaked with great fear, Saurid assembled one hundred and thirty high priests from the provinces and related his vision. The priests took the altitude of the stars and made their prognostication: a deluge would be overwhelming the Earth. "Will it come to our country?" asked the pharaoh. "Yes," they answered, "and Egypt will be destroyed." Since the cataclysm was still three hundred years in the future, Saurid commanded that pyramids ought to be built.[31] Coincidentally, the same time frame for the impending catastrophe was given by seven beings to Enoch the scribe.

Books in possession of Coptic Christians stated how at one time there existed a stela at Giza bearing the inscription, *"I, Saurid, built the Pyramids in such and such a time, and finished them in six years. He that comes after me and says he is equal to me, let him destroy them in six hundred years; and yet it is known that it is easier to pluck down than to build."*[32]

As to the date of construction, the historian Abu Zeyd el Balkhy once provided an ancient inscription that the Great Pyramid was built when the constellation Lyra was in Cancer, or more to the point, when its brightest star Vega was the pole star. This would have been the era of 12,000 BC. It was still considered the *de facto* pole star when the astrological Age of Cancer took place somewhere around the end of the ninth millennium, and while the latter cannot be pin-pointed with great certainty due to the discrepancies in calendrical systems, it still places the date of construction around the general epoch of the great flood.

Chief among the gathered astronomer priests was the god of wisdom Twt — Djehuti, or Thoth to the Greeks —who, upon observing the position of the stars and the impending catastrophe, set about creating an unbreakable repository inside which every book related to knowledge would be preserved from ruin by the impending cosmic collision, reportedly a wealth of knowledge on astronomy, geometry, physics, the use of precious stones, even certain types of machinery.

Did ancient writers believe the Great Pyramid to be this repository? Hundreds of studies prove beyond doubt that when one dissects the numbers hand-wired into the Great Pyramid a wealth of mathematical information is revealed concerning the measure of the Earth, the sky, even the cycle of Sirius. Early Arab chroniclers add to this list a history of past events and of those yet to come. Commenting in the 12th century, the Iraqi physician Abdul Latif remarked of the Great Pyramid: "The stones were inscribed with ancient characters, now unintelligible. I never met with a person in all Egypt who understood them. The inscriptions are so numerous that copies of those alone which may be seen upon the surface of the two pyramids would occupy above six thousand pages."[33]

In a manner of speaking, the Great Pyramid was an antediluvian book in itself.

SERAPEUM. A NO BULL TEMPLE

But I wonder, did Twt have another building in mind, less conspicuous than a pyramid and resembling more a storage room or vault? Eight miles southeast of Giza there exists such a place, an anomalous underground cavern by the name of Serapeum. Although situated in the vicinity of the temple complex of Saqqara, the Serapeum lies well outside the temple boundary. It is a lone wolf, a meandering repository of tunnels and side chambers uncharacteristically hacked out of solid bedrock with total absence of finesse. Nestled tight inside each chamber sits a basalt or black granite box of preposterous size, twenty-four in total, all meticulously shaped — although machined would be a more suitable adjective, the tolerances are engineered to perfection — each topped with a thirty ton lid, too unnecessary to cover a corpse, but perfectly designed to form an air- or water-tight seal.

Each box weighs up to eighty tons and is believed to have been a sarcophagus for aurochs, the enormous bulls representing the sacred *hjpw* or Apis. There's just one problem with this theory: no bulls were ever found inside the boxes or near the Serapeum, and if grave robbers stole the bones, no evidence exists of there ever having been a black market for auroch bones. Even if we accept this preposterous idea, one still needs to explain why it was necessary to carve such cumbersome boxes for these animals when smaller ones would have sufficed.

When Auguste Mariette rediscovered the Serapeum in 1850 it only contained one human burial, that of Khaemweset, a son of Ramesses II; all other boxes were empty. A few bore markings and hieroglyphs. I have examined them up close, and it amazes me how no one is bothered by the rough quality of the scribbles, for that's what they look like in comparison to the refined craftsmanship of the granite boxes. The decorations are crude, etched using a blunt instrument, as though thousands of years separate the boxes from the inscriptions — as though the art of engraving had been lost by the time Khaemweset was intered in 1213 BC. Interetingly the pharaoh was a restorer of historic buildings, temples and tombs. Might he have rediscovered and reused the Serapeum?

Since there is no evidence to prove it was originally intended as a tomb, I wish to propose an outlandish hypothesis: someone working against the clock hastily carved the tunnels and filled them with these water-tight boxes to protect something of far greater importance, such as Twt's documents, from the cascade of water about to descend upon Egypt, then returned

Tourists visiting the Serapeum in 1882, long before the age of pesky vendors.

after the event, retrieved the contents and took them elsewhere. Of course, the obvious problem is, how do you locate an underground repository in a landscape transfigured beyond recognition by a global flood?

Being expert astronomers, the Egyptians were aware of what was about to descend upon them, they would have prepared accordingly. If the Giza pyramids were being erected at this time, two advantages present themselves: first, they weathered the cataclysm; and second, they would have made reliable landmarks. Let's say you are an astronomer on the high

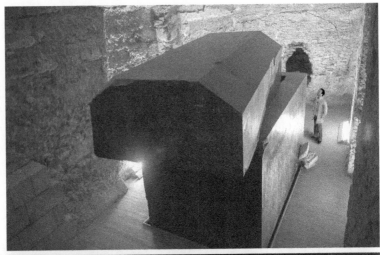

One of the collossal granite boxes in the Serapeum. Below: Compared to the boxes' precision tooling, the etched decoration is of very poor quality.

ground at Giza — marked by Menkaure's Pyramid — after the flood in, say, 9650 BC. Standing in front of the pyramid and looking at the southern sky around midnight on the winter solstice you would have observed the Southern Cross standing upright at 143° and right above the Serapeum, like an X marking the spot. Five hours later, just before sunrise, you would have noted the bright star Ankaa rising with its parent constellation above the same location; the name in Arabic means phoenix, and indeed belongs to the constellation of a bird. The symbolism of the retrieval of valuable knowledge and its rise from the ashes of catastrophe would not have not been lost on people for whom the employment of multiple layers of symbolism was an everyday practice.

To find any location it is necessary to triangulate by establishing three points of reference.

The Serapeum's original entrance tunnel is curiously aligned 100° east and misses the equinox by a long shot. Nothing in temple design was done by accident, so the entrance must be referencing something else. At this latitude in the era of 9650 BC it marks the winter solstice sunrise, but what terrestrial marker was used for this alignment is either lost, buried, or most likely looted for building material.

Which leaves the third point of reference. Like the Giza pyramids, those at Dashur and Meidun to the south are attributed to Sneferu c.2600

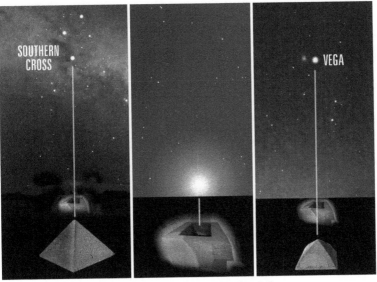

Locating the Serapeum in 9650 BC.

BC, but why should one pharaoh have required so many mausoleums when he only possessed one body? All the evidence linking the pharaoh to this complex is a nearby graffiti written 1200 years after his reign, in which it is stated how the temples "belong to Sneferu," nothing more.[34] The statement does not claim the pharaoh built them, merely that he *owned* them, much like a monarch might own several cathedrals in his kingdom despite the buildings having been in existence centuries before his time.

The Bent Pyramid of Dashur has always been my personal favorite. Up close it has a certain aesthetic quality, in spite of archaeologists believing its two slopes are the result of a mistake. Isolated from Giza it tends to attract few visitors, making every visit personal. Like its neighbors to the north, the Bent Pyramid was not placed where it is by accident. According to Bauval and Gilbert's theory it too forms an integral part of the Orion-Giza matrix established in 10,400 BC and, together with the nearby Red Pyramid, marks the terrestrial counterpart of the Hyades cluster.[35]

Like its peers the Bent Pyramid is aligned to Grid North, making its apex an ideal marker of the celestial pole. Another observer standing at the base and looking north on the winter solstice in 9650 BC would have observed Vega, the nearest to a pole star in that era, appearing at 0° and above the Serapeum at the same time the Southern Cross is referenced from Giza. The third point.

A GAME OF NUMBERS

It would seem that a number of structures in and around the Giza Plateau were planned as part of an antediluvian blueprint, and whoever set it up was conversant with celestial mechanics, not to mention molecular structures, because the Bent Pyramid is not the result of miscalculation. A trigonometric formula applied to its two unusual slopes reveals angles common to the hexagon and pentagon[36] — 6:5 numerically — thus the Bent Pyramid, like Puma Punku before, reflects the numerical relationship of the Earth's precessional cycle. Such temples are analogs of their host planet. Incidentally, human DNA is constructed from alternating six-sided and five-sided crystalline bonds, making us a mirror image of our own celestial sphere.

It wasn't just the architects in Egypt and the Andes that deduced and applied this know-how. The 6:5 ratio is also hardwired into the perimeter of the central temple complex at Angkor Wat in Cambodia, whose structures also depict on the ground the constellation Draco as it appeared in the sky in 10,400 BC.[37] If this is mere coincidence then consider how Angkor is a corruption of Ankh Hor, an Egyptian phrase meaning Life Eternal of Horus, and that the latitudinal distance between the Bent Pyramid and Angkor is precisely 72°, the root number of the Earth's precessional cycle.[38]

It seems we keep bumping into the same architects reading from the same manual no matter where in the world we touch a stone.

Speaking of which, take the smallest of the three Giza pyramids, the one that gets the least attention. Look carefully at the original granite casing stones along the base and you'll notice they are covered with the same protruding knobs common to Saqsayhuaman in Peru, whose name means Place of the Satisfied Falcon.

Consider also how the Viracochas' nickname, Shining Ones, have their antediluvian counterparts in Egypt, the Aku Shemsu Hor, which translates as Shining Ones, Followers of Horus. It seems the same gods *were* present on different continents before and after the flood.

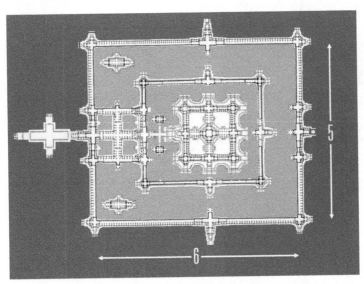

Just like Puma Punku and the Bent Pyramid at Dashur, the Cambodian temple of Angkor Wat is based on the 6:5 ratio.

Tikal's Temple V. It's unusual slope angle is also used in the Great Pyramid of Giza.

THE ITZA,
THE KAAN AND
THE BALAM

"Crocodilo! Crocodilo!" the pilot shouted enthusiastically as he steered the motorized canoe closer to the riverbank. Typically when one is within sight of a twenty-foot reptile with gaping jaws, the sensible thing is to turn the outboard motor in the opposite direction. But Juan Carlos was keen to get me as close to the crocodilo as possible. I believe it was a matter of pride.

We disembarked sensibly a few hundred yards further downstream and onto the mud-laden shore. A short, young woman greeted us and offered a very favorable rate of exchange for *gringo* money. Further up the bank we came to the immigration point, a wooden shack with multiple layers of bright paint, all different colors, all in various stages of decomposition. A turkey calmly strolled out. Beside the shack, another woman vigorously washed clothes in a large metal bowl. An old Toyota truck rolled up and the rear hatch flipped open, revealing a wide assortment of everything one could need for the jungle home: washing powder, razors, stockings, an assortment of packaged food, and that symbol of western economic prosperity, Coca Cola. A dozen women of various ages and walking ability materialized from nowhere as though by teleportation, surrounded the truck and pointed at things inside.

"You show passport now, señor."

This was immigration control Guatemala style. It was simple and honest, my preferred method of travel.

With evidence already procured from around the Pacific, the Near East, Egypt and the Andes validating the existence of a group of antediluvian individuals possessing extraordinary skills, I wanted to focus on how

Central American indigenous people viewed the flood and where they believe their ancestor gods might have come from, particularly with regard to the writings of Plato. In *Timaeus* the Greek scholar outlines the tragic sinking of Atlantis as part oral tradition part allegory. Most historians dismiss Plato's account as pure fiction, partly because they cannot stomach the idea of an advanced civilization existing prior to the twenty-first century, and mostly because they do not understand the mechanics of myth and its ability to convey important information to audiences then and now.

Plato acknowledged his source to be Solon, a scholar and lawgiver who traveled the Nile delta and there learned of the story of a sunken antediluvian civilization from the temple priests at Sais. Solon originally wrote down his account for Socrates' great-grandfather: "I, Solon, was never in my life so surprised as when I went to Egypt for instruction in my youth, and there, in the temple of Sais, saw an aged priest who told me of the island of Atlantis, which was sunk in the sea thousands of years ago... the people were friendly and good and well-affectioned towards all. But as time went on they grew less so, and they did not obey the laws, so that they offended heaven. In a single day and night the island disappeared and sank beneath the sea; and this is why the sea in that region grew so impassable and impenetrable, because there is a quantity of shallow mud in the way, and this was caused by the sinking of a single vast island. This is the tale which the old Egyptian priest told to me." [1]

The Egyptians confided in Solon that, prior to a global flood nine thousand years before his time — marking the event around 9600 BC — the Atlantean empire existed beyond the mouth of the Mediterranean, stretched into southern Europe and Egypt, and records of said civilization still existed when the Greek scholar was in Egypt.

One pearl of wisdom imparted by the priests to Solon concerns an occasion deep in prehistory when the Earth rotated backwards, which led to an Ice Age: "I mean the change in the rising and the setting of the Sun and the other heavenly bodies, how in those times they used to set in the quarter where they now rise, and used to rise where they now set.... At certain periods [the Earth] revolves in the reverse direction...of all the changes which take place in the heavens, this reversal is the greatest and most complete." [2]

Enough ink has been poured on the subject of Atlantis to fill an entire continent — an incomplete catalogue of literature on Atlantis lists 1700 titles, and that was back in 1929[3] — so I feel it unnecessary to regurgitate Plato's well-known story. Suffice it to say the Egyptian priests acquainted Solon with the history of the world as it really is rather than how academics prefer to interpret it. They had kept meticulous records extending deep into prehistory — the King List in the Turin Papyrus alone spans 36,000 years — not for the sake of record-keeping *per se* but as a warning to future generations not to be complacent about the world they live in, to realize that cataclysms are cyclical and bound to come around and undermine the ill-prepared. The achievements and pitfalls of their predecessors became guideposts for future generations.

I wondered what the Guatemalans might have to say on the matter.

The people generally associated with this region — which includes the Yucatan peninsula — are the K'iche' and the Maya. When gold-hungry Conquistadores arrived in the sixteenth century they were astonished to find sprawling temple cities complete with astronomical towers. Everywhere they plundered they saw a people obsessed with the mapping of the sky and the charting of extraordinary spans of time. For example, the Maya employed a number of calendars for tracking the synodic cycle of Venus, Mercury, Mars and Jupiter, along with the cyclic phenomena of eclipses, solstices, and equinoxes. There was a cycle related to the 266-day female gestation cycle, a general 365-day solar cycle, and a 52-year calendar round when the same beginning point in the previous two calendars coincided. Each one interlocks at critical points, demonstrating the interrelationship of the cosmos. Supplemental calendars included a 819-day count, the multiplication of sacred numbers 7, 9 and 13, a 584-day Venus transit that aligns with the Earth and Sun, and Great Cycles comprising 2160 years. Such calculations could only come from incredibly long periods of observation, therefore the Maya or their progenitors must be incalculably old.

The Maya also had absolute knowledge of thirteen dimensions or states of consciousness, and on one level, the development of such intricate calendars was due to this intimate experience, all of which defined their existence on the material plane.[4]

By contrast, the arriving Spanish still believed the Earth to be at the center of a solar system around which rotated the Sun, and thus got by from day to day with a simple solar calendar. Maya cosmology must have reeked of witchcraft. Even to the modern mind their vast astral knowledge seems otherworldly, excessive, unwarranted.

Or is it? Another example is the Maya long count calendar that spans 26,000 years and comes with markers. One marker, the Third World, began c.9600 BC, the period of the great flood; another began around 3113 BC when the maize God directed a group of other gods to set the Universe to order once again, ushering the Fourth World (coincidentally the same period when the first pharaoh of purely human blood is said to have ascended the throne in Egypt). That World reached its apex in 2012 AD and humanity would have a window of thirty years either side to adapt to the changes marking the transit to the next World.[5]

One point of view concerning the origin of the word *maya* is that it derives from a star in the Pleiades seen at its heliacal rising over Yucatan c.3113 BC, heralding the era of the people who took on this collective name.[6] Maya, like Maori or Waitaha, refers not so much to genetics or race but to a way of thinking, it is an overarching principle defining a group of people. According to my good friend, the Maya teacher Miguel Angel Vergara, *maya* refers to a person who has raised their consciousness through the understanding and application of sacred knowledge, it is an allegory, a statement of spiritual consciousness. One is not *born* maya, one *becomes* maya. Such a title is adopted as a collective noun when a group of people share the same spiritual ideal or aspiration.[7] This explains why elders claim the roots of Maya to be much, much older, and the people from whom they descend had different names which reflected the period or World in which they existed.

In one flood myth the K'iche' are said to have migrated from stepping stone to stepping stone in the eastern ocean before arriving in Yucatan.[8] It is their way of describing an island-hopping voyage in search of a new domicile after being displaced from their original land by the flood. Traveling inland from the Yucatan coast, they eventually settled in the highlands of Guatemala and named their main temple city Utatlán, which came under the protection of a regenerating god by the name Q'uq'umatz. Its remains are located barely fifteen miles north of Lake Atitlán, the largest in Central America, beneath whose waters lies the original city, having itself fallen prey to another natural disaster.

The largest Maya groups still live in this region — Tzutuhiles,

Cakchiqueles, Vukumag, and of course the K'iche' — all descendents of an island nation that sank in the Atlantic 11,000 years ago, a place they call Atitlán (or its regional variants Aztalan, Tollan, Tulanzuh). Ascribing the name to the lake and its temple city was a way to keep the memory alive.[9]

There's a strange fatalism involved in making a hazardous journey from a sunken volcanic landmass in the Atlantic only to settle beside a lake resembling an inland ocean in a region crowded with volatile volcanoes! The rest of the history of Lake Atitlán is shrouded in total secrecy, mostly due to the distrust of outsiders, and with good reason, as recent history attests. The Spanish priests who sailed across the Atlantic with Conquistadores butchered everyone in Central America who did not conform to the Catholic opinion of the world. Before they finished their genocide, along with the wanton burning of volumes of technical, spiritual, scientific and historical literature, they extricated a few codices from the Maya. Yet those accounts are but mere tourist guides compared to the knowledge hidden beneath the floors of ordinary Maya homes — which the Spanish were unlikely to search — or better still, held safely in memory by shamans who escaped into the dense jungle of the interior. Today if one wishes to understand Maya prehistory one ought to consult such individuals, for they recall a very different series of events concerning their roots.

After the flood a company of survivors arrived on the northern shores of Yucatan by boat and kept moving inland through the near-flat peninsula and away from water. After what they'd experienced, even I would have been compelled to make for high ground through mosquito and snake and crocodilo-infested jungle just to feel a sense of safety — much in the way the people of the high Andes did when they felt compelled to place their temple cities in truly awkward locations.[11] Those individuals were contemporaries of the K'iche', magician-priests who chose to ride out the tempest and reach survivors in different parts of the world to re-establish the wisdom and the laws upon which new civilizations would be built. With this aim in mind they established the foundation of temple cities throughout Central America.

One such formidable complex is Tikal, of which only an estimated ten per cent has been exhumed from the jungle. The wisdom keepers I befriended are unanimous about the true origin of such places, indicating the buildings are far older than conventionally dated, for what is seen is but one of many skins of an onion. Indeed just about every pyramid in Central America is built in this manner, accommodating the needs and dictums of each successive age and expanding in kind. The pyramid of the magician at Uxmal, for example, is in fact five pyramids encasing a sacred cave. Since neither the stars nor the Earth are fixed, every few thousand years the temple must be realigned to reflect the sky, thus temples were treated like living beings; the Egyptians went so far as to address each room before dawn as though rousing a person from slumber.

Local wisdom keepers state that, outwardly, the current temples date from c.1300 BC, but their foundation is closer to 8000 BC. Over such a long period they have absorbed influences from the Atlantic (Egyptian, Middle Eastern) as well as the Pacific (Asian, Indonesian). Indeed, walking around parts of Uxmal and Tikal one would be mistaken for being in Cambodia or Java or Egypt.

On my first journey to Tikal I felt comfortable there. It is a university reflecting the architecture of the cosmos, a ceremonial centre where the ancient Maya teachers captured sounds from other realities. Tikal is home to the tallest Maya pyramids, and both pyramids and temples reflect the understanding of mathematics, geometry and cosmic calendars. They also act as needles, capturing the telluric energy of the Earth and sky, acupuncturing the ground, and the body. Miguel Angel Vergara has spent a considerable part of his life reassembling and studying the full *Popol Vuh*

Tikal's main plaza. There may be up to nine underground levels.

Pyramid of the Magician, Uxmal. Actually five buildings in one.

and adds the following: "Tikal was once home to the Architects of the Sky, who came from the stars and spoke *He-Suyua-Thau* [the language of light], heralding an era when the city fused science, art, philosophy and religion as one." [11]

Architects of the Sky who spoke the language of light? That paints quite a picture. I wonder which part of the sky they came from?

My walk around the sprawling site led to the pyramid poetically catalogued as Temple V, an imposing structure featuring a broad, steep staircase, in my opinion the most potent of all buildings at Tikal. Its unusual slope of 26° is also employed in the Great Pyramid of Giza — yet another remote relationship. After a couple of hours of solitude away from the incessant cacophony of howler monkeys mischievously wandering the tree canopy above, I wandered over to the main plaza and was joined by Miguel and a K'iche' archaeologist. While Miguel prepared a ceremony to honor the ancestors, I talked to my group about the nine underground layers of construction running beneath the main plaza connecting its two iconic pyramids. I described how the tunnels would have been used particularly by initiates as part of the Mysteries teachings, and how they spent a few days in splendid isolation inside caves concealed within the core of the pyramids before appearing triumphantly at dawn on the summit to observe the rising of Venus, the mark of the risen initiate.

When I finished this spontaneous monologue I looked around to find a lot of stunned faces, particularly that of the archaeologist, who asked me, "How do you know of such things?"

I replied, "Someone here just showed me, a spirit form, perhaps the temple itself is speaking to me, I don't even know if this is true, someone just fed me images and took me to parts of the site no one gets to see."

The archaeologist confirmed all I had said was true. The information has remained confidential because sensitive work is still in progress. Archaeology is a conservative profession, after all. And yes, so far they have discovered five underground levels below the plaza and the pyramids; the rest are in unstable condition due to their remote age, although it is speculated there could be as many as nine levels, a symbolic number in K'iche' Maya tradition.

"What brings you here aside from Tikal?" asked the archaeologist.

"I'm looking for missing people and missing lands."

"You need to go to Lake Peten Itzá and the city of Flores, my friend."

As it turns out, that was precisely where I was staying that night.

HOME OF THE MAGICIANS

Flores is one of those delightful, rambling old towns where every humble home is painted in joyful colors as though someone accidentally dropped LSD into the paint bucket. It once formed the hub for temple cities such as Tikal and Ixlu; many more are known to be hiding in the jungle or beneath deep layers of dirt. Recent discoveries using ground-penetrating radar (LIDAR) include a previously undetected city of 60,000 structures, including plazas and pyramids, capable of supporting some 10 million people.[12]

Flores covers an entire island on Lake Peten Itzá. It is a recent name given by the Spanish to what used to be the religious *axis mundi* of a priestly caste called the Itz or Itzá, the last of the Maya to hold out against the invaders until the city was overrun and razed in 1697. The Spanish referred to it as Tayasal, a corruption of *Ta Itzá* (Place of the Itzá). Yet the Itzá precede that period, they are far older than the Maya, they are the *ancestors* of the Maya.

This was precisely what I had been looking for.

The Itzá called the island Nojpetén (Great Island), except it is not a great island at all. One can comfortably walk from one end to the other in twenty minutes. Its greatness comes from its status as a major spiritual center that once comprised twenty-one temples and a nine-tiered pyramid. The entire island was a temple under the care of the Itzá, accessed only by those who practiced spiritual purity or went there to learn the Mysteries teachings. It was a land set aside from the ordinary world, a primordial mound like Iwnw in Egypt, or the Island of the Sun in Lake Titicaca.

A stela in Flores town square, the only clue this was once a main Itzá religious center.

Aside from a couple of stela now adorning the town square you wouldn't know it was ever so. What gives away its ancient sacred status is the cathedral on the island's highest point, most likely the site of the original pyramid, whose stones were plundered to build the town. The cathedral is not aligned east — a violation of standard Catholic protocol — but rather to the winter solstice sunrise in the era of 7600 BC, when the Sun would have appeared in clear view down the neck of Lake Peten Itzá, thus explaining why the Itzá chose this island over a much larger one nearby and named it Great Island.

The other reason was emotional. Nojpetén was chosen to reflect the original great island in the middle of the Atlantic Ocean that was once the Itzá homeland until the flood consumed it. The sacred book *Chilam Balam* (From the Mouth of the Jaguar Wizard), compiled in the 18th century, actually dates the appearance of the Itzá in Central America: "13 times 400 times, and 15 times 400, plus 400 years, the Itzá lived as heretics." [13] That's a total of 11,600 years since their arrival after "the water swallowed the fount of wisdom," [14] dating their arrival from Atitlán to c. 9600 BC — confirming the date originally given to Solon by the Egyptians, as published by Plato.

(Incidentally the original definition of heretic is 'someone in possession of the facts who is able to choose', referring to a well-informed individual, specifically in matters pertaining to sacred or restricted knowledge).

The Itzá named this land Ma'ya'ab (Land of the Few), and in time established the foundations of the temples and pyramids we know today — an estimated 30,000 of them, the most popular being Chichen Itzá — all of which are recognized by the Maya as astral academies incorporating the teachings brought to this land by a priestly caste. Itzá literally means sorcerer, magician, it is they who are referred to as Lords or Architects of the Sky. They took their name from the god-man Itzamna, a renowned master astronomer, mathematician, and teacher of the laws that underpin a civilized society. Itzamna is depicted on a stela arriving on a raft from the east, surrounded by toppling temples and active volcanoes. He settled in the town of Itzamel before initiating the construction of Chichen Itzá. Ironically the stela was removed from Tikal and taken to Europe, ostensibly for protection, only to be destroyed during an air raid in World War II. Another mural, this time in the Temple of the Jaguar at Chichen Itzá, depicts him as tall, slim, bearded, with large eyes and an olden complexion, and more to the point, with facial features that look decidedly Caucasian. But perhaps the most poignant image of Itzamna is the one painted on a large mural inside a subterranean chamber on the periphery of the central plaza of Tikal.

But Itzamna's background now takes a fascinating left turn. His name is an amalgamation of Izanami and Izanagi, the husband-wife, brother-sister creator gods who appear in Japanese mythology c.8000 BC; the same relationship is attributed to the antediluvian gods of China, Nu Kwa and Fu Hsi. How this god-man arrived from Atitlán only to become etymologically linked to the Far East is confusing at best, except there may exist a bridge between these two disparate trains of thought. Miguel Angel Vergara makes it clear that *two* groups of sages arrived in Central America after the flood: the Itzá of Atitlán, who were represented by the totem Kan/Chan, the serpent, while another, the Olmec, claimed origin from Mu'ul in the Pacific and came under the totem of Balam, the jaguar.[15]

Itzamna paddles to Yucatan after the sinking of Atitlán.

Itzamna also shares an interesting history with the god-man K'uKuulKaan who similarly appears dressed in a long tunic after the flood, from a land lost to the sea to the east. K'uKuulKaan was not so much a given name but the spiritual ideal this individual represented. His cult was based on nonviolence, compassion and humility. It was also obsessed with the mystery of immortality. The people of Yucatan and Guatemala were under no illusion about the physical nature of this god, for they describe him as "fair and ruddy-complexioned with a long beard... a mysterious white man with strong body, broad forehead, large eyes... who came from across the ocean in a boat that moved by itself without paddles." He was also described as such by the Olmec, to whom he was known as Quetzlcoatl.

There is no doubt the incoming Itzá set out to recreate the world they once knew and lost. Only an advanced culture with thousands of years of accumulated science and engineering know-how could have created temple cities such as Copan, Tikal, Chichen Itzá, Palenque, Uxmal, and El Mirador, the largest civic and pyramid complex in the Americas, the product of a fully developed culture. As with other parts of the ancient world the best architecture is found at the lowest layer, its megalithic engineering eclipsing all subsequent construction.

Chichen Itzá, in particular, was a kind of cosmic university to which candidates would flock from all over central America to be educated to the highest levels of mathematics, astrology, astronomy, science, philosophy and the Mysteries, each discipline taught in individual temples, many of which embodied the teachings by mere virtue of measures and decorations hard-wired into the fabric of the buildings. Candidates became masters of the arts and carried the title Ah-Kan-Bezah (Those Who Teach The Path to Wisdom).[16]

Pyramid of K'uKuulKaan, Chichen Itzá.

Geological evidence shows that the Yucatan Peninsula has been habitually destroyed by rampaging tsunamis as tall as fifty feet, necessitating rebuilding programs on a regular basis. This alone accounts for the many layers of style and building design. The central administrative structures of Palenque, for example, exhibit at least four different building periods founded on a lower layer of megalithic stones that are clearly the product of an earlier civilization.

Museums are filled with statues and stela bearing the telltale signs of saltwater erosion from sites deep inland. Everywhere lie buildings half covered with layer upon layer of silt, and yet all rivers throughout the Yucatan are underground, so where did so much silt come from? Recent excavations around the perimeter of the Pyramid of K'uKuulKaan in Chichen Itzá reveals a further two layers of beautifully fitted stone concourses now lying twenty five feet below the present ground level, validating traditions that it was designed long, long ago by the astronomer priest Nohoch-Itz-Tzaab (Great Face of the Rattlesnake), and expanded accordingly from period to period.[17] Like the *moai* on Easter Island, such extreme silting can only come from thousands of years of accumulated debris, from recurring periods of civilization, destruction, fallowness and rebirth. Archaeologists such as Augustus Le Plongeon, who came across such temples covered in dense jungle in the 1890s, remarked on the amounts of river rock and sediment deep inside the buildings, not to mention half-buried buildings, attesting to many violent episodes. The temple of Sayil, some 100 miles from the ocean, appears to have undergone a horrific tsunami which pounded the buildings with such force that great numbers of building blocks have been widely scattered to a point where reconstruction has proved impossible.

Could this be evidence of mega floods and extreme weather that followed the end of the Younger Dryas? One piece of evidence concerns the *sacbe*, the spirit roads that stretch across the Yucatan in ruler straight alignments like umbilical cords linking temple cities to each other. They are identical in character and purpose to the tracks fanning out from Chaco Canyon in New Mexico, or the ruler-straight roads criss-crossing the British Isles

Exposed lower level reveals the pyramid's older layer.

from tip to toe that even in 2000 BC were already described by the Welsh as old beyond memory. Such engineering marvels, ten to twenty-five feet in width, hundreds of miles in length, were built well enough to require little or no maintenance or improvement. They too were constructed from a long accumulation of gathered experience.

Thanks to satellite imagery it is now possible to see where the *sacbe* run into the Gulf of Mexico and continue some thirty feet beneath the present sea level before rejoining land and continuing to the next temple city.[18] At the very least this places their construction before 3000 BC, when the last major sea level rise took place.

Or do such anomalies belong to an earlier epoch? Recent discoveries of 358 submerged cave systems covering nine hundred miles near the temple of Tulum reveals humans were present in the Yucatan earlier than accepted. One recovered human skull was covered in deposits from c.7000 BC. Inside this limestone labyrinth world resembling the arteries of a giant, divers found the remains of enormous sloths, proto-elephants, extinct fauna and, more to the point, Maya artefacts, all deep underwater, trapped by rising water levels between 8000-10,000 years ago, creating a time capsule that places the predecessors of the Maya firmly in this region in the era after the flood.[19]

The historic temple façade, made from small limestone blocks, rests on a course of older megaliths. Palenque.

K'uKuulKaan set the example of ideal conduct that later humans aspired to follow. Here, an initiate reaches such a level and adopts the serpent symbolism associated with this flood god.

*Filfa island seen from the megalithic temple of Hagar Qim. The land
bridge connecting it to Malta collapsed in a major catastrophe.*

SUDDENLY SUBMERGED

"Many have called those straits the Entry of the Mediterranean Sea. Near to the sides of this gullet are set two mountains, one each side, as barriers to shut all in... the Limits of the Labours of Hercules. For which cause, the inhabitants of those parts call them the Pillars of that God; and they believe that by ditches digged within the Continent, the Ocean, before excluded, was let in; and so the Face of the Earth was changed." — Pliny [1]

The St. Vincent Islands were discovered in 1789 by Europeans at 7° 21' N 127° 4' W — roughly between Baja and Tahiti — by Captain Antonio Martinus while sailing from Panama to Macau. An account of the twelve days spent there was written by a missionary aboard the ship, Father Santa Clara, who describes the islands as moderately elevated, about twenty miles in circumference, well wooded and abounding with coconuts. Several small islands lay to the west, with a boat channel in-between providing good harbor. The abundant fur seals on the beach were so tame they would not move out of the way of a landing party searching for food.

Before stocking the ship with five thousand coconuts, two hundred and fifty bread-fruits, four hundred land terrapins and twenty-five green turtles, it was noted how a volcano was ablaze on each of the nine islands. Which might explain why, when Captain Benjamin Morrell sailed there in 1824 all he found after forty-six days of surveillance was discolored water to a depth of 720 feet. [2]

Geologists generally scorn the idea of landmasses disappearing in the blink of an eye, and yet, much to their vexation, suddenly vanishing landmasses are a regular occurrence, even in historical times. Take the case of a Polynesian sailor living on Tuanaki island, part of the Cook group, in 1842. Two years later when a missionary vessel was sent to rescue him, Tuanaki and two other islands had disappeared, the result of a violent earthquake.

Or Davis Island, discovered in 1687, five hundred miles west of South America at 27° south, added to naval charts because it was a huge landmass stretching beyond the horizon. Thirty-five years later captain Jacob Roggeveen went looking for it on his way to Australia but it was no longer above sea level. Still, the journey was not a loss for the Dutchman, for he stumbled upon Easter Island by accident; two islands in the vicinity were put on naval maps as late as 1912 only to vanish in the proceeding years, including Sarah Ann Island in 1932, which failed to be found after a fruitless three-week search by the U.S. Navy.

Chroniclers in the fifth century BC were no strangers to such phenomena. Herodotus noted on his travels that all the land in Egypt south of Menfer and all the way to the highlands of Ethiopia had once been covered by the sea, as were the desert plains of Arabia, corroborating the earlier account from Teotokai Andrew of an island inhabited by the Anunaki having existed in that region during the Younger Dryas.

The historian Pliny likewise was aware of the cutting off of landmasses by rising sea levels, such as Britain from France, and Sicily from Italy. He too referenced a large continent that once was in the middle of the Atlantic, adding, "in our Mediterranean Sea, all men may see at this day how much has been immersed: Acarnania by the inward Gulf of Ambracia; Achaia within that of Corinth... And besides, the Sea has broken through Leucas, Antirrhium, Hellespont, and the two Bosphori."[3] Back in the day the process of geologic renewal was accepted as sudden and catastrophic, such as the total collapse of mountains and hills like Cybotus and Phogium in Ethiopia.[4] As recently as 646 AD a violent earthquake in Chile levelled several mountains, while in China an entire province was swallowed up and replaced by a lake in 1556.[5] And had you been near on the east coast of New Zealand's South Island in 2016, you would've seen ten feet of sea floor rise out of the ocean after an earthquake that lasted a mere two minutes.

With missing lands comes the prospect of lost civilizations and the two go hand-in-hand. A 1966 oceanographic investigation of the Pacific Ocean discovered "two upright columns, about two feet or more in diameter, sighted extending five feet out of the mud. Two more had fallen down and were partially buried, and another angular square-ish block was seen."[6] The official report added that one of the columns bore markings resembling inscriptions. The odd thing was, the worked columns were now at a depth of 6000 feet and fifty-five miles off the coast of Peru.[7] During the Younger Dryas that coastline would have seen the sea 600 feet lower than it is today,[8] still not enough to explain how five man-made objects found their way to the ocean floor. Or perhaps the Andean flood accounts of mountains rising and falling rapidly are not as far fetched as they sound.

What is certain is that 11,000 years ago an unnamed stone mason living in the Sicilian Channel between Sicily and Tunisia cut a 39-foot long, 15-ton limestone monolith, drilled holes into its surface, and transported it 1000 feet to where it was placed upright. In a part of the world where such menhirs are commonplace, it was surprising to find this particular example at a depth of 131 feet below the Mediterranean Sea. The monolith was dated to c.9300 BC based on attached shell fragments, thus it had to have been carved and transported long before being engulfed by encroaching waters. And there's no mistaking its human origins: it has a regular shape and three drilled holes of similar diameter on a block of non-local limestone.[9]

Pliny and others, it seems, were right about the rapid re-shaping of the landscape, particularly the sudden inundation of the Mediterranean.

A MALTESE ENIGMA

Prior to the events of 9700 BC the Mediterranean Sea was much shallower, peppered with archipelagos and landmasses of considerable size that became solitary islands after the drastic rise in sea level at the end of the Younger Dryas, so it is reasonable to ask if we are missing an entire Mediterranean megalithic antediluvian culture whose survivors found themselves scrambling for higher ground? Part of the answer lies in and around the Maltese archipelago, which formed part of Sicily before rising seas transformed it into four islands.

A few years ago I had the opportunity to visit the temples on those sun-kissed islands. Their cloverleaf and womb-shaped internal chambers are unique, as are their adjacent underground temples — *hypogea* — with

Ggantija's unusual double axis, one for the Sun, the other for the Moon.
Bottom: its lower, older wall is better constructed, and better preserved.

whom they form a symbiotic image of the universe, the light above and the dark below. They certainly give the impression of having developed in isolation, the product of a society that wished to remain separate.

One of the oldest temples, Ggantija (Tower of the Giantess), stands on the smaller island of Gozo. It is officially dated to c.3600 BC, based on fragments of debris taken from one of the chambers after the site was cleared during excavations around 1904, casting doubt on the quality of undisturbed organic material. And since the analysis was made long before the availability of radiocarbon testing, the dating appears to be nothing more than an educated guess, to shoehorn it into the academically acceptable timeframe. In 1934 the archaeologist Luigi Ugolini speculated that the lowest habitation layer of another Maltese temple, Tarxien, was closer to 8000 BC.[10] It requires no effort to image how this news was received.

Just like temples in the Andes, Ggantija's oldest stones are also its largest. The original lower courses were cut from hard globigerina limestone and weigh sixty tons apiece and, as one would expect on a small island, they show signs of water erosion. The upper courses are newer, made with smaller, less refined masonry and of a construction aesthetic sufficiently mismatched to suggest a later reconstruction, like an apprentice electrician returning to finish the work of a master carpenter. They are also in a comparatively advanced state of erosion, even the undersides, suggesting they were once scattered on the ground, then reused for reconstruction. The thing is, Malta's regional climate is arid, and has been progressively so for 8000 years.[11]

On the main island, the above is repeated at the temple of Hagar Qim. A number of building periods featuring differing skill levels have been at work here. The older the stones, the better the skill, however, unlike Ggantija, the lower courses of Hagar Qim show extreme weathering to the point of crumbling, as one would expect from limestone closer to the sea and exposed to the elements for a vast length of time. A second period of construction repaired sections of the original temple using blocks of more manageable size and lacking the same finesse, again adding height to the walls; insensitive twentieth century restoration has left predictably appalling results.

Once again the condition of the stone becomes the focal point. If the temples are less than six thousand years old, where did the water come from to produce the advanced level of erosion, because it's been nine thousand years since Malta last experienced the level of sustained precipitation required to create the depth of erosion borne by its temples.

Since the region shares the same climatic footprint as North Africa, it is possible to travel to Giza and observe the same effects on its oldest temples. One of my favorite places to demonstrate the effects of large-scale water erosion is the rectangular temple situated behind the small pyramid credited to Menkaure. In addition to a crowd-free environment, you will be rewarded with a courtyard and avenue composed of massive blocks of limestone, whose upper courses show exactly the same level of water erosion found at Ggantija, Hagar Qim, Mnajdra, and every other Maltese site. A careful examination of this pyramid temple also reveals blocks taken from other sites used to patch and repair after it too incurred heavy damage from some unknown event. If the Giza Plateau was last exposed to profoundly wet climate between 10,500-8000 BC, it follows that the same climate was responsible for weathering the temples on Malta.

As with Egypt, the Maltese temples may be vestiges of a lost antediluvian civilization, after all, sites that once stood on dry land now lie two miles offshore and under twenty-five feet of seawater. One prehistoric temple constructed from "rectangular blocks of unbelievable size" now lies at the bottom of Valletta harbor, still seen in 1536 stretching a considerable distance out to sea.[12] Ggantija itself is a temple of advanced design yet there is no evidence of its gradual development. The temple arrives perfect, on an island too small to accommodate the kind of urban population and architectural civilization required to pull off such an engineering marvel.[13] But what if Ggantija was once part of a megalithic culture on Malta when it suffered a calamity of such magnitude it altered the region beyond imagination and wiped out its ancients architects, leaving the temples to decompose, before the gods returned under more favourable conditions to engage in rebuilding the island's temple culture? Evidence shows parts of Malta have been overwhelmed by tidal waves that swept across the island due to collapsing land bridges, violently stuffing animals, people and artefacts into caves. Figurines of the Earth Mother, carved in a style contemporary with Mediterranean and Near East art between 7000-14,000 BC, were found among accumulated flood debris. Like Jericho, Malta appears to have been at the mercy of unstable climatic conditions following the end of the Younger Dryas, particularly from melting glaciers and collapsing ice dams still covering northern Europe, frequently releasing trillions of gallons of meltwater that rushed into the Mediterranean.

Let us assume Ggantija — and Malta's other twenty-seven known sites for that matter — belongs to a remote age, say, 14,000 years ago, not a far-fetched idea considering the aforementioned shell-encrusted megalith found at the bottom of the sea lies to the northwest of the island. So let's play with this epoch.

Ggantija has two entrances whose axes are slightly misaligned as though tracking two related yet separate objects above the horizon. Due to the effect of precession, the Sun has crept steadily northwards with each passing millennia. By c.12,000 BC it rose in alignment with the upper entrance of Ggantija on the spring equinox, casting a ray of light onto an alcove at the rear of the temple. At this same time, the lower entrance marked the Major Lunar Standstill, the point when the Moon's orbit reaches its southernmost position. Both entrances face a hill across the valley whose summit was entirely levelled to achieve the effect.

Such a remote date is more consistent with weathering on Ggantija's older megaliths, in fact it subjects the temple to not one but two cataclysms — the start and end of the Younger Dryas — inflicting the kind of heavy damage that returning architects would have needed to address. Assuming they repaired the site by 9000 BC, it still left two thousand years of rainy weather to account for the erosion now seen on the upper layers of Malta's monuments.

A CLIFFHANGER OF A DAY

Setting aside the enigma of the Maltese temples for a day, I made a point of examining another of the islands' curiosities — parallel ruts incised deep into the limestone bedrock, resembling tracks made by vehicles following the same, except the evidence points to the tracks having been bevelled and cut out of the bedrock with tools rather than by the repeated passage of wheels.[14] No sensible explanation has been forthcoming as to how they got there or why. The ruts cross the island and often stop at significant megalithic structures; some are interrupted by 3000-year old Punic graves, so at least it is certain they predate this period. Whether they are a clue as to how the limestone blocks were ferried to the temples is a matter of speculation.

The ruts on the north side of Malta cut through towns and gardens, run to the water's edge and continue unobstructed for a considerable distance under the sea. It is true that the north side of the island is sinking, yet the rate at which it is doing so cannot explain the depth to which the ruts descend below sea level; it can be argued that a combination of slippage plus a rise in sea level c.3000 BC is to blame, making the them only five to six thousand years old.

The same cannot be said for the south coast, which, for the most part, is one 600-foot vertical cliff. It was quite an experience to follow the ruts through arid scrub, right up to the cliff edge, and pick up the trail underwater, evidence of how the southern section of the island dramatic collapsed. The historian Louis De Boisgelin visited Malta in the late 18th century and commented on this: "The ruts may be perceived underwater at a great distance, and to a great depth, indeed as far as the eye can possibly distinguish anything through the waves." [15]

It appears the island was subjected to an impact of such magnitude that caused enough pressure to split the bedrock along a fault called the Pantalleria Rift. Unlike the northern coast that slopes gently into the water, the southern coast borders a deep canyon which in 16,000 BC was already filling with seawater, but the coastline still lay a considerable distance from Malta. It took a stupendous rise in sea level at the end of the Younger

Hagar Qim and its various, and progresively smaller stages of construction.

Dryas for the Mediterranean to finally reach the cliffs of Malta, a process that concluded by 7000 BC. The question that remains is what might have caused the cliffs to collapse in the first place?

One candidate is a massive wall of ocean water that rammed through the deep, narrow canyon then separating Morocco and Gibraltar — as ancient writers claim — inundating the Mediterranean basin, collapsing land bridges, and turning landmasses into islands. This was also the opinion of De Boisgelin: "A variety of phenomena prove that there must have been a great extent of land towards the south and west [of Malta], and that it must have been destroyed by some very violent cause out of the common course of nature. It appears that this destructive shock came from the west, and that it acted with the greatest force... we can only attribute the present state of things to an immense body of water... it also destroyed that part of the mountain which united the three islands, and this inundation has stripped them of all vegetable earth." [16]

And as far as the tracks at the edge of the cliffs are concerned, "this circumstance gives every reason to suppose that the ground must have sunk very considerably in this spot." [17]

A sudden subsidence of land was most certainly the case because the ruts along the top of the southern cliffs continue underwater for three miles and reappear 500 feet above the sea, along the top of the tiny island of Filfla, still seen there by visitors in 1911.

The enigmatic 'cart ruts' of Malta.

A THOUSAND MISSING HEADS

I need little excuse to spend time in medieval Valletta, a limestone city of steps worn smooth by the feet of the Knights of Malta, numerous Arab traders, ancient Phoenician voyagers, and the odd pirate or two. When opposing cultures collide, like asteroids, the result is often messy, but here they blend into a warm, romantic and sensual urban paradise.

After the obligatory two-hour outdoor lunch, I made my way to the Museum of Archaeology in central Valletta to get a sense of who the megalithic builders might have been and when they might have lived. Two carved limestone slabs grace the entrance hall, removed from the temple of Tarxien for their own protection. Visitors walk by, pose for selfies, and move on, oblivious to an extraordinary connection. The four spirals carved on each slab reflect the essence of life: the solstices, the equinox, and a central circle referencing the force holding this recurring rhythm of life in perpetual balance. And yet the first time I saw the panels they had a

Inundation map of the Mediterranean around Malta.

familiarity about them. Indeed I had seen them before, in the museum at Tiwanaku and, except for a slight artistic difference, they may as well have been carved by the same ancient artist.

It is by no means the only link between Malta and the Andes. In 1902, workers digging a cistern accidentally broke through the ceiling of a well-preserved subterranean ritual temple that became known as the Hypogeum of Hal Salflieni. Sometime in the distant past the bedrock was hollowed into thirty-three contiguous halls and chambers on three floors with a footprint of a quarter of a square mile, and may have served as the underground component of the nearby temple of Tarxien.

Like many of its kind, the Hypogeum was intended as a place of ritual, an environment where one can connect with another level of reality, and recent acoustic research proves it was deliberately tuned to a resonant frequency known to shut down mental processing in the brain and induce altered states; the same frequency has been detected in the Kings Chamber of the Great Pyramid.[18]

Red ocher paintings were daubed on several walls, one featuring a bull reminiscent of Palaeolithic cave art from 8000-30,000 BC. But something less artistic lay concealed in layers of dirt: over seven thousand human remains violently mixed with those of animals and sundry debris as though dumped into the caverns by a wall of water. What made the find significant were the hundreds of skeletons with elongated skulls identical to those in Paracas, on the coast of Peru.

Back at the museum, I'd arranged to meet with the director to see these dolichocephalic skulls. I had been forewarned by my colleague, the investigative journalist Graham Hancock, to expect a less-than-warm reception when inquiring about matters of discomfort to archaeologists. He'd been there earlier only to find that, of the hundreds of unusual skulls removed from the Hypogeum, only six could be accounted for. Even so Hancock still had to press the staff to show him the paltry collection.[19]

I was to be presented with even fewer: none. In fact the director palmed me off with a box of typical *Homo sapiens* skulls while stating there never was evidence of dolichocephalic skulls found in Malta.

There was no avoiding the drop in barometric pressure in the room. I pressed that the skulls are a matter of record rather than a figment of imagination.[20] And in case such a trap popped up, I presented photographs that Graham had lent me from his visit which clearly show said skulls — held by a member of her staff no less — including that of an adult's with a missing fossa median, a seam common in human skulls that allows the plates to expand during childbirth. We are definitely looking at a very different species of person living on Malta — a whole tribe, according to the original find — and given the outlandish concentration of temples on such a small piece of land, they may have formed a reclusive culture, a special society set apart from ordinary humans, precisely as I've speculated all along with regard to the antediluvian gods.

At this point in my brief meeting, the director of the Museum of Archaeology of Malta left the room and my visit was terminated.

The abrupt shutting down of uncomfortable evidence follows the topic of ancient civilizations wherever one travels, whether it's the archaeological cabal of Indonesia seeking to discredit Danny Hilman Natawidjaja at Gunung Padang, or Graham Hancock and myself in Malta — or another fellow by the name of Silva who lives on the remote Atlantic archipelago.

THE UNDERWATER MOUNT THAT IS A PYRAMID

While on my way to Portugal to research potential antediluvian sites, I landed on the island of São Miguel in the Açores to stretch my legs and work my way through a plate of those addictive little custard pastries, pasteis de nata. An article in the morning newspaper announced an exceptional discovery proving the Açores was indeed the location of the lost continent of Atlantis. Sometimes the universe has impeccable timing.

Diocleciano Silva is a veterinarian by day and a sport fisherman by the weekend. He was on his boat casing the fertile fishing banks between the islands of São Miguel and Terceira when his sonar picked up something that ought not be there: a 180-foot tall perfectly square structure with several diminishing levels, oriented to the cardinal points — a step pyramid, larger than a football stadium and, according to the bathymetric reading, 120 feet below sea level. A long experience of the sea has given Diocleciano many surprises but none quite like this.

This was not entirely fresh news. Mr. Silva had made the discovery eight months earlier but hesitated to divulge it. Given the ferocity of personal attacks and slander by the academic mafia that follow such explosive discoveries, I can't blame him, and yet the discrediting on this occasion came from the Portuguese Navy, just for a change, who claimed the lucky fisherman found nothing more anomalous than an underwater sea mount, one of many in the region. How the ocean is capable of sculpting such a perfect structure, they could not explain. Nor could they explain why the pyramid they claim to be a mount lies in a totally different location to the GPS coordinates provided by Diocleciano.

Unperturbed, the Commander of the Açores Maritime Zone insisted the GPS reading was an error. One wonders, given such shoddy equipment, how Diocleciano has managed to sail to and fro for years in the middle of the ocean and return home safely each time! Nevertheless the Portuguese navy quickly dismissed the find as a natural feature on the basis of older charts of their own while never investigating the specified site.

The alleged pyramid appears on the slope of a large submarine volcano that makes up much of the João de Castro sea bank, a treacherous area filled with perilous undersea volcanoes. One eruption sank two ships in 1718 before building up to a circular island one mile long and eight hundred feet high. Ravaged by the Atlantic Ocean, the island finally disappeared within four years. Strong seismic activity afflicts this region and the entire archipelago, it is a highly volatile part of the Earth's crust, the kind of place where a landmass could quickly and violently vanish. Still, marine life loves it here and it has been an important fishing ground for centuries, perhaps longer.

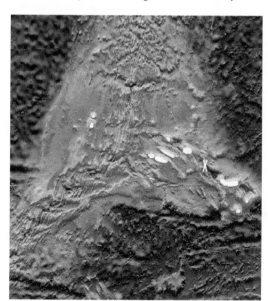

Bathometric map of the Açores reveals a shape not unlike that of Atlantis in medieval maps. X marks the underwater pyramid.

Eight years after the discovery nothing has moved forward. Or has it?

In my book *The Divine Blueprint* I presented a hypothesis

that many of the oldest sacred sites were placed mathematically on a world grid. Most might have even been in place before the flood. By extraordinary coincidence Graham Hancock found the same grid using a different computation.

To paraphrase the hypothesis, if an ancient civilization wished to build temples as markers around the world they would base the plan on a mathematical or geometric grid reflecting the host planet. The ancients recognized the Earth as a living organism, and living organisms are formed on cellular bonds using pentagonal geometry. The base angle of the pentagram is 72°; its divisors are 18, 36, 54, 108, 144. If one locates a declared Navel of the Earth, such as Iwnw in Egypt, and converts those numerical values to longitudes, the vertical lines hit notable sacred places with remarkable accuracy. Graham's version uses the numbers inherent in the Earth's processional cycle, whose main divisor is 72. Predictably, we both reached similar conclusions albeit independently.

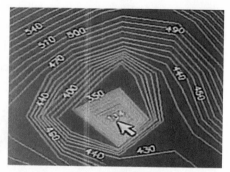

Sonar image of underwater pyramid.

Incidentally, the same series of numbers are hard-wired in the fabric and features of major temples, sacred texts and myths.

One of the things that vexed me during this research was the lack of longitudinal markers in the Atlantic. Not surprisingly I was excited by Diocleciano's discovery, even if it came after the book went to press. I still had to wait a couple of weeks before returning home to locate the underwater pyramid on my map, and as much as I would have loved a happy ending, Silva's discovery is 3.5° west of the mark, close but not close enough. I suspect Diocleciano was given a taste of things to come, and should an underwater search be conducted slightly to the east it might yet yield something more provocative.

11,000 years ago all this would have been another matter. Even discounting a major subsidence in the mid-Atlantic Ridge due to damage from comet impacts and rising sea levels, the Açores still formed a formidable island chain. In 1963 the Russian physicist Dr. Maria Klionova recovered rocks sixty miles north of the Açores at a depth of 6600 feet bearing signs of exposure to oxygen c.15,000 BC, while sediment taken from the Mid-Atlantic Ridge revealed the remains of freshwater plants as well as beach sand created along an ancient shoreline. Even rainwater was found trapped in fossils and limestone deposits. These are indications that this part of the Atlantic was above sea level just before the onset of the Oldest Dryas. A similar situation was observed in 1898 by the crew of a ship laying underwater cable in the archipelago. As grappling hooks scraped the ocean bottom two miles below, they turned up unfamiliar particles of lava whose peculiar glassy structure could only have solidified in the open air.[21]

Plenty of discussion has taken place since Plato's time establishing this as the most likely area of Atitlán/Atlantis so I need not revisit this scenario. What is worth pointing out is that, in myths, Atitlán is said to have collapsed in three stages, in conjunction with the three Dryas events that took place over a 3000-year period. It is therefore feasible that in 13,000 BC the archipelago still formed a considerable landmass, and bathometric maps of the region offer a glimpse of the roughly triangular format of the original island continent, just as depicted on ancient maps.

Coincidentally, Plato's dialogue in Critias describes a sunken Atlantis much in the same way navigators in the Pacific did when looking for other missing lands in the 19th century, "...when afterward sunk by an earthquake, became an impassable barrier of mud to voyagers sailing from hence to any part of the ocean." [22]

Underwater pyramid aside, there exist 140 step pyramids on the island of Pico itself, built with small basalt stones locally referred to as biscuits. They reach up to forty feet in height, contain hidden chambers, many of which are astronomically aligned.[23] Deposits of ancient artefacts unearthed by archaeologists Nuno Ribeiro and Anabela Joáquinito point to the structures being much older than the accepted date of the discovery of the Açores by the Portuguese in 1427. In Nuno's words: "We have found a rock art site with representations we believe can be dated back to the Bronze Age... we have an epigraph from Roman times, according to two scientists who were invited to interpret the inscription... megalithic structures, and an important set of structures scattered throughout the islands that need to be interpreted in new ways." [24] Phoenician coins from the 2nd century BC have also been discovered on the adjacent island of Corvo.[25]

As exciting as these discoveries are, none of the above are proof of remote antiquity, they merely show that life continued to thrive in the middle of the Atlantic in spite of unimaginable forces that once afflicted the region. The ferocity of seismic events past and present preclude that little if any conclusive evidence of Atitlán may ever be found. Yet, like sonar images, there are other signs pointing to an antediluvian presence in the Açores — a series of cart ruts on the island of Terceira that, like those on Malta and Easter Island, run to the edge of cliffs and into the sea.

A KIND OF CUBAN REVOLUTION

If parts of the Açores dropped two miles to the bottom of the Atlantic, and five megaliths stand 6000 feet off the coast of Peru, then a submerged city at 2300 feet should be relatively easy to explain.

"It is stunning. What we see in our high-resolution sonar images are clear man-made, large-size architectural designs. It looks like when you fly over an urban development in a plane and you see highways, tunnels and buildings," announced offshore engineer Paulina Zelitsky who, with her husband Paul Weinzweig and their son Ernesto, discovered megaliths "of a kind you'd find at Stonehenge or Easter Island... Some structures within the complex may be as long as 400 metres wide and as high as 40 metres... They show very distinct shapes and symmetrical designs of a non-natural kind. We've shown them to scientists in Cuba, the U.S. and elsewhere, and nobody has suggested they are natural." [26]

The team had originally been scheduled to locate shipwrecks off Cuba's western coast, where hundreds of vessels are believed to have sunk over the centuries, but they became understandably sidetracked. And who can blame them. The structures they stumbled upon while scanning the seabed with side-scan sonar and videotape equipment bear a remarkable resemblance to Mayan pyramids in nearby Yucatan. Invited scientists saw what appear to be streets, bays and structures similar to wharves in a port. [27] Stone blocks up to fifteen feet long, cut in perpendicular and circular shapes, were recovered from the ocean floor. "The stone is very polished granite. All of this peninsula is limestone, very fractured limestone. So, geologically, it [megalithic granite blocks] is totally foreign to Cuba. But it's also not known in Yucatan because Yucatan is also limestone, not granite." [28] An anthropologist at the Cuban Academy of Sciences analyzed stills taken from the videotape and claimed some of the stones appear to contain symbols and inscriptions.[29]

Like Malta, this submerged metropolis lies on what used to be a land bridge connecting the island with Yucatan, a plateau adjacent to a deep fault line.[30] Vestiges of the site might still exist above water because, three decades earlier, archaeologists excavated a megalithic structure along Cuba's western shore, a few miles from the underwater discovery.

The geologist affiliated with the underwater project, Manuel Iturralde, made a valuable observation: the volcanic glass covering the ocean floor could only have been formed on the surface while it was in contact with oxygen, suggesting the land upon which the city once stood must have been above water, and the last time a shift in both sea level and seismic activity of such magnitude took place in the region was around 11,000 years ago. A secondary indication that a severe cataclysm collapsed the entire surface lies in stones extracted from the ocean floor that show concentrations of fossilized escaramujos, a crustacean that lives at a depth of only six feet.[31]

"You would not think that a reasonable woman of my age would fall for an idea like this," [32] Zelitsky remarked, yet the team returned to reconnoiter the site with a remotely operated vehicle controlled from the mother ship via fibre-optic cable. Its cameras confirmed the earlier findings, including vast granite-like blocks between six and fifteen feet that were cut in perpendicular and circular designs.[33]

Amid the piles of sonar-enhanced maps spread over Zelitky's desk lay a well-worn copy of Comentarios Reales de las Incas, the account of Inka and pre-Inka history by Garcilaso de la Vega, the same tome that describes the great flood in the Andes and the arrival of Viracocha and his seven Shining Ones. Zelitsky was particularly fascinated by the account of ancient ruins at the bottom of Lake Titicaca — which have since been confirmed — and the sense of irony they present.[34]

Predictably, like other discoveries that would alter the history of civilization, this story has been buried very deep ever since.

VENICE OF THE PACIFIC

Temptation draws me magnetically back to the Pacific. No other place on Earth reflects such an absence of terrain, only the outstretched tips of drowned lands and submerged volcanoes peek above water like lips daring to be heard. A spaceman could look at the Pacific Rim — the most volcanically active region on Earth — and recognize, with detachment, how this ring of fire exists due to an impact of such magnitude it dislodged a roughly elliptical section of the Earth's crust.

A window on Nan Madol. Thousands of basalt columns larger than these were moved from the other side of the island to build an entire city.

One of the first Europeans to search the Pacific in the 16th century, the Portuguese navigator Pedro de Quierós, proposed the theory that its islands were the remains of a now submerged continent, a view accepted by his peers at the time. It may not be the most scientific hypothesis but it is nevertheless an accurate observation based on folklore collected directly from island people by such explorers. Soviet scientist V.V. Belousov discovered that in the recent geologic period, and certainly during the age of Homo sapiens, "the Pacific ocean grew considerably at the expense of great chunks of continents which, together with their young ranges of mountains, were inundated by it. The summits of these mountains are to be seen in the island garlands of East Asia." His findings were supported by another scientist, George H. Cronwell, in a paper delivered to the Tenth World Pacific Congress, in which he reported the discovery of such anomalies as coal on Rapa Island, irrefutably proving that there once existed a continent in that part of the Pacific.[35]

As we have already seen, many islands such as Tahiti retain standing stones, moai, ahu and other fragments of a lost megalithic culture. Others like Pohnpei tried to rebuild in the image of what once was. Unique to Pohnpei (Upon a Stone Altar) is the ka tree, an odd choice of name because it is the Egyptian word for soul. Even more unique is a roughly pentagonal temple city by the name of Nan Madol, consisting of a group of small artificial islands linked by a network of canals. Its core features some one hundred artificial islets contained within a mile-long perimeter wall, up to thirty feet high, built in alternating layers of large columnar basalt blocks and infill, all of which had to be laboriously transported from the opposite side of the island.

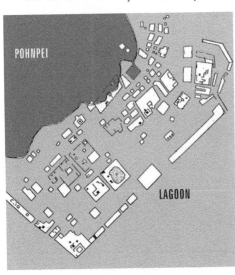

Sections of Nan Madol still above sea level.

Pohnpeians originally called this enchanted citadel Soun Nan-leng

(Reef of Heaven). According to legend it was created by the sorcerers Olisihpa and Olosohpa upon arriving from a sunken land to the west called Kanamwayso, and indeed the remains of another citadel have been located offshore at a depth of ninety feet. The two brothers sought a place to build Soun Nan-leng in honor of Nahnisohn Sahpw, god of agriculture, whereupon they performed rituals and levitated the huge stones with the aid of a flying dragon.

There's a resemblance here to the exposed structures made from columnar basalt atop Gunung Padang on the island of Java, but what is really striking about this out-of-place megalithic wonder is that it was designed to form a restricted sanctuary, it was designed to be separate from the island, much like a sacred enclosure, as though its inhabitants wished to create an isolated society. Like the long heads of Malta, these people were different, particularly the two brothers who were said to be much taller than the natives.

TAIWAN AND TULAN, PLACES OF REEDS

The Taiwanese flood myth describes how the giant snake Bonum blocked the flow of rivers until the entire world was submerged except the highest peak, Tongku Saveq (Mountain of Shelter). Two people were forewarned by gods to listen to a great change in the sound of the sea at the time of the full moon, whereupon they were to make haste for the

Menhirs at Sao Pa, below the Mountain of Shelter.

Megalith at Sao Pa. Same knobs as in the Osirion, Menkaure's Pyramid, and Andean temples.

mountain. There they received refugees from a sunken land called Tulan, from which Taiwan takes its name.[36]

Tulan or Tolan, if we recall, is the name also given by the K'iche' Maya to a missing homeland, the Place of Reeds.

Below the mountain lies Sao Pa and its large concentration of megaliths, twenty-one feet tall by a few inches slim, not unlike the proportions of the stone pillars of Göbekli Tepe, and Stennis, a stone circle on the remote northern Scottish island of Orkney. And just as Stennis was designed by people with a keen knowledge of astronomy, so the site at Sao Pa was carefully chosen to mark the Tropic of Cancer where, on the summer solstice, an upright stone casts no shadow.

Geodetically, Sao Pa also sits precisely 90° east of Giza.

One of the flat-faced megaliths was taken to the Taiwan Museum. It features a pair of large cubes carved in relief. Anyone who's climbed to either Naupa Huaca or the Moon Temple of Wayna Picchu in Peru will recognize the same design protruding from their respective centerpiece megaliths. Again we must ask, is this evidence of a group of astronomer architects from the same academy regrouping and rebuilding after the flood, and if so, what evidence remains of their previous work?

The answer may lie seventy miles east of Taiwan and eighty feet below sea level, on the island of Yonaguni. The megaliths of Sao Pa mark the Tropic of Cancer in the present era, but had they been erected ten thousand years earlier they would have missed the mark by one degree of latitude, an unacceptable margin of error to any self-respecting architect of the sky.[37] Back then the slow-moving imaginary line of the tropic would instead have passed through Yonaguni and its submerged citadel, a vast ledge of shaped steps, roads, passages, platforms and pillars, some astronomically oriented. To quote the geologist Robert Schoch: "Since Yonaguni is close to the most northerly position the tropic reaches in its lengthy cycle, the island may have been the site of an astronomically aligned shrine." [38]

Prior to the flood this hand-carved mesa would have resembled a kind of ceremonial island, its shape reminiscent of carved bedrock outcrops found throughout Peru called intihuatana, whose angles are designed to mark significant solar, lunar and stellar events. Yonaguni may have been a larger version. A model of the entire mesa, based on measurements and photos taken over the years by divers, even resembles the enigmatic carved boulders scattered throughout Peru, with their steps, staircases and ledges leading nowhere.

The parallels abound and astound.

LAND OF THE RED HILL

A rapidly encroaching ocean lost India a considerable amount of land, and today several cities lie far out to sea beneath the murky, sediment-laden waters of the Indian Ocean, one of the most evocative being Mahabali-puram, the City of Bali the Giant.[39] But the greatest loss to the flood was the land to the south of India which once connected today's island of Sri Lanka to the mainland. The region was called Kumari Kandam.

The focal point of this ancient land of the Dravidian culture is Arunachela, the Red Hill, a Navel of the Earth where the laws and knowledge of the gods were deposited as an insurance policy against any further infringements of the sea. "Oceans will not submerge it, even at the time of the great deluge."[40] The extreme antiquity of Arunachela may well be correct because the Dravidian language alone is more than 10,000 years old.[41]

The Red Hill takes center stage in the most ancient Tamil literature, the Tolkappiyam, itself based on an earlier work, which in turn was part of a library of truly ancient texts going back a further 10,000 years. These were housed in the First Sangam (academy), a city of knowledge founded at Tenmadurai during the age of gods by no less a figure than Siva himself.[42] This antediluvian academy was composed of 549 members, among them the sage Agattiyanar, the hill god Murugan, Kubera the Lord of Treasure, and patronized by eighty-nine kings over an unbroken period of 4440 years before being consumed by a major transgression of the ocean.[43]

The survivors moved north and established the Second Sangam at Kapatapuram, which persevered for a further 3700 years until it too was consumed by the sea, along with the rest of Kumari Kamdan. One survivor, a Tamil prince named Thirumaaran, managed to rescue literary classics such as the Tolkappiyam and swam with them to Uttara Madurai, closer to continental India, establishing there a Third Sangam which continued for 1850 years.[44] Alas it too was inundated and now sits at the bottom of the Indian Ocean to the south of present-day Madurai, a city that remains a place of great scholarship in India as though channelling its predecessors.

The scholarly argument is that the last Sangam disappeared between 350-550 AD. If we accept this at face value and calculate backwards from the years ascribed to each Sangam, we arrive at the following founding dates: Third Sangam, 1500 BC, Second Sangam, 5200 BC, First Sangam, 9600 BC, give or take a hundred years.[45] This places the first Academy of the Gods firmly around the period of the flood, again confirming Tamil oral traditions, not to mention those of the K'iche' Maya and the date given to Solon by the priests at Sais. That three unconnected sources should use the same calendrical point of reference is beyond coincidence. And there's no mistake about it, the oldest Tamil texts make reference to the submergence of no less than 700 kavatham (1000 miles) of Tamil land that once consisted of forty-nine counties filled with forests, rivers and hills that, due to three major submersions by the ocean, including the great deluge, forced people to move further and further north.[46] This original territory was said to have once belonged to the oldest of dynasties, one of whose kings was a man by the name Nedyon, which transliterates as Tall One.[47]

The descriptions of three sudden losses of land and their location between southern India and modern day Sri Lanka fit remarkably well with the three major rises in sea level that characterize the Dryas periods in this region,[48] and presents a good case for the Sangams dating to at least the time of the flood, when Sri Lanka, India and Kumari Kamdan formed a whole. However, when Buddhist monks in the fourth century AD began writing down the oral traditions of Sri Lanka and compiling them into the Mahavamsa, Dipavansa and Rajavali, they describe the loss of large swathes of land beyond Sri Lanka due to three great deluges, one of which washed away "twenty miles of coast, extending inland."[49] An older account appears to take place in antediluvian times and describes how the giant king Ravana, ruler of a citadel with twenty-five palaces, was punished by the gods for his heinous behavior.[50]

So could the three Sangams be the product of an earlier tradition? Speaking at the Fifth International Conference of Tamil Studies, chairman N. Mahalingam presented further evidence from the Mahavamsa, in which it is stated that Kumari Kamdan originally extended 4900 miles further south. He further states that "the first great deluge took place in 16,000 BC, when a large part of Lemuria was submerged under the sea.

Meenakshi Temple, Madurai The city's temple and academic culture is inherited from antediluvian academies, long since overwhelmed by the Indian Ocean.

The second one occurred in 14,058 BC when parts of Kumari Kandam went under the sea. The third one happened in 9564 BC when a large part of Kumari Kandam was submerged. The fourth deluge is said to have occurred between the years 2939 BC and 2387 BC and almost coincides with the birth of the Kaliyuga age." [51]

The periods outlined in the Mahavamsa fit within the geological parameters of the three Dryas events. And since it mentions a fourth rise in sea level — the one that altered the coastline of the Persian Gulf and whose general dates are accepted among the scientific community — it leads us to presume the more remote dates to be equally valid. But more to the point, the Mahavamsa states that the First Sangam was itself preceded by four earlier academies,[52] meaning that we are now looking at a tradition of knowledge, gods and civilization extending well into the prehistoric era, all suddenly vanished.

Those mysterious knobs, this time on the altar stone of Naupa Iglesia. Peru.

Manu with the Seven Rshis. Although only one woman is part of such brotherhoods, she often holds the most important position, as teacher of secret knowledge and propagator of the divine bloodline.

SEVEN TALL SAGES AND OTHER IMMORTALS

"They could endue with power the substances on earth." — Building Texts

Myths materialized around the world to record for posterity the crashing of aerial projectiles and the terrifying flood that ensued. Without exception the stories describe pockets of survivors being assisted by groups of unusual looking people who appeared from the sea to teach them the accoutrements required for starting, or re-starting, civilization.

11

Each group consisted of seven individuals led by a charismatic eighth; the leader is always partnered with a wife who is also his sister: Osiris and Isis in Egypt, Enlil and Ninlil in Mesopotamia, Fu Hsi and Nu Hwa in China, Izanami and Izanagi in Japan, Viracocha and his unnamed wife in the Andes, and Kiwa and Hotu Matu'a on Easter Island.

At this point it might be useful to recall Manu, the Indus Valley flood hero who is identified in the *Bhagvata Purana* as Satyavrata, Lord of Dravida (south India). Predictably this righteous man is forewarned by the god Vishnu, who comes to him disguised as a fish. Vishnu promises to return seven days later, during which time Manu is to gather seeds and animals. "On the seventh day after this, the three worlds [Third World perhaps?] shall sink beneath the ocean of dissolution. When the world is dissolved in that ocean, a large ship, sent by me, shall come to you." [1]

Vishnu follows up on his promise in time for the fireworks to commence. "The sea, augmenting as the great clouds poured down their waters, was seen overflowing its shores and everywhere inundating the earth." [2]

It strikes me that Manu was not alone aboard this ship. As Vishnu continues: "Surrounded by the Seven Sages... you shall embark on the great ship and shall move without alarm over one dark ocean." And further along: "In the world thus confounded, the Seven Sages, Manu and the fish were beheld... the fish unwearied drew the ship over the waters, and brought it at length to the highest peak of Himavat [Himalaya]. Smiling, he gently says to the Sages, "'Bind this ship without delay to this peak.' They did so accordingly." [3]

Here we are faced once more with a group of seven wisdom keepers led by an eighth, who appear within an antediluvian environment and survive the flood. They are renowned seafarers (hence the fish symbolism), they bring the gifts of civilization to the surviving human population, wear simple tunics, shun meat in favor of vegetables, grow their hair long, perform their spiritual attuning at high altitudes, and set examples of spiritual decorum that society may imitate — the foundation for the Hindu principle of *dharma* and the Egyptian *maat*. The Seven Sages advised rulers, but when those rulers stepped beyond the rules of civilized behavior, they would take on the role of kingship themselves until a legitimate individual was procured and appointed. If kings abused their power the Sages would curse them, sometimes with severe consequences.[4]

If these were the same magnificent seven led by Viracocha, K'uKuulKaan, Quetzalcoatl, Fu Hsi and so on, they must have had supersonic means of transportation at their disposal, because they appear simultaneously in a multitude of locations around the world. Realistically I suspect what we are dealing with here is a brotherhood, an institution emanating from a central location, or locations, each secluded from ordinary humans until circumstances force them to establish direct contact. The *Mahabaratha* agrees with part of this hypothesis when it claims, "there are many Seven Sages." [5] And given their comfort with the open seas, they may all have lived on islands.

The *Vedas* specify that the closing of every Yuga or a Great Age is accompanied and defined by a major *pralaya* (catastrophe), whereby all traces of the former Yuga are erased. It is at these junctures that such groups of wisdom keepers are selected to ride out the storm so that the accumulated wisdom may be repromulgated, ensuring the resurrection and continuation of knowledge that underpins civilization.[6]

Izanami and Izanagi raise Japan from the ocean. Like all antediluvian gods, in addition to being married, they were also brother-sister.

From the surviving accounts in the *Rgveda*, the Seven Sages or *Sapta Rsis*, are mortal individuals who have been raised to the status of gods through their knowledge of sacred things, ostensibly knowledge handed down since the dawn of time, which they memorized, practiced, and shared with others so that the human condition might be elevated in their time. They knew of the forces of nature and how to control them, they possessed unique gifts of telepathy and clairvoyance, and generally mastered the arts leading to spiritual refinement. Not surprisingly they were esteemed as second only to the one supreme God.[7] While there is no doubt this institution was replenished by fresh recruits, the Vedas do hint of incarnation, even an extraterrestrial element, because it is said these people come to Earth periodically in order to renew Vedic knowledge.[8]

So what are we to make of this, because the Seven Sages also feature prominently in the *Building Texts* of Egypt, in which they are described arriving from an island to the south named Ta-Neterw, "the Homeland of the Primeval Ones," following its destruction by a great flood in which the "majority of its divine inhabitants drowned."[9] The gods Hor/Horus and Twt/Thoth subsequently appear on the scene accompanied by Seven Sages, who are referred to as Aku Shemsu Hor — Shining Ones, Followers of Horus.[10]

THE GODS LIVE LONG. AND PROSPER

Although they cover a substantial portion of the perimeter wall of the temple of Edfu, the existing *Building Texts* are a mere fragment of a vast Egyptian prehistoric record recovered by Alexander the Great and the Ptolemaic pharaohs who followed. It is a fascinating narrative describing the arrival of gods and the creation of temple culture, even if it sometimes makes for confusing commentary.

It speaks of the First Occasion, when humans were given the gifts of civilization by a group of puissant male and female gods who governed the land from their seat at Iwnw and various satellite temples along the Nile. To quote the Egyptian historian Hassan: "The Egyptians believed that in the beginning their land was ruled by a dynasty of great gods, of whom Horus, the son of Isis and Osiris, was the last. He was succeeded by a dynasty of semi-divine beings known as the Followers of Horus, who, in turn, gave place to the historical kings of Egypt." [11]

If the First Occasion is dated correctly to 10,400 BC then the *Building Texts* describe the company of gods arriving in Egypt following the *first* destruction of Ta-Neterw at the start of the Younger Dryas, meaning part of their island was still extant until the events around the great flood finished it off for good. Once settled in Egypt, Hor and his merry companions had barely seven hundred years in which to re-establish new temple cities before facing the great flood, after which they returned to rebuild a project already in motion. This hypothesis is consistent with the level of erosion at buildings such as the Valley Temple and the Menkaure Pyramid Temple, both of which show considerable weathering of their original limestone slabs by water and a subsequent retrofitting with harder granite to fix the damage.

Like the gods in whose footsteps they followed, the Aku Shemsu Hor are described as physically elegant, and possessing supernatural powers that gave them control over the forces of nature, and for this reason their collective name, Neterw, makes no distinction between an aspect of nature, an individual or a god. The three were interchangeable because their qualities were reflected in each other. For example, it was said the seven Shining Ones had the ability "to endue with power the substances on earth," foretell the future, and provide magical protection by means of symbols and the giving of names. They were creators of civilization,[12] real rather than abstract beings, capable of succumbing to human frailties. It was not uncommon for later individuals to take on the names of these gods as totems whenever they portrayed the qualities of the gods, hence there existed many Osiris, Twt, and Isis, just as there were many Quetzalcoatl.

One striking feature of these physical gods was their ability to rule for immense periods of time, they were practically immortal by human standards. Of Ra it was said he ruled for so long that in time he became a stumbling old man with saliva running down the side of his mouth. His successor Shu also got tired of reigning for hundreds of years, particularly after a major tempest lasting for nine days tested his limits and finally convinced him to abdicate in favor of his son Geb.[13]

Egyptian scholars such as Maspero considered the prehistory of their country to date back 36,000 years.[14] Later compilers such as Manetho, Diodorus and Syncellus followed suit with a range between 36,000 to 39,000 years. These seem unrealistic lengths of time, yet a papyrus discovered in Luxor in 1824 sets out the timeline in graphic terms. Dated c.1400 BC, it was taken to Turin for examination (it is known as the Turin Papyrus), but by the time it was finally opened the papyrus disintegrated. Despite its condition it was still possible to establish a total of nine dynasties belonging to pre-dynastic pharaohs. The oldest belonged to the Venerables of Memfer

A section of the Building Texts at Edfu.

— Neterw such as Ra, Osiris, Isis, Hor, Set and Twt who reigned for 23,200 years. They were succeeded by Venerables of the North, the Aku Shemsu-Hor, who settled at Iwnw, and reigned for 13,420 years until the time of Menes, described as the first pharaoh of "purely human bloodline," who gained the throne c.3113 BC. A total of 36,620 years.[15] The main point of interest here concerns the 13,420-year reign of the Aku Shemsu Hor until the time of Menes, indicating that the Followers of Horus were not merely a group who survived the great flood, they were in existence 6000 years before the founding of Iwnw, a continuous tradition of sages.

Roman scholars such as Mela and Herodotus offer additional information based on accounts provided to them by the priests at Iwnw who insisted such numbers were not pure fantasy, the events described actually occurred and were based on physical observation. "The Egyptians pride themselves on being the most ancient people in the world. In their authentic annals one may read that since they have been in existence, the course of the stars has changed direction four times, and that the sun has set twice in the part of the sky where it rises today."[16]

If these commentators are referring to the passage of time through the houses of the Zodiac, then in Herodotus' time, when the sun rose in Aries and set in Libra at the spring equinox, two completions of this cycle would have begun 39,000 years before his time.[17]

The historical timeline of Egypt and the dazzling longevity of its early rulers would seem aberrant were it not for other civilizations claiming the same biological magic, such as the Sumerians and their breathtaking King List. The best-preserved specimen is the Weld-Blundell Prism, a vertical cylinder made of clay inscribed with cuneiform c.2170 BC. The document provides a comprehensive list of the Sumerian Kings from the beginning when "kingship descended from heaven, the kingship was in Eridug... In five cities, eight kings; they ruled for 241,200 years. Then the flood swept over." The prism was found a few miles to the north of Ur, at Larsa, home of the fourth antediluvian king Kichunna.

Such numbers seem almost abstract, even if we allow the Sumerians the possibility of having employed a method of computation now lost to us; the Egyptians themselves are known to have employed a calendar based on the motion of Sirius. This Sothic Cycle synchronizes with the solar year with only a margin of error of one month every 1460 years. According to

Manetho, recorded Egyptian history is composed of 25 periods of 1460 Sothic cycles, or one full revolution around the Zodiac, which again takes us into the region of 23,000 BC.[18]

Ancient writers in other parts of the world routinely assert how dynasties in remote civilizations spanned eccentric spans of time. The *Troano Manuscript* describes how twelve Maya Kaan dynasties reigned for 16,000 years, while the Chinese *Tchi* mentions twelve dynasties reigning 18,000 years, as do Hindu records which state, "in those times men lived as long as they chose to live and were without any fear of [the god of Death]."[19]

THE GODS GO FLYING

The *Kujiki* forms the backbone of Japan's prehistoric texts concerning deities and the descent of kingship from the sky. They are estimated to be at least 10,000 years old. In the narrative, a period of 1,722,475 years elapses between the descent of the Sky Kami (a god or spirit form) and the first imperial family who became its earthly representatives and continued its values into historical times.[20] The Sky Kami brings a civilizing influence to bear on a desolate and violent world, flying to Earth in a Sky-Rock-Boat to a place called Tsukushi, the Center of the World — a navel by any other name — identified as the island of Kyushu on the south-western tip of Japan. In one account, in order to reach this island it was necessary to travel eastwards, implying that the point of origin of the gods might have been the Korean peninsula.

Japan's oldest religious practice, Shinto (Way of the Gods) describes antediluvian heroes moving around in flying boats, the legends born from observation and likely handed down through Japan's oldest culture, the Jomon, who state their ancestors were gods who settled the region some 12,000 years ago. They may be right because the Jomon were already established by 14,000 BC, thus not only did they experience all the Dryas cycles, they would have observed the gods dispensing the virtues of civilization after each cataclysm.

The flying rock boats are easy to locate. To the east of Kyushu, near Osaka, stands a 500-ton Ishi-no-högen (The Departing Stone). This upright monolith is cut to look as though it floats over a sacred spring that never dries, even during drought. It's a massive cube marked with deep, vertical grooves and a pair of rectangular incisions on the top; a pyramid extrudes from its side which required the removal and re-shaping of half the block, and yet not one tool mark is visible. It is impressive as it is alien, and neatly conveys the image of a rock ship flown by the prehistoric gods. Legends speak of two gods, Okunisushi (Great Land Master) and Sukuna-biko-na setting out to build a temple in the course of one night but only got as far as creating this monolith due to a local rebellion breaking out among other gods.

Another example is Iyefune (rock ship), located in dense forest to the east of Osaka on Mount Miwa, one of Japan's most sacred mountains, an area filled with the type of machined megaliths common to the Andes. This single granite slab weighs 800 tons, and features deep, rectangular sections incised from the top all the way through to the core as though made by a surgeon armed with a laser.

Many eastern traditions unambiguously state that in the time of gods, people had the capacity for flight, be it using a ladder, magical rope, flying Vimanna craft, or in the case of Japan, stone boats. The stories are common to the Jorai of Indochina, the Koryaks of Central Asia, and is especially mentioned in the Indian epic *Mahabharata*: "Visvakarma, the architect among the gods, built aerial vehicles for the gods... You descendent of the Kurus, that wicked fellow came on that all-traversing flying vehicle known as Saubhapura and pierced me with weapons... He entered into the favourite divine palace of Indra and saw thousands of flying vehicles intended for the gods lying at rest... Indra, the Lord of Heaven came with a special type of flying vehicle which could accommodate 33 divine beings." [21]

I can't help but recall the earlier story of the Waitaha receiving a group of master craftsmen with narrow eyes from the north after the flood, magicians capable of "shaping rock without breaking its spirit," because all around the island of Kyushu lies evidence of antediluvian gods possessing extraordinary skills in masonry,

Iyefune, the boat of the gods. Mt. Miwa.

*Botanist Philipp Franz Siebold sketched Ishi-no-högen while he was
stationed in Japan in the 1920s. Again the mysterious protruding knob
so unique to ancient architecture. But what is it for?*

particularly on the Korean peninsula which is but a short boat ride away.
Before the flood, both locations were joined as one landmass, and included
Taiwan to the south. The Korean peninsula itself contains the greatest
concentration of *dolmen* in the world, a tradition that is now seen as

originating here before migrating westwards to Europe. For one thing, *dol* is the Korean word for stone.

TALL, SHINING AND LONG-HEADED

Between South Korea and Kyushu lies the small island of Jeju, home to an unusual concentration of 12-foot tall statues carved from porous basalt. They are called Dol Hareubang (grandfather stone), and are said to depict in size and style the ancestors who came here after the flood, outsiders who were very tall magicians. An earlier name, Beoksumeori, means 'head of the shaman'. A number of statues bear a striking resemblance to those of Viracocha around Lake Titicaca, right down to the position of the hands above and below the navel.

Throughout our quest I've made references to very tall people (as opposed to giants) whose lives straddled the boundary at the close of the Younger Dryas. I want to revisit this topic, along with that of elongated skulls, because both overlap in Egypt. The *Building Texts* describe intermediaries between gods and humans as Urshu, a term applied in conjunction with the half human, half divine Aku Shemsu Hor. The texts put their height at 5 cubits. Depending on the type of cubit used, the Royal or the Sacred, these individuals would have stood between 8.5 and 10.25 feet tall.

Mesopotamian tradition follows suit. Post-flood Apkallu (Sages) such as Lu-Nanna are said to have been two-thirds Apkallu one-third human,[22] while the flood hero Gilgamesh, who was himself part Apkallu, is described in the *Book of Giants* as *lugal*, meaning 'big man or giant';[23] in the Hittite version of the epic, Gilgamesh was said to be 11 cubits tall, or 18 feet, meaning that his statue currently on display in the Louvre Museum is depicting this man life-size.[24]

The Aku Shemsu Hor were also biologically different in that their skulls were naturally elongated, just like the people we dealt with earlier in Peru, Malta, and the region around the Black Sea. I refer to them affectionately as Long Heads. In the words of the prominent Egyptologist Walter Emery: "Towards the close of the fourth millennium BC we find the people known traditionally as the Followers of Horus forming a civilized aristocracy or master race ruling over the whole of Egypt. The theory of the existence of this master race is supported by the discovery that

A Dol Hareubang in Korea. Always the focus on the navel, and large eyes.

graves of the late pre-dynastic period in the northern part of Upper Egypt were found to contain the anatomical remains of a people whose skulls are of greater size and whose bodies were larger than those of the natives, the difference being so marked that any suggestion that these people derived from the earlier stock is impossible. The fusion of the two races must have been considerable, but it was not so rapid... The dawn of the historic period of Egypt was divided into the two rival kingdoms of the North and the South, both ruled by a royal house and aristocracy of the same race and both known traditionally as the Followers of Horus — the demigods of Manetho's history. The original capitals of those two states appear to have been Buto in Lower Egypt and Hieraconpolis in Upper Egypt; but at the time of the final unification, the chief cities of the two powers were apparently Sais in the north and Thinis (or Abydos) in the south." [25]

The dissertation by Walter Emery is correct in many respects except for the date. The Followers of Horus may indeed have been the offspring of the antediluvian gods, but the *Building Texts* have them well established in Egypt long before the flood.[26] Hor himself was venerated much earlier. The city of Buto, formerly known as Tell El Fara'in (Hill of the Pharaohs) once featured a renowned monolithic sanctuary dedicated to this antediluvian god. The city's importance was built on cultural developments spanning ten thousand years, from the Paleolithic to 3100 BC, implying that the cult of Hor was already well established there around the time of the Oldest Dryas. Likewise Hieraconpolis, formerly Nekhen, was a mound city with similar prehistoric roots, also under the tutelage of Hor.

Although half human, half divine, the Followers of Horus were loathe to couple with human women for the obvious reason that a man twice as tall as a woman raises life threatening complications at birth for the mother. The second reason was to maintain the purity of bloodline of a people who appear to have kept one foot in the astral world while simultaneously living in a physical body. This underpinned the Shining Ones' declared ability to work their magic, to control the laws of nature. For this reason they developed skulls elongated in the rear and capable of housing a larger parietal cortex, the area of the brain associated with spiritual and dream states.[27] By comparison, humans have a more developed frontal cerebral cortex in order to process information.

The lineage of the long-headed Followers of Horus was still evident in Amenhotep III.

But thousands of years after their appearance, the lineage of the Followers of Horus began to thin out. They were faced with a grim choice: accept annihilation or find a way to successfully interbreed with human women, the results of which are confirmed by Emery's findings. This successful transition between two races ultimately culminated in Menes, "first pharaoh of a totally human bloodline" c.3113 BC.[28] That said, remnants of the Followers of Horus survived well into the second millennium BC, as attested by Amenhotep III with his elongated skull, and likewise his son and grandson, Akhenaten and Tutankhamun, although the problems of long-term interbreeding had by then led to obvious physical deformations.

One branch of this lineage of sages may have survived into our era. In the early twentieth century there existed in China's Schechuan province a race called the Lolos. Inhabiting an area the size of Wales, these highly independent people were taller than Caucasians, with prominent cheekbones, broad, arched noses, and pointed chins. They possessed a unique pictographic script and a belief that for each person on Earth there is a corresponding star in the sky. They also possessed an I-Pu, an ancestral tablet composed of wooden pieces cut from the Pieris tree, the same type from which the ark in their flood myth was constructed. They believed in patriarchs who live in the sky, among whom are the Creator gods A-chi and A-li — who appear to be variations of the Mesopotamian antediluvian gods Enki and Enlil — and Tse-gu-dzih, the one attributed with causing the great flood after becoming frustrated with the wickedness of humans. These patriarchs lived outrageously long lives of 660 and 990 years respectively. After Tse-gu-dzih opened the sluice gates of the sky to release torrents of water, only one man, Du-mu, was saved in a hollowed out log along with his four sons.[29]

MAGICIANS AND WIZARDS

There is no shortage of magician gods in Egypt. Twt, who is attributed with authorship of every branch of knowledge both human and divine, is also described as the Great Lord of Magic who could move objects with the power of his voice.[30] He understood "all that is hidden under the heavenly vault" and was described as "the counter of stars and the measure of the Earth." He also is said to have invented writing, was a great mathematician and surveyor, and would bestow his wisdom on anyone smart enough to handle such knowledge.[31] Shortly before the flood he is said to have inscribed the sum of all knowledge in books of a material that is resistant to damage by conflagration, hiding them in Egypt and throughout the Earth, to be rediscovered "only by the worthy," individuals who would apply the information to elevate a society reduced to rubble.[32]

Isis was said to be "more intelligent than countless gods, of knowing everything in heaven and earth, being strong of tongue... perfect both in giving command and in saying the word. She possessed the understanding of the power of words, incantations and spells with which to bend nature and the known laws of physics." [33]

Her consort Osiris was considered one of the original Wise Ones in the Egyptian pantheon. The name is a Greek phonetic transliteration of the original WSR (pronounced Asar), a word which became the root of *vizier*, and ostensibly, *wizard*. Osiris is portrayed as a bearded god, a civilizer who brought with him the knowledge of agriculture, animal husbandry, astronomy, writing, architecture and music, and not forgetting, a spiritual science underpinning a rightful life and laws leading to the immortality of the soul. He also led the way to building cities, temples, and implementing just laws. Business cards must have been awkwardly long back then.

Tiki from New Guinea, and Hiva Oa in the Marquesas. Although stylized depictions, the thin lips, bulging eyes and elongated skulls are characteristics described by cultures who came in contact with flood sages.

Thankfully he was rewarded with a short nickname, 'the Good One' — as was his Irish counterpart Daghda Mor, 'the Good God', who is similarly depicted with a ceremonial beard and a white robe with a thin waist sash; just as the Shining Ones wore beards and white robes with beaded sashes; as did the civilizing god of the Indus region, Zarathustra, whose teachings are claimed by his followers to have been already fully implemented by 7500 BC.[34]

It seems both Osiris and Viracocha might have been separated at birth, because in physical description and deed they belong to the same brotherhood of seven sages. Many overlapping legends exist of Viracocha throughout the Andes but they generally agree that this blue-eyed, white man possessed a power over the forces of nature, while his words and deeds earned him the image of a scientist, engineer, astronomer, architect, teacher and healer all rolled into one: "He caused the terraces and fields to be formed on the steep sides of ravines, and sustaining walls to rise up and support them. He also made irrigation channels to flow from the living stone... and he went in various directions, arranging many things." [35]

Such terraforming and stonework are evident in the epic works at Ollantaytambo. Only in the fifteenth century did the Inka inherit and restore this citadel, adapting it for their own needs, along with the 15,000-mile network of roads that everyone in the region knew full well had been the work of "white, auburn-haired men who'd lived thousands of years earlier."[36]

Viracocha achieved it all with the assistance of seven *Hayhuaypanti*, each a specialist in his or her field. Writing in the first decade of the seventeenth century, the chronicler Garcilaso de la Vega reminds us of the magic once imbued in Cuzco by Viracocha and his Shining Ones. Garcilaso describes how the streams flowing under and around the Qorikancha, where the Navel of the Earth stood, were endowed with special properties. He goes on to lament the state of disrepair of the water system after the Spanish conquest, particularly one stream that rose a little to the west of the city, the water of which had been so prized for its fecund properties that special piping had to be laid underneath the city to take it from the royal vegetable garden to the temple. The special plumbing was necessary, Garcilaso wrote, because its water caused such vigorous plant growth that it would have damaged the buildings had it leaked onto the land beneath the city's walls and pavements.[37]

Likewise, Hawaiian folklore is filled with stories of the *Menehune* from the islands of Molokai and Kauai, legendary people with magical powers who were able to control the forces of nature. Like their counterparts elsewhere, they were known for their ability to miraculously build temples of stone overnight.[38]

Such innate abilities of the antediluvian gods are affirmed in the *Popol Vuh*. "They were endowed with intelligence; they saw and instantly they could see far, they succeeded in seeing, they succeeded in knowing all that there is in the world. When they looked, instantly they saw all around them, and they contemplated in turn the arch of heaven and the round face of the earth. The things hidden in the distance they saw all without first having to move; at once they saw the world, and so too, from where they were, they saw it. Great was their wisdom; their sight reached to the forests, the lakes, the seas, the mountains, and the valleys." [39] These individuals worked many miracles,[40] but alas their magical abilities led to a number of them developing arrogance and abusing their gifts, ironically leading to their demise,[41] when their folly ran foul of the tolerance of greater gods who pressed the reset button by unleashing a cataclysm.[42]

A sage from Kumari Kandam would agree with the above account from Central America, because the same descriptions, the same events, the same issues, and the same final outcome are recorded throughout the Vedas.

*Practically invisible in its cave setting, Betatakin was the original
home of the Hopi Snake Clan after the great flood.*

PEOPLE OF
THE SERPENT

Early Roman chroniclers refer to an ancient people living in the western Iberian Peninsula as Lusitanii, the People of Light. Physical traces of their existence are now scant, but they live on in legends which paint them as autonomous, highly religious people who followed the ways of nature and harnessed its magical qualities, the knowledge of which they shared throughout the region, hence their depiction as traveling gods. They constructed impressive stone temples and were said to have been unusually tall.

12

This land is today called Portugal, and aside from the Morbihan region of Brittany, it possesses some of the oldest stone circles, dolmens and passage mounds in Europe, some tentatively dated to 5300 BC, based on the lower habitation layer of accumulated debris. Realistically they are likely to be far older. The mountainous north became the Lusitannii center of operation, a region where one comes across anomalous structures such as carved granite boulders near the village of Panoias. One is the size of a house and has had its top incised with square and circular holes, some with bevelled edges that look like slots for inserting upright slabs, not unlike the technique employed at Göbekli Tepe. The boulders feature a series of deep, rectangular tanks; shallow and perfectly level ledges connect each feature without any sign of tool marks. On the side, steps cut in relief are impractically high for people of this region who tend to be rather short.

I have seen almost a dozen similar structures in Peru, three in and around Saqsayhuaman and Quillarumyioc alone, their ledges astronomically aligned, with features illustrating certain creation myths as well as Mysteries teachings. The wear on the steps at Panoias attests to their great antiquity, yet there is little indication as to the purpose of such hillside monuments. Aside from the obvious visual connection it is impossible to prove any further link between Panoias and Peru, although, ironically, when the Portuguese president Salazar invented an artificial folk identity to galvanize the Portuguese in the 1940s, he copied the traditional dress patterns and colors of indigenous Peruvians. Perhaps the old dictator inadvertently channelled an ancient connection!

Like the stone boats of Japan's antediluvian gods, the enigmatic boulders may be the handiwork of the People of Light, who may themselves have been the progeny of a far older group — the Shining Ones, as the name implies — who fled across the Atlantic in search of high ground. Portugal, after all, is conveniently the first dry land east of the Açores, the first landfall being a mountain called Sintra.

The Greek historian Strabo describes in his *Geographica* a people of different appearance living around Sintra, specifically on a promontory extending from the mountain for a considerable distance out to sea. Strabo may have been relying on a far older source because that promontory collapsed into the Atlantic thousands of years before his time, taking with it a citadel. Such a large piece of land could only have disintegrated through the action of some titanic force, perhaps the same wall of water that afflicted the Maltese islands in the Mediterranean, after all Sintra and Malta would have shared the same trajectory of waves originating in the central Atlantic; they also share the same geology, both are underpinned by vast subterranean tunnels, and sit on delicate fracture zones. Additionally, a deep layer of stretches covers 40 miles from Sintra and into central Portugal, evidence of a massive tsunami that smashed the region in prehistoric times.

Trekking among the eucalyptus groves of Sintra is one of life's unique pleasures. By its very location adjacent to the Atlantic, the mountain creates its own cool microclimate, handy for days when temperatures on the surrounding plains force one to seek the shelter of shade or a café. Colossal moss-covered granite boulders lie everywhere, discarded like crumbs on a giant's dinner plate.

One of Sintra's summits is connected by a honeycomb of underground galleries to another hill thirty-five miles away, to the point where the sea is able to penetrate these inland caverns, leading Arab chroniclers to describe

Sintra as a hollow mountain.[1] Although a good number are of volcanic and sedimentary origin, other cavities have been purposefully carved by human hands. According to a former caretaker of the Moorish castle on one such summit, Sintra is a big subterranean city criss-crossed with miles of underground tunnels, one linking the castle with a Capuchin monastery three miles away.[2]

Sintra takes its name from the Mesopotamian lunar goddess Sin. Lunar cults have practiced here since 7000 BC,[3] with human activity already established between 8000–10,000 BC.[4] Whoever these peopel were they certainly had a flair for the dramatic. During one of many visits, I came across a local legend of a passage linking the east-west spine of the mountain, each entrance forming a portal to the Otherworld. It was impossible to pass up such a tempting opportunity, so I spent two days clambering through boulders, undergrowth and mist to be rewarded with the sight of the remains of a large passage mound on the western edge of the mountain, its earthen canopy long since washed away by the ocean-driven rain that typically pours here, its stones almost blending with the bedrock, and further dislodged by earthquakes, for Sintra lies on a highly volatile subduction plate. Perched high on a ridge, the entrance features an

Panoias megaliths bear a strong resemblance to those in the Andes. particularly in Saqsayhuaman (bottom).

unobstructed view of the equinox sunset over the Atlantic — obviously the gods were romantics — so I hazarded a guess that the exit would fall along the same alignment to the east, to face the sunrise.

It did, at another megalithic passage mound conveniently located inside the entrance to the grounds of Pena Palace four miles away. Standing inconspicuously amid the overgrown ferns and still resembling a dolmen, it is easily overlooked by thousands of visitors unless they forego the taxi ride and leg it up the steep footpath. The connecting tunnel, claimed to link the two sites, has long since been blocked with rubble from thousands of years of seismic activity.

A week rummaging through Sintra leaves you in no doubt that the people described by the Greek commentators were comfortable working on a megalithic scale, and did so on a mountain that, to all intents and purposes, functions in isolation to its surrounding territory, much like an island. In remote times the region was known as *Promontorio Ofiússa* (Promontory of the Serpent), its residents being the *Ofiússa* (People of the Serpent).[5] Furthermore, the Portuguese coast appears in legends and traditions as the cradle of a royal or sacred bloodline descended from an antediluvian race, with Lisbon itself founded by Ophiusa, literally Serpent Woman, and like the Anunaki of Mesopotamia, she was portrayed as half-human half-fish.[6] Strabo, it seems, was on the right track.

Passage mound in Sintra, home of the People of the Serpent.

The association with serpents has nothing to do with the worship of snakes *per se*. The serpent or dragon refers to the entwining telluric currents of electricity and magnetism that flow along and through Earth and space. Since these forces are invisible to the eye, the serpent was adopted as the animalistic metaphor to visually express their movement. It is one of the oldest culturally shared symbols. However, there is also a second layer of meaning. Anyone who sensed, controlled or manipulated such forces was considered a serpent priest, a magi (magician), or sorcerer (one who works with the source). These sages were also symbolically associated with an amphibian creature, the newt — *ewte*, to coin its etymological origin, which means 'resplendent mind' — thus anyone who works with Earth energies also develops numinous qualities. One of the last cults to embody these principles was the Druid, whose titles were enumerated thus: "I am a Druid; I am an architect; I am a prophet; I am a serpent." [7]

The writer and spiritualist Paul Brunton made an erudite observation about telluric forces and the qualities of people who personified them: "The serpent is self-moving; it is unassisted by hands, feet or external limbs. So too is the Creative Force entirely self-moving as it passes from form to form in its building of a whole world or a single creature... [its symbolism] stood for the working of the Force which freed the soul of man during initiation, a force which slowly crept through the body of the entranced initiate almost exactly like the slow creeping of a snake." [8]

Magicians? Earth energy? Special powers? This should all be familiar territory by now. Etymology and symbolism aside, there is no surviving evidence of these People of the Serpent having come to Iberia overland from the east via Europe. What if their point of origin was from the west, across the water from Atitlán or what remained of it? Let's see if a connecting thread exists on the other side of the Atlantic that might improve our understanding of the antediluvian gods.

KAANUL, A SERPENT BY ANY OTHER NAME

The earliest foreigners in Yucatan were the Itzá sages who arrived on boats from the east following the loss of Atitlán. They were generally referred to as Kaanul — literally People of the Serpent — led by the magician priest Itzamna, whose title was Serpent of the East. In time their progeny, the Maya, also came to refer to themselves as People of the Serpent; their secondary title, Descendents From Cosmic Wisdom, offers a clue to the knowledge they inherited from the Itzá.[9]

As we already know, Yucatan has three central flood heroes: Itzamna, K'uKuulKaan and Quetzalcoatl. All three individuals arrived in modern-day Coatzelcoalcos from across the Atlantic on a boat "with sides that shone like the scales of serpent skins." [10] Up until now their overlapping attributes have led many to believe they are one and the same entity. However, the responsibility of a large-scale reconstruction of their original homeland in this region couldn't possibly have fallen upon the shoulders of one person alone; as Indian texts state "there were many Seven Sages," so I am inclined to follow the common sense hypothesis that these were three separate individuals in charge of three brotherhoods, each linked to the same institution and race. The description of Quetzalcoatl is not dissimilar to that of Itzamna: a tall, white man with broad forehead, large eyes and flowing beard, dressed in a long white robe reaching to his feet. He condemned the killing of things except for fruits and plants, taught people the use of fire for cooking, how to build houses, and demonstrated that couples could live together. He introduced writing and the calendar, taught the secrets of masonry and architecture, mathematics, metallurgy, medicine, divination (dowsing), astronomy and the measure of the Earth, and agriculture, specifically the introduction of domesticated corn, the staple of this region. He was a patron of the arts, and a peacemaker who, when addressed on the subject of war, plugged his ears with his fingers. To these qualities can be added civilizer, founder of laws, cities and temples.[11]

The Maya know exactly where their wisdom comes from and the qualities of the gods who provided it: "In truth, they were admirable men... They were able to know all, and they examined the four corners, the four points of the arch of the sky, and the round face of

K'uKuulKaan. Labnah, Yucatan.

the earth." [12] These People of the Serpent were specialists in their fields. K'uKuulKaan's companions are described as "two were gods of fish, two others gods of agriculture, and a god of thunder." [13] And according to the *Popol Vuh*, "they were not men... they were giants." After spending ten years establishing laws, temples and administrative buildings in the temple city of Mayapan, K'uKuulKaan is said to have joined a raft of serpents, and together they set sail towards the rising sun and returned to where they'd originated,[14] implying there may have been parts of Atitlán still above the sea after the flood, ostensibly today's Açores. In any event, they were compelled to live in seclusion from humans, much as they had done before their arrival.

But not everyone returned. K'uKuulKaan and his sages left Itzamna and company to journey inland towards Guatemala to erect the temple cities of Tikal and Palenque, which were referred to as Serpent Cities in homage of founders such as Nohoch-Itz-Tzaab (Great Face of the Rattle-snake), the astronomer priest responsible for the original Pyramid of K'uKuulKaan in Chichen Itzá. In turn, Chichen Itzá's original name Yucc Yabnal (Seven Great House) pays homage to the seven Kaanul priests as well as the Pleiades.

A tall stela in the temple of Ek Balam shows a ruler surrounded by a feathered serpent, identifying him as a member of the Kaanul dynasty, According to the *Troano Codex* this divine bloodline had already run for 16,000 years by the time the Spanish arrived in the sixteenth century, implying that either the dynasty was already established in Yucatan before the flood, or it originated in Atitlán itself. Ek Balam's main building contains 108 chambers, one of which features a doorway surrounded by thirty-three large teeth and elaborate images, all in stucco. Among them are seven *An-Hel* (Beings of Creation), each winged figure representing the original Itzá flood teachers. The approach to this stepped rectangular structure is marked by a building romantically named Structure X whose original footprint appears to be aligned to the spring equinox in the era of 7000 BC.

When the Balam (Jaguar) wisdom keepers arrived from the Pacific — for the same underlying reason as the Itzá — their teachings overlapped at Palenque, whereupon future Maya masters of the city took on combined Mu'ul-Atitlán titles such as Lord Kaan Balam.

The serpent emblem became synonymous with future individuals who personified the traditions of the original People of the Serpent. They adopted the names of these gods and became an example to others,[15] hence there have been many K'uKuulKaan — an honorary title meaning 'feathered serpent'. "The title is in allusion to a spiritual mastery in science and spirituality," explains Miguel Angel Vergara. "KuKuul represents the feathers, the sacred spiritual knowledge of the cosmos; Kan represents science, technology, mathematics, astronomy, geometry. When the two practices are harmonized, the initiate takes on the composite name." [16]

The same practice was followed in Egypt and the Middle East.

The lineage of the People of the Serpent was still active throughout Guatemala well into the eighth century. Temple cities such as Holmui carried the snakehead emblem of the royal house, although by historical times the clans had descended into feuding families whose warring and bickering bore little resemblance to the ethics of the original lineage [17]— ironically the kind of behavior that once led the creator gods to flood the Earth 11,000 years ago, according to the myths. An altar dated 544 AD at Guatemala's La Corona site suggests the Kaanul dynasty of Snake Kings acted like its namesake in slowly squeezing the life out of the rival kingdom of Tikal. It even depicts the ruler Chak Took Ich'aak attempting to conjure two gods from a shaft in the form of a snake.[18]

SERPENTS IN THE EAST

We now have a clearer picture of the lineage of wisdom keepers who escaped Atitlán to found new homelands east and west of the Atlantic. However, this is only half the story. The progenitors of the Olmec are said to have arrived in Central America from the sunken Pacific island of Mu'ul, as did a tribe in Arizona, who now provide a further link to the Pacific and beyond.

The Hopi were originally defined by a number of separate yet interconnected clans, one being the Snake Clan. One narrative describes how Hopi ancestors lived in or close to Patowahkacheh (Great Water). Somewhere on this ocean lay an island where the original Snake People once lived; nearby was a second island belonging to Koyanwuhti, the goddess of wisdom. The story involves a young man who goes on an

Two Itz shown as winged An-Hel, a possible precursor of angel. Ek Balam, Yucatan.

adventure to these islands and marries a beautiful maiden, and although on one level the tale appears to depict the allegorical path of an initiate, it also commemorates actual events from long ago, for the Snake Clan is very real. It was forced to sail eastwards from an island in the Pacific consumed by the flood. Following a considerable period of migration, the clan settled at Kawestima in Arizona (today known as Betatakin), where they

were known as Hisat-Sinom. It was a home they shared with unusual beings called *katcisam*; this will be of great importance later. Finally they moved to Walpi, a Hopi village on First Mesa, Arizona.[19] What is fascinating is the linguistic trail linking their story to the central Pacific, for example, the Hopi word *tsu'a* (snake) is the same as the Samoan *sua*.[20] Therefore it is likely that, in addition to Atitlán, the People of the Serpent had a base in the East.

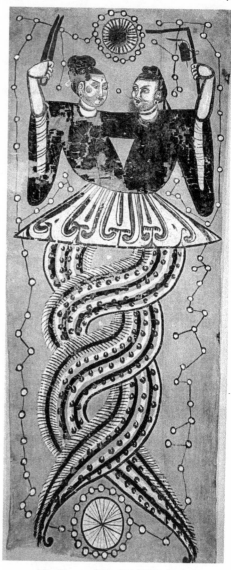

Nü Kua and Fu Hsi, founders of China's dragon bloodline.

A divine hierarchy of dragon lords is known to have been present within Chinese culture for at least 7000 years,[21] although the association stretches into antediluvian times. According to legend, both Chinese primogenitors were closely related to *lóng* (dragons). At the end of his reign the first ruler was himself immortalized into a dragon and ascended to the sky; the next was born by his mother's telepathy with a dragon, and ever since, the ancient Chinese have self-identified as descendants of the dragon,[22] suggesting the presence of a divine bloodline borne of the mating between gods and humans. This symbolic as well as probable genetic connection is enforced by the lineage of Chinese monarchs who took on the title Son of Heaven whenever they cemented a matrimonial bond. The phrase was interpreted literally in China and Japan, whose monarchs were considered half-human half-divine — just as in Iberia, India, Scythia, Egypt and Mesopotamia — or regarded as the living image of gods,[23] insinuating once again how they were offspring of the original People of the Serpent.

The Chinese antediluvian goddess Nü Kwa and her consort Fu Hsi are said to have molded humans from clay when they descended onto the sacred mountain Hua Shan after the flood. They taught them how to hunt, fish and cook their catch, the art of writing, and provided the laws necessary for the foundation of a civilized society, while knowledge of agriculture and medicine came from a Divine Farmer by the name of Shennong.

Nü Kwa is of central interest to our quest because she is credited with repairing the sky after Gonggong, a water god with red hair and a tail like a serpent, damaged the pillar supporting the heavens, essentially knocking the Earth's axis off kilter and causing the planet to tilt to the southeast and the sky to the northwest — a story often used to explain why the rivers of China generally flow to the southeast. The remote period when this cataclysmic event befell the Earth is described in the *Huainanzi*: "Going back to more ancient times, the four pillars were broken... Heaven did not completely cover [the Earth]; the Earth did not hold up [Heaven] all the way around [its circumference]. Fires blazed out of control and could not be extinguished; water flooded in great expanses and would not recede. Ferocious animals ate blameless people; predatory birds snatched the elderly and the weak. Thereupon, Nü Kwa smelted together five-colored stones in order to patch up the azure sky, cut off the legs of the great turtle to set them up as the four pillars, killed the black dragon to provide relief... and piled up reeds and cinders to stop the surging waters. The azure sky was patched; the four pillars were set up; the surging waters were drained... blameless people [preserved their] lives." [24]

Written in enigmatic style, the book uses allegory to describe how a god with knowledge of earth magic balanced the elements of nature after the heavens fell out of alignment and the sky was punctured with holes, when deep fissures opened in the ground, and entire regions caught fire while others were flooded — a fair picture of a planet damaged by the impact of a disintegrated meteor. There's no mistaking the prehistoric setting, a time when oversize "predatory birds snatched the weak."

Nü Kwa and Fu Hsi also come from the sister-brother wife-husband tradition, like other pairs — Anu and Antu, Zeus and Hera, just to add new names to the ever-growing list. But there's another revealing aspect to this Chinese pair, they are portrayed as half-snake, half-human, thus shown to herald from the People of the Serpent, setting in motion the divine dynasty of Dragon Emperors in China, ending with the last emperor in 1912. In the Forbidden City it is possible to see the Throne of Supreme Harmony featuring the seven tiers commemorating the lineage of the original Seven Sages.

Just as the Seven Sages and the People of the Serpent are always associated in some form with the sea, so the dragon was associated in China and Japan with water. The famous Japanese Dragon King Ryo-Wo was revered as the god of the sea and was said to live in an underwater grand palace called Ryugu, from where he controlled the ocean. The association also appears in Korean legends, in which mortals and dragons are always connected to each other via an intermediary fish.[25]

Interestingly, while the serpent or dragon was associated with Emperors and water, the Empress was identified with the phoenix, the bird of resurrection, together painting a vivid symbolism of the rebirth of a divine lineage after the flood.

VENOM THAT PROLONGS LIFE

Earlier we looked at the unusual ability of antediluvian gods to live outrageously long lives. The same was true of the People of the Serpent, and this overlap may reveal how they achieved it. This surreal longevity appears to have been partly genetic, as though these people originated from an environment that differed significantly from Earth's, much like a citizen of Mars adapting to a planet whose orbit around the Sun is shorter, making a day seem like an hour. The method was also partly induced. Somehow they found that snake venom is rendered harmless when mixing with a certain blood type, producing an elixir that boosts the body's immune system and retards the aging of cells, thus extending longevity while creating the illusion of immortality. As strange as this might seem, Chinese herbalists still use diluted snake venom to prolong the shelf life of food.

The relationship between longevity and serpent venom became central to the symbolism of the Greek god of medicine Asclepius who, legend has it, killed a snake, then watched another slither into the room with a herb in its mouth. With this herb Asclepius was able to resurrect the dead snake, putting his healing abilities on par with those of another group of serpents in the east called the Naga priests.

THE CULT OF NAGA

The long sovereignty of the People of the Serpent and their influence on human affairs covers the regions of Thailand, Cambodia, Laos, India, and many Pacific islands, and in every case the sages belonging to this select group are referred to as Naga (serpent).

Fijians claim they originated in Central Asia, then migrated to Egypt, and continued south to Tanganika before sailing across the Indian and Pacific oceans to their present homeland. A secret initiation called Baki was once practiced in Fiji inside walled temple enclosures called *naga*, the name also given to a seafaring race whose ships resembled serpents. The Fijian civilizing god Degei arrived on such a canoe from his sunken abode after a *ualuvu levu* (great flood), landing on the Ra coast of Viti Levu where he built a village at Vuda (origin), and taught agriculture to local people. Degei also acts as the guardian of two caves on the island said to lead to the Otherworld, a job similarly ascribed to Osiris.

One Naga progenitor of the royal house of Japan is Izanagi, whose etymological connection to the Itzá makes his name a compound word meaning 'serpent magician'. According to Japan's prehistoric text *Kujiki*, he and his sister-wife Itzanami gave birth to the islands of Japan by raising the land out of the ocean, or to be geologically correct, when Japan separated from mainland Asia by rising seas at the end of the Younger Dryas to become an archipelago. The *Kujiki* itself is estimated to have been compiled before the flood, with one document, *Takenouchi*, describing two sunken landmasses in the Pacific called Miyoi and Tamiara, the result of dozens of *tenpenchii* (cataclysms) that afflicted the Earth due to an imbalance between humans and the divine source.[26]

Incidentally the *Takenouchi* states that the Five-Colored Peoples (humanity) coexisted for millions of years and only through growing degeneration in society have the Yuga cycles (world ages) generated a periodic wiping out of civilization.[27]

Naga tradition extends to Viet Nam, where the first person to unite the Cham people of the region and teach them agriculture and medicine was an Empress by the name Po Nagar. In Laos, the Naga kings were intertwined with water spirits, just as they were in Cambodia. In the legend of Nagi Soma, for example, a prince meets the daughter of the Naga lord of the land — who is half human half, snake — by the seashore, whereupon he marries her and founds a royal race.[28] The Naga tradition was maintained for millennia at Angkor, where each year the ruling king united with a symbolic Nagi to recall and revive the prehistoric origins of the cult.[29] As indeed he should, because a study by John Grigsby of the orientation and position of Angkor's main temples suggests the site is far older than the official 12th century founding date. Just as the Giza pyramids model the belt of Orion in 10,400 BC, so the main temples of Angkor mirror the coils of the celestial serpent, the constellation Draco, as it appeared above Cambodia in the same era.[30]

The further you walk away from the heavily visited temples of Angkor and toward outlying sites such as Phnom Bakheng, the more anomalies begin to appear that point to a retrofitting and expansion of an earlier megalithic site. Walls damaged by earthquakes and strife reveal megalithic blocks taken from elsewhere to patch up holes. In several cases these blocks look no different to the high precision masonry prevalent in Puma Punku, they bear the same precision-drilled holes and a finish that looks as though the stone was poured like cement. What I find most interesting is how one wall near this site has partly collapsed, revealing refined and meticulously fitted megalithic core masonry. Contrary to common sense, this advanced masonry was subsequently encased by smaller, cruder, comparatively less precise stonework, the kind consistent with the 12th century, the era when the whole fifteen square miles of Angkor was allegedly built from scratch. There is also the curious case of a solitary megalithic block that, stylistically, could have been taken from Puma Punku and dropped here. Or vice versa. It even features the double staircase design common to the Andes that forms the basis of the *chakana* or Andean Cross.

If you are inclined to walk around Angkor, mark down the number of steps, statues, platforms and carved serpents. You will discover the mathematical values common to the Earth's precessional cycle are hard-wired into the fabric of the buildings. Like the Great Pyramid, it seems Angkor too has been rebuilt to maintain the ongoing tradition of knowledge first set down by the antediluvian sages.

One of the more unusual remarks concerning the Naga comes from the *Mahabharata* and Vedic *Purana* texts of India, in which it is said they assumed human form when a situation demanded it — such as a global cataclysm, or the necessity for mass social reformation due to degeneracy in the human race. When describing the domain of the Naga, the *Puranas* are specific yet paradoxically vague, probably because they tried to conceal their precise whereabouts, compelled as they were to lead a separate existence. As always, the ocean theme is prevalent. The Naga would arrive on the seashore, typically in groups of seven led by an eighth: "Rishi Kashyapa begot the seven great serpents," [31] thereby revealing the People of the Serpent to be the same as the Seven Sages. Once their mission is accomplished they return to a land beyond the horizon, to Patalaloka (Nether Regions), somewhere amid the ocean. Hindu mythology describes their capital as a subterranean location called, appropriately enough, Bhogavati (peopled by snakes).[32]

And yet if their original homeland sank, to where were they returning? Were portions of their island still remaining after the flood? Are the allusions to underwater domains mere descriptions of former lands now inundated?

The irony is that, for all their efforts risking their lives to bring civilization to human shores, the Naga race was almost obliterated in India by Aryan king Kuru in a massacre at Takshashila when his clan came to possess their land. Just as in Yucatan and the Andes we see the same pattern of groups of humans turning on the flood heroes or their offspring, even though the Indian account appears to have occurred well into historical times. The cliché 'power corrupts' is an apt observation here, for once humans had been raised from a state of barbarity, some figured out that the only thing better than imitating the gods is to usurp power and pretend to be one.

Nagas in Indian temples. The seven serpent halos
acknowledge the flood Rshis.

Itzamna as a wise, and bearded, old man.
Chichen Itzá.

Nevertheless, as with the Shining Ones in Egypt and the People of the Serpent in Guatemala, the Naga bloodline persevered for thousands of years after the flood and into historical times. Naga kings and queens in India ruled over a dozen cities throughout the subcontinent, including the northwest of India where they held court at Patalpuri, as well as at the aforementioned city of Takshashilla, once home to one of the world's oldest universities. Today, traces of these People of the Serpent can be seen in the symbolic rituals performed by the cult of Shiva and its practitioners, the Naga Sadhu,[33] a comforting thought because the aim of these ascetics is to become "well disposed, kind, willing, effective or efficient, peaceful, secure, virtuous, honourable, righteous, noble," [34] in other words, "a good man or woman who chooses to live on the edge of society to focus on spiritual perfection." [35]

Not unlike the gods who set the example 11,000 years ago.

There's one further aspect about the People of the Serpent which will take us west of India and into Mesopotamia and its antediluvian gods. Ninlil, sister-wife of the god Enlil, bore the title Great Mother Serpent of Heaven, and was appropriately pictured with a serpent's tail.[36] It's one of two times when the serpent title is raised in Mesopotamia, the other being a Watcher by the name Kâsdejâ, "who was son of the Serpent named Tabââ'êt." [37] These magicians formed a reclusive enclave on a mountaintop somewhere in the Middle East, a settlement by the name Gar-sag,[38] where they went by the collective name Anunaki.

Or as they were known throughout India, Annunagi.[39]

Sumerian figurine depicting Lord Anu himself.

A MEETING WITH THE LORDS OF ANU

At this point it is worth recalling my conversation with Teokotai Andrew, the wisdom keeper of Tongareva, and how his tribe's ancestors were the tall, bearded, red-haired Tupenake/Anunaki, "great sages, star navigators and intelligent human beings" who originated from an island called Te Pitaka, and how it sank somewhere in the region of what is now the Arabian Peninsula during the great flood.[1]

13

Inundation maps of this region prove his people's tradition to be generally correct. A dramatic rise in sea level 10,600 years ago breached the Straits of Hormuz and caused the fertile plain between Persia and Saudi Arabia to become what today is known as the Persian Gulf.[2] That's the equivalent of flooding the British Isles.

The same situation prevailed along the western coast of the Arabian Peninsula, which became the Red Sea. Sumerian traditions identify this waterway as the general region from where the civilizing flood god Ua-annu once emerged with his seven sages.[3] Given how its earliest name was Sea of Reeds[4]— Aaru to the Egyptians — it makes for a tantalizing hypothesis, because the K'iche' and the Olmec refer to one of the points of origin of the antediluvian sages as Tolan, the Place of Reeds.

MANY GODS, ONE PEOPLE

By now it should be obvious that the Aku Shemsu Hor, the Followers of Horus, the Shining Ones, the Hayhuaypanti, the Urukehu, the Huari, the People of the Serpent, the Naga, the Kaanul, the Ofiússa, the Seven

Rshi, the Apkallu, and the Anunaki are interchangeable. They are one and the same group of antediluvian gods — civilizing flood heroes and magicians sharing the same maritime symbolism, "fish-men... who worked many miracles" to quote the *Popol Vuh*,[5] all interconnected by physical description, deeds and ideals, from Iberia to the Atlantic and Yucatan, from Japan and China to Cambodia, from Polynesia and Indonesia to India, and from Egypt to Anatolia and Mesopotamia.

The global link completes with the Dogon of Mali, an ancient people of the Sahara whose creation myth describes their culture as founded by a group of sea or water people called Nommos. The name means 'Instructors, Monitors' — Watchers by any other name. Created by the sky god Amma, the Nommos are described as inhabiting a world orbiting Sirius, from where they descended long ago in a vessel pouring thunder and fire; because they required a watery world in which to live they were subsequently dubbed Gods of Water, not unlike the People of the Serpent.[6]

The Dogon inherited a substantial amount of hermetic knowledge from the Egyptians, which might have included the understanding of Sirius and its lesser-known twin star, Sirius B, whose existence was only proved with the advent of advanced optics in the twentieth century.[7] The Dogon ceremonial headdress, with its extended rays and oblong patterns, resembles the equally out-of-place *katsina* costumes of the Hopi, which we'll discuss later; paintings depicting the Nommos with fish tails seem oddly similar to the Mesopotamian Apkallu, who are themselves depicted with fish tails or as men wrapped in fish skins and wearing distinctive double-stranded beards indicative of their divine rank of office.

Just to clarify, Apkallu are not a people but a distinction, a title meaning 'sage'. They are Anunaki (People of Anu), the descendents of Anu, a god of the sky. Let us now examine how they and Mesopotamia fit into the antediluvian picture.

THE MISSING LAND OF THE ANU

The Sumerians believed there once existed a land called Dilmun which they identified as the Garden of the Gods. It has been argued that Dilmun was nothing more than a myth, partly because it was said to be inhabited by immortals, and yet, as we have seen, antediluvian people were attributed with superhuman life spans that, to any person and their great, great, great, great grandchildren, would make them seem impervious to death. Since it is a view shared by so many disparate cultures, at the very least we ought to treat the notion as a valid observation, even if it sounds outlandish, because there is plenty of circumstantial evidence in support of Dilmun as a physical location.

During his tenure as trustee of the British Museum in the late 19th century, Sir Henry Rawlinson was perhaps the first to suggest the location of Dilmun in modern-day Bahrain, based partly on the region's Old Mesopotamian name, Karsag Dilmun,[8] and the plethora of archaeological sites found there which were conservatively dated to the Bronze Age. Aside from the sites being far too young to be linked to an antediluvian culture, the theory has a few problems in itself, namely that Sumerian texts describe this home of the Anunaki as filled with groves of cedars and towered by twin mountains, neither of which exist in the vicinity of Bahrain. In Rawlinston's defence, the Earth was a very different place 11,000 years ago, mountains fell and rose in the blink of an eye, landmasses sank, seas became deserts, deserts became seas. Only now are geologists beginning to grapple with the idea of how a cosmic calamity rearranged the planet beyond recognition.

Fish symbolism and flood gods: Nommos and U-annu.

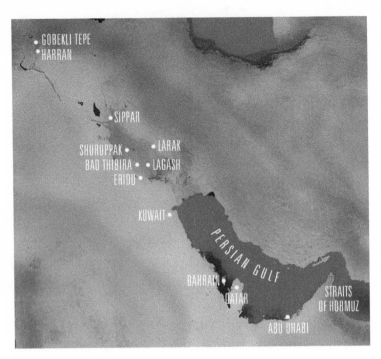

It must also be emphasized that the Sumerian tradition Rawlinson used for reference was borrowed from older Mesopotamian texts describing events that had taken place five thousand years earlier. Given such a span of time, transliterating from a dead language into another would have posed enormous problems, artefacts are certain to have crept into the texts, in fact the Sumerians most likely faced the same obstacles later Greek historians did when translating Sumerian and Akkadian into their own language; even in Egypt most people by 1500 BC had no clue what the hieroglyphs were trying to tell them.

That said, in the fourth millennium BC, around the time of Sumer, a people called Dilmun or Telmun did live around the Persian Gulf, specifically in Qatar, Kuwait, portions of eastern Arabia, and Bahrain.[9] One inscription to king Ur-Nanshe of Lagash mentions "the ships from Dilmun brought him wood as tribute from foreign lands," so clearly neither the ship, its cargo or port of origin were imaginary.[10] Could the Dilmun of the Sumerians have been a remnant of an earlier, much disfigured land, the home of the Anunaki? For one thing, evidence of an intermediate civilization lying between Mesopotamia and India has already been found in the general area of Bahrain.[11]

Rawlinson's theory was later expanded and refined by Frederich Delitzsch, who believed Dilmun to be further east and near the head of the Persian Gulf, by the Straits of Hormuz. I believe he might have been on to something.

Like North Africa, Arabia was severely reshaped by events at the close of the Younger Dryas. The fertile plain that existed prior to the creation of the Persian Gulf once supported a sizeable population 75,000 years ago. That all changed c.9000 BC when the sea at the Gulf of Oman broke through the Straits of Hormuz and drowned much of the region; by 6000 BC the entire area was underwater. Archaeologists have turned up evidence of a sudden wave of human settlement along the shores of the gulf c.5500 BC and, more importantly, they believe that precursor civilizations existed yet still lie hidden beneath the waters. [12]

There is additional support for this in Mesopotamian legend. It claims how an Anunaki god by the name of Enki founded the antediluvian city of Eridu in southern Mesopotamia, yet Enki himself was said to originate from Dilmun, a land filled with springs, and free of disease and death. It was referred to as "the land from which the Sun rises." Assuming this isn't just a metaphor, it places Dilmun east of Bahrain, either near the Straits of Hormuz —as Delitzsch speculated — or further out in the Indian Ocean but now missing.

Egyptian papyrus 1115 may have something to say about this. Stored in the Hermitage Museum, this remarkable document details the story of an Egyptian sailor journeying with others down the Red Sea. The ship was caught in a storm in the Indian Ocean, and all but one — the narrator — survived, only to be shipwrecked on an island. At first he believed it to be uninhabited, but in time he came to meet its ruler, who gave the sailor a new boat and some gifts and sent him home to Egypt. At the farewell, the ruler remarked to the sailor, "after you depart from this place you will never see it again, for it will turn into waves."

Although the papyrus itself is more than five thousand years old, the era in which the event took place is unknown. What is interesting is how the ruler of the island had foreknowledge of its disappearance, so either the story took place just before the flood, or the flood had already taken place and the island would soon be consumed by rising seas. We can only speculate. However, the description of the ruler offers an insight into the kind of people living there, for the sailor describes him as a serpent with blue eyes and a beard. It seems our shipwrecked sailor inadvertently stumbled upon the island of the People of the Serpent — the Annunage, as they were known in India. The unique papyrus comes as close as any document linking the Anunaki to a home somewhere in the vicinity of Arabia or the Indian Ocean. It is worth recalling that the Anunaki were referred to as Shining Ones — as in Shining Ones, Followers of Horus, and the Egyptians believed these gods originally sailed from Ta Neterw, the homeland of the gods, which lay to the south, the general direction of the Red Sea and the Indian Ocean.

Mesopotamian accounts contribute a few morsels to this mystery. They describe the assembly of the Anunaki as being located at the summit of a very tall mountain, and in relation to northern and eastern Arabia the only area that fits such a description is the peninsula of Musandam, an exclave of the Sultanate of Oman, which juts dramatically into the Persian Gulf to form the lower portion of the Straits of Hormuz. It's a ragged piece of land, ironically still sliding into the sea, with an interior packed with mountains over 6000 feet in altitude, the highest in the region by a very long margin. The name of its main city, Khasab, may be a modern corruption of Karsag, the assembly of the Anunaki, but like so many ancient riddles in Arabia it is not known how the small city acquired this name, or for that matter, its history before the Portuguese built a fort there in the eighteenth century.

Teotokai Andrew was right, locating Te Pitaka will prove difficult due to the drastic rearrangement of terrain following the flood.

THE SAGES OF MESOPOTAMIA

"I learned the craft of Adapa the sage, which is the secret knowledge... I am well acquainted with the signs of heaven and earth... I am enjoying the writings on stones from before the flood." [13] So spoke Ashurbanipal, 7th century BC Sumerian king. What else might the monarch have gleaned from writings that, by his time, were nine thousand years old?

Sumeria's flood myth is widely accepted among scholars as being the source for the story depicted in the Old Testament, minus the obvious cultural and religious alterations. The Sumerians in turn inherited theirs from the Mesopotamians, the most complete account being the Schoyen

Tablet. It begins with the emergence of humans and animals on Earth. After a frustrating thirty-seven lines of missing text the story resumes in a different era, a time of high civilization when "kingship was lowered from heaven" [14] during an antediluvian period in which an unnamed god "perfected the rites and the exalted divine laws... founded the five cities... in pure places, called their names, apportioned them as cult centers." The cities are Eridu, Badtibira, Larak, Sippar and Shuruppak.[15] Although they are conventionally dated to c.5400 BC, excavations reveal the foundations of the main temples to have been built much earlier; for instance, the Eridu ziggurat rests on seventeen previous temples, attesting to these sites having indeed been founded in deep antiquity, exactly as claimed in the tablets.[16]

After another series of missing lines the story has jumped far into the future, when a pious priest-king by the name Zin-suddu (Life of Long Days) is being advised by the god Enki to prepare for "a flood that will sweep over the cult centers, to destroy the seed of mankind," due to it having reached a level of corruption beyond what was acceptable to the gods.[17] Enki instructs Zin-suddu to bury all the tablets in a safe place in the city of Sippar, so that survivors "may relearn all that the gods had taught them."[18] What follows is predictable: after being instructed to build a *vara* (a large enclosed boat), and taking on board seven Apkallu, Zin-suddu describes the flood overwhelming the cities to the accompaniment of exceedingly powerful windstorms, and for seven days and nights his mighty ship is tossed about the waters.

After yet another frustrating break in the text — the tablets were found damaged — the story picks up with a dazed Zin-suddu standing in the

Mesopotamian flood epic. Still a best-seller in 700 BC.

presence of the high gods Enlil and Anu who expresses dismay — and remorse — at the appalling destruction that has befallen humanity and the Earth. Zin-suddu is then instructed to return to Sippar, dig up the tablets "and turn them over to mankind." [19] He does and "they built cities and erected temples to the gods."[20]

A second and parallel flood narrative, *Epic of Gilgamesh*, provides a little more detail. The hero Utnapishtim — a descendent of the Apkallu who bore the title Atrakhasis (Unsurpassed in Wisdom) — is forewarned by Enki, who lives in a cube-shaped structure beneath the sea. After the conflagration, Utnapishtim's ship runs aground on Mount Nisir (Mount of Salvation),[21] where he is approached by seven Apkallu and told that they expect the knowledge stored in the tablets previously buried in Sippar to survive a *future* cataclysm. For all his efforts Utnapishtim, like Zin-suddu, is rewarded with immortality.

A substantial part of what we know about ancient Mesopotamia comes from *History of Babylonia* compiled by the Chaldean astronomer-priest Belreusu, who wrote his accounts from whatever public records and temple archives were still available in the third century BC, information which, he stated, had been maintained and preserved for "over 150,000 years."[22] Obviously the Sumerians were very comfortable with the antiquity they inherited. The accounts describe how the sage Ua-annu — a man of letters and sciences, an architect, temple builder, lawgiver, geometrician, and agriculturalist — brought the civilizing arts to humans who, in that period, behaved no better than wild beasts. Ua-annu's full name and

Enki with another Anunaki sage.

title is Uannadapa, *adapa* meaning 'sage, wise',[23] the root of *adept*. Over the course of several thousands of years this sage, who was "endowed with comprehensive understanding," together with his band of Apkallu — which included An-Enlil-da, "conjurer of the city of Eridu" — created the antediluvian cities and formed a great civilization. These people are described as conjurers, magicians, sorcerers, engineers, craftsmen, stonecutters, and masters of "the chemical recipes" and practical magic. The foundations they implemented during antediluvian times, plus all future renovations of the sites, were attributed to their knowledge,[24] the purpose of which was to establish the plans of heaven on earth.[25]

Notice how the Apkallu built civilization *before* the flood. This Golden Age and its cities were already long established before the events that unfolded at the end of the Younger Dryas, implying these magicians were indeed capable of living for hundreds of years. This explains why scholars are at pains to account for the sudden and fully formed Sumerian civilization — or the Egyptian, or Yucatec, or Andean, for that matter — unless they accept it as the renovation of a previous endeavor. For example, Sumerian language, like Aymara, is peculiar in that it is not related to any other world language and yet when it appears it does so fully developed.[26] Given such comparative idiosyncrasies, whoever injected this instant culture heralded from one which developed parallel to that of ordinary humans.

Early chroniclers like Belreusu go to great pains to point out that the rise of Sumerian civilization owed everything to the knowledge of the Apkallu. What they brought to the region was about as perfect as it gets, and the cuneiform texts describe in no uncertain terms how, through their intervention, humanity experienced "exceptional splendor and plenty, the golden age before the flood." [27] The Sumerians were still crowing about Ua-annu thousands of years after the flood: "There is nothing he brought that has been added by way of improvement." Together with seven Apkallu he rebuilt the decimated region and prescribed a moral code.[28] As his name implies, Ua-annu is one of the People of Anu.

Incidentally, one variant of his name, Ou-anaa, bears such a close resemblance to Ouaraa, the ruler of Easter Island c.800 AD, that it makes one wonder just how long the lineage of the Anunaki was maintained throughout the Pacific, especially in light of Teotokai Andrew's revelation of the Anunaki's presence in the Cook Islands around 3000 BC.

ENOCH MEETS ENMED-URANNA MEETS ENOCH

Four miles south of Harran —twenty-six from Göbekli Tepe — lies a permanent settlement on a mound called Tell Idris dating to c.8000 BC. In the *Qur'an*, Idris is the name given to Enoch, the Hebrew antediluvian prophet and great-grandfather of Noah, who is also identified in Islam with the Egyptian Twt, inventor of writing, astronomy and sacred buildings.[29] According to 9th century Persian philosopher Abu Mashar, Idris — and Enoch and Twt, for that matter — may not have been a name but a title, "its first bearer, who lived before the Flood... The Harranians declare his prophethood... He wrote many books whose wisdom he preserved on the walls of Egyptian temples lest it be lost. It was he who constructed the pyramids." [30]

It seems even the Persians believed the pyramids to have been built before the flood by one of the Shining Ones.

Enoch's published work, *Book of Enoch*, was discovered in Ethiopia. Written in Ge'ez, the Ethiopian sacred language, it is the most enthralling and unique of gospels and yet was excluded from the biblical canon, marginalized as an apocryphal work; it also predates the official gospels by at least two centuries. But before we get deep into the Hebrew version of things, a lesson in geopolitics.

The Babylonians made quite clear their displeasure of the Hebrews, how, during their captivity, they purloined Babylonian accounts concerning the creation, the antediluvian Earth, the flood myth, its hero, and tales of unusual beings called Apkallu or Watchers. Whether we agree with this or not, the point remains that the Babylonians themselves received their accounts from the Chaldeans and Sumerians, who in turn inherited theirs from remote sources, and by the time the Hebrews got their hands on the material, the Babylonians themselves had added a few prejudices of their own. A case of the pot calling the kettle black. Regardless, there is one point of interest. In the Babylonian/Sumerian narrative, the seventh antediluvian hero is a man of letters who is invited to a high location where he receives insights into divine wisdom from two heavenly beings or gods named Adad and Shamash. This hero Enmed-uranna was also king of Sippar, founder of the guild of *bârûs* or diviners, and a recipient of revelations — in other words, a wise man or magician, as his surname clearly indicates.[31] (In Sumerian the name means 'meeting place of heaven').[32]

The description of Enmed-uranna and his experience — ascent to a mountain, direct contact with the gods in their abode, the dictation of specialist knowledge, the offering of drugs of immortality by the god Anu, the dressing in divine linens, the anointing with oil — is remarkably identical to that of Enoch's, who is similarly listed in *Genesis* as the seventh in line from Adam. The sixth century itinerant Nestonian monk Cosmas Indicopleustes wrote an account during his travels in the region that juxtaposes, with great precision, the Chaldean and Hebrew accounts right down to their respective flood heroes Zin-suddu and Noah. Indeed the Mesopotamian traditions provided the model that biblical writers deliberately modified, inverted and reinterpreted, with the intent to show off the superiority of Jewish cultural foundations.[33] Furthermore, as the scholar Amar Annus points out, "Jewish authors systematically discredited the Mesopotamian primordial sages [*apkallu*] as the Watchers and Nephilim, while making them part of national history. In Jewish reinterpretation, Mesopotamian antediluvian sages became illegitimate and wicked teachers of humankind." [34]

There is another name entering the conversation here, the *nephilim*, and we shall come to them soon.

The Anunaki appear in the *Book of Enoch* as *a-nan-na* and its variant *a-nun-na*. They are sages who live in a settlement called Gar-sag, which Hebrew writers erroneously equated with a heavenly paradise by mistranslating the Akkadian description of the settlement as *shamu*, a 'lofty, walled enclosure', later transliterated in Persian as *paeri-disa*. This large compound on the summit of Mount Ardis featured the Building of Knowledge, and a restricted building where the Wise Ones — the high assembly of the Lords of Anu — held council. One of them, Enlil, was both Lord of the Air and Lord of Cultivation,[35] while his wife Ninlil bore the title Nikharsag and was referred to as Serpent Lady.

After the Lords of Anu settle on Ardis, several hundred teacher-craftsmen named Watchers descend and assist in the enterprise. This took place in the days of Jared, father of Enoch, hundreds of years before the flood.[36]

WATCHERS OR ANGELS?

Enoch is described as "a truthful man... writer of the truth," a faithful scribe who is trusted enough to be regularly taken to the compound of the Anu, aboard of what can only be described as a flying device that airlifts him to the summit: "The men called me. They lifted me up and placed me on what seemed to be a cloud, and this cloud moved, and going upwards I could see the sky around and, still higher, I seemed to be in space. Eventually we landed on the First Haven and there they showed me a very great sea, much bigger than the inland sea where I lived."[37] The Greek account from which this is taken describes the vehicle as *pneuma* (air), so we can deduce Enoch boarded an air-chariot — probably the same *husen-gal* (great bird) in which Enlil flew, as described in Sumerian tablets.

Enoch is allowed to see the Anu's other abodes, which totalled seven because he describes reaching a final, and highest, location called Seventh Haven. Here he accompanies two guardians whom he describes as messengers,[38] otherwise known as Watchers. The original term *watcher* comes from Aramaic and means 'to be awake'.[39] Later Greek translators used *egregoroi*, which carries two meanings: 'those who watch or guard' and 'those who are awake'. Thus the Watchers are awake or enlightened people performing supervisory roles, exactly as the name implies.

In the *Book of Enoch* as well as the *Book of Daniel*, the Watchers are described as angels, leading to the misunderstanding they were ethereal beings. To clarify, the early Greek version calls them *aggelos* — messengers — and since humans observed and interacted with them, they must have been physical people. The *Dead Sea Scrolls* compiled by the Essenes incorporates all three interpretations, stating how "the angels of the Lord descended upon earth — those who are named the Watchers — that they should instruct the children of men, that they should do judgment and uprightness upon earth." [40]

The Watchers were distinguishable from humans insofar as they possessed knowledge of the mechanics of nature and how to manipulate it, thus they were compared to gods — a view held by the Egyptians, who referred to them as both Urshu (Watchers) and Neterw (elements of nature or gods).

GODS WITH SHINING SKIN

Like a wide-eyed traveler, Enoch continues walking into the abode of the Anu, accompanied by the Watchers whom he describes as having the appearance of men but far taller; Sumerian figurines depict them with elongated heads. Once inside the assembly he describes how the Lord of Anu, to allay Enoch's trepidation and make him feel at home, asks one of the main Watchers by the name Mika-el to "strip Enoch of his clothes and anoint him with fine oil, and dress him like ourselves." [41]

The oil had an odor like myrrh and gave the Watchers' skin a lustrous, luminous quality, hence their nickname *Elohim*, Shining Ones. Enoch further describes them as white or light-skinned — much as the antediluvian gods are described elsewhere — implying the Anunaki heralded from more northerly or southerly latitudes. Clearly it was a genetic trait because a later remark by Enoch adds another layer to their physical description. It is of his grandson Lamech, whose wife gives birth to a son whose body was "white as snow and red as the blooming of a rose; and the hair of his head was in long locks which were as white as wool, and his eyes... lighted up the house like the Sun. His father Lamech was afraid of him... he resembles the sons of the Lord." [42]

The implications are tantalizing. For the descendents of Enoch to look like the Anunaki, Enoch himself must have been part of that bloodline, a highly likely scenario if we recall that Hebrew Enoch is none other than Mesopotamian Enmed-uranna, the antediluvian magician-king of Sippar, whose Anu lineage is reflected in his surname.

Alternatively, did Mrs. Lamech have a fruitful encounter with one of the Anu? Gossip abounds.

There is a second point to consider with regard to the Watchers' physical appearance. In Enoch's other apocryphal work, *Books of Adam and Eve*, he mentions how one couple leaving the enclosure at Gar-sag for the first time, for the valley below, noticed a change in the substance of their bodies, how living at lower altitude made them appear denser than before. [43] Siberian and Iranian peoples made the same observation, claiming the ancestors were less dense, their skin was pale or radiant, their hair often white. The Kalmucks and Tibetans of Central Asia go so far as to say these peoples' bodies gave off light to the point where they were compared to stars. They lived for hundreds of years, fed by the fruit of a forgotten tree, but the more they associated with the physical world the denser they became, and consequently their lifespan shortened to resemble that which humans consider normal. This is a culturally shared notion even among people in remote places such as Vanuatu in the South Pacific.[44]

One gets the impression the Watchers were humanoid yet not entirely of Earth.

Let's return to Enoch's account. He describes the grand assembly of the Anu as consisting of forty-nine lords overseen by Lord Anu himself. That's seven groups of seven sages. The four central Watchers of the assembly are "Mika-el, the kind and patient one; Rapha-el who is responsible for treating illnesses and wounds among the people here; the third was Gabri-el, and the fourth was Uri-el who is responsible for dealing with those who are selected to receive an extension to their normal life-span." [45] These would become known in the Bible as archangels.

Enoch describes how the Watchers/Anunaki were split into groups of seven and given responsibility and jurisdiction over an assigned Earthly precinct, to attend to the raising of humans from their primitive state. Each was given additional responsibilities and chores while living at Gar-sag: Gabri-el was in charge of the walled enclosure containing the central buildings of the Anu, as well as a special garden from which all manner of fruit trees and shrubs were grafted to seed places in the lowlands where humans would learn to grow their own crops. Gabri-el — GBR in its original form, root of the word *governor* — was Governor of *paeri-daeza*, the garden of the gods, as well as overseer of other People of the Serpent who lived there.[46] And here is where the Bible has it all wrong concerning the garden of Eden, upon which this fragment is based: when Eve is talking to a serpent about eating the fruit from the Tree of Knowledge she is actually talking with Gadre-el, a Serpent person, one of the Watchers living in the compound at Gar-sag. [47]

THE LOCATION OF GAR-SAG

But where are Gar-sag and Mount Ardis located? Several writers have attempted to place it at Mount Hermon in Lebanon, some well reasoned,[48] others with a need to justify the borrowed biblical narrative, after all, the slant given by the Hebrews to the *Book of Enoch* includes shifting the assembly of the Anu from the Middle East to the Levant in order to justify a religious dogma. However, as far as we know, all the original cities in the region founded by the Anu were located in Mesopotamia, well to the east.

There is one point worth considering in this argument. *Hermon* may be a transliteration of Armen, a Watcher who lent his name to Armenia,[49] thus it can be posited that the original assembly of the Anu may have been located along the northwestern periphery of Mesopotamia. Enoch himself describes one region of the Anu as highly volcanic, from whose peaks he saw a kind of ocean, which could feasibly be the Caspian Sea as seen from the volcanoes of northern Armenia. Enoch further tells us that the assembly was located in a secluded environment on a tall mountain yet with a climate pleasant enough to grow fruit trees. On another journey he appears to be describing a region *above* the Earth from the vantage point of a space rocket: "I saw that the winds spread out the heights of heaven, and are stationed between heaven and earth; they are the pillars of heaven. And I saw the winds which cause the sky to turn and the orb of the sun to revolve, and all the stars.... I saw the paths of the angels; I saw at the ends of the earth the firmament of the heavens above." [50]

It's an account full of paradoxes, yet it is possible that by the time Enoch's words were compiled the originals were no longer accessible, let alone translatable. We are given lots of salivating detail about the home of the Anunaki but, like a missing land, it remains stubbornly out of sight.

In time Enoch receives advance notice of an impending global deluge from the Lords of Anu, and how his great-grandson Noah would be further instructed on what to do because the event would occur in his lifetime, not

Ninlil in council with other Anunaki.

Enoch's. The Lords of Anu clearly had foreknowledge of a danger lurking in the sky, demonstrating their proficiency at astronomy, while at the same stroke validating the statement made earlier about ancient Egyptian sages learning of the great flood two hundred years in advance and preparing accordingly by building pyramids and other safe houses to protect the knowledge, to be recovered afterwards by another group of Shining Ones, the Aku Shemsu Hor.

Although everyone was destined to perish, the Lords of Anu promised Enoch there would be exceptions: "all the children of men may not perish through all the secret things which the Watchers have disclosed and have taught their sons." [51]

THE FALL OF (SOME) WATCHERS

How did the Watchers, who taught the civilizing sciences to humans then returned after a global catastrophe to do so again — traits generally associated with educated and gentle people — become depicted in the Bible as demons? Overlapping traditions, religious dogma and a smattering of translation errors have obfuscated the original narrative, so let's examine the facts in the available source material and clarify this important point.

Miniature figurines may not seem like supporting evidence, but in this matter they might just be. Sets of alloy figurines depicting Apkallu were found buried in the foundations of Mesopotamian buildings as a prevention to ward off evil spirits. Clearly if such apotropaic guardians were protecting people's homes they could hardly have been terrorists too. The figurines were called *massarê*, meaning Watchers. The term is applied in Akkadian ritual texts and incantations, just as it is in Aramaic as *yryn* (wakeful ones), the other term given to guardian Watchers.[52] These protective *massarê* were still employed in the magical defence of later Neo-Assyrian palaces, as seen in relief along the walls, even as free-standing sculptures made of stone or precious metal.[54]

One of the most tantalizing images of an antediluvian Earth appears in the *Book of Giants*, a component of the *Book of Enoch* discovered among the *Dead Sea Scrolls*. It is also, frustratingly, one of the most damaged. The fragments give the impression of a world populated by ordinary people, and by god-like people of very tall stature — the Watchers — who possessed secret knowledge of science and the hidden mechanics of nature. It is clear from Enoch's eyewitness reporting that the Watchers were adamant on maintaining a strict code of behavior and a distance between themselves and humans, as instructed by the Lords of Anu.

The trouble began when a group of two hundred Watchers reneged on this explicit mandate by intervening directly in human affairs. They abandoned their abode at Gar-sag to live among humans, teaching secret things to undeveloped, unsophisticated hunter-gatherers which inevitably led to their corruption.[54] The names of nineteen defectors are recorded in the *Book of Enoch*, led by "Shemhazah [who] taught spell-binding and the cutting of roots; Hermoni taught the loosening of spells, magic, sorcery and sophistry. Baraqel taught the auguries of the lightning; Kokabiel taught the auguries of the stars; Zikiel taught the auguries of fire-balls; Arteqif taught the auguries of earth; Simsel taught the auguries of the sun; Sahrel taught the auguries of the moon. And they all began to reveal the secrets to their [earthly] wives." [55] This may not seem so egregious, but as recent history will attest, even accidental contact with secluded aboriginal people at a different stage of development can corrupt a tribe's natural evolution and cause irreversible harm. Simply stated, advanced knowledge and inexperience make poor bedfellows.

As did taller Watchers with shorter human women. A ringleader by the name Yeqon led a smaller group astray by copulating with such women, who predictably gave birth to what can only be described as abominations. The Watchers' progeny were an unfortunate group of misfits called *nephilim* (giants), who ran amok throughout the land,[56] and while ordinary people did not seem unnerved by the appearance of the Watchers, they were certainly disturbed by the *nephilim*.

Obviously an incompatible genetic pairing existed between Watchers and humans, and explains why so many offspring of the gods in post-diluvial civilizations — kings, queens, pharaohs — interbred for practical reasons.

A few renegade Watchers were seduced by Earth and exploited its bounty. Their advance knowledge made them arrogant, they pushed the boundaries of their powers by undertaking genetic experiments with animals such as donkeys, asses, goats and sheep, followed by a program of miscegenation that resulted in monsters, many of which turned on their makers.

It is widely accepted among academics that humans mostly foraged for food for the best part of 300,000 years. The sudden domestication of whole species of wild animals and plants c.8000 BC is one of the great conundrums of history because it played an enormous part in the development of human civilization. Animals and plants became objects of organized agricultural and material activity without a known precedent. Is it possible this evolutionary leap is proof of the Watchers' original experiments, corrected after the great cleansing? Skeletal remains of wolf, wild boar, auroch, bezoar, moufflon and wild cat have been unearthed in Jericho, the city of giants, buried in a ten-thousand-year old sedimentary layer, yet in a layer barely a hundred years younger these species have been replaced with the domesticated dog, cat, pig, sheep, goat and cow — an unprecedented evolutionary leap.

Interbreeding with human women led to similar disastrous consequences, they begat monstrous beings. Lacking wisdom, these offspring barbarians ran amok, killed people for sport, and eventually perished through they own foolishness. This genetic breeding program, with haunting parallels to our present era, is claimed to have caused great corruption upon the Earth, and numerous world myths share the belief that this catastrophic experiment precipitated the cleansing of the world. The myths agree that a disintegrating meteor was merely the tool; the cause was the will of the Lords of Anu over the forces of nature combined with the timing of a near-Earth space object. As the Lord of Anu himself confided in Enoch, '"the things which you see at rest and in motion were completed by me. I will tell you now... what things I created from the non-existent, and what visible things from the invisible. Not even to my Watchers have I told my secrets." [57]

Yet the Watchers retained powers of their own, particularly the gifts of clairvoyance and telepathy, as exemplified by Mahway, a *nephilim* of the renegade Watcher Barakel. After a shamanic dream, he reveals to the other renegades their demise by a flood. The dream was deliberately induced by the Anunaki Ohya, who shows the giant a stone tablet with all the *nephilim* names carved upon it, drowned in water along with the roots of two hundred trees burned by fire. It is interesting how a frightened Mahway turns to Enoch for an interpretation of this prophetic vision, placing the scribe in the same time frame. Mahway and his monsters await Enoch's advice,[58] but all they receive is a confirmation of their demise and hope they repent for their licentiousness, because the land and its human victims are crying out, complaining about their misdeeds and the harm they have inflicted.[59]

The renegade Watchers crossed the line, and the problem wasn't confined to Mesopotamia, it was global. The Wichita of Oklahoma recall in their mythology how, before the flood, there existed people with supernatural powers, and through their ability to control the forces of nature, death was unknown; some lived to be an extraordinary amount of years. This was one of the things that led to a terrible imbalance in nature and society. The stories also describe how the wife of a chief was impregnated and gave birth to four monsters who played with other children at first, but as they grew in stature into giants, they took to violence and other barbaric acts. Such perversions of nature were seen as omens that a reckoning was imminent.[60] Legends among the Hopi and Zuni describe how few, if any, of the pregnant human mothers survived giving birth to babies who emerged the size of grown infants from the womb. Similar stories exist in the tradition of the Yaghan of Tierra del Fuego.

Enoch was brought before the Lords of Anu, at a location undisclosed even to his peers, to witness the four main Watchers decrying the actions of the renegades: "Asael... has taught wrong-doing, and sins upon the earth, and all manner of guile in the land; he revealed the eternal mysteries prepared in heaven and made them known to men, and his abominations the initiates among children of men make for themselves." [61] For the corruption of humanity with physical perversions, the sharing of restricted information, and the manufacture of weapons, a number of renegades were rounded up and imprisoned by Uri-el.[62] The leader of the group, Satanail, was incarcerated in one of the desolate penal volcanic regions; another, Azazel, was not so lucky, he was bound hand and foot and tossed into a cave, sealed in, and dumped into lava. Although Uri-el and Gabri-el made a concerted effort to curb the lawlessness, the *nephilim* abominations were still out of control. In an emotional appeal to the Lord of Anu, Uri-el expresses his frustration, he senses that something is being kept from the other Watchers overseeing operations at Gar-sag. It is at this point we discover that the Lord of Anu possessed the power of prediction, he was aware of the impending global disaster, whereupon he instructs Enoch,

"Tell [Noah] from me, 'Hide yourself', and inform him of what is to happen, that all the Lowlands will be destroyed in a flood which will wipe out everything on it. And give him instructions on how he may escape so that his descendents may be preserved for all time." [63]

The Lord of Anu also sends another Watcher, Sariel, to warm Lamech and Noah: "Heal the earth which the Watchers have ruined, and announce the healing of the earth, that I shall heal its wounds and that the children of men shall not altogether perish on account of the mysteries which the watchers have disclosed and taught.... The whole earth has been devastated by the works of the teaching of Asael."

Meanwhile Gabri-el is instructed to "go to the giants [Nephilim], the bastard offspring, the children of fornication, and destroy those sons of the Watchers from among the sons of men... that they should not expect to live an eternal life, but that each one should live five hundred years" [64]

AFTER THE FLOOD

An unspecified period passes after the flood. The groups of Seven Apkullu are no longer taking part in spreading knowledge, replaced instead by two-third Apkallu beings — part human, part divine.[65] Their lineage endured in many royal households well into historic times, for example, Nebuchadnezzar I, king of Babylon, described himself as a "seed preserved from before the flood;" [66] the architect of Angkor is described as half human, half divine; the lineage of the Aku Shemsu Hor continued into 14th century BC Egypt through Amenhotep III, and his son Akhenaten.

As for the secret knowledge of the Anu and the Apkallu, it was promulgated for thousands of years by new groups of sages, among them the leading Essenes of the Qumran community, priests of the Enochian tradition who referred to themselves as Sons of Light,[67] as did the Druid priests of northern Europe.[68]

As for the *nephilim*, not all were wiped out. According to Genesis, "Nephilim were on the Earth in those days — and also afterward — when the sons of God went to the daughters of humans, and had children by them. They were the heroes of old, men of renown." [69]

They were still evident c.1300 BC when Israelite scouts entering Canaan reported "all the people we saw there are of great size. We saw the

Nephilim there, the descendants of Anak... We seemed like grasshoppers in our own eyes, and we looked the same to them." [70]

Perhaps the living giants of the Solomon Islands and other remote places are a faint reminder of this distant and regrettable episode in human history.

The Shining Ones, Followers of Horus. Temple priests disfigured specific effigies deliberately to prevent outsiders from misusing their energy. The Egyptians believed everything in the temple was imbued with a life force since the time of the First Occasion.

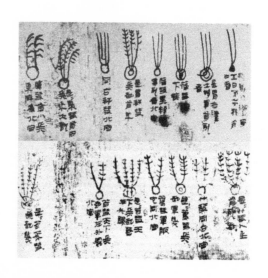

*The Chinese kept meticulous records of comets (top),
which they referred to as "vile stars." Even in 4th century
Europe (below) comets were associated with cataclysms.*

THE MECHANICS OF A COMET

Disaster: dis (negation of) astor (a star)

Donald Gault and Charles Sonnett, two scientists of the Department of Planetary Sciences at the University of Arizona, set out to demonstrate the impact of a large space rock in the ocean.[1] They theorized that the first result would be the generation of a large plume of vaporized debris consisting of seawater, seabed rock, and matter from the meteorite itself. This plume would be sucked high into the atmosphere by the reduced barometric pressure created by the descending projectile.

14

Not surprisingly the release of such titanic energy would generate an equally powerful and wide circular wall of water, both upwards and outwards, which could travel very long distances without loss of energy. The vast amount of energy transferred from a high-speed meteoric impact to a body of water, both in terms of potential and kinetic energy, means that the resulting wave is both extremely tall and speedy.

The first wave forced out by the impact would travel at a speed of 397 miles per hour. But that's just the beginning. The original impact site is temporarily replaced with a three-mile tall circular wall of water with a base pressure of some 3.5 tons per square inch, and highly unstable at that, so when this high pressure water rushes back to fill the hole created by the impact, a second massive wave is generated, packing a punch with 60% of the energy of the first.

This sobering model is based on a sound understanding of water waves and the formulae which exist for calculating the speed, height and pressure of waves regardless of whether they are caused by a meteorite, a ship or a duck.[2]

In a nutshell, the height of the first tsunami from a meteorite impact at sea will match the depth of the water at the point of impact. Therefore if fragments from the disintegrating meteorite of 9703 BC hit deep parts of the Atlantic or Pacific oceans, the tsunami they generated could potentially have been as high as three miles. And even though these projections are extrapolated from projectile velocity experiments carried out in a controlled environment, they nevertheless validate oral traditions of waves crossing the Rocky Mountains to penetrate North America, or reaching the Himalaya as far as Tibet.

Seas rising to cover mountain ranges seems like an improbable proposition, fantastical even, yet there exist many bodies of water far from the ocean or at high elevation containing salty sea water, and virtually all of them are regions from where flood myths arise. Take the Ararat Massif in Armenia, for example, on whose slope rests the petrified hull of a massive ship, ostensibly Noah's ark.[3] Ararat has been a sacred mountain to Armenians since the dawn of their culture (the name derives from a Sanskrit word meaning 'holy ground'), and the earliest variant of the name c.3000 BC was Urashtu [4] — a variant of the Egyptian term Urshu (Watcher), perhaps. The mountain's adjacent lakes, Van and Urmia, are both salt water despite being 5400 feet and 4160 feet above sea level respectively. To the southwest lies another mountain range featuring sea-sand beaches — at 7000 feet. To the north there are two large landlocked bodies of water, the Aral and Caspian seas, both of which are salt water and still feature marine life that is more at home in the ocean, and yet the closest possible inlet is 500 miles away.

At 13,000 ft in the Andes, Titicaca is the world's highest navigable lake and was once a vast inland saltwater sea, in fact, sea horses still live there. In southern Australia, Lake Eyre is a sea salt lake in a basin that is 300 miles from the ocean.

Are such bodies of water merely examples of coastlines stranded by millions of years of uplift, or did their water become contaminated by an incursion of the sea? Because the ability of a high-speed projectile transferring its kinetic power to water is such that it was once capable of generating a wave that took the bones of humans, mammoths, sabre-toothed cats and marine animals and dumped them on the summit of a mountain deep inland in Vermont.

It is also worth bearing in mind that the peaks of tsunami are lower as the shockwaves travel through wide open sea, they are merely seen as giant rogue waves, much like the Urukehu experienced on their way to New Zealand when such waves capsized one of their *waka*. Had these navigators been closer to shallow water they would not have survived to tell the tale, because a tsunami regains its original height once it reaches a coast.

Is this what motivated ancient people to build temple cities far inland and at high altitude? Cuzco, 11,000 feet above sea level; Pisac, 10,000 feet; Tiwanaku, 12,000 feet; Kura Tawhiti, 3000 feet; Arunachala, 2400 feet, Göbekli Tepe, 2500 feet.

In Arizona, the Anasazi place of emergence, Tuuwanasavi, located at the three mesas, is 6300 feet above sea level, while the Sipapuni of the Hopi is in Canyonlands, whose average altitude is 6000 feet above sea level. It is characterized by a mineral dome along the Little Colorado River, below Black Mesa. The site is purely symbolic,[5] representing as it does the moment in tribal tradition when the messenger god Masau'u assisted the Hopi at the end of the Third World. One of the lesser-known aspects of this myth is an instruction by Masau'u that the people ought not rest too long in the same location, that sixteen years is more than ample time to set down roots before becoming complacent. Thus Hopi settlements were impermanent. Historians still paint the nomadic movement of such tribes as due to creeping desertification over the past four thousand years, necessitating the need to live close to sources of water which, in the desert Southwest, rapidly diminished with climate change. This much is true, however, such an opinion is now contradicted by archaeological finds at Black Mesa that place human habitation there some ten thousand years ago, proving that migration by native tribes took place within sixteen hundred years of the flood.[6]

A CRASH COURSE IN COMETS

Outwardly the scientific world has doggedly resisted the overwhelming evidence that the Earth was nearly destroyed by the impact of a fragmenting meteor 11,000 years ago and with it whatever high civilization may have once existed. They are, however, starting to open up to the possibility that another event of equal magnitude took place barely one thousand years earlier and triggered the Younger Dryas. In 2007 a team of twenty-five prominent and accredited researchers met at the American Geophysical Union in Acapulco to cite several inquiries and present evidence that the Clovis culture — a subjective collective term describing early North American peoples — vanished suddenly from the historic record due to the impact of a wayward comet that entered the atmosphere c.10,800 BC, fractured into pieces and exploded in giant fireballs, the debris scattering across North America — Canada in particular — and Europe.[7] It is estimated that while large fragments plunging into the two-mile thick Laurentide Ice Sheet destabilized it, those parts of North America not covered by ice were scorched by wildfires.[8] The effects were a rise in sea level, extensive biomass burning, megafaunal extinctions, and a cooling of the atmosphere, creating the onset of the Younger Dryas.[9]

Additional research by sixty-three scientists from sixteen countries advocating a cometary impact theory has now displaced the glacial melt theory as the leading cause of the Younger Dryas. Dozens of peer reviewed scientific publications from the National Academy of Sciences provide supporting evidence, such as the presence of nanodiamonds and microscopic grains associated with impact events coinciding with the onset of the Younger Dryas c.10,800 BC.[10] To compound their claim, studies of 129 core samples from lakes across the world demonstrate a clear spike in sediment charcoal levels, evidence that a mass burning was in effect on a worldwide scale which consumed around 10 per cent of the landmass. The dramatic rise of carbon released into the atmosphere further contributed to a sudden drop in temperature.[11]

Undaunted, humans rebuilt. Within three hundred years of the onset of the Younger Dryas cold snap, the Egyptians were celebrating Zep Tepi, a defining event when everything that was clean, good and wholesome began once more. It marked the foundation of temples along the Nile and the whole paraphernalia upon which civilization is erected, a point of view shared by the Mesopotamians and a number of similar cultures.[12]

All this effort would be undone within seven hundred years by a second impact that closed the Younger Dryas. Around 9645 BC a steep temperature rise of 14° F. took place over a fifty-year period, more disastrous than the most pessimistic doomsday global warming scenario today and experienced in one lifetime![13] Backed by Greenland ice core data, the mathematician Flavio Barbierro proposed a model to explain this sudden warming of the climate. Because the Earth behaves like a giant gyroscope, a strike from an asteroid of considerable size, at the right angle and in the same direction as the gravitational pull of the Sun and Moon, could feasibly disturb the planet's torque and shift its spin axis, even if for a brief moment. Since the Earth is also a semi-fluid object — oceans on the surface and a liquid core inside a liquid lithosphere — a change in centrifugal rotation affects the behavior of its layers, deforming and displacing landmasses. There would also be a displacement of the poles, forcing the ocean's water to shift towards the new equator with considerable force, buckling and reshaping the Earth's surface. A change in the mantle establishes the new rotation of the axis in a matter of days or minutes. The consequences would be devastating. Large parts of the crust would rise and fall, volcanic activity would increase, titanic earthquakes would be unleashed, accompanied by hurricane force winds, torrential rain, wildly fluctuating sea levels, and tidal waves hundreds of feet tall crossing entire continents.[14]

Barbierro's hypothesis neatly accounts for all the descriptions of what took place geologically and climatically around the world as recorded in nearly two hundred indigenous traditions.

Once again we must ask, could these two events, barely one thousand years apart, be another factor explaining the two separate yet complimentary megalithic building styles found consistently throughout the world?

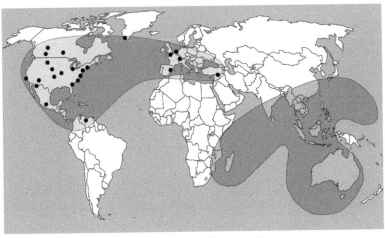

Known impact sites and debris fields from first Younger Dryas event.

The effect of a large meteor striking the Earth was researched by the French astronomer Pierre Laplante back in 1796, whereupon he reached similar conclusions: "The axes and rotational movement will be changed, the seas forsaking their age-old positions and rushing towards the new equator; most of the human race and the beasts of the field will be drowned in this universal deluge or destroyed by the violent shock imparted to the terrestrial globe, entire species annihilated, every monument to human endeavour overthrown." [15]

Laplante's observation was not taken seriously until 1994 when comet Shoemaker Levy arrived from outer space to be captured by Jupiter's gravitational pull, the pressure of which split the rock into twenty-one fragments that pummelled the giant planet, causing a plume of debris thousands of miles high. This time it was Jupiter's turn, the same could have happened to Earth, in fact, David Levy, one of the two astronomers after whom the comet is named, went on to state as much, it is but a question of time.

ONE CATACLYSM IS NOT ENOUGH

From 22,000 BC to 9000 BC alone, the Earth experienced wild climate fluctuations. During that era the most stable habitable region was the territory between the tropics of Cancer and Capricorn, coincidentally the region where most of the oldest megalithic sites are located as well as the aforementioned homelands of the gods.

Ancient writers alluded to recurring conflagrations, and their words are now vindicated by geologists and climatologists. As the Egyptian priests once explained the capriciousness of life on Earth to Solon: "In mind you [Greeks] are all young; there is no old opinion handed down among you by ancient tradition, nor any science which is hoary with age. And I will tell you why. There have been and there will be many and diverse destructions of mankind, of which the greatest are by fire and water, and lesser ones by countless other means... For in truth the story that is told in your country [Greece]... has the fashion of a legend, but the truth of it lies in the occurrence of a shifting of the bodies in the heavens which move around the earth, and a destruction of the things on the earth by fierce fire, which recurs over long intervals... Just when you and other nations are beginning to be provided with letters and the other requisites of civilized life, after the usual interval, the stream from heaven, like a pestilence, comes pouring down, and leaves only those of you who are destitute of letters and education; and so you have to begin again like children, and know nothing of what happened in ancient times." [16]

Compare the statement with the Mayan *Popol Vuh*: "Again there comes a humiliation, destruction and demolition. The [people of that time] were killed when the Heart of the Sky devised a flood for them. A great flood was made; it came down on the heads of the [people], they were killed, done in by a flood. There came a rain of resin from the sky... the earth was blacked because of this; the black rainstorms began, rain all day and rain all night." [17]

An Akkadian legend called the *Erra Epic* was authored by a writer of the period by the name Kabti-ilani-Marduk, yet he states that he was merely transcribing an old visionary dream recounted by Erra himself. Erra is a god who is roused from slumber by his advisor Išum and Seven Sages, sons of heaven and earth, "champions without peer," each of whom is assigned a destructive destiny by Anu. However, the narrative is then tainted with a political agenda: these Anunaki are made out to be terrorists whose services Erra hopes to employ in the destruction of the Babylonians. When the obvious propaganda is removed and the remaining text is read in its original context, an element of astronomy and warning rises to the surface. The narrative is placed in the mouth of another god, Marduk: "Once long ago indeed I grew angry, indeed I left my dwelling, and caused the deluge. When I left my dwelling, the regulation of heaven and earth disintegrated. The shaking of heaven meant the positions of the heavenly bodies changed, and I did not restore them. The quaking of netherworld meant the yield of the furrow diminished, being thereafter difficult to exploit. The regulation of heaven and earth disintegrating meant underground water diminished, high water receded." [18] As with other flood narratives, there is a description of the regular order of planets and stars being disrupted by an outside force. Marduk may have been an astral object, a comet that "left its dwelling" causing the "regulation of heaven and earth" to be disintegrated. It was not uncommon in the ancient world for astral bodies to be personified and awarded the status of gods because they were considered living entities in their own right. Where the above text diverges from others lies in its mention of the retreat of aquifers, along with the receding of high water, strongly suggesting the oceans suffered a serious drop in sea level as a result of this encounter, whereas comparative flood myths describe an *overabundance* of water. What the *Erra Epic* appears to be describing are conditions during the Last Glacial Maximum around 22,000 years ago, when the Earth experienced a steep drop in aquifers and sea level due to most of the water being trapped as ice. If so, this prehistoric event is compatible with the traditions of the Sumerians, who claimed their history had been maintained and preserved for "over 150,000 years." [19]

ON EARTH AS IT IS IN HEAVEN

Those great students of the stars, the Chaldeans, were under no illusion that planetary orbits are in any way fixed, but undergo periodic change. Writing about their knowledge, Diodorus of Sicily said, "Each of the planets, according to them has its own particular course, and its velocities and periods of time are subject to change and variation." [20]

One such event took place not so long ago. In the *Bamboo Books* of China it is stated that in the tenth year of the reign of Emperor Kwei c.1578 BC, "the five planets went out of their courses. In the night, stars fell like rain. The earth shook." [21] And further along: "At this time the two suns were seen to battle in the sky. The five planets were agitated by unusual movements. A part of Mount T'ai Shan fell down." [22]

The Pawnee describe a time when the Earth's poles switched places, when the southern star and the north star swapped positions and that "when the time comes for the ending of the world, the stars will again fall to the earth," [23] an idea shared by Egyptians who once accepted south as up and north as down. Such drastic reversals were understood to occur periodically in relation to the Great Year — the Earth's processional cycle — and were accompanied by great conflagrations, leading learned people such as Philo of Alexandria and the Stoics to comment, "by reason of the constant and repeated destructions of water and fire, the later generations did not receive from the former the memory of the order and sequence of events." [23]

As pointed out earlier, a collision between the Earth and a large projectile is capable of altering its rotation and, consequently, affecting the way calendars are calculated. Surprisingly enough, most world calendars were originally based on a 360-day year and a 30-day lunar month, until the 8th century BC when five days began to be added to the solar year, and the lunar calendar was reduced to 29 days, thus synchronizing the seasons with current heavenly motions, leading to speculation that at one time the Earth spun faster on its axis and the Moon's orbit differed from what it is today.

This was certainly the view of Hindu chronology outlined in the *Aryabhatiya*, an Indian treatise on mathematics and astronomy, in which it is argued that with the closing of Great Ages and their associated catastrophes, slight differences in the motions of heavenly bodies come into play. [24] The notion was employed by their neighbors, the Assyrians and Babylonians, who applied the same numerical values in their buildings. The walls of ancient Babylon were 360 furlongs in length, "as many as there had been days in the year," [25] while the Egyptians composed their year into 360 days, as did pre-Inkan cultures, and the Maya.[26] The Chinese went a stage further: they divided the sphere into 360 degrees, each degree corresponding to the passing of the zodiac over the course of a full solar year. When five-and-a-quarter days were added to compensate for the Earth's new rotation, they divided the sphere into the same number, thus harmonizing the new length of solar year with terrestrial geometry.[27]

It seems chaos still ensued in the heavens and on Earth leading up to the 8th century BC that forced a reformation of calendars. Addressing the emperor of China at the time, the astronomer Y Hang announced that the order of the sky and the movement of planets had changed sufficiently to make it impossible to predict such things as eclipses, further adding that in earlier times Venus orbited 40° south of the ecliptic and even eclipsed the star Sirius, something it does not do today.[28]

Ancient traditions keep reminding us the cause is periodic. All we need do now if figure out when it is next likely to occur.

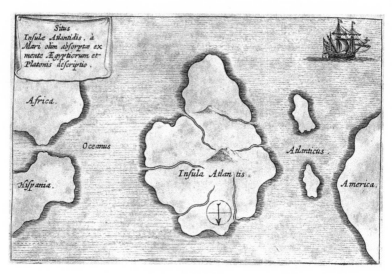

Map of Atlantis, when North was South.

MISSING COASTS

*"If you examine [ancient Egyptian] art on the spot, you will find
that ten thousand years ago (and I'm not speaking loosely, I mean
literally ten thousand), paintings and reliefs were produced that are
no better and no worse than those of today."* — Plato[1]

When caliph Al-Ma'mun attempted to force his way into the Great
Pyramid in the ninth century, one of his priorities was to find maps of
the world, said to have been deposited there by Twt, whose accuracy once
allowed the gods to move unhindered about the planet. It is
not known if he succeeded, but a number of anomalous maps
subsequently surfaced around the Mediterranean showing
islands, continents and other features yet to be discovered at the time, or
no longer exist.

15

One such map appears in *Mundus Subterraneus*, a geological opus
compiled in 1684 by Athanasius Kircher, a scholar and polymath who's
been compared to Leonardo da Vinci. It depicts the island continent of
Atlantis prominently in the middle of the Atlantic Ocean; Kirchner
claimed the map was based on Plato's works along with five pages from
additional sources including rare Egyptian accounts. The result is a map
of the Atlantic oriented with south at the top, with America to the right
instead of left, Africa and Iberia to the left instead of right and, on the
island of Atlantis itself, a compass pointing south instead of north.

The thing is, Egyptians once considered south to be north, while the
Hopi and other ancient commentators claim a rapid movement of the poles
did occur in remote times and led to an ice age. In his studies of the Indian
sacred book *Mahabharata,* the scholar Lokamanya Yilak points out that

"the Earth's magnetic field is tied up in some way with the rotation of the planet. And this leads to a remarkable finding about the earth's rotation itself... the axis has changed also. In other words, the planet has rolled about, changing the location of the geographical poles." [2] Coincidentally, the last known geomagnetic reversal completed around 10,400 BC.[3]

In addition to a sudden pole shift, in 1837 Louis Agassiz proposed a hypothesis that the Earth's crust once suffered a major displacement, an idea that only gained traction in the late twentieth century, and with some merit. The planet's rotation and tilt have clearly been a factor, even a trigger of sudden glacial epochs. Einstein himself once considered the uneven distribution of ice at the poles to be capable of destabilizing the Earth through centrifugal momentum causing a slippage of its top-most skin, which is barely 30-miles thick and rests over a lubricating layer. Theoretically this would cause the polar regions to slide to the equator. In such an event the Sun would indeed be seen to rise and set in completely different parts of the sky, in contrast to its present east-west trajectory. This scenario might have taken place between 14,500–12,500 BC, with aftershocks up to about 9500 BC.[4]

Antarctica is a good example of crustal displacement. A map of this snowbound landmass created by French geographer Orance Fine in 1531 uses sophisticated map projection and spherical trigonometry accurate enough to allow fifty points of reference to be located today. The problem is, the map was drawn three centuries before said continent was discovered.[5] Another anomalous map by Philippe Buache accurately shows Antarctica's sub-glacial topography, an extraordinary leap of imagination considering the last time the south pole was ice-free is estimated at 14 million years ago.[6] Or is academia wrong? Certainly Antarctica was once 2000 miles further north — where the capital of Chile is today — ice free, with only a small portion of its landmass inside the Antarctic circle; Queen Maud Land in particular would have been a most agreeable place for agriculture and a developing island civilization. There is also evidence that sediment-carrying rivers were still active in the Ross Sea as late as 4000 BC,[7] so clearly Antarctica has not been as snowbound as we might believe. The only thing we can be certain about this continent is that much of what we know is uncertain.

Adding weight to the crustal displacement theory is the 1513 map of

Turkish admiral Piri Reis, collated from twenty different ancient source documents, and showing the coastlines of South America and Africa with a high degree of accuracy, even the remote Falkland Islands are located with pinpoint precision. It correctly depicts the Amazon River and its source, yet in the sixteenth century all this had yet to be located or explored by westerners. The large island of Marajo, which ought to appear at the mouth of the Amazon, is missing, leading to the conclusion that the source map was made around 13,000 BC when said island was still part of the mainland. But more importantly, Queen Maud Land is depicted free of ice, a situation that only occurred before 4000 BC. The map also shows a large landmass over the sub-oceanic Mid Atlantic ridge, 500 miles to the east of Brazil and just north of the equator; with rising of sea levels, only fifteen pinnacles of rock remain above the water today, collectively named the Rocks of Peter and Paul.

Not only does the Piri Reis map depict the Earth's landmass prior to major geological changes and upheavals, its unusual projection is based on an ancient astronomical observatory centered on the Nile island of Elephantine, once Egypt's legendary southern border. This was validated by the US Air Force. However, on the Piri Reis map the island is not located

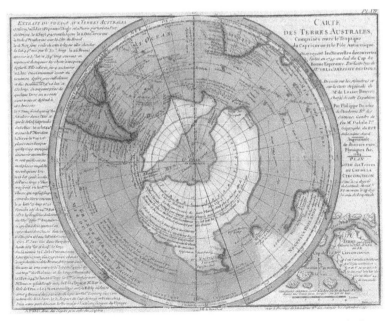

Buache shows Antarctica as two islands, just as it appears beneath the ice.

north of the equator but two thousand miles to the south, in present-day Tanzania. The US Air Force office was similarly impressed by the ability of this 16th century cartographer to have projected his map as though from space. Since the map is based on extremely ancient sources, it follows that the original cartographer must have known the Earth to be spherical.

We are regularly told the Greeks were the first to figure out the Earth was round and yet the Avestans before them were certainly aware of the existence of the poles by the time they wrote the *Mahabharata*, for they describe the Arctic Circle as a place where "the stars, the moon and the sun are only once a year seen to rise and set, and a year seems only as a day." [8] An Icelander reading this passage would see an accurate description of the behavior of the sky at extreme northern latitudes. The text is conservatively dated to 800 BC but eastern scholars claim it too is a copy based on extremely ancient sources, like so many other texts of the Indian region. Even Pliny knew the spherical attributes of the Earth when he noted in 79 AD, "Human beings are distributed all around the earth and stand with their feet pointing toward each other.... Another marvel, that the earth herself hangs suspended and does not fall and carry us with it." [9]

Maps, it seems, are a remarkably reliable method of recording what exists as well as what no longer does.

In historical times around the Mediterranean it was commonplace for seafarers to copy maps without realizing the source documents recorded

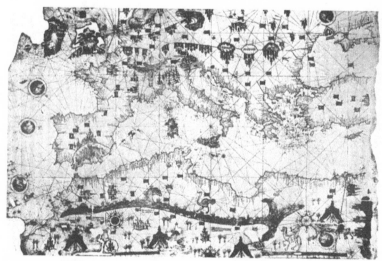

Ben Zara's map still shows glaciers in Europe and a river along the Sahara.

alandmasses no longer extant. For example, a map drawn in 1487 by Yehudi Ibn Ben Zara depicts glaciers further south than Sweden, and what the coastlines of the Mediterranean, Adriatic and Aegean seas might have looked like before the melting of Europe's ice caps following the end of the Younger Dryas.[10] It also shows a substantial river running east to west in the middle of the Sahara emptying into the Atlantic Ocean, yet no such river existed in Ben Zara's time, only though satellite imagery has this hitherto unknown body of water been located beneath the sand. The desertification of northern Africa began around 9700 BC due to a change in the Earth's orbit and interplay with changes in atmosphere, sea levels and sea ice,[11] with the region between Egypt and the west coast of Africa finally succumbing to desert by 3000 BC. Thus Ben Zara's source map must have been created when the river was still in full flow, which again takes us to around the time of the Younger Dryas.[12]

REBUILDING THE FORMER HOME OF THE GODS

The Apkallu were said to have arrived in Mesopotamia from their residence in Apsû (Ocean of Wisdom or deepwater abode) until the god Marduk — who is perceived as an errant celestial object — forced them to retreat to the safety of this location during the flood, so clearly this is not a metaphorical or otherworldly environment but a physical location — quite possibly Te Pitaka, the missing land of the Anunaki described in the Tongarevan tradition.

There is a parallel to this account in the *Building Texts*, where "the homeland of the Primeval Ones" is identified as an island in the ocean, home to a prosperous civilization whose survivors set out in ships, re-settling in a number of locations to "rebuild the former world of the gods." [13] The *Building Texts* make it clear that 12,000 years ago there were two races on Earth: hunter-gatherers with little knowledge of civilization, and an altogether different race of people who lived remotely, far more advanced in engineering, metallurgy, large-scale architecture, natural magic, civic cohesion and navigation. And perhaps in technology too, because there is an odd passage describing how the source of light on Ta Neterw came from a Sound Eye, alluding to a device by which the entire island was artificially illuminated. It too was destroyed by the great flood, causing darkness to fall on the domain of the gods.[14]

The late English scholar Eve Reymond published an incisive study of the *Building Texts* that reveals much about the origin and home of the antediluvian gods of Egypt. To read them is to travel to a bygone era of high civilization, of survival and new hope, to place yourself front and center of a rebuilding project that attempted to revive a destroyed wonderworld. One can almost taste the bittersweet endeavor as the texts describe a period in prehistoric times called the Early Primeval Age of the Gods, in which we find the ancestors of the ancient Egyptians arriving from the Home of the Primeval Ones, a sacred island amidst a great ocean where "the earliest mansions of the gods" were founded.[15]

These gods were accomplished sailors who traversed the seas, but when a meteorite and a flood destroyed their island, "companies of gods" lucky enough to be caught at sea survived. The texts describe the calamity as "the great leaping snake pierced the domain of the gods," eerily reminiscent of the Waitaha description of a comet and its tail, "Auahi Tu Roa [Firebird] who carries messages across the darkened skies for the Sky Father." Upon sailing back to see what remained of their homeland, all the gods saw were reeds and mud that made the sea impassible to navigation and hindered further exploration.[16] Reluctantly the group wandered the world as the "crew of the Falcon" in search of suitable locations where they might recreate their former home;[17] chief among this group of wandering gods was Hor and Twt.

When Diodorus was compiling his history of Egypt, informants told him that the decision by the gods to rebuild there was due to southern Egypt's geographical advantage in a period marked by extreme cold and the absence of sunlight. Close to the equator, conditions were warmer and humid, and the extra rainfall following the flood benefitted this region well as an ideal place for the regeneration of new forms of life.[18]

Each of the gods were assigned specific tasks: the Shebtiw possessed the ability to "enbue with power the substances of the earth", they could "magnify things" and provide magical protection through the careful use of symbols and words; a second group, the Builder Gods, were in charge of constructing sacred architecture "according to what the Sages of the primeval age revealed to Twt"; then there were the Seven Sages, Followers of Horus, each an expert in their field, whose knowledge was superior even to that of Twt.[19] We may as well be describing the Lords of Anu, the Anunaki or the Watchers.

But where exactly was their original land? The Egyptians believed Ta-Neterw lay to the south — assuming that in the period being described south meant south, not north — a maritime land across a large expanse of water that could only be reached by boat; on occasion the gods would invite a human there to see it. Part of it was still in existence during Zep Tepi, when the territorial reign of the god Ra gave rise to a golden age which later Egyptian cultures looked on with great fondness and regret, since it was "a time of truth that came down from the sky and united with those who were here on Earth. The land was in abundance, bodies were full, there was no year of hunger in the Two Lands. Walls did not fall, thorns did not pierce in the time of the Primeval Gods." [20] It is described as an Island of Fire, "a mystic land of origin beyond the horizon," presided by Hor; it was also the abode of Twt, where he "made shrines for the gods and goddesses," validating it as a real location, least of all because the Egyptians recorded its name as Ta-Ur, land of the old city.[21]

The island is described as "intersected by canals filled with running water, which caused them to be always green and fertile. On these grew luxuriant crops of wheat and barley, the like of which were unknown to earth. The *Papyrus of Nu* says that "the wheat grew to a height of five

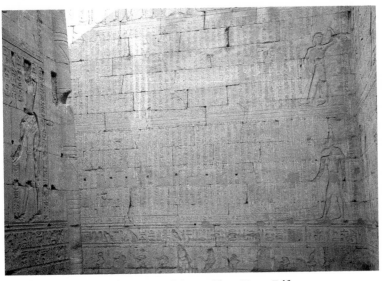

A small section of the Building Texts. Edfu.

cubits, the ears being two cubits long and the stalks three; the barley grew to a height of seven cubits, the ears being three cubits long and the stalks four. Here lived the spirits of the blessed dead, who were nine cubits high, and the reaping of these crops was, it seems, reserved for them, and for the Souls of the East." [22]

Such a description of abnormally large crops is strangely similar to the way Viracocha and his Shining Ones potentized the water in and around the Qorikancha in Cuzco that made vegetation grow to extravagant height.

The deciphering of the *Building Texts* soon revealed they did not originate at the temple of Edfu, they are a synopsis of an ancient and vast archive of material that fell prey to millennia of political and environmental caprice. It has to be remembered that when explorers reached the site in the early nineteenth century, its once grand interior was being used as a storehouse for animals and corn. Vast amounts of rubbish were piled in and around the site, and state rooms had been turned into sleeping quarters and kitchens, while campfires lit inside the buildings led to the fine, painted hieroglyphs being covered in thick layers of soot. An architectural wonder had been transformed into a hovel. It was wise of the Greek restorers in the 3rd century BC to physically carve the information onto the walls of Edfu lest the knowledge of the origins of the gods be lost — especially as the *Building Texts* state how they constitute nothing less than "the words of the Sages... the only divine beings who knew how the temples and sacred places were created," for they were the very creators of that knowledge. [23] They dictated it to Twt who compiled it into a number of books, all lost for the time being: *Sacred Book of the Temples, Book for Planning the Temple, Sacred Book of the Early Primeval Ones,* and *Sacred Book of Atum.* Another work, *Specifications of the Mounds of the Early Primeval Age,* contained the master plan upon which Egypt was to be laid out, including an inventory of all the original mounds upon which the historical temples would be built, all part of the plan to resurrect the former age of the gods during and following the Younger Dryas.

A CONTINENT HIDDEN BEHIND A MURAL

Twt's tomes were not the only ones to be concealed. At some point in the early eleventh century, an archive of up to 50,000 documents was

Wang Yuanhu at Dunhuang.

sealed up in a chamber inside one of the caves of Mogao (Peerless), part of a system of 492 temples located in a remote corner of northwestern China.

The nearby city of Dunhuang was once a strategic religious and trading point along the Silk Road, and in time the site became a major Buddhist place of veneration, with over 1000 caves used for meditation, each elaborately painted and filled with statues, reliefs and other objects used as visual representations of the quest for enlightenment. The entrance to what is now referred as the Library Cave was further concealed behind a wall painting. Nine hundred years later, visiting Daoist monk Wang Yuanhu wondered what lay hidden behind the mural, and upon discovering the cache of historical, mathematical and folkloric texts written in a dozen languages including Old Uyghur, Tangut, early Tibetan, Sanskrit, and the undeciphered Nam language, he appointed himself guardian of the cave temples.

The first Western expedition to reach Dunhuang arrived in 1879, followed two decades later by French explorer Paul Pelliot, who took to the daunting task of sorting and arranging the endless sea of documents, as he graphically illustrates in his letter: "During the first ten days I attacked nearly a thousand scrolls a day." News of the cache reached John MacMillan Brown, philologist and Chancellor of the University of New Zealand, who took to studying whatever texts were made available outside China. Something must have impressed him because, soon after, he became a leading western advocate for a lost continent in the Pacific. Like the 16th century European navigators collecting stories from island to island, he too remarked that today's Pacific islands are the remnants of an older root civilization, a theory he based upon examination of certain texts from the Mogao caves written in a lost language, Tocharish, which included a map of the original Pacific detailing the location of a missing landmass.

Frustratingly, the map has vanished along with the texts MacMillan was reviewing.

THE HOPI OF MUIA

The trail picks up with the Hopi, who refer to their original homeland as Muia, an island in the Pacific lost to a global catastrophe. "Those people

The entrance to Mogau caves today. The mural in Cave 16 in 1921.

who got here, the flood destroyed most of them but a few survived. They were the remnant of something big... But these Hopi people know that they came from across the ocean and migrated here," recalls Homer Cooyama Kykotamovi of the Hopi Coyote clan. [24] A long time ago the ancestors of the Hopi were seafarers whose oral tradition included descriptions of this land, knowledge of which is typically transmitted to initiates during coming-of-age ceremonies. Bamboo and reeds are used throughout creation myth and storytelling in the kivas, plants totally out-of-place in the arid desert landscape of Arizona.

This missing land in the Pacific is emphasized in Samoan tradition, where it is still referred to as Mu, the Mu'ul of the Olmec. During his time in Tibet, Paul Schliemann, grandson of the noted archaeologist, came across a Chaldean text in a Buddhist temple in Lhasa, written approximately 4000 years ago, in which the island's final days is recounted: "When the star Bal fell on the place where is now only sea and sky the Seven Cities with their Golden Gates and Transparent Temples quivered and shook like the leaves of a tree in storm. And behold a flood of fire and smoke arose from the palaces. Agony and cries of the multitude filled the air. They sought refuge in their temples and citadels. And the wise Mu, the hieratic of Ra-Mu, arose and said to them: 'Did not I predict all this?' And the women and the men in their precious stones and shining garments lamented: 'Mu, save us.' And Mu replied: 'You shall die together with your slaves and your riches and from your ashes will arise new nations... The land and its inhabitants were torn to pieces and swallowed by the depths in a few months." [25]

Funny how the essence of the Egyptian god Ra is sprinkled throughout the Pacific as much as its islands — places such as Ra-Iatea in Fiji, literally 'white skinned people of Ra'.

Other Polynesian people refer to this lost land as Havai'iki, which in time has been shortened to Hiva. According to Hawaii folklore the gods created an ideal land for the first humans in Kahiki-homua-kele, once situated along the present Hawaiian chain of islands but since submerged, which ties in perfectly with the island's tectonic record, and perhaps why the translation of this lost paradise is The Land That Moved Off. Survivors became forest-dwelling races such as the Nawao, large-sized hunters descended from Lua-nu'u, the Mu people, and the Wa people. [26] Another Hawaii tradition states that during the Era-of-Overturning, the people's homeland was called Hoahoamaitru. There, a man by the name of Nu'u built a big boat in which to survive the flood whose waters overflowed the land except for the Hawaiian peak of Mauna Kea.[27]

Academia loves to trash the idea of the missing continent of Mu as much as they do Atlantis. They particularly direct they scorn at the one person who expounded the idea in the late nineteenth century, James Churchward, but regardless how much of Churchward's work is pure research or conjecture, the fact remains that just about every Pacific culture validates the existence of this land, regardless of what it was originally called. During his time and travels in India and Burma, Churchward was informed by the Naacal, an elevated class of priests and wisdom keepers who originated from said lost continent some 15,000 years ago. Much of their information, which includes detailed and accurate descriptions of how the cosmos and the earth works, millennia before NASA, was written in symbolic form on hundreds of clay tablets which Burmese priests claim have been systematically looted from their temples. That's quite a long time to hold a grudge. Among the symbols is the seven-headed serpent representing the formative aspects of nature and the seven Serpent People who once taught them, as written in religious texts such as the Hindu *Manava Dharma Sastra*, the *Rg Veda*, and the Nahuatl teachings of Yucatan, with the most scientific of texts found among the Marquesans. The language in which they were written was called Naga-Maya, whose closest translation is serpent-water. Given what is known about the People of the Serpent and their relationship to water places the quackademics on a back foot, to quote the late John Anthony West.

The *Ramayana* goes so far as to describe the Naacal priests as Maya adepts, "starting from the land of their birth in the east, as missionaries of religion and learning, went to Burma and there taught the Nagas. From Burma they went to the Deccan in India, whence they carried their religion and learning to Babylonia and to Egypt." [28] This is somewhat validated in the *Troano Codex*, the written accounts of the Maya during the Spanish invasion, where Mu is referenced using the same symbols found in India and Burma. One script in a temple at Uxmal confirms "the lands of the west from where we came... that land of Kui... birthplace of our sacred mysteries." A stela in the temple of Akab Dzib in Chichen Itzá likewise describes the lands of the West being shaken to their foundations by earthquakes before being engulfed by the flood. The *Troano Manuscript* fixes the date of cataclysm at 9937 BC, remarkably close to the Younger Dryas boundary, and further states that the dominant race was light-skinned, great navigators and sailors, learned architects, and builders of great temples in stone.[29] The *Codex Cortesianus* picks up the narrative: "Mu, the country of the hills of earth, was submerged... The place of the dead ruler is now lifeless, it moves no more, after having twice jumped from its foundations... the king of the deep, while forcing his way out, has shaken it up and down, has killed it, has submerged it... Twice Mu jumped from her foundations; it was then sacrificed by fire... By kicking it, the wizard that makes all things move... sacrificed it that very night." [30]

In describing this missing land as "having twice jumped from its foundations," the account tallies with the two geological upheavals marking the start and close of the Younger Dryas.

Seven plus one Lookers. Horseshoe Canyon, Utah.

STAR PEOPLE

Four-thirty a.m. is the perfect time to go for a walk, even if, like me, you're not a morning person. Just before sunrise, the desert is the quietest place on Earth. I like the desert, it is a place to find answers, to bring closure. As the song goes, "in the desert you can remember your name."

The meeting point of Utah, New Mexico and Arizona has always felt like a second home to me — along with Kura Tawhiti in New Zealand and Luxor in Egypt — even back when I was a wee nipper living in Europe. Although I've made several journeys to this region, the one place I desired to experience above all was a panel of petroglyphs in one of its most remote canyons, requiring a seven-hour hike, typically in 100° heat, while carrying a backpack 90% stuffed with water.

16

The images on the panel are like no other. Painted in red ochre, the seven figures stand over seven feet tall, draped in long tunics, with a central eighth whose eyes stare with a self-assured alertness. These people look nothing like the Hopi or Zuni, they belong to another time and place, and it's probably for this reason that the frieze has been inappropriately labelled the Ghost Panel.

Before departing on the trek into Horseshoe Canyon I discussed the panel and its figures with Zuni elder, Clifford Mahooty, a man never short of fascinating stories about Native American tribespeople and their traditions. My quest was as personal as it was exploratory, I wished to learn more about the part these ancient people might have played in the flood narrative and the gods who facilitated their appearance in North America, after all, people are known to have been present in this canyon since 9000

BC. Clifford was attentive to my obvious passion to come face-to-face with the cloaked figures. "I feel as thought I've known them for a long time, " I said, "they're awfully familiar, even with the gowns draped to their ankles."

Clifford gave me a puzzled look. "But you *do* know who they are, you've come across them before. We call them Lookers."

THE FOUR WORLDS OF NATIVE AMERICA

According to Hopi tradition the First World, Tokpela, was destroyed by a fire of global proportion.[1]

In the Second World, Tokpa, the Earth bore little resemblance to the previous one. Where there had been land now there was water and vice versa. This period came to a close when the poles spun out of control and the world "rolled over twice... it froze into solid ice," a remarkably good fit with the period of the Older Dryas.[2] The Earth turned on its axis, north became south — the Hopi describe it as "south-facing world" — the consequence of which was an ice age. Members of the Hopi were warned in advance and instructed to follow a cloud of unusual shape by day and a moving star by night that led them to a mound of the Ant People. Once safely inside, the Hopi lived underground until conditions allowed them to return to the surface.[3]

In the Third World — the one we are immediately concerned with, the period of the Younger Dryas — the population grew rapidly and achieved remarkable progress, building cities and a world civilization.[4] Although many people lived in harmony with nature and the spirit world, there developed a parallel and technologically advanced society that used its creative power unwisely which ultimately led to wars. They built "flying shields," aerial craft capable of traveling quickly to different places in the world to devastate entire cities.[5] As expected, this did not sit well with the creator gods, whereupon they decided the world must be destroyed yet again, this time by a great flood, and recreated from scratch. Predictably, instructions were sent out to place selected people on boats — "inside tall plants with hollow stems," was the expression.[6]

When the survivors emerged they were shocked to see the great landmass where they'd once lived reduced to the top of a tall mountain surrounded by water, lots of water. They took to boats and sailed from island to island, the remains of former lands, slowly migrating eastwards and slightly to the north. The Hopi narrative states how they finally reached a large, flat island, covered with trees and plants, settling there for a short time before being ushered to North America, presumably due to ever rising seas. Upon reaching a mountainous region, they paddled upstream through deep canyons, searching for the Place of Emergence, which they eventually found. From a high elevation they looked west and south and saw the islands from whence they'd migrated, the tips of mountains where once a landmass had been. They were now living in this, the Fourth World.[8]

The Place of Emergence refers to a symbolic mound at the base of the Grand Canyon. However, the Hopi suggest the description of the labyrinthine journey taken up the Colorado River to this site is an allegorical representation of the journey as a whole, for the mound itself is far too young to be the original — the level of the river 11,000 years ago was much higher than it is today, the mound would have been submerged. Hopi tradition claims the true Place of Emergence lies "down below" in Central America, which the ancestors reached after the mother continent, Kásskara, sank in the central Pacific at the same time as another in the Atlantic by the name Talawaitichqua, the Atitlán of the Itzá. Kásskara is said to have covered a fair portion of the central Pacific south of the equator.[9]

Katcina dance, c.1900. Note the painted white face. If this commemorates an ancient event, who is the white person representing?

A messenger god by the name Massau'u was instructed to stay with the Hopi and oversee the initial settlement and the migrations that would follow. An amalgam of legends depict this individual as a decrepit old man of grey complexion concealing a younger, robust man who lives somewhat remotely among the tribe to whom he gifts knowledge written on stone tablets. Masau'u possesses the power of flight, the ability to traverse vast expanses of territory as though superhuman, and to interact between worlds. In many respects he acts as an observer, a Looker.[10] Could his name be related to Mâsu, the name of the mountain in the *Epic of Gilgamesh* where the seven Apkallu alighted after the flood, and one of the oldest names of Mount Ararat, the resting place of the ark, according to the Bible? [11]

OF RED ANTS AND ANUNAKI

One fascinating aspect of the Hopi tradition is their vivid recollection of helpful outsiders, especially at times of extreme crisis, the most alluring being the Ant People. What on earth possessed the Hopi to describe them this way?

The Ant People are associated with the color red, but whether this is purely symbolic or descriptive of a physical characteristic, such as red hair, is not known for certain. However, Red Ant People are also central to Maya legends, which link them to the building of temple cities, and *saqbe*, the ruler-straight spirit roads, all of which took place during the time of First Creation. The traditions of Central America state how the Red Ant People possessed magical powers which enabled them to control the laws of nature, and how they used sound to move and raise megaliths to create stupendous temples in the course of a single night. The Yucatec called them *Chac Zay Uincob* (Red Ant Men) because they labored to create order in nature, just as industrious red ants do.[12]

To the Maya and Hopi, Red Ant People were linked with Orion, specifically its belt, whose central stars are regarded as the tripartite body of an ant. But it's their terrestrial link that reveals their place in the list of antediluvian gods, specifically a group in the Middle East, for the Hopi word for ant is *aanu*, while the word *nàaki* means reddish yellow sand; the derivative *naakwatsim* means 'friend'. One variation, *aanu-nàa-kii*, literally means 'ant-father-home'. Whichever interpretation one cares to pick, the overall description of ant people is father figures with a complexion akin to reddish-yellow sand, or who originate from such an environment, such as the Middle East. And it gets better. The offspring of the Anunaki are described as *nemalah,* an old Hebrew term for ant. [13]

The Hopi recall the leader of the Ant People as an individual by the name Anu-Sinom (ant man or being). In the legend, this unusual humanoid is described as generous and hardworking, willing to provide food to the people and teach them methods of food preservation so they could ride out the prolonged upheaval taking place outside their protective cave.[14] This is not as far fetched as it may seem because vast man-made cave systems exist throughout the world. One excellent example, Derinkuyu, lies two hundred miles west of Göbekli Tepe and once comfortably housed 20,000 people while they patiently waited out catastrophes caused primarily by mass coronal ejections.[15]

WATCHING THE KATSINA

Straddling the Arizona-New Mexico border are another ancient and equally fascinating people, the Zuni. Just like Sumerian and Aymara, Zuni language is not related to any other, it appears to have been invented, a designed language spoken for at least 7000 years. It also contains a high proportion of Japanese words. Zuni and Japanese people share the same frequency of Type B blood as well as near-identical flood traditions, the only difference being that the Zuni categorically state they arrived in North America from a sunken land somewhere in the Pacific.

Ant People also feature prominently in Zuni tradition; an excellent life-size depiction of them is painted in red ochre on a wall in Sego Canyon, Utah, a far less strenuous trek than Horseshoe Canyon. They are credited with helping the people relocate after the flood to the region around modern-day Zuni village; the Zuni even have a term of endearment for them — Lookers.[16]

There's a sensational observation made in the tradition. It turns out the Zuni gave them the sobriquet Ant People because of the antennae sticking out of their helmets.[17]

If you find antennae and helmets out of place in the desert southwest then you'll love the unusual dancers called *katsinam*, a Hopi collective term for 'spirit beings', although the phrase isn't limited to an ethereal entity, as one might expect. The Navajo consider *katsinam* to be real beings with a more developed mystical outlook, to whom they refer as Air-Spirit People: "They are unlike five-fingered earth-surface people who come into the world today, live on the ground a while, die at a ripe old age, and then leave the world. They are people who travel in the air and fly swiftly like the wind." [18]

Certainly it's an odd choice of word because the syllable *ka* is not native to Hopi, it appears to have been imported from a visiting Egyptian, it is the word for 'soul' or 'spirit'. The etymological root of *katsina* is speculative yet suggestive: it may be a compound of the words *kátci* (spread out or surface of the Earth) and *náa* (father),[19] in essence an 'overseer of the Earth', a father figure. As for the plural *katsinam*, it applies as much to nature spirits as it does to physical intermediaries who possess a working knowledge of the laws of nature and how to bend them — Lookers such as Massau'u and members of his entourage, who similarly assisted another tribe, the Hisat-Sinom, better known as Anasazi.

The *katsinam* are commemorated in art and ritual wearing unusual and technical-looking headgear, sometimes with what appear to be antennae, certainly not the type of practical garb one wears in the extreme heat of desert plateaus. Hopi elder Don Talayesva offers an eye-opening portrayal of the relationship between the *katsinam* and the original people of this land: "My fathers and uncles showed me their ancestral masks and explained that long ago the real Katsinam had come regularly to Oraibi [Third Mesa] and had danced in the plaza. They explained that since the people had become so wicked — since there were now so many Two-Hearts in the world — the Katsinam stopped coming in person and sent their spirits to enter the masks on dance days." [20]

Cultural traditions agree that *katsinam* appeared at the crossing point between the destruction and creation of world ages, that they inhabited two worlds, and traveled here from very far away. They are regarded as ancestors but not progenitors of the people during the migrations after the great flood.[21] The unique nature of the *katsina* dances suggests an immortalization of physical people whose ideas, dress and appearance became ritualized and remembered because these benevolent outsiders were instrumental in the cultural, civic and architectural development of the Hopi and Anasazi during their time of origination. Even more surprising is how so many petroglyphs in northern Arizona depict the *katsinam* in a rectangular format with arms upraised, like a kind of hallmark bearing a passing resemblance to the Orion constellation.

Zuni tradition brings a layer of understanding to the relationship between *katsinam* and the "flying shields." The Zuni claim the *katsina* ceremony commemorates pilots communicating with each other, each *katsina* representing real people who once were referred to as

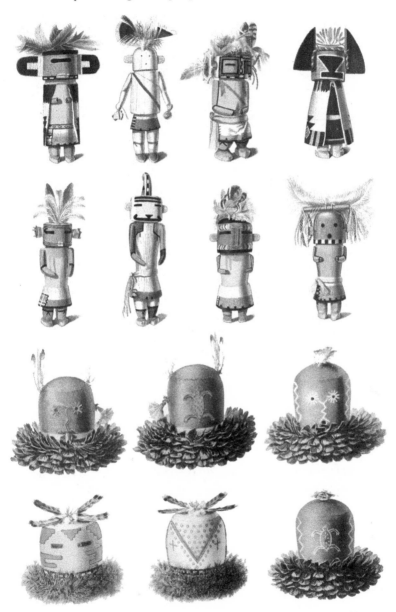

Seen together, these katcina dolls and Zuni masks of gods and goddesses offer a vivid, if stylistic portrait of the Red Ant People.

gods.[22] As for the flying shields themselves, Hopi legends refer to them as *paatuwvota* — literally 'magic flying shield used as vehicle' — whose derivative, *paatsöviw*, is an insect that skates on the surface of water. That paints quite a picture of vessels hovering over the sea.[23] These aerial craft have a curious parallel in the Indian sacred text *Visuddhi-Magga*, where an "air-katsina" is described in the context of a trance-inducing tool, one of ten items inherited from the time of gods.[24]

One of my favorite stories featuring the flying shields is that of a young Hopi bride accompanying her *katsina* husband back to her village: "This time on their way home, the two were going to travel by flying shield. Together they climbed onto the shield and the girl firmly shut her eyes. As the shield lifted off, the katsinam all gave out a boisterous yell. The spectacle was incredible; every sort of katsina conceivable was present. All of a sudden as the couple flew along, flashes of lightning were visible in the air and the rumble of thunder could be heard. When the shield rose higher, drizzle began to fall. The katsinam were now accompanying them. They actually followed the pair in the form of clouds... Customarily, a bride is returned to her residence in the morning. Therefore the parents had headed to the edge of the mesa at this time to look out. Looking down from the rim of the mesa, they saw an incredible number of people coming across the plain. To their amazement all were katsinam, singing and crying out their calls." [25]

THE WATCHERS OF WALPI

The Hopi believe themselves to be one of the first inhabitants of the American continent, and certainly their village of Oraibi is the oldest continuously occupied settlement in the United States.[26] Two other centers of habitation cling to vertiginous, six hundred-foot high mesas whose alignment bears a passing resemblance to the belt of Orion, and together with other main cult centers, form a close resemblance to the entire constellation across the American southwest.[27]

It is the village of Walpi that is of greatest interest to our quest. Located on First Mesa, the name literally means Place of the Watchers.[28] Referred to as *Tuuwalaqa* (Protectors), one of their central figures is an individual called Sótuknang (Heart of the Sky God), a messenger of the creator god

Taiowa, whose mission was to travel to Earth and create a landscape fit for habitation after the flood.[29] Obviously this now establishes a direct link between the Hopi, the Watchers and the Anunaki, and opens up all kinds of possibilities. For one, if the Watchers and the *katcinam* are one and the same people, were they literally capable of inhabiting two worlds, as the Hopi and Zuni suggest? Is the collective term coined by the Hopi and Zuni for these individuals — Star People — merely a metaphor, or is it an accurate description of their astronomical knowledge as well as ability to travel among the stars? And if so, are these Star People the same as the Starwalkers — the Urukehu of New Zealand, Easter Island and Tiwanaku?

It seems as though Hopi and Zuni traditions are finally intertwining a number of loose threads, so let's see where the association with the stars takes us.

The peaceful Hopi people believed their ancestors came from outside the Earth, specifically the Pleiades, and it is said the general demeanour of Pleiadians is reflected in Hopi lifestyle. Dakota legends give similar weight to this star cluster – Tiyami they call it, their ancestral homeland. The Cree people believed that in a time before history, their ancestors arrived from the stars in spirit form, only to become humans on Earth. The Lakota speak of mysterious celestial beings that manifest as spheres of light and often choose particular children to follow them on a journey through space and time. No wonder Native Americans perceive the issue of alien visitation in a spiritual manner, as Plains Cree author Stephane Wuttunee explains: "[My people] give far greater attention to the seeking of the spiritual understanding of things rather than going after "the truth" as people from dominant cultures do. This is part of the reason why we tend to stand back and view or listen at first rather than bare in with questions or take the hard, direct approach." [30]

Growing up in a tight-knit community, Stephane listened attentively to the stories passed down by the elders of his tribe. He says they spoke of "distant relations and Star People living amongst the stars many times, mainly around campfires and during traditional ceremonies. Far from being anything to be feared, Star People was just another term I grew up around. I remember listening in awe and fascination at the thought of us having relations that lived off and outside our world, and sometimes spoke to them in my silent moments at night. I wanted to know who they were and what they looked like, if they had families like us, etc... It wasn't until my later teens that I discovered that people from the dominant cultures were talking about the same "people" as my elders did, though each side's sense of perception of these people seemed radically different from one another." [31]

One common characteristic among all the gods of the flood we've encountered so far is their advanced knowledge of astronomy, and the sentiment is shared by many indigenous people of North America: "My people tell of Star People who came to us many generations ago," recalls Richard Wagamese of the Wabaseemoong First People. "The Star people brought spiritual teachings and stories and maps of the cosmos and they offered these freely. They were kind, loving and set a great example. When they left us, my people say there was loneliness like no other. If Star People did come to the Ojibway, where did they go? Where did they come from? Who brought teachings to them? What scientific magic did they own that allowed them to make such an incredible journey – and is it possible for us?" [32]

This puts a better perspective on the aforementioned flying shields. Native Americans openly talked about them long before the recent ancient alien craze. The late Oglala Sioux holy man Black Elk describes one of his personal experiences: "So when I went to vision quest, that disk came from above. The scientists call that a... Unidentified Flying Object, but that's a joke, see? Because they are not trained, they lost contact with the wisdom, power and gift. So that disk landed on top of me. It was concave, and there was another one on top of that. It was silent, but it lit and luminesced like neon lights. Even the sacred robes there were luminesced, and those tobacco ties lying there lit up like little light bulbs. Then these little people came, but each little group spoke a different language. They could read minds, and I could read their minds. I could read them. So there was silent communication. You could read it, like when you read silent symbols in a book. So we were able to communicate... They are human, so I welcomed them. I said, "Welcome, Welcome..." [33]

All this brings a little twist to our adventure. We have been looking all along for terrestrial homelands for these ancient architects, but it appears we need to expand our gaze. Whoever these individuals were or where they came from, they certainly possessed an understanding,

Flying shields depicted on a petroglyph panel. Three Mesas, Arizona.

a technology even, that was far and above that of the average ancient human. But why should a group of Watchers have felt compelled to stay after the flood and assist in rebuilding Earth's decimated population, then disappearing, leaving future communication to be made through more subtle means such as telepathy and shamanic journeying?

I was sharing my thoughts with Clifford Mahooty, who has himself experienced close encounters with these beings on many occasions and feels they are nothing less than benevolent people. Then, in the middle of a conversation about the great kiva at Chaco Canyon, which I've always felt to be oversized for its intended purpose, Clifford remarked, "That's because it was never a kiva. That's what archeologists think. If they'd asked us we would have told them the real purpose. It was never used for ceremony, it was used as a space port." [34]

104 DEGREES IN THE CANYON

By the time I reached the Ghost Panel, Horseshoe Canyon was becoming toasty. Beneath a vertical limestone canopy, seven hooded figures in red ochre stand alongside a distinctive eighth. They are tall, elegant. Amid the stillness of the canyon floor, the silence is deafening. Yes, I had encountered them three times on my travels, and yes, the Hopi and Zuni are right, they communicate in a very unusual way. One experience was during an unplanned visit to Kephren's pyramid, when the same hooded, cloaked people emerged from the walls of the Kings Chamber and, as three of my colleagues will testify, we saw them as clear as daylight amid absolute darkness. The full account is given in my book *The Divine Blueprint.* The experience has stayed with me to this day, partly because I wasn't expecting it, partly because it proves the indigenous traditions are correct, but mostly because it is as humbling as it is overwhelming.

A few years later I would take a private group to the Kings Chamber during one of my tours to sacred places. As I began a meditation I had the unexpected pleasure of watching the same figures reappear and position themselves behind each of the sixteen participants. Later at dinner, I asked for their impressions. Without prompting, a quarter of them felt a tall person stand behind, arms outstretched, and the feeling of being protected if they were to fall backward, like a sign of trust.

It's exactly how I'd seen it.

Clifford was right, I did know the people pictured on the Horseshoe Canyon panel, they refer to themselves as Watchers.

Lookers, indeed!

KNOWLEDGE OF THE FEW

My mentor, the late historian and antiquarian John Michell once argued that prehistoric monuments all over the world "were all designed in accordance with one scheme of proportion in units of measurement which are everywhere the same... relics of a former elemental science, founded on principles of which we are now ignorant... At some period, thousands of years ago, almost every corner of the world was visited by people with a particular task to accomplish. With the help of some remarkable power, by means of which they could cut and raise enormous blocks of stone, these [people] created vast astronomical instruments, circles of erect pillars, pyramids, underground tunnels, cyclopean stone platforms, all linked together by a network of tracks and alignments, whose course from horizon to horizon was marked by stones, mounds and earthworks." [35]

This "former elemental science" is precisely what people like the Hopi

Lookers with distinctive antennae. Sego Canyon, Utah.

and the Tamil describe as having been part of a development of innovation during the Younger Dryas, in complete contradiction to the backward-cave-dweller-human model expounded by historians. Echoes of this knowledge are all around if one cares to look, and it begins to explain the spontaneous flowering of human civilization around 8000 BC. Humans suddenly discovered civilization because it had already been established before the flood.

To illustrate the point, during the reign of pharaoh Geb — one of the original Neterw — it is said he came into possession of a golden box long protected inside a fortress somewhere along Egypt's eastern frontier. This talisman contained effects belonging to his grandfather Ra. The story goes that, once he ascended the throne, Geb ordered said box to be brought to him to be unsealed. In hindsight it proved to be a careless move because the moment the box was opened, "the breath of the divine serpent" sent out a bolt of fire of such force it struck dead all Geb's attendants and gave the pharaoh what appears to be third-degree burns.[36] The tale is remarkably similar to the later Hebrew story of the Ark of the Covenant, so much so that it makes one wonder whether this was the same device — Palestine and the Levant having once been part of the kingdom of Egypt — or whether there were many golden boxes of a scientific nature passed on from an earlier and technologically advanced culture. In both the Egyptian and Hebrew narratives each box contained a rod (Ra and Aaron's respectively) and both killed or maimed anyone who failed to handle its contents without understanding the instruction manual, as the Philistine guards found out when they contracted hemorrhoids.

The priests of Sais once confided in Solon, "in our temples we have preserved from the earliest times a written record of any great or splendid achievement or notable event which has come to our ears."[37] Fifteen hundred years later the Egyptian historian Ibn Abd El Hakim was still remarking on how so many of the temples were designed to protect the ancient knowledge and technology of the antediluvian gods. With regard to what was placed inside the pyramids, he describes, "arms that did not rust, and glass which might be bent but not broken... an idol of black granite... when anyone looked upon him, he heard on one side of him a voice which took away his sense, so that he fell prostate upon his face and did not cease until he died." He further describes another protective device, a statue to which one was magically drawn "until he stuck to it, and could not be separated from it until such time as he died." [38]

When caliph Al-Ma'mum and his men attempted to enter the Great Pyramid in the same era, they did so by blasting their way in because by then no one knew where the entrance was located. Only by blind luck and dynamite did they dislodge a limestone plug securing the ascending passage leading to the interior of the building, only to face a further succession of massive granite plugs. The building was still sealed. Ma'mum hadn't been driven by the promise of monetary treasure, but the certainty it contained objects from a high civilization, such as exotic metals, spells that held power over nature and, as we saw earlier, "a secret chamber containing maps and tables of the celestial and terrestrial spheres. Although they were said to have been made in antediluvian times, they were supposed to be of great accuracy." [39] Like the pharaoh Khufu three thousand years before him, Ma'mum had sought out another temple somewhere on the Giza plateau said to contain a room called Inventory, where the books and objects once owned by Twt were stored. Like Khufu, he was to be thwarted.

Many pyramids in Egypt are problematic for the pyramids-are-burial-chambers cartel. The Pyramid of Sekhemkhet at Saqqara was found completely sealed along with its 'sarcophagus' which, when opened, was found to be empty. The Pyramid of Meidum was likewise sealed and contained nothing inside, not even a box. Perhaps the treasures that glory hounds such as Ma'mum sought were the buildings themselves, because anyone interested in numbers or astronomy is able to extract all manner of useful information. Take the Great Pyramid, for example, it encodes the precise value of the Earth's polar radius. It is a scale model of the northern hemisphere on a scale of 1:43,200, a number deliberately chosen to reflect the seconds in a 12-hour day, making the building time-commensurate as well. The number is not an accident, it reflects the Earth's full axial tilt (21,600 years x2), a recurring number expressed in myths as 432, 4320, 432,000 and so on. From its base divisor of 72 we can derive the age of each house of the zodiac, 2160 years. Twelve houses in the zodiac equals 25,920 years, otherwise known as the Great Year or the Precession of the Equinoxes.[40] And this is just a quick synopsis of one antediluvian building.

The smaller pyramid, the one attributed to Menkaure, is especially puzzling. The lower sixteen courses are faced with megalithic blocks of red granite, interlocked in a jigsaw pattern much like those at Saqsayhuaman, and features the same protruding knobs. Its descending passage and innermost chamber, which are fitted inside solid bedrock, are made from chocolate granite composed of feldspar, mica and quartz, an extremely hard material to work with under any circumstances. Mica was the material of choice in Central American temples. An extensive layer of sheet mica was found sandwiched between two upper levels of the Pyramid of the Sun at Teotihuacan; more sheets were discovered nearby in the aptly named Mica Temple. Two additional 90 square feet pieces were discovered under a thick slab floor, and of a specific elemental variety found four thousand miles away in Brazil.[41]

Mica is generally used as an electrical insulator and capacitor, a clue as to the ultimate purpose of the buildings.

Inside Menkaure's pyramid, ancient architects made it even harder for themselves by allowing little room in which to maneuver the huge blocks of stone — from as little as two feet down to a few inches. There is no headroom in which to place lifting equipment, nor is the inner chamber large enough for more than a handful of people, who would be physically incapable of lifting the stones anyway. The only possible explanation is that the granite blocks were hydraulically raised into place. Which begs a further question: why line the interior of these passages and chambers, which are carved out of solid bedrock, the ceiling is not likely to collapse?

Rumours of technology from a bygone era and protected from damage

Part of the lower course of red granite is still attached to the pyramid attributed to Menkaure. This hardest of rocks is eroded by water, in a region that hasn't seen significant rainfall in over 6000 years. Note the same protruding knobs common to Andean temples. Giza.

by the great flood are rife throughout Egypt. When Setnau, one of the sons of Ramses II, came across the story that Twt had hidden one of his books in a repository somewhere near the Giza Plateau, he set out with his brother to find it: "On the third day they found it... went down into the place where the tomb was. When the two brothers came into the tomb they found it to be brilliantly lit by light which came forth from the book."[42] It can be argued that the story is metaphorical, the Mysteries of the ancients were always veiled in this manner, and since we are talking about a book of wisdom it is not inconceivable that what shone from the book was something akin to light — enlightenment. Conversely, it is worth remembering the earlier story of the antediluvian Yim who was provided inside his ark with a 'window, self-shining from within'.[43] "There are uncreated lights and created lights,"[44] explains the god Ahura Mazda, who gave Yim other goodies such as a jeweled glass throne or chariot capable of flight and a miraculous cup in which one could see everything that was happening anywhere in the world.[45] Over in Central America, Quetzalcoatl's nemesis, the Tula leader Tezcatlipoca, is said to have had at his disposal a kind of smoking mirror which enabled him to see the activities of men and gods from afar, much like a cross between close-circuit television and radar. It was made from a stone called Tezcat, and from it, other mirrors were manufactured to be used by magicians trained in the art of divination.[46]

Statues of Viracocha depict him holding two unusual objects, although they are so worn they cannot be properly identified. In central Mexico, a better-preserved group of nine-foot tall statues of Tula warriors are depicted in the same upright pose. Legends state how these gods — called *Atlantes* — armed themselves with *xiuhcoatl* (fire serpents) which emitted burning rays capable of piercing and dismembering a human body. I wonder whether this may have been the device with which many of those megaliths were cut and carved like butter, after all, in Cuzco and Saqsayhuaman the stones show clear signs of having been subjected to intense heat.

The central argument in many texts and myths maintains that the events which shook the Earth 11,000 years ago resulted from the abuse of power and the careless sharing of inappropriate technology with comparatively immature humans. The culprits are said to have been a group of renegade Watchers. Before this abuse took place we are informed that the knowledge was willingly passed along to responsible individuals who would preserve it and share with survivors after the Earth was wiped clean. On this matter, the Estonian scholar Amar Annus elegantly points out, "One way to preserve the knowledge was to inscribe pre-flood wisdom in its entirety on different tablets or stones and either bury them or to install the knowledge carriers on high places to escape the perdition." [47]

In Mesopotamian tradition, such a divine source of restricted information was the *Tablet of Destinies*, originally in the possession of seven Apkallu,[48] which corresponds to the divine secrets in the *Pargod* in *3 Enoch*. Enoch was probably describing this momentous occasion when he wrote in his own words: "Then the Lord [Anu] called one of his Archangels named Uriel, who was the most learned of them all, and said: 'Bring out the books from my library and give Enoch a pen for speedy writing, and tell him what the books are about'. And Uriel hurried and brought me the books, smelling of myrrh, and handed me a pen." [49]

Atlantes with their fire serpents. Tula, Mexico.

Another panel of Lookers/Watchers with the snaking emblem, identifying them as People of the Serpent. Horseshoe Canyon, Arizona.

Comet over Mount Taranaki, New Zealand. Indigenous people
the world over are wary of passing space rocks.

THE TERRIBLE TAURIDS

Peruvians need little excuse to take to the streets to celebrate, be it a festival, a notable figure or religious occasion, in fact, one would be forgiven for believing an underground movement exists solely for the invention of obscure saints. One day I was walking through old Cuzco looking for misplaced megaliths among its residential buildings — I found an entire wall inside a gift shop — when it became progressively more difficult to get from one side of the street to **17** the other. The population had tripled, a sea of people flowed towards the central plaza. Of course! The beginning of November, everyone must be out celebrating the fertility festival popularly known as May Day. Peru lies in the southern hemisphere, the calendars are reversed.

In Europe, May Day is a Christian feast day, cunningly usurped from the Celts who'd been practicing it thousands of years earlier as Beltane. Its mirrored opposite is Samhain, the cross-quarter in the solar calendar marking the fallow days when nature has yielded its bounty and retreats into a period of gestation from which life is born anew on the winter solstice. This too was usurped and renamed All Souls Day, that annoying November ritual when peer pressure forces intelligent people on the evening prior to participate in a gruesome desecration of children's otherwise healthy teeth.

But this was not the case in Peru. Everyone was out commemorating Aya Marcay Killa, literally 'the month of carrying corpses'. They were honoring the dead. To confuse matters, it's been traditionally regarded as a water or rain ceremony, yet November is already the wet season in the Andes, so why the need for a rain festival when it is already pouring?

Besides, up to the time of the Inka, a second festival took place in May to honor the spirit world, exactly as it is done in the northern hemisphere every November.

Two feasts commemorating the dead? What is going on here?

DAYS OF THE DEAD

This calendrical mix-up is not an anomaly restricted to the Andes. Before colonization by Catholics, the people of Tonga and other Pacific Islands south of the equator also held a remembrance for deceased ancestors early in November, as did Australian aborigines, in ceremonies culminating around the seventeenth of the month; Hindu, Persians and Japanese did likewise in the northern hemisphere. In Yucatan and Guatemala, and specifically the Lake Petén region associated with the Itzá, it is tradition to bake cakes from the very best corn and hang them from branches of sacred trees or at crossroads and isolated nooks, typically around the 17th of November.

All this is most odd because places in opposite hemispheres shouldn't be holding common observances in the same month. And it gets stranger. The ancient remembrance of the dead doesn't just occur in every corner of the world, it does so when the Pleiades occupy a conspicuous position in the sky that has nothing to do with their folkloric role as heralds of spring and the planting season.[1] At one time in India — north of the equator — November was regarded as the Month of the Pleiades, despite the Pleiades not being prominent in the sky until April. This makes even less sense when one considers that every two thousand years this seven-star cluster rises in a different month,[2] and yet the November festival remains constant. Since the timing is of no practical use to people such as farmers, who rely on the exalted position of the stars to mark the return of Spring, is it possible the Indians might have been commemorating an event in which the Pleiades played a pivotal role?

In Arizona, on the first day of the New Moon in November — also called the Initiates or Hawk Moon — members of the Hopi *kiva* prepare, fast and cleanse before undertaking a private ceremony called Wúwutcim. On a symbolic level it marks the time when the Earth lies cold and barren, and by extension the individual. But there's more to it. Wúwutcim marks the beginning of the new ceremonial year and recalls the first phase of Creation — a ritual generally reserved for the winter solstice. During the restricted ceremony, an elder representing Masau'u shares with young initiates the teachings of this antediluvian Watcher, while the *kachinam* appear for a brief time on Earth. In many ways it is similar to the feast of Samhain, when the barrier between worlds is thinner and honor is given to ancestors and protective spirits. The Hopi ceremony begins with a New Fire ritual the moment the belt of Orion appears above the *kiva*,[3] and closes sixteen days later when the Pleiades appear in the same position at midnight. On the seventeenth day, the entire village celebrates.

The Pleiades are generally regarded by ancient cultures as a group of heavenly luminaries dispensing knowledge and wisdom. Temples were raised throughout the world in honor of this cluster of faint stars and their positive influence upon human affairs, so it is both odd and contradictory to find the Pleiades also looked upon as the seven Stars of Death — as they were throughout Persia and Mesopotamia, where November was called *Mordad* (Angel of Death), the month when the festival of the dead culminated with the ascendency of the Pleiades at midnight on the seventeenth of the month. In Egypt it was performed as a three-day festival dedicated to At-Hyr (Hathor) in commemoration of a world-destroying deluge and the souls who perished in it,[4] a stance also adopted in the Hebrew account of the flood: "Now the deluge was caused by the male waters from the sky meeting the female waters which issued forth from the ground. The holes in the sky by which the upper waters escaped were made by God when he removed stars out of the constellation of the Pleiades; and in order to stop this torrent of rain, God had afterwards to bung up the two holes with a couple of stars borrowed from the constellation of the Bear. That is why the Bear runs after the Pleiades to this day; she wants her children back, but she will never get them till after the Last Day." [5] Strange how the same story appears in the Aboriginal tribal lore *Water Girls of the Pleiades,* who emerge from a hole in the sky in Orion prior to a major catastrophe.[6] The *Talmud* also contains a legend associating the Pleiades with the world flood: "When the Holy One wished to bring the deluge upon the world, he took two stars out of the Pleiades and thus let the deluge loose," [7] a passage eerily reminiscent of the Andean flood account of the farmer looking up at the sky and watching "angry stars gathering close to the Sun."

Later, misinformed Aztecs took the association to its extreme. They regarded the rising of the Pleiades at midnight every fifty-two years as a cosmic sign that the sky was falling and the world was about to end, and sacrificed up to 50,000 people a day to forestall the event.

In the south Pacific the cluster is at its most prominent towards April and May, and yet in the Society Islands and other cultures, where the Pleiades were known as Matari'I, the Festival of the Dead began at the end of October to welcome the god of paradise in commemorating those who had departed and to share in the joy of the living. At the end of the occasion, the Breath of God was instilled once more across the Earth.[8] That was prior to Christian missionaries arriving on Tahiti to change the calendar and put an end to all the fun.[9]

The question now is, what took place so long ago in the region of the Pleiades during November that made this star cluster synonymous with death in so many parts of the planet?

UNWANTED VISITORS FROM SPACE

The forty-two books written by the antediluvian god Twt were said to cover every facet of knowledge.[10] Naturally the tomes were zealously guarded and handed down from one remote generation to another, from the Followers of Horus to the pharaohs, and maintained by the priesthood at Iwnw. Twt's particular focus appears to have been astronomy and geography, in essence corroborating Plato's remark about the Egyptians having carefully observed stars for ten thousand years. Why would anyone be so obsessed with marking the motions of the heavens to a level far in excess of what is required for agriculture or navigation? Likewise the Itzá, the Olmec and the Maya assiduously marked time spans covering over 140,000 years, too long to be of practical use for a species with an average life span of seventy years. It's a fixation common to all the gods we've encountered so far.

The following statistic might clarify things. It is estimated that an average of 200,000 tons of debris falls onto the Earth from interplanetary space every year.[11] Hardly surprising, then, that even as late as the 7th century the Chinese astronomer Li Ch'un Feng was compelled to describe comets as "vile stars. Every time they appear... something happens to wipe out the old and establish the new." Maori peoples didn't care much for such space junk either, they looked upon a Tunui-a-te-ika (comet) as a tormenting demon whose appearance was a precursor to certain death,[12] while the Sumerians put such incoming projectiles into perspective with the word *agh-hu-bua* — great celestial inundation.

The Native American Ojibwa, like the aboriginal cultures of Australia, have a long memory of events that took place deep in prehistory, such as the recurring orbit of a large comet whose tail sows unimaginable destruction across the Earth: "The star with the long, wide tail is going to destroy the world some day when it comes low again. That's the comet called Long-Tailed Heavenly Climbing Star. It came down here once, thousands of years ago. Just like the Sun, it had radiation and burning heat in its tail. The comet burned everything to the ground. There wasn't a thing left. Indian people were here before that happened, living on the earth. But things were wrong; a lot of people had abandoned the spiritual path. The holy spirit warned them a long time before the comet came. Medicine men told everyone to prepare. Things were wrong with nature on earth... Then that comet went through here... It flew so low the tail scorched the earth... The comet made a different world. After, the survival was hard work. The weather was colder than before." [13]

The Navajo have an even older recollection. One of their sky gods streaked down from heaven as a flaming serpent and left a calling card in the shape of Meteor Crater in Arizona. The impact is estimated to be 50,000 years old.

The word *comet* is used as a general term, but it is useful to distinguish between the types of rocks flying around in space. The general agreement among astronomers is that a comet consists of a nucleus of ice and dust, and develops a tail of gas and dust when approaching the Sun. By comparison, an asteroid is a small rocky body orbiting the Sun, although 'small' is a relative term, some asteroids are 600 miles in diameter. A meteor, on the other hand, is a body of matter that enters the Earth's atmosphere and disintegrates, while a meteorite is the type that makes full body contact.

The latter is the type that concerns us.

Mounting evidence suggests the Earth crossed a stream of cosmic debris around 10,800 BC containing fragments of a once massive planetary object, now disintegrated, portions of which crashed to the ground and triggered the Younger Dryas,[14] the irony being that Earth crossed the same path 1100 years later and closed said glacial period,[15] when "seven burning mountains hurtled towards the Earth," to put it in the words of Enoch the scribe.[16]

A scientific paper from the University of California provides a visual dimension to events leading up to the Younger Dryas. The scientists involved were examining the sudden mass extinction of camels, mastodons, horses and sabre-toothed cats in North America, along with a major decimation of human population around 11,000 BC. The paper posits that meteorite impacts in the northern hemisphere, many smashing directly into the great ice sheets, were responsible for the abundance of nanodiamonds distributed over 20 million square miles across the face of the Earth. This material is produced by the kind of temperature variations, pressure and oxygen levels associated with an extraterrestrial collision which leaves a thin, black, carbon-rich layer in subsurface soil. Additional glassy materials such as cosmic impact spherules, high-temperature melt-glass, grapelike soot clusters, carbon spherules and platinum were also formed at temperatures in excess of 2200 degrees Celsius, all consistent with a meteorite impact. Altogether the field of debris covers 10% of the planet.[17] Thirty-two sites on three continents were analysed, revealing a large concentration in North America and Western Europe. As one of the scientists summed up, "Our hypothesis challenges some existing paradigms within several disciplines, including impact dynamics, archaeology, palaeontology and palaeocean-ography/palaeoclimatology, all affected by this relatively recent cosmic impact." [18] To give a sense of perspective, one impact crater discovered beneath the Hiawatha Glacier in Greenland measures nineteen miles in diameter and was produced by a mile-wide object.[19]

This is what triggered the Younger Dryas. For evidence of the closing event one can look to the large meteorite craters dating from 10,000 - 8,000 BC found along the eastern and south-eastern seaboard of North America. They are hard to miss, there are over one hundred thousand of them, concentrated along the coastline between Florida and Virginia. The field of impact is called the Carolina Bays and its discovery dates back to 1931 when a new survey of the eastern seaboard called for a photogrammetric experiment, for which a company specializing in aerial photography was commissioned. When the films were enlarged and examined in stereo they revealed vivid images of an impact site composed of gigantic mud-filled craters, so much so that pilots looking at them drew comparisons to the bomb craters of battlefields from the First World War.

The area is scarred with three thousand troughs, half of them longer than 1300 feet, one hundred longer than 5250 feet. In total they cover an elongated elliptical area of 63,500 square miles. The longitudinal axes of the craters run parallel, indicating the descending meteorites must have been traveling in the same direction and, given the shape of the craters' thrust walls along the southeast, suggests the space rocks arrived from the northwest. Since the craters are both elliptical and circular, the indication is of a descending body that disintegrated and exploded, leaving two different sets of impressions along with a mess of overlapping craters.[20] The sand around the crater rims also displays evidence of excessive heat caused by the impacts.

Naturally the consequences were immediate, even on the opposite coast of North America where more than one billion fish were found petrified on the former seabed off the coast of California around the period of impact.

It seems Enoch's description of "seven burning mountains" was a tad understated, it was nothing short of a swarm.

EARTH'S DANCE WITH DEATH

The *Mahabharata* paints the offending meteorite that generated the global flood in graphic terms as a horrific one-eyed bird with one wing in the night sky, screaming and vomiting blood. According to various world accounts the Earth was subsequently covered in a thick, chocking

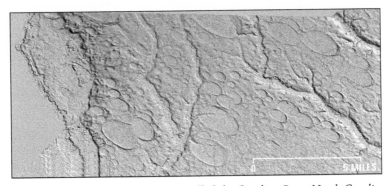

LIDAR image of oval impact craters called the Carolina Bays. North Carolina

dust, accompanied by rough winds, and fireballs that crashed with hissing sounds. Darkness covered the land. Survivors used torches to light their way at midday. Mountains collapsed onto the plains. It was said to have appeared during the Indian month of Kartitika, the middle of October to early November, and was said to have obscured the normal view of the Pleiades. There is only one known culprit who arrives like clockwork from this sector of the sky at the same time each year: the Taurid meteor shower.

The Taurids are named after their radiant point in Taurus, the constellation standing between the Pleiades and Orion, from where they are seen to emerge in the sky. Due to the gravitational perturbations of planets, Jupiter in particular, the Taurids have spread out over time to become two separate showers: the Southern Taurids, active from approximately September 10 to November 20, are the remains of Comet Encke, while the Northern Taurids, active from approximately October 20 to December 10, originate from an asteroid. Still, the Taurids are believed to be remnants of an even larger body that disintegrated within the last twenty or thirty thousand years, otherwise the asteroids would have spread around the inner planetary system and no longer be recognizable as a stream.[21] Even so it is still the largest stream in the inner solar system. It takes two weeks for the Earth to pass through it — a timeframe that coincides with the period allocated to ceremonies performed by people such as the Hopi. Every late October to mid-November the Earth plays a dangerous game of Hit and Run while we stare up at the night sky, marvelling at a spectacle we believe to be benign but in reality comes with a history of devastation that would make a Hollywood special effects team blush.

And now for the second instalment of this uplifting story. Because the Taurids' twenty-million mile wide trail of debris follows an orbital path, the Earth replays this game once more every June, except this time the stakes are a higher, because cross sections of the stream approach from the Earth's daytime side and cannot be visually observed.

The Taurid stream has a cycle of activity that peaks roughly every 2,500 to 3,000 years, when its core passes nearer to Earth and produces either more intense showers or total annihilation. It's pure luck. Sometimes Earth wins, but on occasion, it loses. On June 25, 1178, a monk at Canterbury Cathedral witnessed a fragment of the Taurids colliding with the Moon, creating what would become known as the Girodano Bruno crater. The impact sent out a tail of debris tall enough to be seen for several nights. The date coincides with a series of notable meteorite impacts on Earth catalogued by Chinese astronomers of the period, some impacting New Zealand to form the Tapaniu craters on the South Island. The event was recorded by the Waitaha, who describe the catastrophic forest fires that led to a mass extinction of bird species.

The most recent Taurid event took place in June 30, 1908, when a fireball streaked across the northern hemisphere and exploded over Tungusta, Siberia. A Russian scientific paper published an analysis of results of micro-samples recovered from the peat bog near the epicenter and revealed the origin to be meteoric.[22]

Since the end of the Younger Dryas, the Earth has been on the receiving end of dozens of such minor hits, reminders of the importance of monitoring the sky and, if necessary, developing inconveniently long calendars, and hard-wiring the warning into standing megaliths or the walls of massive temples.

Why were the ancients afraid of comets? Because they had reason to be.

Hopi Snake Clan member enters kiva. Arizona.

The Hopi village of Walpi stands on one of three mesas that appear to mirror the belt stars of Orion. Arizona.

ORION THE UBIQUITOUS

"The Watchers could take on human form when they wanted to."
— Book of Enoch

Yucatan. January.

Uxmal is another of my 'second homes'. The centrepiece of this temple city is its distinctive curved Pyramid of the Magician, erected in a single night, so the legend goes. Like other organic temples it grew over time, adapting to the changing skies, becoming **18** five pyramids in one. Its grandiose staircase is lined with the inescapable effigies of Cha'ac, God of Rain. An enclosure skirts the base, built in a style more common to Saqqara and Angkor than Yucatan. Out of the blue, my good colleague Miguel Angel Vergara tells me, "There's a phrase associated with this temple, a mantra used to connect with and open the records embedded inside: Nak-He-Nah-Tun, it means Pyramid of Precious Stone of the Children of the Turtle. The Children of the Turtle is humans."

"The phrase sounds remarkably like Akh-en-Aten," I replied.

Now, what would the name of an Egyptian pharaoh be doing in Yucatan describing the function of a pyramid, I wonder? Miguel looked surprised too, he'd never even heard of Akhenaten.

And there's a lot of Egyptian in the Yucatan, for example, the Maya supreme god Ahau is the nickname given to the Followers of Horus; like Osiris, both K'uKuulKaan and Quetzalcoatl are depicted in blue-green (as is Siva, for that matter), while both Egyptian and Maya dynasties trace their lineages beyond the Oldest Dryas. The Maya words *hom* (ball court), and *ik* (air) are Egyptian — *hem* (little ball), *ikh* (suspend in air) — as are the words for canoe, reed, well, house and snake.

Watching the low-angle light from the setting Sun pick out the detail of the Pyramid of the Magician is one of life's great pleasures. The other is watching the shape of Orion dominate the sky above it at night, as though the two were made for each other; at this latitude its belt stars rise above it like a flagpole. The Maya look upon Orion as the First Father Hunhunahpo, a grain god who figuratively dies and resurrects — like Osiris — and they placed great importance on three specific stars in this constellation: Saiph, Alnitak, and the great blue giant Rigel. Together they represent the Three Stones of the Hearth, the very foundation of Maya cosmology and its associated temple culture. Directly in the center of this equilateral triangle lies Nebula M42. The Maya call it K'ak, the very flame of creation.

This hearth is physically represented by three standing stones in the center of an altar in Uxmal's quadrangle, the enclosure of the wisdom keepers — or at least they did until the Spanish removed them during their purge of un-Christian idolatry. Yet the relationship was so integral to Maya belief that the triangular three-stone hearth was a feature in all traditional homes. The center of the Orion triangle is referred to as Heart of the Sky, the same term given by the Hopi to the *katcina* Sótuknang.

If you've been paying careful attention throughout this adventure you will have noticed I've been dropping subtle hints here and there about Orion, the most obvious being the Giza pyramids that mirror its belt starts, with Osiris as the constellation's earthly representative. There are other examples: Teotihuacan's three main pyramids echo the belt of Orion when its main avenue, the Way of the Soul, aligned to the constellation's apogee on the winter solstice c.10,400 BC. Teotihuacan is one of the homes of Quetzalcoatl, Osiris' doppelgänger in Mexico. The K'iche' Maya linked Orion with a certain Jun Rakán, or *huracán*, a strong wind that is said to have accompanied Quetzalcoatl during the deluge.[1]

To the people of Tonga, Orion was the most important of constellations. They called it Toloa and marked it it terrestrially with the collossal megalith Ha'amonga a Maui, along with large mounds, now heavily eroded, although the place name still survives.[2] Perhaps this is what the Olmec had in mind when they referred to the homeland of the antediluvian gods as Tollan, the

Place of Reeds, the very same description offered in Egypt.

While there is no doubt the gods lived on missing lands such as Atitlán, Mu'ul, Hiva Oa, Ta Neterw, Apsû, Bhogavati, iw titi and Te Pitaka, my travels and research have led me to entertain the idea that their point of origin, the ultimate missing land, might lay elsewhere. It may not even be terrestrial at all.

Let's see where this thought takes us.

THE ORION CONNECTION

The word Orion, of course, is a recent variant on an ancient name. Its earliest linguistic root comes from the Anunaki sage Ur-annu (a variant of U-annu), whose name translates as 'light of heaven' and 'Red Man of Anu', a probable reference to his hair color. Babylonian star catalogues list the constellation as Sipa.Zi.An.Na, another relationship to the Anunaki because it literally means True Shepherd of Anu.

The Greeks later transliterated Ur-annu into *Oarion* (boundary), suggesting the constellation marks some unspecified periphery, a frontier into another realm perhaps. Its Arabic name Al Jabr provides a further layer of interpretation: 'giant' and 'broken bones', a nod to Osiris, the hero who is figurative dismembered during his initiation into the Otherworld.

Orion takes on related symbolism and purpose across multiple cultures. In India he is Praja-pati, master of created beings, which no doubt influenced the Celtic view of the constellation as the source of divine kingship, while in Scandinavian lore, Orion's bBelt becomes the staff of Frigge, the goddess responsible for making the Earth fertile. Collectively, Orion appears to represent a place of high office as well as a source of life.

One of the oldest people to adopt Orion as a talisman were the Anasazi, or as they were originally called, Hisat-Sinom, a rather revealing name because it breaks into two parts: *hisat* (people of remote times) and *sinom* (people or man), and it suggests a link to the Watcher and Red Ant person Anu-Sinom. If so, the name is describing 'people belonging to the remote time of Anu-Sinom'. As the tribe began to disappear, their traditions were blended into the Hopi worldview, including the belief in the influence of stars on the development of human psyche during its carnal entrapment. Such a sky-ground correspondence was taken to its pinnacle when the

Hopi came to choose the locations for their terrestrial universe in a remote corner of Arizona desert — the First, Second and Third Mesas. These three natural sandstone tables, rising hundreds of feet above a parched plain, once resembled islands twelve thousand years ago when northern Arizona, like ancient Egypt, was blessed with abundant rainfall. The alignment of the mesas bears an uncanny resemblance to the pattern formed by the belt stars of Orion, with additional centers such as Betatakin, Canyon de Chelly, Homol'ovi and Wupatki completing the body.[3] The Lakota or Sioux claim to have created a similar relationship with their sacred sites in the Black Hills of South Dakota.

The relationship is reproduced again on a personal level. Leading up to the Hopi winter solstice ceremony of Soyal, the elders retire to a *kiva* in early November to observe the passing in the night sky of Hotòmqam, the brightest star on the belt of Orion, through an opening in the roof. As we saw in the previous chapter, once all three stars are framed by the opening, with the center star above the fireplace, the ritual of Wúwutcim commences in accordance with the pattern first laid down on Earth.[4] The ritual serves a number of purposes. On one level it marks the rite of passage of the initiate and involves a symbolic death and rebirth, as practiced in the Mysteries of Osiris and other figuratively resurrected heroes throughout the ancient world.[5] On a secondary level it serves to convey and commit to memory the knowledge of past events, and to honor the people from whom the rituals originated. The Hopi ceremony recounts the Emergence legend, when the creator god Taiowa encouraged his Watcher emissary Masau'u to make the long journey from the old world to establish the current world with the ancestors of the Hopi-Anasazi. The important thing to bear in mind is that the story is communicated inside the *kiva* the moment the central star of Orion's Belt passes directly over the fire pit. Like other ancient Mysteries schools teachings, the rest of the ceremony remains a closely guarded secret: "On the fourth day of the proceedings, visitors are barred from the pueblo and all trails are closed. This is a night of mystery and terror. People are forced to remain indoors and forbidden even to glance outside... Concurrently, in the kivas underground, a most esoteric and awe-inspiring ritual is being performed which no white observer has ever glimpsed." [6]

In yet another relationship between two ancient cultures on opposite sides of the planet, when Osiris ascends to Sahu (Orion) he becomes an example for others to emulate, he is now an intermediary between sky and ground. The same relationship appears in Arizona. A Hopi *katsina* by the name Sohu is described as an intermediary god between Orion and Earth. He is portrayed wearing a row of three dots on his chest representing the belt of Orion, which in turn is reflected in the alignment of the Three Mesas. The Hopi word for mesa is *tuukvi*; its derivative *tuukwavi* means bead or necklace. In turn, the cognates of the Egyptian word *sahu* are *sa-t* (beads), and *saa-t* (wisdom).[7]

By this point the word coincidence becomes redundant.

TRAVEL BETWEEN TWO WORLDS

There exist a number of curious overlaps between astral and physical travel to and from Orion, to the point where the lines between the two become blurred. One incidence is illustrated in Egypt. A foreman working in Saqqara in the 19th century came face-to-face one dawn with a jackal beside the ruined pyramid of Unas. "It was as if the animal were taunting his human observer... and inviting the puzzled man to chase him. Slowly the jackal sauntered towards the north face of the pyramid, stopping for a moment before disappearing into a hole. The bemused Arab decided to follow his lead. After slipping through the narrow hole, he found himself crawling into the dark bowels of the pyramid. Soon he emerged into a chamber and, lifting his light, saw that the walls were covered from top to bottom with hieroglyphic inscriptions. These were carved with exquisite craftsmanship into the solid limestone and painted over with turquoise and gold." [8]

The inscriptions would become known as the Pyramid Texts. They describe in minute detail the path taken by the initiate, while still alive, into the Otherworld, and the return to his or her living body. Allegedly carved around 2320 BC, they portray a thorough and scientific understanding of another level of reality that would seem above and beyond the capability of people in this supposedly unsophisticated age. The Egyptologist Raymond Faulkner succinctly described their importance: "They disclose to us a vanished world of thought and speech, the last of the unnumbered aeons through which prehistoric man has passed, till finally he... enters this historic age." [9]

How old is this vanished world? Writing in 1934 Wallis Budge, former Keeper of Egyptian Antiquities in London, made a valid observation that the Pyramid Texts appear to have been brought *back* into use around the time of Unas, because the high number of unknown words used and the awkward sentence construction suggests the texts were cobbled together from older sources, so much so that the engravers etching the hieroglyphs onto the chamber walls did not fully comprehend what the original scribes had written, as though the material had been handed down from a remote age and the workers in the twenty-third century BC were having difficulty translating it into the language of the day.

One of the many enigmas of the *Pyramid Texts* concerns the aspiration of the candidate — often a pharaoh, although the practice was open to anyone of moral integrity — to be reborn as "this Great Star, the Companion of Orion, who traverses the sky with Orion... you ascend from the east of the sky being renewed in your due season, and rejuvenated in your due time." [10] They describe the means by which the gods enable the ascent of the individual into their abode using a special throne made from the metal *bja* — not a far cry from the flood hero Yim and his flight-capable jeweled glass throne, or the 'cloud' that air-lifted Enoch to the domain of the Anu. Other references are made to "a ladder for you to ascend to the sky," and the Hnw-bark, a celestial canoe that propels the individual

Section of the Pyramid Texts inside the pyramid of Unas. Saqqara, Egypt.

across the heavens.[11] The texts depict the work of a graceful poet if not an erudite astro-physicist and, like Enoch, the original writer may have been improvising while attempting to describe something beyond his level of comprehension, hence a symbolism and syntax that, at times, appears obtuse to us.

Since the central theme of the *Pyramid Texts* deals with the spiritual resurrection of the individual, it may be that the ancient source of these instructions is none other that the transformation of Osiris, a mortal being who becomes as a bright star, a god, and subsequently takes on the form of Sahu, whereupon the god-man is described in the manner in which Orion appears to the eye: "his leg is long and his stride extended." Strangely enough the same attribute is shared by the Indian antediluvian god Vishnu who, like Osiris, is also depicted with blue skin.[12] Perhaps there is more to this than mere allegory, because one of the Seven Sages of India, Visvamitra, is described in both the *Ramayana* and the *Mahabaratha* to have transferred a king of ancient India named Trianku to the sky *in bodily form* "where he now shines as the constellation Orion." [13] Aboriginal tribes in Northern Australia certainly believe in a material connection because they identify the Watchers as *Nurrumbunguttias,* and claim they physically arrived on Earth from Orion.[14] The association stems back to the Watchers before the great flood, because the term used to describe their first offspring, *nephilim,* derives from *nephilâ,* the Aramaic for Orion. Furthermore, when Shemyaza, the leader of the renegade Watchers, was finally apprehended by the Anu lords, he was tied and bound before being made to hang upside down for all eternity in Orion.

As much as the idea vexes western thinkers, such examples are not just hinting at an experience far and beyond a spiritual or shamanic journey, they are indicating a *physical* link between the terrestrial world and Orion, with the belt stars serving as a kind of portal into the domain of gods; and the candidate, having gained access to their knowledge, returns with raised intellectual capacity that places the individual on par with the gods themselves. The association between the two is said to have fostered the advent of gods on Earth that led to the development of human culture. In the *Building Texts* it is described how, on occasion, the gods would even allow a human to visit their remote abode, from which the lucky individual returned enlightened, with a greater understanding of the world.

Are we mature enough to accept such a leap in understanding? Perhaps. Recently NASA announced the existence of magnetic tubes that open every eight minutes linking the Earth to the Sun, the space agency even using the word portals in the press release. By all accounts the antediluvian gods possessed an intimate knowledge of the mechanics of nature as well a thorough understanding of the stars. Certainly they were master navigators, but what if their expertise in navigation extended beyond the ocean? It might be the realm of science fiction, and yet for all their efforts NASA has merely rediscovered what sages in the Indian subcontinent already knew about planetary and solar mechanics. As far back as 8000 BC these portals were described in the *Yayurveda* as "serpents which move along the ground and are mirrored in the sky, which are the arrows of sorcerers." If it took modern humans 10,000 years to discover a mechanism by which the Earth is tethered to the Sun, what else might still be discovered in this decade, that these portals also connect the Earth with other stars?

WAITAHA GRANDMOTHERS' VIEW

For the final piece of evidence on this matter we turn once more to the words of the Waitaha, whose ancestors were the Starwalkers, long distance voyagers who settled on Easter Island and intermarried after the flood consumed their earthly domain. Turning to the oral traditions of the Elder Grandmothers, we gain a new perspective on the relationship between the antediluvian Urukehu, Orion, and the inhabitants of Earth. In their own words: "Kurawaka [school of the canoe] is the name given by our ancient ancestors to the great snare constellation Te Kupenga o Te Au [The Net of the World, Orion]... The name is also given to our Kurawaka ancestors who travelled on the great tides of the ocean... They are the *tuakana* [elder brother, sister] of the nation of Waitaha. Many of our *whanau* [families] and *hapu* [family groups] descend from these original elder voyaging ancestors... Rakaiwaka is the name given to the *hapu* and *whanau* named after the central star in the Belt of Orion [star Alnilam]. Utilizing these identifiers, Pakau waka is included as the third star.

"These three founding groups are the ancient people of Waitaha. It is these families who gave the sacred social pattern to join and become as one nation that would live happily in peace and plenty in the lands and outer islands of Waitangi ki Raro [Easter Island]."[15]

Notice how the grandmothers make a point of describing Easter Island not as a single island but as it once was, a *group* of lands.

The three Waitaha family groups each took on the name of a star in the belt of Orion: Kurawaka (star Mintaka) was composed of elder *whanau*, the leaders, thinkers, planners; Rakaiwaka (star Alnilam) were investigators, researchers, contractors; Pukauwaka (star Alnitak) were the knowledge keepers and dreamers of the nation.[16] Orion itself was referred to as The Sacred Fish Trap of Outer Space (Punga Tapu o Te Atea) and Net of the World, a name that conjures an image from the *Building Texts* at Edfu, where the Followers of Horus set off on a raft across the ocean, using a net for a sail. And yet it was also the title given to the female flood hero of the Waitaha, Hotu Matu'a, at a stroke linking the Urukehu with the Aku Shemsu Hor.

The Waitaha grandmothers add that contact with these ancestors took the form of regular visitations which considerably extended the knowledge base of the tribe concerning the mechanics of nature and the universe, not to mention social and moral codes and other valuable information for the establishment of a healthy coexistence between people and planet. These were physical interactions rather than shamanic communications.[17]

That was many thousands of years ago. Something occurred whereby the Urukehu stopped coming in physical form, but frustratingly there is no explanation as to why. From this point, the elder Waitaha seers remained in contact with the Urukehu within the spirit houses of the stars of Orion's Belt, which they considered to be both doorways to the spirit world and access points to the Waitaha's extended family. The communication continues today. Still, the Elder Grandmothers remain unequivocal about the physical contact between the Waitaha and people from Orion, as the following quote illustrates: "In all the ancient teachings, they speak of our teachers and healers as having direct communication with our ancient learned ancestors who came to us in our old world villages and helped in the development of our cultural and traditional knowledge base. We understand that the teachings of the very highest orders were for those trusted souls who have the ability to overcome ego and use the knowledge for the greater good of the people." [18]

I believe this clarifies the conundrum of whether the ultimate missing land of the antediluvian gods was figurative, symbolic or physical. It's all of the above. Ancient cultures had no issue with overlapping physical reality, metaphor and symbolism, their worldview was holistic, the Universe an interconnected web of energy. A temple was a mirror of the sky, a plant was a physicalization of consciousness, and so forth. To them, the physical is nothing more than the non-physical reduced in frequency, much like science now understands that accelerating audible sound frequency forty octaves above human hearing produces sonoluminescence, the transmutation of sound into visible light. Conversely, looking at the head of a needle under the microscope reveals this simple solid object to be nothing more than a geometric aggregate of atoms, electrons and molecules vibrating at exceptional speed, yet all such phenomena only became accepted when the discovery of the electron microscope made the unseen visible to the eye.

In the same manner, ancient sources unanimously claim there once existed a time when two races co-existed on Earth. After the evaporation of the last world by a flood, groups of Seven Sages led by an eighth volunteered to remain behind to sow the seeds of rejuvenation before they too returned to their boats and flying shields and vanished across the seas. Up until now it's been a mystery as to where they went, but the accounts all point to a non-terrestrial source. As strange as it may seem to modern ears, Orion may well be the ultimate missing land.

Ancient cultures do not seem to mourn the gods' lack of physical presence because they understand there is little difference between physical and non-physical states, it's all a matter of shifting one's perspective and adapting accordingly, thus they are comfortable in maintaining the umbilical cord of communication through shamanic means. The Waitaha call it Mind Journeying: "The ancient ones sent their minds and spirits soaring inside envelopes of thought, and the sounds contained in the words had carefully been selected for just such a mind journey. Te Rere Wairua [the flight of the spirit] enabled them to communicate their requests to the ancient elders. The elders utilized a form of fasting in their preparation, and during this time the remainder of the process was locked very carefully inside the inner teachings of the Waitaha Wananga [university of learning], under the strictest control of the teachers and healers." [19]

The point is reiterated by the Hopi and Zuni, who do not blink when describing a time in the remote past when contact with the *katsinam*

Watchers was physical, and how nowadays the interaction is subtle, even though, on occasion, physical contact still takes place. This implies the Lords of Anu really did possess control of the laws of nature to the point where they were able to morph their physical state. As Enoch the scribe himself remarked, "the Watchers could take on human form when they wanted to," [20] just as the *Mahabharata* and *Puranas* of India make the same comment about the Naga and how they could assume human form when a situation demanded it — such as a global cataclysm.

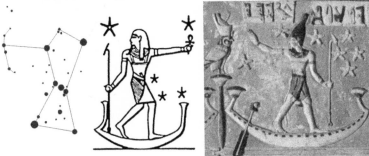

The Net of the World, portrayed by the Followers of Horus at Edfu.
Below: Osiris boards the solar boat as Sahu-Orion.

Temples such as Luxor are proven to emit as much energy as
that created by a group of people in meditation.

THIS
UNSHELTERING SKY

"The name of this Fourth World is Tuwaqachi, World Complete. You will find out why. It is not all beautiful and easy like the previous ones. It has height and depth, heat and cold, beauty and barrenness; it has everything for you to choose from. What you choose will determine if this time you can carry out the plan of Creation on it or whether it must in time be destroyed too... You will have help from the proper deities, from your good spirits. Just keep your own doors open." — Sótuknang, Hopi katcina [1]

Failing to grasp the understanding of their predecessors, the Aztec adopted a belief that the only way to stop the inevitable destruction of the world — for they learned it had occurred four times before — was to systematically sacrifice 100,000 people a year, ripping out victims' beating hearts to appease the god of creation into postponing the end of the current Fifth Sun.[2] Unlike the Aztecs we have a chance to learn from the antediluvian gods and their emissaries.

19

Faced with certain annihilation 11,000 years ago, groups of sages gathered their accumulated knowledge and carved it onto the faces of pyramids, buried it in sacred places, or hard-wired it into the very fabric of monuments built with stone of cumbersome size. We can deduce two things from this behavior: one, they wished future generations to know there once existed an advanced civilization who reached its apogee in astronomy, mathematics, telluric sciences and spirituality to create a golden age across a swathe of the Earth; and two, they wished to remind us, lest we forgot, that the near-destruction of the Earth is cyclical, its recurrence is part and parcel of life on this planet, it is an accepted line item on the contract of incarnation. Obliteration occurred before, it will again, and life resumes. Why else build megalithic structures that defy cataclysms and common sense unless they are meant to serve as building blocks for the survivors? Why else did these enlightened people work with complex calendrical systems marking vast tracks of time when simple agricultural calendars would have sufficed?

Western religion treats humans as sinners the moment their umbilical cord is severed and labels every natural catastrophe a sure sign of divine retribution. Any belief system founded on such fearmongering serves no one except those who created it in the first place. As religious books go, the Qur'an may not be perfect either, but at least it makes an important distinction between the warning of a grievous day and a grievous punishment, and the applied Arabic term means a day that would be remembered for generations to come as a future warning.[3] My direct experience of ancient temples coupled with the words of the ancestors tells me that all we have read up to this point in this adventure is preparation for a major overhaul.

DISTANT EARLY WARNING

With rare exceptions, as a society we stopped building sacred sites after 200 BC — at least according to their original recipe and purpose. No longer are temples built over the intersecting paths of the Earth's telluric currents,[4] nor are their proportions designed to influence the human biological field, nor do they stimulate its consciousness.[5] In their stead we have erected facsimiles promoting ideologies that do next to nothing to advance the spiritual development of the human race. By its very nature the word *religio* means 'reconnect with the source', and yet religion is often designed to achieve the very opposite. The consequences have proved disastrous, because one of the purposes of the original megalithic sites was to create environments where the perceived distance between the individual and subtler levels of existence is reduced. We have lost contact with the land, the sky, ourselves and, ultimately, with the gods who assisted us on this present experience.

As I illustrated earlier, it is believed by indigenous people the world over that contact with the Watchers and other sages by-and-large stopped taking place on a physical level some time ago, resuming instead through subtler means. But just because one no longer possesses a physical body doesn't mean one can't be useful. As the Watcher Sótuknang once reminded the Hopi, "you will have help from the proper deities... Just keep your own doors open." [6] So it is reassuring to know that the Watchers are very much involved at this present time.

Since the late 1970s indigenous wisdom keepers have assisted researchers such as myself come to grips with perhaps the most wondrous, most artistic form of communication taking place on this planet right now. The subject of crop circles raises excitement and ire in equal proportions when broached. My first book *Secrets In The Fields* painstakingly lays out the evidence that crop circles were created by an intelligent consciousness, and the unusual anomalies upon which the designs are made are incapable of being reproduced by people: cellular changes in plants, their bending without damage, the superheating of liquid in a fraction of a second, alteration of the local electro-magnetic and geomagnetic field, and manipulation of soil chemistry are just a few of its anomalies. To save repeating myself I will merely direct you to the evidence presented in the book, if only at least to dispel the false impression that the phenomenon is perpetuated by people. Such an idea was borne from the careful crafting by elements within the British Secret Service to debunk the subject just as it was gaining worldwide traction, even among the quality press. The idea of a fraud was proved to be a fraud in itself, misdirection with the intent of manipulating the public's perception.[7]

The central thesis focuses on the creators of the mysterious symbols, who identified themselves to indigenous wisdom keepers and others who keep their doors open. To quote one of the many communications: "You ask the meaning of your circles in the fields. You have been made aware of the presence of the Watchers. Watchers is a name of a collective intelligence which guides you mortal humans. It is an intelligence from outside the planet... We have been coming for years and years in physical form, and this has happened many times... We have communicated before many times, usually through thought processes, but now it needs to be seen." [8]

And the signs certainly caught the world's attention, especially when the majority of the original crop glyphs began clustering around a conical man-made hill in southern Britain named Silbury, literally Hill of the Shining One.[9] The association couldn't be more obvious. Early glyphs resemble petroglyphs found in Native American territories, which themselves reference the Lookers, or Watchers. One extraordinary crop glyph near Alton Barnes in 1990 — an event made famous when it depleted most car batteries in that hamlet — resembles a petroglyph carved near First Mesa in Arizona depicting the flying shields of the *katcinam*. With its circles and connecting avenues, the glyph indicates communication between the upper and lower worlds, using the symbolic language known to indigenous peoples.

I am condensing a very complex subject into manageable paragraphs because never in my wildest moments did it cross my mind to add crop circles to a project concerned with the nature of antediluvian gods and their domains. However, while writing this closing chapter it dawned on me that I've been sitting on a vital piece of information for over twenty years whose enormity only now becomes apparent. And it makes for sober reading.

Five years after the Alton Barnes glyph, a rural field named Longwood Warren, near the English town of Winchester, hosted an exceptional 240-foot diameter crop glyph, a replica of the inner solar system right down to the planetary orbit ratios around the Sun, each indicated by a majestic sweep of thin, barely eight-inches wide rings made of standing plants; a necklace of sixty-seven grapeshot circles plus three outlying circles represent the asteroid belt, that thick ring of debris orbiting between Mars and Jupiter. The information is 99 percent accurate, so whoever was behind this artwork is proficient in astronomy — not to mention geometry, mathematics and sound because Euclidean theorems and diatonic ratios are concealed in its design matrix.[10]

The author was bent on communicating an important piece of information because all the planets are accounted for except the Earth, which is missing. The puzzle nagged scientists and researchers alike for months. Then, an astronomer versed in Euclidean mathematics and a passion for Stonehenge examined the glyph. The late Gerald Hawkins, Astronomer General of Boston University, took the exact alignment of planets indicated by the glyph and calculated the two occasions during the twentieth century when their positions appeared as such in the solar system. The first, November 6, 1903, is remembered as the day the Wright brothers proved at Kitty Hawk, North Carolina, that, given wings, man could fly. The second, July 11, 1971, marked another milestone in flight: Mariner 9, the first spacecraft ever to orbit Mars, was making its way to our red neighbor.

The analysis was fascinating yet hardly earth shattering. Why should the Watchers wish to commemorate our past achievements in aviation?

One plausible theory was that by providing a freeze-frame of the sky and linking it to two notable historical events, the design might be communicating a future date, not least because the sixty-seven year span between the two events coincides with the number of 'asteroids' in the design, placing the next conjunction in 2038. But still the nagging thought, why was the Earth missing? Was the glyph's appearance in the middle of June, amid the second Taurid stream, more than a coincidence?

WHEN THE SKY FALLS

If the earlier chapter on the Taurids kept you awake at night, perhaps you might consider reading this part in daylight. Perseverance shall be rewarded with a potential happy ending.

Unlike others of its kind, the Taurid stream is filled with chunks of debris hurtling through space at phenomenal speed. Among the kamikaze rocks of this dross is a 3-mile wide remnant of comets Encke and Rudnicki, along with a volatile Earth-crossing projectile by the name of Olijato, first observed in 1876. These are accompanied by "one to two hundred asteroids of more than a kilometer in diameter." [11] As the astrophysicists Clube and Napier bluntly point out, "this unique complex of debris is undoubtedly the greatest collision hazard facing the Earth at the present time." [12]

If all this makes for sombre reading then consider that Clube and Napier's research further reveals a 19-mile wide behemoth orbiting the heart of the Taurid stream, invisible to optical equipment due to its current inert behavior, and will remain so until gases building up inside are released, making the object visible once again. Large fragments accompany this giant, all of which pose extreme danger to Earth. To quote Professor Emilio Spedicato, a mathematician with a passion for celestial mechanics: "It is predicted that... around the year 2030, the Earth will again cross that part of the torus that contains the fragments, an encounter that in the past has dramatically affected mankind." [13]

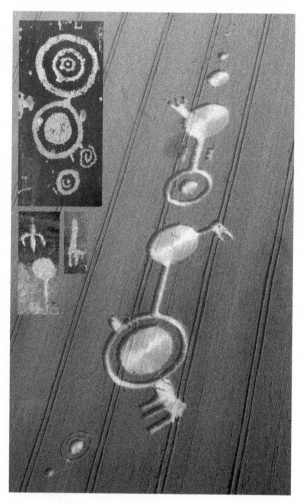

*Alton Barnes crop glyph. Note similarities to the flying
shield petroglyph and its adjacent panel.
Opposite page: Longwood Warren crop glyph depicts the
inner solar system with a missing Earth.
The overlay shows its well-calculated Euclidean geometry.
The area between the asteroids and inner perimeter is
defined by a square, whose mathematical ratio generates
the musical note D (second octave).*

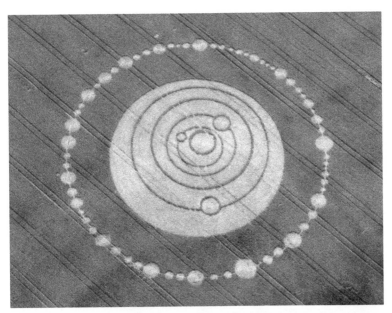

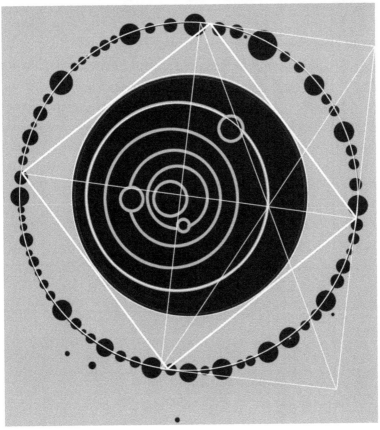

This brings into sharp focus the reason why barely a month goes by without space agencies issuing press releases announcing a new asteroid, a meteor or some other near-Earth projectile, the irony being they now share the same obsession with the sky as did the gods of old.

We are hardly clueless to near-extinction scenarios. There exists evidence in support of devastating meteorite impacts in 7600 BC, 4400 BC, 3150 BC, 2345 BC, 1628 BC, 1159 BC, 207 BC, 536 AD and 1178 AD [14]; there is additional mounting evidence of extraterrestrial plasma events which sometimes occurred in tandem with impacts. These electrical events are caused by gamma ray outbursts from stellar phenomena or by mass coronal ejections from the Sun. They cause extraordinary displays of light phenomena, intense heat, incineration of flammable material, melting of ice caps and vaporization of water. One incident known as the Carrington Event occurred as recently as 1859 and damaged 130,000 miles of telegraph cables throughout Britain; some operators were electrocuted, while others were able to operate equipment without power due to the extra induced current.

And that was a relatively minor outburst.[15] In 1989 a billion-ton cloud of gas and plasma ejected from the Sun with the energy of thousands of nuclear bombs. Within hours, six million people in Canada found themselves without electricity. They should consider themselves fortunate, in earlier times one particular strike was so intense it vitrified stonework, buildings, even entire ancient cities. Some well-researched cases can be seen in the so-called hill forts of Scotland, Wales, Germany and Turkey,[16] many of which were used as sacred places as early as 8000 BC. Evidence suggests such an intense burst of heat would have been made possible by a bolide, an incoming projectile blowing apart in the atmosphere, generating destruction over wide area, as was the case in 1908 above Tunguska which, incidentally, took place when the Earth again crossed the Taurids. A similar incident in the 6th century altered the climate sufficiently to cause crop failures, plagues and devastation that ushered the Dark Ages in Europe.

THE END OF THE WORLD IS (MAYBE) NIGH

By now it should be crystal clear why antediluvian architects were obsessed with the sky and why they built megalithic structures engineered to withstand ten thousand years of pillage and politics, into which they poured the sum of their experience, reminding future generations of the importance of understanding not just a shared evolutionary journey, but also the Earth's place in own celestial drama.

It seems to me the gods also wished to warn of the danger of complacency. They experienced global upheaval — twice — and enough individuals survived the second to promulgate the knowledge that rekindled human civilization, reminding us that nothing in life really dies, it merely reconstitutes and reinvents itself. The non-event that was the end of the world on the winter solstice of 2012 served one useful purpose beside promoting prophets of doom: it demonstrated why the ancients marked time in great cycles. The most important feature of the misinterpreted Mayan Calendar is not a firm date for global calamity, but rather a pivotal moment within a sixty-year window stretching from approximately 1982 to 2042 — coincidentally spanning the dates calculated by professors Hawkins and Spedicato, and indicated by the crop glyph. It merely reflects the motion of one cycle as it dissipates into another. During such periods the Earth falls under the influence of changes taking place in the machinery of heaven, when order turns to chaos and chaos returns to order, much like the change in tides at the beach. One such mechanism involves the Earth overturning on its axis, "the earth turned upside down," [17] as the Egyptians say on the Harris and Ipuwer papyri. As tragic as this may have been, it is reassuring to know that although the only constants in the universe are order and chaos, the higher the level of chaos the greater the potential jump to a higher level of order.

We have already seen how the Maya inherited complex calendars from people who'd acquired long-term observation of the cycles of the heavens and the benefits and harm such motions bring. According to the Maya, the previous age was destroyed by flood, and this present cycle is predicted to close with global destruction by fire and earthquakes. The clock began ticking for this age c.3114 BC, a date roughly coinciding with a comet or plasma event c.3150 BC that impacted climate worldwide. By the same token, the previous cycle began around 8240 BC, coinciding with the 'sudden' global outbreak of agriculture and civilization.

Another mechanism at work is the geomagnetic reversal of the poles, the last one having occurred around 10,400 BC,[18] the period commemorated by a number of the world's oldest monuments. The next is expected to take place around 2030.[19]

If the expression May You Live in Interesting Times is anything to go by, the third decade of the twenty-first century is shaping up to prove it.

Ancient cosmologies mark the passing of each age and its associated catastrophe with the symbol of a new Sun. The Maya refer to these as Fire Sun, Hurricane Sun, Earthquake Sun, Water Sun. By comparison, Nahua tradition lists Chicon-tonatiuh or seven Sun cycles forming an annular cosmic drama,[20] as do the aborigines of North Borneo;[21] Buddhist scriptures, whose six previous Suns were each brought to an end by water, fire or wind, state that this present seventh sun will end with the Earth breaking into flames, a view shared by the aborigines of Sarawak.

The *Visuddhi Magga* and the *Bahman Yast*, two books of the *Avesta* claimed to span hundreds of thousands of years, similarly describe seven cycles,[22] each beginning with the cosmic mechanism winding itself up and unravelling at each close, accompanied by "signs, wonders, and perplexity which are manifested in the world at the end of each millennium." [23]

The Avestic Aryans of ancient Iran, who state in their scriptures how the original homeland Airyana Vaejo was destroyed at the close of an age defined by a devastating lowering of temperatures that brought ten months of winter across the Earth and with it a period of glaciation. Predictably a man of high renown — whose wife also happens to be his sister, naturally — was instructed by a god to ride out the snow and bitter cold inside a large underground enclosure, after which he builds a boat to house all manner of species.[24] The story appears to depict climatic conditions at the onset of the Younger Dryas, and is reiterated by the Toba people in the border region of Paraguay and Chile, who recall the same difficult cold period when the Sun was barely able to warm the Earth.

AN OUTCOME NOT SET IN STONE

The Hopi have been foreseeing the future for over a thousand years: people speaking to each other across great distances via spider webs (telephone wires), the riding of wagons without horses on black ribbons (asphalt roads), the gourd of ashes falling to the Earth and burning people (the atomic bomb), the End Times people living in the sky (International

Space Station). Given such a track record it would be unwise to ignore their knowledge of world ages. The Hopi speak of three previous worlds and are very clear in their description: "The first world was destroyed by fire that came from above and below. The second world ended when the terrestrial globe toppled from its axis and everything was covered with ice. The third world ended in a universal flood. The present world is the fourth. Its fate will depend on whether or not its inhabitants behave in accordance with the Creator's plans." [25]

Indeed Sótuknang did remind the Hopi at the onset of this current world, "what you choose will determine if this time you can carry out the plan of Creation on it or whether it must in time be destroyed too... You will have help from the proper deities, from your good spirits. Just keep your own doors open." [26] Taken at face value, the advice offered by this Watcher implies the destruction of this current world is a potential rather than a foregone conclusion. And this is where the good news comes in.

On my travels around the world I meet countless people keeping their door open in the face of relentless negativity about the current state of world affairs. I am encouraged by what I see. At any given moment 95% of the world is at peace, a vast improvement from two hundred years ago. Every week inspired people bring new ideas to fix the environment, from ocean plastic-eating machines to wind powered devices that make drinking water out of thin air. And yet, paradoxically, there is no escaping the brutal fact we are living on borrowed time. At the time of writing, by early August humans will have consumed more of nature than the planet is capable of renewing in a whole year. We now find ourselves in a situation where the human population is consuming 1.6 planets a year and the date falls back six days with each passing year.[27] For the first time in living memory we as a society have forsaken the natural order and embarked on the suppression of nature, abstractionism and mathematical analysis at the expense of observation and empathy, and a divesting of personal responsibility in favor of artificial intelligence. In short, we are at the threshold of progressive innovation whilst undermining our biological viability. The balance can tip either way. Since we are an inherent part of nature, when we abuse this connection, nature sends unmistakable warning signals. By way of analogy, when we work our own body in ways it is not meant to operate, the muscles and bones turn on the host and cause incalculable pain.

It is no different for this biological organism called Earth and the warnings are loud and clear: overpopulation, environmental degradation, resource depletion and famine, to which NASA and other space agencies add near-Earth asteroids, comets and other projectiles that could spell the end of this Fourth World, ironically prophesied by the very cultures who, in little over a century, have been almost eradicated at the hand of 'advanced' society.

During a radio interview in which I was making the point between gods, the integrity of temple culture and the uplifting of the human condition, there came a moment in the broadcast when we discussed the coincidence between the fall of temple culture and the fall of civilizations. Uncharacteristically, part of the conversation grew increasingly pessimistic and ended in that most awkward moments on live radio — absolute silence — at which point I began to speak off the cuff, the inspiration just hit me while on air, you could say I had an epiphany. It's a risk speaking into a live microphone without preparation. Nevertheless I felt compelled.

I recalled the aforementioned quote by Sótuknang — that the future isn't always written in stone — along with the following flood myth from the region of Viet Nam, Laos and Thailand. Back in the days when celestial beings and humans could travel back and forth to visit one another, when people lived for three hundred years, and the region was named Muang Lum (Lower World), there lived in northern Thailand three unusual lords, Pu Langxoeng, Khun Kan and Khun Khet, earthly representatives of a celestial being named Thaen. All that Thaen required was for people to honor him at meal times and follow the rules set down for good conduct. But gradually the three lords neglected this simple courtesy, they fell out of favor with the heavens, and a great flood wiped out everyone and everything — except the three lords, who built a raft, took aboard their wives and children, and met Thaen in the sky, reassuring him they had learned from their error and from now on they would be more respectful.

Thaen agreed and sent down a messenger to teach people all the crafts necessary upon which to build a civil society.

Soon the Earth became overpopulated and the three lords took to regular intoxication. This time Thaen recalled the lords and replaced them with his messenger Khun Bulom and seven sages. When Thaen was convinced the people could look after themselves once more, he had the bridge to heaven collapsed so that humans could no longer visit.[28]

The central point to the story is not how it echoes so many other accounts we've already covered, it's the one small detail about Thaen retracting the bridge to heaven. It brought to mind all the traditions in which the Watchers and others of their ilk sowed the seeds of civilization then disappeared across the sea, never to be seen again in physical form, thereafter appearing sporadically or not at all, then abruptly making their presence known at the close of the twentieth century through messages encoded in crop glyphs.[29]

My point is this. Long ago humans established a relationship with gods who, on occasion, would feed morsels of knowledge in what seems to have been a carefully orchestrated plan to assist human society evolve gradually towards a more civilized state; on occasion they would allow a lucky individual into their world so the person could share a favourable impression with his peers upon return. Looking at the myriad of ancient cultures and their stories, as a species it seems we ultimately relied on outside assistance, perhaps to the point of dependency, especially after each overturning of the world. So my question is, what if the lesson to be learned in this present age is to discover the spark of divinity in ourselves, to recognize the god within? Was Sótuknang daring humans to do better, was he offering us a challenge?

THE POWER OF HUMAN POTENTIAL

What if by losing our connection to divine assistance we discover our own supernatural potential?

Tibetan Buddhist monks are no strangers to the extraordinary, such as using the body to heat freezing water by simply applying the power of thought and intention. Seated in meditation in a drafty monastery one mid-winter, monks took part in an experiment, draped in sheets drenched in cold water despite the air temperature being already close to freezing, and yet, instead of freezing, the monks began to sweat, to the point where the sheets dried within an hour. The Harvard cardiologist Herbert Benson monitored the event.[30] Such is the ability of ancient traditions like Buddhism and Qigong to place particular emphasis on peak attention and guided intent to achieve the extraordinary.

The energy inherent in thought and emotion has been the subject of recent experiments on the nature of consciousness. A group of scientists working at Princeton Engineering Anomalies Research (PEAR) demonstrated how global collective consciousness had a marked affect on a computer's output hours *prior* to tragic incidents, such as the terrorist attack on the twin towers in New York in 2001, as though a psychokinetic effect was experienced by six billion people worldwide. Clearly an event of great magnitude unified world consciousness even before it occurred. The implications reveal important details about human consciousness. First, a collective group appears to have a psychokinetic effect on any micro-physical process; second, the effect of a greater number of people holding the same intent is stronger than a single person's, with an impending catastrophe corralling people's focus and inherent ability like no other. Essentially it was proved that an event of great magnitude is capable of uniting world attention.[31]

The PEAR experiments were expanded to measure the influence of ancient temples on human consciousness. They revealed that an Egyptian temple by itself is capable of generating an energy field equal to that of a meditating group, and yet the results were highest when such a group interacted with the temple.[32] This interrelationship between people and megaliths was further discovered when acoustical analysis of monuments such as the Great Pyramid of Giza, the Hypogeum of Hal Safflieni in Malta, and Newgrange in Ireland show each one to have been designed to a specific frequency which is proven to shut down the mental processing area of the brain and switch it towards an active receptive state of consciousness.[33] The Followers of Horus, the Anunaki, the People of the Serpent, the Watchers and every other

Maharishi Manesh Yogi, who introduced the Trancendental Meditation technique

brotherhood would hardly have built such places and described them as locations that transform the individual into a god, into a bright star unless they wished humans to discover their co-creative potential and evolve beyond their perceived physical limitation.

What if intention were added to this equation? A number of high profile cases have shown how intent is capable of affecting a given target. One early peer-reviewed intention experiment involved a group of sixteen volunteers in London who were able to influence biophoton emission in single-celled algae called *acetabularia* stored in a laboratory run by the scientist Fritz Popp — in Germany.[34]

PEAR took the concept to the next stage. Conducting a group of people focussed on the same aim, their combined intent was shown to influence the output of a computer to the point where it became possible to alter a regular electronic drumbeat.[35]

If people united by a single thought can do this to a machine, how about their environment? In 1998, 15% of the Brazilian state of Roraima succumbed to an out-of-control fire. Over 1500 firefighters from three countries joined in to quell the flames, all to no avail. 13,200 square miles of land were torched. Then, experts in weather modification were flown in: two Caipo Indian shamans. Two days after a ritual dance, the heavens opened, rain poured in abundance and 90% of the fire was extinguished.[36]

Since the 1960s, over 500 studies conducted by the Maharishi Effect of Transcendental Meditation have been shown to reduce conflict and suffering. The most notable were performed using directed group focus targeting American cities during times of high crime. One study of twenty-four cities showed that whenever 1% of the population was engaged in transcendental meditation, the crime rate dropped 24%. In a follow-up study of forty-eight cities, half of those with the requisite 1% of meditators experienced a 22% decrease in crime and an 89% decrease in the crime trend. In the other half of cities without the threshold percentage of meditators, crime increased by 2% and the crime trend by 53%.[37]

If just one percent of the population of a city is capable of influencing its environment, by extension it would take just over 8000 people to affect the entire world — or less if the level of focussed intent is intense, as proved by the PEAR experiments and the Tibetan monks.[38] As we are now aware that the universe is not a series of isolated events but an interrelated mechanism-organism, and our thoughts and intent are capable of influencing the world around us, surely it would be possible to influence the potential course of, say, an earthbound meteor?

Suppose one day the world wakes up to news of a space agency declaring, with absolute certainty, civilization as we know it is about to end due to an unavoidable collision with a large space rock — the kind of story already rolling out with ever greater frequency yet picked up only by an audience with an interest such matters. On rare occasions, when such objects pass between the Moon and Earth, the press release makes international headlines. But what if one day that bulletin offered even odds of annihilation? As history, and now experiments in consciousness show, it often takes an incident of global proportion to galvanize the world into action. At first glance our present situation may look fractured beyond repair, but given such a scenario I wonder if the validation of the supernatural power latent in the human temple, welded to a sign of mutually assured destruction, is enough to generate a bulwark of energy capable, in all likelihood, of affecting and altering the outcome of an incoming cosmic monster, and in the process unite this dysfunctional human brotherhood?

Probably.

Besides selectees in laboratories and monks, we know there exist others who already understand how the universe works and how it can be tailored by the magical power of concentrated will. We called such individuals by many names but they all belonged to the same guild. One of them was the Lord of Anu, who once confided in Enoch, "the things which you see at rest and in motion were completed by me. I will tell you now… what things I created from the non-existent, and what visible things from the invisible."[39] That's quite the power.

Perhaps what the antediluvian gods might have wanted with us all along was for us to discover the very same power within ourselves, to develop the gumption to alter the course of our own destiny and thus discover, in the end, that we too are gods.

References

CHAPTER 1

1. Betts, M. Ancient Language may Prove Key to Translation System, Computerworld, vol. IX, no. 8, 25 Feb, 1985, p.30; and Sunday Times, London, November 4, 1984

2. Edgar Mejita, personal communication

3. Waters, Frank, Book of the Hopi, Ballantine, New York, 1972, p.16

4. Song of the Waitaha: The Histories of a Nation, Being the teachings of six Waitaha elders as told to author Barry Brailsford, Wharariki Publishing Ltd, 2003

5. Wong, Kate. Ancient Fossils from Morocco Mess Up Modern Human Origins, Scientific American, June 8, 2017

6. Shreeve, James, The Neanderthal Enigma, William Morrow & Co, 1995

7. Ruhlen, M. Linguistic Evidence for Human Prehistory, Cambridge Archaeological Journal, 5/2, 1995, p.265-8

8. "Stone Bracelet is Oldest Ever Found in the World," Siberian Times, May 12, 2015; "Could this stunning bracelet be 65,000 to 70,000 years old?" 2 August 2017

9. Rudgley, R. Lost Civilizations of the Stone Age, Century, 1998

10. Marshack, Alexander. The Roots of Civilization, McGraw Hill, 1972

11. P. Spurny, J. Borovicka1, H. Mucke, and J. Svoren. Discovery of a new branch of the Taurid meteoroid stream as a real source of potentially hazardous bodies, Astronomy & Astrophysics, May 20 2017

12. Hughes, D. Focus: Visitors From Space, Astronomy Now, Nov. 1997

13. Wou-Foung in G. Schlegel, Uranographie Chinoise, 1875, p.740

CHAPTER 2

1. Plato, Timaeus, trans Bury, 1929, 22 C-D

2. Dorsey, G.A. The Mythology of the Wichita, Carnegie Institution of Washington, 1904, p.291-5

3. Bellamy, Hans Schindler. Moons, Myths and Man, Faber and Faber, London, 1938, p.277

4. Clark, E.E. Indian Legends of the Pacific Northwest, U. of C. Press, Berkeley, 1963

5. ibid

6. Popol Vuh, le livre sacre, ed. Brasseur 1861 CH III, p.25

7. Brasseur, Sources des nations civilisees du Mexique, I, p.55

8. Brasseur, Sources de l'histoire Primitive du Mexique, p.28-9

9. ibid, p.40

10. de Sahagun, Bernardino. Historia general de las cosas de Nueva Espana, 1938, p.481

11. Gomara, Conquista de Mexico, II, 261

12. Williamson, Robert Wood. Religious and Cosmic Beliefs of Central Polynesia, vol. I, Cambridge University Press, 1933, p.8, 37

13. ibid, p.44

14. The Epic of Gilgamesh, trans Thompson, Luzac & Co, London, 1928, tablet 11

15. Charles, R.H. Apocrypha and Pseudepigrapha of the Old Testament, Oxford University Press, Vol. II, 1963, 13-28

16. ibid

17. Howarth, H.H. The Mammoth and the Flood, Sampson Low, Marston, Searle and Rivington, London 1887

18. Salomon, Frank, and Urioste, George L. Huarochirí Manuscript: A Testament of Ancient and Colonial Andean Religion, University of Texas Press. 1991

19. Posnanski, Arthur. Tihuanacu: Cradle of American Man, vol. III, J.J. Augustin, New York and La Paz, 1957, p.142

20. Osbournem H., South American Mythology, Hamlyn Press, 1968

21. Ferguson, J.C., Chinese Mythology, Archaeological Institute of America, 1928, p.29

22. Holmberg, Uno, The Mythology of All Races, Vol. IV, Cooper Square Pubs., 1964, p.364-8

23. ibid p.369

24. Turner, An account of an embassy to the court of the Teshoo Lama in Tibet, Cambridge University Press, 1800

25. MacCulloch, J.A. The Mythology of All Ages, vol. II, Archaeological Institute of America, Boston, 1930, p.188

26. Warren, Henry Clarke, World Cycles, Buddhism, HArvard University Press, 1896, p.328

27. Andree, Richard. Die Flutsagen, F. Vieweg und Sohn, Braunschweig, 1891, p.115

28. Nair, Roshini. "Archeological find affirms Heiltsuk Nation's oral history settlement on B.C.'s Central Coast dated back to 14,000 years," CBC News, March 30, 2017

29. Yao, Universal Lexicon, Leipsig and Halle, 1732-1754, vol LX; Schoch, Robert, and McNally, Robert. Voyages of the Pyramid Builders: The True Origins of the Pyramids from Lost Egypt to Ancient America, Tarcher/Penguin, New York, 2003

30. Holmberg, op cit, p.369

31. The Kalevala, trans. Martin Crawford, Robert Blake Co., Cincinatti, 1888, p.xiii

32. On The Eternity of the World, Vol IX, trans Colson 1941, 146-147

33. Diodorus of Sicily, trans. Oldfather, The Library of History, II, 31

34. The Mahabharata, cited Tilak, Lokamanya, The Arctic Home of the Vedas, Tilak Bros., Poona City, 1903, p.420

35. Peder Steffensen, Jorgen. N.I.B. Center For Ice and Climate, University of Copenhagen, 11, Dec. 2008

CHAPTER 3

1. Ansell, John. Kupe's Descendant Confirms Other Races Were Here First, elocal, National Archives, Waipoua Forest Stone City, May 10, 2013

2. ibid

3. Cowan, James. Legends of the Maori, Vol. 1, Southern Reprints, 1987, p.238-9

4. Timaru Herald, February 24, 1875, p.3

5. Lesley, Chris. http://greaterancestors.com/timaru-herald-from-new-zealand-1875-reports-of-giants-remains/

6. ibid; and N.Z. Truth, 29 September 1965, p.13

7. Plumm, Gabbi, and Marsh, Peter, Skeletons in the Cupboard, Ep. 1, The Redheads, Plummtree Productions, Wellington, 2014

8. Transactions and Proceedings of the New Zealand Institute, vol. VII, Trubner & Co, London, 1875, p.144-6; and investigative researcher Gary Cook,

personal communication

9. Plumm, Gabbi, and Marsh, Peter, op cit

10. Ansell, John. op cit

11. Hill, Marika. "Ngapuhi leader: Red-heads, fair skins beat Maori to NZ", New Zealand Press Herald, 28 December, 2012

12. Thorsby, Erik. "The Polynesian Gene Pool: An Early Contribution by Amerindians to Easter Island", Royal Society Publishing, vol. 367, Feb 6, 2012

13. Phillipps, W.J., Journal of the Polynesian Society, Volume 57, Auckland, 1948 p.30

14. Brailsford, Barry. Song of the Waitaha: The Histories of a Nation, Being the teachings of six Waitaha elders as told to author Barry Brailsford, Wharariki Publishing, Christchurch, 2003, p.33

15. Papakura, M kereti. The Old Time Maori, Victor Gollancz, London, 1938

16. Brailsford, op cit, p.27-8

17. ibid, p.34-5

18. ibid

19. ibid, p.39-40

20. ibid, p.42

21. ibid, p.57

22. ibid, p.185-87

23. ibid

24. ibid, p.187

25. Schoch, Robert, and McNally, Robert. Voyages of the Pyramid Builders: The True Origins of the Pyramids from Lost Egypt to Ancient America, Tarcher/Penguin, New York, 2003

26. ibid, p.135, p.287-8

27. Smith, Deborah. Dreaming lead to ancient crater, Sydney Morning Herald, Dec 28, 2009

28. Brailsford, op cit, p.53

29. Michell, John. A Little History of Astro-archaeology, Thames & Hudson, London, 1977, et al

30. Brailsford, op cit, p.43

31. Te Korako, Makere and Te Porohau Ruka, Whispers of the Waitaha, Wharariki Publishing, comp. Barry Brailsford, Christchurch, 2006. p.201

32. Brailsford. op cit, p.34

33. ibid, p.55

34. Posnanski, op cit

CHAPTER 4

1. Schmidt, Gavin, and Frank, Adam, The Silurian Hypothesis: Would it be possible to detect an industrial civilization in the geological record?, Cornell University, 2018

2. Leon, Pedro Cieza de. Chronicle of Peru, Hakluyk Society, London, 1864 and 1883, Pt. 1, Ch. 87

3. Osborne, Harold. Indians of the Andes: Aymaras and Quechuas, Routledge and Kegan Paul, 1952, p.64

4. Silva, Freddy. The Divine Blueprint, Invisible Temple, Portland, 2012, p.33-41

5. Posnansky, Arthur, Tiahuanacu: The Cradle of American Man, Ministry of Education, Vol. II, Ministry of Education, La Paz, 1957, p.88

6. ibid, p.91

7. ibid, p.89

8. ibid, p.89; and Mueller, Rolf. Der Sonnentempel in den Ruinen von Tihuanacu, Dietrich Reimer, Berlin, 1931

9. Bellamy, Hans Schindler, and Allen, Paul. The Calendar of Tiahuanaco: A disquisition on the time measuring system of the oldest civilization in the world, Faber and Faber, New York, 1956, p.47

10. Posnansky, op cit, p.98

11. ibid, vol. II, p.99

12. Posnanski, op cit, p.141

13. ibid, p.140

14. Based on 1:1.2, the same ratio as 6:5

15. Mueller, op cit

16. ibid, p.90

17. Gamarra, Jesus, and de Jong, Jan Peter. The Cosmology of the Three Worlds, J&J Productions, 2012

18. Popular Archaeology, Vol. 14, March 1, 2014

19. Kruzer, A., The Question of the Material Origin of the Walls of the Saqsayhuaman Fortress, isida-project.ucoz.com

20. ibid

21. Vega, Garcilaso de la. The Royal Commentaries of the Inca Garcilaso de la Vega, 1539-1616, Orion Press, 1961, p.237

22. ibid, p.233-35; Markham, Sir Clemens, The Inca of Peru, Smith, Elder & Co, London, 1911, p.33

23. Vega, op cit, p.4-6

24. Darmestester, James, and Mills, H.L. The Zend Avesta, 1895, Atlantic Pub reprint, New Delhi, 1990, Part 1, p.5

25. ibid, p.15-18

26. Fernandez-Baca Tupayachi, Carlos, Saqsaywaman: A Model of Atlantis, the Untold Story, Munaypacha, Lima, 2006, p. 161

27. Dillehay, Tom, et al, Chronology, mound-building and environment at Huaca Prieta, coastal Peru, from 13 700 to 4000 years ago, Antiquity Pubs., 86, 2012, p.48-70

28. Sullivan, William. The Secret of the Incas, Crown, New York, 1996, p.119

29. Personal communication from Teokotai Andrew, wisdom keeper of Tongareva

30. Sullivan, op cit, p.219

CHAPTER 5

1. Vega, op cit, p.132

2. Edgar Caceres, personal communication

3. Kondratov, Alexander, The Riddles of the Three Oceans, Progress Publishers, Moscow, 1971, p.79-80

4. Thompson, William. Te Pito Te Henua, or Easter Island, Government Printing Office, Washington, 1891, p.502

5. Schoch, Robert, Forgotten Civilizations, Inner Traditions, Rochester, 2012, p.78-9

6. Kondratov, Alexander, The Riddles of Three Oceans, Progress Publishers, Moscow, 1971, p.34

7. Brown, J. Macmillan. The Riddle of the Pacific, T. Fisher Unwin, London, 1924, p.279

8. Heyerdahl, Thor. The Kon-Tiki Expedition, Unwin Paperbacks, London, 1882, p.141

9. Wolff, Werner. Island of Death: A New Key to Easter Island's Culture through an Ethno-psychological Stuidy, J.J. Augustin, New York, 1948, p.156-7, citing Metreux, Alfred. Mysteries of Easter Island, Yale Review 28, 1939, p.771; and Fox, Charles Elliot. The Threshold of the Pacific, Kegan Paul, London, 1924, p.338

10. Englert, Father Sebastian. Island at the Center of the World: New Light on Easter Island, Robert Hale & Co, London, 1970, p.45

11. ibid, p.46-7

12. Maziere, Francis. Mysteries of Easter Island, W.W. Norton, New York, 1968, p.40; Brailsford, op cit, p.35

13. Heyerdahl, op cit

14. Schoch, op cit

15. Schoch, ibid, and private communication

16. Jo Anne Van Tilburg, personal communication

17. Te Korako, op cit, p.201

18. Brailsford, op cit, p.66

19. ibid, p.160-1, and personal communication

20. "Rano Raraku Exterior Quarry: Moai sketches and neck tracings (RR-002-077),"Notes from the Easter Island Statue Project Database, www.eisp.org/983/

21. Validated by Teokotai Andrew.

22. Thomson, William. Te Pito Te Henua, or Easter Island, in Report of the US National Museum, Under the Direction of the Smithsonian Institution, June 30, w1889 1891, p.462

23. Brailsford, op cit, p.35

24. Jenkins, Jere, and Ephraim Fischback, and John Buncher, et al. "Evidence for Correlations between Nuclear Decay Rates and Earth-Sun Distance," Cornell University Library, 2008

25. Jenkins, Jere, and Ephraim Fischback. Perturbation of Nuclear Decay Rates during the Solar Flare of 13 December 2006," Cornell University Library, 2008;

26. Schmidt, Klaus, Göbekli Tepe: The Stone Age Sanctuary in South-Eastern Anatolia, Ex Oriente, Berlin, 2012, p.243; How Old Is Göbekli Tepe? The Tepe Telegrams, 6/12/2016

27. ibid

28. ibid

29. Brailsford, op cit, p.189

30. Andrew Collins and Rodney Hale, www.andrewcollins.com/page/news/P43.htm

31. Michael Anissimov, www.wiseGEEK.com

32. Bauval, Robert, cited in Hancock, Fingerprints of the Gods, Crown, New York, 1995, pp.444-5

33. Bauval, Robert, and Gilbert, Adrian. The Orion Mystery, Crown Publishers, New York, 1994, p.192-3

34. Prag, Kay. The 1959 Deep Sounding at Harran in Turkey, Levant 2, 1970, p.71-2

35. Hassan, Selim, Excavations at Giza, Vol VI, Government Press, Cairo, 1948, p.45

36. Green, Tamara. The City of the Moon God: Religious Traditions of Harran, E.J. Brill, Leiden, New York, 1992 p.21, 25, 95-7, 100, 121

37. Al Masudi, Muruj al-dhahab was ma'adin al-jawahir c.960

38. R.H. Charles, The Book of Jubilees, Adam and Charles Black, London, 1902, pp.71-2

39. Lloyd, Seton and Brice, William, Harran, Anatolian Studies, Vol I, British Institute of Amkara, 1951, p.71-2

40. Klaus Schmidt, They Built The First Temples, Verlag C.H. Beck, Munich, 2006

41. Enix, Linda. The Ancient Architects of Sound, Popular Archaeology, March 2012

42. Personal communication from Mayan teacher Miguel Angel Vergara

44. For example, Silva, Freddy, The Lost Art of Resurrection, Invisible Temple, Portland, 2015, p. 53-6

45. Personal communication, Miguel Angel Vergara

46. Silva, op cit, p.141-44

CHAPTER 6

1. Burpee, Lawrence J. (Ed.): Journals and Letters of Pierre Gaultier de Varennes de la Vérendrye and His Sons. New York, 1968

2. Fenn, Elizabeth A. Encounters at the Heart of the World: A History of the Mandan People. Farrar, Straus and Giroux, 2014

3. Andrew Teokotai, personal communication

4. ibid

5. ibid

6. ibid

7. ibid

8. Silva, op cit, p.189-191

9. Melville, Herman. Typee: A Peep AT Polynesian Life, London, 1846

10. Willey, Keith. Assignment New Guinea, Jackaranda Press, Brisbane, 1965, p.70-72

11. cited in Frazer, Sir James George, Folklore in the Old Testament, Vol. I, MacMillan and Co., London, 1919, p.223

12. Hancock, Graham, Magicians of the Gods, Thomas Dunne Books, New York, 2015, p.406

13. Teokotai Andrew, personal communication. His mother witnessed the event.

14. Boyrayon, Markus. Solomon Islands Mysteries, Adventures Unlimited Press, 2010

15. Ginsberg, Louis. The Legends of the Jews, The Jewish Publication society of America, Philadelphia, 1988 Vol I, p.162

16. Darmestester, James, and Mills, H.L. The Zend Avesta, 1895, Atlantic Pub reprint, New Delhi, 1990, Part 1, p.18

17. ibid, p.20; and 1989 translation p.14, note 87

18. Journal of the Anthropological Institute, Vol. VI, Trubner & Co, London, 1877

19. Gray, Jonathan, The Lost World of Giants, Teach Services, Thames, 2006

20. Brailsford, op cit, p.34-5

21. Spoehr. Alexander. Marianas Prehistory: Survey and Excavations on Saipin, Tinian and Rota, 1957

22. Te He Grace, John, Tuwharetoa: A History of the Naori People of the Taupo District, A.H. & A.W. Reed, 1959, p.115

23. Cowan, James, Journal of Polynesian Studies, Vol. 30, pt. 2, Auckland, 1921, p.96, 141

24. Brown, J.M., The Riddle of the Pacific, London, 1934, p.236

25. Heyerdahl, Thor, American Indians in the Pacific, Victor Pettersons, Stockholm, 1952, p.370

26. Bolton, Kerry R., "Enigma of the Ngati Hotu", Antrocom Online Journal of Anthropology, vol. 6, n. 2, 2010

27. Matamua Monica et al, Brief of Evidence in the Matter of the Treaty of Waitangi Act 1975, Waitangi Tribunal, Wellington, 2008; Antrocom Online Journal of Anthropology 2010, vol. 6, n. 22008; Plumm, Gabbi, and Marsh, Peter, op cit

28. Fuente Magna, the Controversial Rosetta Stone of the Americas, April Holloway, The Epoch Times, Oct 2, 2014

29. Heyerdahl, Thor. The Ra Expeditions, Doubleday, New York, 1971, p.17

30. Price, Michael, Strange, elongated skulls reveal medieval Bulgarian brides were traded for politic, Sciencemag.org, March 12, 2018

31. www.ancient-origins.net/news-history-archaeology/breaking-new-dna-testing-2000-year-old-elongated-paracas-skulls-changes-020914

32. ibid; and Marzulli, L.A., Nephilim Hybrids, Spiral of Life, 2016

33. Foerster, Brien, Elongated Skulls Symposium, Los Angeles, 2018

CHAPTER 7

1. Cook, Gary. The Secret Land: Journeys Into the Mystery, Stoneprint Press, Oamaru, 2002, p.17-19

2. ibid

3. Best, Elsdon. The Maori, Journal of the Polynesian Society, Vol. I, 1924, p.288-91

4. Cook. op. cit

5. Lowe, David, and King, Carolyn. The Drama of Conservation: The History of Pureora Forest, Springer, Auckland, 2015, p.1-17

6. Solihuddin, Tubagus, A drowning

Sunda Shelf Model during Last Glacial Maximum and Holocene: A Review, Indonesian Journal of Geoscience, vol. I, no.2, August 2014, p.99-107

7. Nature, 518, February 12, 2015, p.228-31

8. Schoch, Robert, The Case for a Lost Ice Age Civilization in Indonesia, Atlantis Rising Magazine, March 2014, p.41

9. Hancock, Graham, Magicians of the Gods, op cit

10. ibid, p.409

11. ibid

12. The Oklahoman, June 29, 1969, p.1

13. ibid

14. Thom, Alexander. Megalithic Sites in Britain, Clarendon Press, Oxford, 1967

15. The Jewish Encyclopedia, Funk and Wagnalls Co., Vol. 5, London, 1916, p.659

16. Ess, Margarette van, and Rheidt, Llaus, Baalbek-Heliopolis: 10,000 Jahre Stadtgeschicte, Zabern Phillip Von GmbH, 2014

17. ibid

18. Alouf, Michael. History of Baalbek, 1914, p.39-40

19. ibid, p.41, 42, 86

20. Hartoune Kalayan, Notes on the Heritage of Baalbek and the Beka'a, p.53

21. Ruprechtsberger, Erwin, Von Steinbruch zum Jupitertempel von Baalbek, Linzer Archaeologische Forschungen, 1999, 30, 7-56

22. Hassan, Selim. The Great Sphinx and its Secrets; Historical Studies in the light of recent excavations, (Excavations at Giza 1936-7, vol. III), Government Press, Cairo, p.49, 264-7

23. N. Wyatt, Religious Texts from Ugarit, Sheffield Academic Press, 1998, p.378ff

24. Miriam Lichtheim, Ancient Egyptian Literature, vol III, University of California Press, Berkeley, 1980 p.148; Budge,

E.A. Wallis. Osiris and the Egyptian Resurrection, vol. II, Philip Lee Werner, London, 1911, p.180

CHAPTER 8

1. Goenka, Himanshu. Egypt Ancient History: 7300-year old city Found in New Excavation Along the Nile, IBT Times, 11/24/2016

2. Diodorus of Sicily III, 55, trans C.H. Oldfather, Loeb Classical Library, 1939

3. The Times, London, 17 March 1914

4. Frankfort, Henri. The Cenotaph of Seti I at Abydos, 39th Memoir of the Egypt Exploration Society, London, 1933, p.18

5. Also stated by John Anthony West in The Traveler's Key to Ancient Egypt: A Guide to the Sacred Places of Ancient Egypt, Quest Books, Wheaton, 1996, p.392

6. Frankfort, op cit

7. Strabo, Geography, vol. VIII, p.111

8. Bauval and Gilbert, op cit

9. West, John Anthony. Serpent In The Sky, Quest Books, Wheaton, p.184-242

10. ie. West, op cit

11. Wells, Ronald A., and Christopher Walker, ed. Astronomy Before the Telescope, St. Martins Press, New York, 1996, p.29–32

12. Massey, Gerald, Ancient Egypt: The Light of the World, Vol. II, T. Fisher Unwin, London, 1907, p.613-4

13. "Pyramids Seen as Stairways to Heaven", Tim Radford, The Guardian, May 14, 2001

14. Wells and Walker, op cit, p. 35

15. In The Heart Of Cygnus, NASA's Fermi Reveals A Cosmic-ray Cocoon, Nov. 28, 2011, www.nasa.gov/mission_pages/GLAST/news/cygnus-cocoon.html

16. Higgins, W.H., Stars and Constellations, p.22

17. Massey, Gerald, op cit

18. Clark, Rundle, Legend of the Phoenix, University of Birmingham Press, 1949, p.17

19. Reymond, Eve, Mythical Origins of the Egyptian Temple, Manchester University Press, 1969, p.13, 87

20. For example, Bauval, R., and Gilbert, A., The Orion Mystery, Random House, New York, 1994; Hancock, G., Heaven's Mirror, et al

21. Bauval, R., and Gilbert, A., op cit, p.192-3

22. Reymond, op cit, p.169, 279

23. Hoffman, Michael. Egypt Before The Pharaohs: The Prehistoric Foundations of Egyptian Civilization, Marlboro Books, 1979, p.29, 88

24. Reymond, op cit, p.13

25. Bauval and Gilbert, op cit, p.100-2

26. Hassan, Selim, The Sphynx: Its History in Light of Recent Excavations, Government Press, Cairo, 1949, p.75

27. Breasted, James Henry. Ancient Records of Egypt: Historical Documents from the Earliest Times to the Persian Conquest, Histories and Mysteries of Man Ltd, London 1988, pp.83-5; and Lehner, Mark. The Egyptian Heritage, p.128-9

28. ibid

29. A similar view expressed by Graham Hancock in Fingerprints of the Gods, p.303

30. Lichtheim, Miriam, Ancient Egyptian Literature, Vol. I, University of California Press, 2006, p.218

31. Greaves, John. Pyramidographia, Thomas Birch, London, 1737, p.81-3

32. ibid, p.7

33. cited in Brunton, Paul, A Search in Secret Egypt, Philosophic Foundation, 1936

34. Edwards, I.E.S., The Pyramids of Egypt, Penguin, London, 1993, p.78

35. Bauval and Gilbert, op cit, p.142-3, p.191

36. My thanks to Alex Sokolowski, editor of World Mysteries.com, for the calculations

37. Hancock, Graham, Heaven's Mirror, Crown, New York, 1998, p.167-9

38. ibid

CHAPTER 9

1. Higginson, Thomas Wentworth, Tales of the Enchanted Islands of the Atlantic, Macmillan and Co., London, 1898, p.1-3

2. Plato, The Statesman or Politicus, trans. Fowler, 1925, pp.49-53

3. Gatteford, J., and Roux, C. Bibliographie de l'Atlantide et des questions connexes, Bibliotheque de Lyon, 1926

4. Calleros, Miguel Angel Vergara. The Sacred Knowledge of the Maya, 2011, p.24

5. Men, Humbatz. The 8 Calendars of the Maya, Bear & Co, Rochester, 2010, p.12

6. Maya teacher Miguel Angel Vergara, personal communication

7. Calleros, op cit, p.13

8. Popul Vuh, the Sacred Book of the Ancient Quiche Maya, University of Oklahoma Press, Norman, 1950

9. Miguel Angel Vergara Calleros, personal communication

10. ibid

11. Calleros, op cit

12. Scientists discover ancient Mayan city hidden under Guatemalan jungle, Associated Press, The Independent, Feb 3, 2018

13. Men, op cit

14. ibid

15. Miguel Angel Vergara Calleros, personal communication

16. Calleros, op cit, p.16

17. ibid, p.42

18. Micol, Angela. Satellite Archeology Research Society, personal communication

19. Zachos, Elaine. Maya Artifacts Found In World's Largest Underwater Cave, National Geographic, February 2018

CHAPTER 10

1. Pliny, History of Nature, bk. III, p.151

2. Morrell, Benjamin. A Narrative of Four Voyages, J&J Harper, New York, 1832

3. Pliny, bk II, p.128

4. ibid

5. Brown, John, A Dictionary of the Holy Bible, H.C. Southwick, Albany, 1816, p.111

6. Tufty, Barbara, "Found In The Pacific," Science News, Vol. 89, no.15, 9 April 1966, p.239

7. ibid; and R. Menzies, Duke University Marine Laboratory and Edward Chin, Marine Laboratory of Texas A&M, Cruise Report, Research Vessel Anton Bruun, Cruise 11

8. ibid

9. Underwater Discovery: Stone Age Humans Precisely Carved a 15 ton Stone Pillar and Carried it 300 Meters, Journal of Archaeological Science, vol. 3, Sep 2015, p.398-407

10. Ulogini. Luigi. Malta: Origini della Civilita Mediterranea, La Libreria dello Stato, Rome, 1934, p.244

11. Zdruli, P. and Trisorio Liuzzi, G. (Eds). Status of Mediterranean Soil Resources: Actions Needed to Support their Sustainable Use. Mediterranean Conference Proceedings, Tunis, 26-31 May 2007. Medcoastland Publication

6. IAM Bari, Italy, pp 330; Lang D.M. Soils of Malta and Gozo, Colonial Office Colonial Research Studies Report No. 29, HMSO, London, 1960

12. Milfsud, Anton and Simon. Dossier Malta: Evidence for the Magdalenian, Malta, 1997, p.128; Sultana, Chris, et al, Malta: Echoes of Plato's Island, The Prehistoric Society of Malta, 2000, p. 42

13. Renfrew, Colin, Before Civilization: The Radiocarbon Revolution and Prehistoric Europe, London, 1999, p.163

14. cited Hancock, Graham, Underworld, Crown, New York, 2002, p. 331

15. de Boisgelin, Louis, Ancient and Modern Malta, Vol I, G. & J. Robinson, Paternoster Row, 1804, p.49

16. ibid, p.127

17. ibid, p.49

18. Enix, Linda, et al, Ancient Architects May Have Been Chasing a Buzz From Sound Waves, OTS Foundation, http://www.otsf.org/background-reading.html

19. Personal communication

20. Evans, J.D, The Prehistoric Antiquities of the Maltese Islands: A Survey, University of London, 1971, p.58

21. cited in Stearn, Jess, Edgar Cayce: The Sleeping Prophet, Doubleday, New York, 1967. p.229

22. Plato, Critias, trans. Jowett, guttenburg.org, 1998

23. Pimenta, Fernando et al, Land, Sea and Skyscape: Two Case Studies of Man-made Structures in the Azores Islands, Culture and Cosmos, Vol. 17-2, 2003, pp.107-32

24. Prehistoric rock art found in caves on Terceira Island, Carolina Matos (Ed.), Portuguese American Journal, Aug 27, 2012

25. 'Det Götheborgska Wetenskaps och Witterhets Samhallets Handlinger', 1778

26. "Evidence of ancient city found

in depths off Cuba 1/2 Mile Down",
Michael Posner. The Globe and Mail.
Montreal, December 7, 2001

27. Electronic Edition of the Diary of
Yucatan, Merida, October 9, 2004

28. Posner, op cit

29. ibid

30. Explorers Return To Study 'City' On
Ocean Floor Off Cuba. Las Vegas Sun
5-19-02

31. Electronic Edition of the Diary of
Yucatan, op cit

32. Las Vegas Sun, op cit

33. Posner, op cit

34. Ancient Temple Found Under Lake
Titicaca, BBC News, August 23, 2000

35. Tompkins, Peter, Mysteries of the
Mexican Pyramids, Harper & Low, New
York, 1978, p.373

36. Miguel Angel Vergara Celleros,
personal communication

37. Hancock, Underworld, op cit, p.596-
624

38. Schoch, Robert, Voices of the Rocks,
Harmony Books, New York, 1999, p.111-
112

39. Hancock, op. cit, p. 89-289

40. Subramanian, M.C., Glory of
Arunachela, Sri Ramanasraman,
Tiruvannamalai, India, 1999, p.104

41. Hancock, op cit, p.234

42. Dikshitar, C. Ramachandram, Studies
in Tamil Literature and History, The South
India Sauiva Siddhanta Works Publishing
Society, Madras, 1983, p.7

43. ibid

44. Devakunjari, D., Madurai Through
the Ages, Society for Archaeological,
Historical and Epigraphical Research,
Madras, p.26. And cited Hancock,
Graham, Underworld, op cit, p.248-49

45. Hancock, op cit, p.250

46. Dikshitar, op cit, p.13-14, cited
Hancock op cit

47. Kanakasabhai, V., The Tamils Eighteen
Hundred Years Ago, Sauiva Siddhanta,
Madras, 1966, p.21; Ramachandran, D.,
Studies in Tamil Literature and History,
South India Sauiva Siddhanta Works Pub
Soc., Madras, 1983 Ch 1, p.8-9, p.32-33

48. cited Hancock, op cit, p.254

49. Kanakasabhai, op cit

50. Spense, R. Hardy, The Legends and
Theories of the Buddhists, Sri Satguru
Publications, Delhi,1990, p.6

51. Mahalingham, N., Kumari Kamdan
The Lost Continent, Proceedings of the
Fifth International Conference of Tamil
Studies, International Association of
Tamil Research, Madurai, January 1981,
p.2-54; Dundes, Alan, Ed, The Flood
Myth, University of California Press,
1988, p.294-5

52. Mahalingham, ibid

CHAPTER 11

1. Satpatha Brahmana, Part I, Motilal
Banarsidass, Delhi, 1994, p.186-92

2. ibid

3. Muir, J. Original Sanskrit Texts, Vol I,
Trubner & Co, London, 1890, p.199

4. Mitchener, John, Traditions of the
Seven Rishis, Montilal Banarsidass,
Delhi, 1982, p.218-225

5. cited in Mitchiner, John. Yuga Purana,
The Asiatic Press, Calcutta, 1986, p.293

6. Mitchener, Traditions of the Seven
Rishis, op cit, p.206-09

7. Griffith, Ralph. Rgveda, vol I, E.J.
Lazarus, Benares, 1916, p.285-351

8. Mitchener, op cit, p.196

9. Reymond, op cit, 9, p.90

10. ibid, p.28, 33, 41

11. Hassan, Selim. The Sphinx,
Government Press, Cairo, 1949

12. ibid, p.25, 28, 41, 91, 159, 289

13. New Larouse Encyclopedia of Mythology, Hamlyn, London, 1959, p.9-13

14. Manetho, The Aegyptica of Manetho, Harvard University Press, 1940, p.3-5

15. Wilkinson, J. Gardner, The Hieratic Papyrus of Turin, T. Richards London, 1851; Schwaller de Lubicz, R.A., Sacred Science, the King of Pharaonic Theocracy, Inner Tradition International, New York, 1982, p.87; Schaweller de Lubicz, R.A., Sacred Science, the King of Pharaonic Theocracy, Inner Tradition International, New York, 1982, p.87

16. Mela, Pomponius. De Situ Orbis, Sumptibus, 1816; and Herodotus, History p.193

17. Hancock, Graham. Fingerprints of the Gods, op cit, p.545

18. Murray, Margaret. The Splendour That Was Egypt, Sidgwick and Jackson, London, 1950, p.12

19. Mahabharata, Santiparvan, Moksadharma. Quoted in Lovejoy, Arthur, and Boas, George. Primitivism and Related Ideas in Antiquity, Johns Hopkins Press, Baltimore, 1935, p.436

20. Wheeler, Post, The Sacred Scriptures of the Japanese, Henry Schuman, New York, 1952, p.91

21. Dileep Kumar Kanjilal, Vimana in Ancient India, Sanskrit Pustak Bhandar, Calcutta, 1985, p.18-19

22. Kilmer, A.D., The Mesopotamian Counterparts of the Biblical Nephilim, in E.W. Conrad and E.G. Newing (eds.), Perspectives on Language and Text: Essays and Poems in Honor of Francis I, Andersen's Sixtieth Birthday, July 28, 1985, Eisenbrauns, Winona Lake, p.39

23. Wise, M. and Abegg, M and Cook, E, The Dead Sea Scrolls, Harper San Francisco, 1996, 4Q531 Frag 1

24. D. Arnaud, Aula Orientalis Supplementa 27, 2007, no. 42; A. R.

George, Aula Orientalis 25, 2007: 240; A. R. George, Aula Orientalis 25 (2007): 247-248; cited Annus, Amar, "Louvre Gilgamesh (AO 19862) is depicted in life size, University of Tartu, 2012

25. Emery, Walter, Archaic Egypt, Penguin Books, Harmondsworth, 1972, p.38-9

26. Reymond, op cit, p.112-14

27. "Neural Correlates of Personalized Spiritual Experiences," Lisa Miller Iris M Balodis et al, Cerebral Cortex, bhy102, Oxford Academic, 29 May 2018

28. de Lubicz, R.A. Schwaller, Sacred Science: The King of Pharaonic Thocracy, Inner Traditions, Rochester, 1982, p.111

29. Henry, A, in The Journal of the Anthropological Institute of Great Britain and Ireland, Vol. 33, 1903, p.98-103

30. Budge, E.A. Wallis, Gods of the Egyptians, vol. I, Gilbert and Rivington, London, 1904, p.414

31. ibid

32. Fowden, Garth. The Egyptian Hermes: A Historical Approach to the Late Pagan Mind, Princeton University Press, 1993, p.33

33. Budge, Egyptian Myths, p.44 ; and Gods of the Egyptians, vol. II, p.214

34. Tavaria, Phiroz Nasaevantji, A Manual of Khshnoom: The Zoroastrian Occult Knowledge, States People Press, Bombay, 1971

35. Markhem, Clemens, R., trans. and ed., Narratives of the Rites and Laws of the Yncas, Hakluyt Society, London, 1873, vol.c XLVIII, p.124

36. Donelly, Ignatius. Atlantis: The Antediluvian World, Harper & Brothers, New York, 1882, p.394

37. Vega, Garcilaso de la, Comentarios Reales de los Incas, Ediciones La Republica, Tomo XXIII, Montevideo, 1992, pp. 2185-2186

38. Pali Jae Lee & Koko Willis, Tales from

the Night Rainbow, Night Rainbow, 1990

39. Goetz, Delia, and Morley, Sylvanus (Eds.). Popol Vuh: The Sacred Book of the Ancient Quiche Maya, University of Oklahoma Press, 1991, p.168

40. ibid, p.156

41. ibid, p.169

42. ibid, p.90-3, p.178

CHAPTER 12

1. Abu Mahmud Ibn Al-Qazwini, al-Buldân Ajâ'ib, Wüstenfeld, Göttingen, 1849-51

2. Account of Abilio Duarte, cited in Adrião, Vitor Manuel, Sintra, Serra Sagrada, Comunidade Teurgica Portuguesa, Sintra, 1994

3. O Domingo Ilustrado, Vol. 2, n.57, 1898

4. Sintra: Patrinomio da Humanidade, Câmara Municipal de Sintra, Sintra, 2011 web.archive.org/web/20110807005808/ http://www.cm-sintra.pt/Artigo. aspx?ID=3383

5. Gandra, Manuel Joaquim, O Eterno Feminino no Aro de Mafra, Mafra, 1994

6. cited Martins, Hugo, Comunidade Teurgica Portuguesa, no. 69, July 2013, p.36-7

7. Davies, Edward, Mythology and Rites of the British Druids, J. Booth, London, 1809, p.536

8. Brunton, Paul. A Search in Secret Egypt, London, Rider, 1965, p.262

9. Miguel Angel Vergara Celleros, personal communication

10. Irwin, Constance. Fair Gods and Stone Faces, W.H. Allen, London, 1964, p.139

11. Ignatius Donnelly, Atlantis: The Antediluvian World, Harper & Bros, New York, 1882, p.165; The Mythology of Mexico and Central America, p.161

12. Goetz and Morley, op cit, p.168

13. Hamlyn, Paul, New Larousse Encyclopedia of Mythology, London, 1989, p.439

14. ibid

15. Calleros, op cit, p.13

16. Personal communication

17. Yuhas, Alan. Secret Mayan tombs lend rare insight into rule of mysterious 'snake kings', The Guardian, 14 Oct 2016

18. Associated Press, Sep 14, 2018

19. Hill, Kenneth, and Malotki, Ekkehart. Hopi Dictionary/Hopìikwa Lavàytutuveni: A Hopi-English Dictionary of the Third Mesa Dialect, University of Arizona Press, 1998, p.137; Courlander, Harold, The Fourth World of the Hopis, University of New Mexico Press, 1987, p.85

20. Martinez, Susan, The Lost Continent of Pan, Bear and Co., Rochester, 2016, p.211

21. Howard Giskin and Bettye S. Walsh. An introduction to Chinese culture through the family. State University of New York Press, 2001, p. 126

22. Zai, J., Taoism and Science: Cosmology, Evolution, Morality, Heath and more, Ultravisum, 2015

23. Dull, Jack. "The Evolution of Government in China", Heritage of China: Contemporary Perspectives on Chinese Civilization. University of California Press, 1990

24. Major, John S.; et al., eds., The Huainanzi: A Guide to the Theory and Practice of Government in Early Han China, Columbia University Press, New York, 2010

25. Piggott, Juliet, Japanese Mythology, Hamlyn, 1969

26. Morrow, Avery, The Sacred Science of Ancient Japan, Inner Traditions, Rochester, 2014, p,101

27. ibid p.121

28. Gaudes, Rudiger, Kaundinya, Preah

Thaong, and the Nagi Soma, Asian Folklore Studies, Vol. 52, Nanzan University, 1993, p.333-358

29. Bonnefoy, Yves (ed.), Asian Mythologies, University of Chicago Press, 1993, p.150

30. Grigsby, John, The Temples of Angkor, cited Hancock, Graham, Heaven's Mirror, p.124-32

31. Varaha Purana

32. Gopal, Madan, and Gautam, K.S. eds., India Through the Ages. Publication Division, Ministry of Information and Broadcasting, Government of India, 1990, p. 78.

33. Singh, Singh, Bipin, The legend of Annu-Nagi, Mythology and History of Naga People and Queen Gaidinliu of Naga, p.6-7

34. Monier Williams Sanskrit Dictionary with Etymology, Oxford University Press, p.1201

35. Flood, Gavin. An Introduction to Hinduism, Cambridge University Press, Cambridge, 1996, p.92

36. Monaghan, Patricia. The Book of Goddesses and & Heroines, Llewellyn, St. Paul, 1993, p.255

37. The Book of Enoch, R.H. Charles, ed., Bungay, London Society for Promoting Christian Knowledge, 1917, LXD: 8-12

38. O'Brien, Christian. The Genius of the Few, Turnstone Press, Wellingborough, 1985

39. Singh, op cit, p.1

CHAPTER 13

1. Personal communication

2. Hancock, Graham, Underworld, op cit, p.43-6

3. Verbrugghe, Gerald, and Wickersham, John, eds., Berossus and Manetho, University of Michigan Pres, 1999, p.43

4. Exodus 2:3; and 1 Kings 9:26

5. Goetz, Delia, op cit, p.155-69

6. Griaule, Marcel. Conversations with Ogotemmeli: An Introduction to Dogon Religious Ideas. International African Institute, Oxford University Press, Oxford, 1965

7. Cited in Temple, Robert, The Sirius Mystery, St. Martins Press, London, 1976

8. De Lafayette, Maximillien. Comparative Encyclopedic Dictionary of Mesopotamian Vocabulary, Dead and Ancient Languages, Vol. 10, Times Square Press, New York, 2014, p.63

9. Crawford, Harriet E. W., Dilmun and its Neighbors, 1998. p. 9; Glassner, Jea-Jaques, The Invention of Cuneiform, 1990, p.7; Nayeem, M.A., Prehistory and Protohistory of the Arabian Peninsula: Bahrain, 1990, p.32

10. Kramer, Samuel Noah, The Sumerians: op cit, p.308

11. Kondratov, Alexander. Three Oceans, Progress Publishers, Moscow, 1971, p.156

12. Rose, Jeffrey. "New Light on Human Prehistory in the Arabo-Persian Gulf Oasis," Current Anthropology 51:6, Dec. 2010

13. Fincke, Jeanne. The Babylonian Texts of Nineveh: Report on the British Museum's Library Projects, Archiv fur Orientforchung 50, 2003-4, p.111

14. Kramer, Samuel. History Begins at Sumer, University of Pennsylvania Press, 1991, p.149

15. Hallow, William. Journal of Cuneiform Studies, vol. 23, 61, 1970

16. Kramer, Samuel. The Sumerians, op cit p.108

17. ibid, p.151

18. Verbrugghe, op cit, p.49-50

19. ibid

20. ibid

21. Scolnic, Benjamin Edidin. If the Egyptians Drowned in the Red Sea where are Pharaoh's Chariots?: Exploring the Historical Dimension of the Bible, UP of America, 2005 p.40

22. Verbrugghe, op cit, p.43

23. Annus, Amar, On the Origin of the Watchers, Journal of the Study of Psedepigrapha, Vol. 19-4, 2010, p.285

24. For example, Annus, ibid p.289

25. ibid; Verbrugghe, op cit, p.17, p.44; Lansberger, Benno. Three Essays on the Sumerians II: the beginnings of civilization in Mesopotamia, Udena Pubs, Los Angeles, p.174

26. Cavalli-Sforza, Luca, et al. The History and Geography of Human Genes, Princeton University Press, 1994, p.215

27. Annus, Amar, op. cit. p.287

28. Lansberger, Benno, op cit, p.174

29. Green, Pamela Tamara, p.170

30. ibid, p.137-8

31. see Lambert, W.G., The Qualifications of Babylonian Diviners, in S.M. Maul (ed.), Festschrift fur Rykle Borger zu seimen, 65, Geburtstag am 24 Mai, 1994, Styx, Groningen 1998; and Collins, J.J., The Apocalyptic Imagination: An Introduction to Jewish Apocalyptic Literature, Eerdmans, Grand Rapids, 1998, p.45-6

32. George, A.R. Babylonian Topographical Texts, Peeters Pubs., 1992, p.261

33. Annus, Amar, On The Origin of the Watchers, op cit, p.280; and Hallo, William, Origins: The Ancient Near Eastern Background of Some Modern Western Institutions, Brill, Leiden, 1996, p. 1-17

34. Annus, ibid

35. O'Brien, Christian. The Genius of the Few, Turnstone Press, Wellingborough, 1985, p.38-39, p.73

36. The Book of Enoch, R.H. Charles, ed., Bungay, 1917, VI:6; 1 Enoch, ed. Matthew Black, E.J. Brill, Leiden, 1985 p.28

37. Book of the Secrets of Enoch (2 Enoch), Slavonik version, ed R.H. Charles, Oxford, 1896, III:1

38. ibid, XXI:2 - XXII:12

39. Black, op cit, p.106

40. The Book of Jubilees, in Eisenman, R. and Wise, M. The Dead Sea Scrolls Uncovered, Element, 1992

41. Book of the Secrets of Enoch (2 Enoch), op cit, XXI:2 - XXII:12

42. The Book of Enoch, R.H. Charles, op cit, CVI: 1-8

43. Platt, Rutherford, Jr. The Forgotten Books of Eden, Bell, New York, 1980, p. 6-7

44. Mahabharata, Santiparvan, Moksadharma. Quoted in Lovejoy, op cit, p.436

45. The Book of Enoch, R.H. Charles, op cit, L:1-10

46. ibid, XX: 6-8

47. O'Brien, op. cit, p.145

48. ie. O'Brien

49. Baty, John. The Book of Enoch the Prophet, Samuel Jefferson, London, 1839

50. I Enoch, ed. Matthew Black, op cit, p.35

51. RThe Book of Enoch, H. Charles, op cit. p.37

52. Amar Annus, op. cit, p.283

53. Wiggermann, F., Reallexikon der Assyriologie und Vorderasiatischen Archaologie 8, 1994, p.222-44

54. Charles, op cit, p.31-40

55. I Enoch, ed. Matthew Black, op cit, p.28-9

56. Charles, op cit, p.5-6, p.42; George Nickelsburg and James VanderKamm, 1 Enoch: The Hermenia Translation,

Augusburg Fortress, MN, 2012

57. The Book of the Secrets of Enoch, Charles, o pcit,, XXIV-1

58. Nag Hammadi Texts, 4Q530 Frag 2

59. Wise, M: Abegg, M.: and Cook, E. The Dead Sea Scrolls, A new Translation, Harper San Franscisco, 1996

60. G.A, Dorsey, The Mythology of the Wichita, Carnegie Institution of Washington, 1904 p.291-5

61. I Enoch, ed. Matthew Black, op cit,p.29-31

62. The Book of Enoch, R.H. Charles, op cit, XIX: 1-2

63. ibid, X: 1-12

64. I Enoch, ed. Matthew Black, op cit, p.30

65. Kilmer, Anne. The Mesopotamian Counterparts of the Biblical Nepilim, in E.W. Conrad and E.G. Newing, Perspectives on Language and Text: Essays and Poems in Honor of Francis I Andersen's Sixtieth Birthday, July 28, 1985, Winona Lake, p.39-40

66. Annus, op. cit, p.295

67. Eisenman, R., James the Brother of Jesus, Faber & Faber, 1997

68. Knight & Lomas, Uriel's Machine, Element, Shaftsbury, 1999, p.289

69. Genesis 6:4, New International Version

70. Numbers 13: 32-3

CHAPTER 14

1. Sonnett, C., and Gault, D., The Oceanic Impact of Large Objects, Advances In Space Research, Vol. 11, Issue 6, 1991, p.77-86

2. Stoker, J.J., Water Waves: The Mathematical Theory With Applications, Wiley Classics Library Edition, New York, 1992

3. There exists verifiable proof on the ground. See the pioneering work of Ron Wyatt, http://wyattmuseum.com/discovering/noahs-ark

4. Diakonoff, Igor, First Evidence of the Proto-Armenian Language in Eastern Anatolia, Annual of Armenian Linguistics, 13: 51-54, Cleveland State University, 1992; also spelled Urartu, after a nearby settlement.

5, Personal communication with Zuni elder Raymond Mahooty; Waters, Frank, op cit, p.115

6. Prehistoric Culture Change on the Colorado Plateau: Ten Thousand Years on Black Mesa, ed. Shirley Powell and Francis E. Smiley, University of Arizona Press, 2002, p.162

7. Pringle, Heather, Did a Comet Wipe Out Prehistoric Americans?, New Scientist, May 22, 2007. The date was revised from an earlier estimate of 10,600 BC

8. ibid; and "Bayesian chronological analyses consistent with synchronous age of 12,835–12,735 Cal B.P. for Younger Dryas boundary on four continents" www.pnas.org/cgi/doi/10.1073/pnas.1507146112

9. Firestone, R.B., West, A., Kennett, J.P., et al, Evidence for an extraterrestrial impact 12,900 years ago that contributed to the megafaunal extinctions and the Younger Dryas cooling, PNAS, vol. 104, no. 41, Oct 9, 2007, p.16016-20

10. Kinzie, CR Hee, SSQ Stich, A et al. Nanodiamond-rich layer across three continents consistent with major cosmic impact at 12,800 cal BP, Journal of Geology, 122(5), 2014-01-01

11. Toward end of Ice Age, human beings witnessed fires larger than dinosaur killers, University of Kansas, Science Daily, February 1, 2018; Wendy S. Wolbach, Joanne P. Ballard, et al, Extraordinary Biomass-Burning Episode and Impact Winter Triggered by the Younger Dryas Cosmic Impact 12,800

Years Ago. 1. Ice Cores and Glaciers. The Journal of Geology, 2018; 000 DOI: 10.1086/695703 ; Wendy S. Wolbach, Joanne P. Ballard, et al., Extraordinary Biomass-Burning Episode and Impact Winter Triggered by the Younger Dryas Cosmic Impact 12,800 Years Ago. 2. Lake, Marine, and Terrestrial Sediments. The Journal of Geology, 2018; 000 DOI: 10.1086/695704

12. Clark, Rundle. Myth and Symbol in Ancient Egypt, Thames & Hudson, London, 1978, p.263

13. Alley, Richard, and Michael Bender, Greenland Ice cores Frozen In Time, Scientific American, Feb 1998, p.80-85; Dansgaard, W., et al, The Abrupt Termination of the Younger Dryas Event, Nature, vol. 339, June 15, 1989, p.532

14. Barbiero, Flavio, "On the Possibility of Very Rapid Shifts of the Poles," Quaderni del Dipartimento di Matematica, Statistica, Informatica ed Applicazoni, Universita degli Studi di Bergamo, Italy, 1997, no. 7, 1-20

15. Laplace, Pierre. Exposition du Systeme du Monde, 1796

16. Plato, Timaeus, trans Bury, 1929, 22 C-D

17. Tedlock, Dennis. trans. Popul Vuh: The Mayan Book of the Dawn of Life, Simon and Schuster, New York, 1986, p.84

18. Foster, B., Before The Muses: An Anthology of Akkadian Literature, CDL Press, Bethesda, 2005, p.887

19. Verbrugghe and Wickersham. op cit

20. Diodorus of Sicily, trans. Oldfather, The Library of History, II, 31

21. Legge, James. The Chinese Classics, III, pt. I, Trubner & Co, London, 1865, p.125

22. Winger, L., Textes historiques, 2nd ed, 1922, I, 50

23. Philo, On The Life of Moses, ii

24. The Aryabhatyia of Aryabhatta, trans. W.E. Clark, 1930, p.51; and Surya Siddhanta: Burgers E., A Text Book of Hindu Astronomy, 1860

25. Gilmore, John, The Fragments of the Persika of Ktesias, MacMillan, New York, 1888, p.38

26. Lockyer, Norman. The Dawn of Astronomy, Cassell and Co, London, 1894, p.243

27. Murray, H., and Crawford J., A Historical and Descriptive Account of China, 1836, p.235

28. Gaubil, Antoine. Histoire de l'astronomie Chinoise, Rolin, Paris, 1732, p.73-86

CHAPTER 15

1. Laws II, in John Cooper, Plato: Complete Works, Hackett Publishing Co, Cambridge, 1997, p.1348

2. Yilak, L.B.G. The Arctic Home of the Vedas, Tilak Bros., Poona City, 1903, p.61

3. Nature, vol. 234, 27 December, 1971 p.173-4

4. Hancock, Fingerprints of the Gods, op cit, p.470-2; Flem Ath, Rand, and Rose. When The Sky Fell, St. Martins Press, 1995

5. Hapgood, Charles. Path of the Pole, Chilton Book Co, 1970, p.111

6. ibid, p.99

7. ibid, p.107

8. Tilak, op cit, p.64-7

9. Pliny, Natural History, II, 45

10. Henry Patton et al, Deglaciation of the Eurasian ice sheet complex, Quaternary Science Reviews, May 19, 2017

11. "Sahara's Abrupt Desertification Started By Changes in Earth's Orbit, Accelerated by Atmospheric and Vegetation Feedbacks." American Geophysical Union, Science Daily, July 12, 1999

12. Skonieczny, C. et al. "African humid periods triggered the reactivation of a large river system in Western Sahara, Nature, 6, 8751, 2015

13. Reymond, op cit, p.122-134

14. ibid, p.108

15. ibid, p.8, 55, 90, 105

16. ibid, p.109, 202

17. ibid, p.190

18. Diodorus p.26

19. Reymond, op cit, pp.25, 28, 41, 91, 310

20. Brandon, S.G.F., Creation Legends of the Near East, Hodder & Stoughton, London, 1963, p.48

21. Rundle-Clark, R.T.. Myth and Symbol in Ancient Egypt, Thames & Hudson, London, 1959, p.140, 222, 246

22. Budge, Gods of the Egyptians, op cit pp.7, 287; Budge, Osiris and the Egyptian Resurrection, vol, I, Medici Society, 1911, p.97-8; Faulkner, R.O., Pyramid Texts of Pepi I, vol. II, Oxford University Press, Oxford, 1998, p.316

23. Reymond, op cit, p.273

24. Courlander, Harold, Hopi Voices: Recollections, Traditions, and Narratives of the Hopi Indians, University of New Mexico, Albuquerque, 1982, p.37 and p.97

25. Schliemann, Paul. How I Found the Lost Atlantis, The Source of All Civilization, CreateSpace reprint, 2013, p.18

26. Beckwith, Martha Hawaiian Mythology. University of Hawaii Press, 1970, p. 321-323

27. Thomas, Lowell. Hungry Waters, the Story of the Great Flood, Philadelphia, 1937, p.188

28. Churchward, James. The Lost Continent of Mu, 1932, p.324

29. ibid

30. ibid

CHAPTER 16

1. Waters, Frank, Book of the Hopi, Penguin, New York, 1977, p.1

2. ibid

3. ibid, p.6

4. ibid

5. ibid

6. ibid

7. ibid

8. ibid

9. ibid, p.115; Blumrich, Josef. Kásskara und die sieben Welten die Geschichte der Menschheit in der Überlieferung der Hopi-Indianer, Indianer, Knaur; Auflage, 1999; also cited Hamilton, Shawn. Nexus Magazine, Feb-Mar 2016, p.59-63

10. ibid, p.137

11. Ararat's name originates from the M šu (Mashu) mountain mentioned in the Epic of Gilgamesh. Armen Petrosyan, cited Panossian, Ramik. The Armenians: From Kings and Priests to Merchants and Commissars, Columbia University Press, New York, 2006

12. Thompson, Eric. Maya History and Religion, U. of Oklahoma Press, Norman, 1970, p.340

13. Hill, Kenneth, and Malotki, Ekkehart. Hopi Dictionary/Hopìikwa Lavàytutuveni: A Hopi-English Dictionary of the Third Mesa Dialect, University of Arizona Press, 1998, p.31, 190, 270, 271; David, Gary. The Orion Zone: The Ancient Cities of the Southwest, Adventures Unlimited Press, Kempton, 2006 p.292

14. Waters, op. cit, p.16

15. Schoch, Robert. Forgotten Civilizations: The Role of Solar Outbursts in our Past and Future, Inner Traditions, Rochester, 2012

16. Clifford Mahooty, personal

communication

17. ibid

18. Zolbrod, Paul. Diné Bahané: The Navajo Creation Story, University of New Mexico Press Albuquerque, 1984, p.36

19. David, op cit, p.154

20. Talayesva, Don, and Simmons, Leo. Sun Chief: The Autobiography of a Hopi Indian, Yale University Press, 1963, p.86

21. Parsons, E.C.. Pueblo Indian Religions, University of Nebraska Press, vol. I, 1996, p.275

22. Clifford Mahooty, personal communication

23. Hill and Ekkehart. Hopi Dictionary op. cit, p.376

24. Warren, Henry Clarke. Buddhism in Translations, Harvard University, Cambridge, MA, 1909 p.322

25. Malotki, Ekkehart, and Lomatuway'ma, Michael. Earth Fire, Kiva Publishing, 1987, p.58-61

26. Walters, Frank, op cit, p.ix

27. David, op. cit, p.28

28. Mindeleff, Victor. A Study of Pueblo Architecture: Tusayan and Cibola, Government Printing Press, Washington, 1891, p.136

29. Adams, F. Charles. The Origin and Development of the Pueblo Katsina Cult, Library of Arizona Press, 2017, p.4

30. UFO Digest, Sept 2008

31. ibid

32. Wagamese, Richard. Star People, wagamese.writer.wordpress.com, 2011

33. Black Elk, Wallace, and Lyon, William. Black Elk: The Sacred Ways of the Lakota, p.90-1

34. Clifford Mahooty, personal communication

35. Michell, John, The New View Over Atlantis, Harper & Row, San Francisco, 1984, p.83

36. New Larousse Encyclopedia of Mythology, p.14

37. Plato, Timaeus and Critias, Penguin Classics, p.35-6

38. Greaves, John, Pyramidographia: Or a Description of the Pyramids in Egypt, George Badger, London, 1646, reprinted Robert Lienhardt, Baltimore, p.96

39. Tompkins, Peter. The Great Pyramid, Penguin, London, 1978, p.6

40. Stecchini, Livio. in Tompkins, Peter. Secrets of the Great Pyramid, Penguin, Hammondsworth, 1973

41. Bloomingarden, Richard. The Pyramids of Teotihuacan, Editura S.A. Mexico, 1993, p,16

42. Budge, E.A. Wallis. Egyptian Magic, Kegan Paul, Trench, Trubner and Co., London, 1901, p.143

43. Darmestester, James and Mills, H.L. The Zend Avesta, 1895, Atlantic Pub reprint, New Delhi, 1990, Part 1, p.18

44. ibid, p.20; and 1989 translation p.14, note 87

45. Encyclopedia Iranica, Jamshid i and Jamshid ii

46. Spence, Lewis. The Magic and Mysteries of Mexico, Rider, London, 1922, p.51

47. Annus, Amar. On The Origin of the Watchers, op cit, p.284

48. Denning-Bolle, S. Wisdom in Akkadian Literature, Ex Oriente Lux, Leiden, 1992, p.28

49. The Book of the Secrets of Enoch (2 Enoch), Charles, R.H. op cit

CHAPTER 17

1. Olcott, William Tyler. Star Lore of All Ages, G.P. Puttnam's Sons, New York, 1911, p.411

2. Haliburton, R.G. The Festival of the Dead, Royal Astronomical Society of

Canada, Ottawa, 1863, p.24

3. Waters, op. cit, p.149 p.168-87

4. Haliburton, op cit, p.1; Olcott, op cit, p.412

5. de Santillana, G & von Dechend, H. Hamlet's Mill. Nonpareil Books, Boston 2007, p 386, quoting Sir James Frazer, Folk-Lore in the Old Testament, 1918, vol. 1, pp. 143f

6. Knight and Lomas, op cit, p.12

7. Olcott, op cit, p.412

8. Haliburton, op cit, p.25

9. Henry, Teuira. Ancient Tahiti, Bernice Bishop Museum, Hawaii, 1928

10. Budge, Gods of the Egyptians, vol. I, op cit, p.414

11. Steel, Duncan. Rogue Asteroids and Doomsday Comets: The Search for the Million Megaton Menace that Threatens Life on Earth, John Wiley and Sons, New York, 1995

12. Best, Elsdon. Tuhoe: The Children of the Mist, A.H. and A.W. Reed, Wellington, 1929, p.853

13. Archaeoastronomy: The Journal of the Center for Archaeoastronomy, Vol. VIII, nos. 1-4, January 1985, p.99

14. Napier, W.M. Paleolithic Extinctions and the Taurid Complex, Monthly Notices of the Royal Astronomical Society, Vol. 405, issue 3, July 1, 2010, p.1901-6

15. Clube, Victor, and Napier, Bill, The Cosmic Winter, p.150-3; Hoyle, Fred, and Wickramsinghe, Chandra, Life on Mars? The Case for a Cosmic Heritage, Clinical Press Ltd., Bristol, 1997, p.176

16. Tollmann, E. and Kristan. Terra Nova, vol. 6, no.2, 1994, p.209-17

17. Kinzie, Charles, et al. Nanodiamond-Rich Layer Across Three Continents Consistent With Major Cosmic Impact at 12,8000 Cal BP, Journal of Geology, 122(5), 1.1.2014

18. Cohen, Julie. Nanodiamonds Are Forever, The Current, University of California, August 28, 2014

19. Kjar, Kurt, et al. A large impact crater beneath Hiawatha Glacier in northwest Greenland, Science Advances, Nov. 14, 2018

20. Mitrovic, George. Goodbye Siberian Woolly Mammoth, self-published monograph

21. Clube and Napier, op cit, p.150; Babadzhanov, P. B.; Williams, I. P.; Kokhirova, G. I., "Near-Earth Objects in the Taurid complex", Monthly Notices of the Royal Astronomical Society. 386 (3): 1436–1442, 2008; Whipple, F.L., "Photographic meteor studies. III. The Taurid shower", 1940; Kla ka, Jozef, "Meteor Streams of Comet Encke. Taurid Meteor Complex", 1999

22. Kvasnytsya, Victor; et al. "New evidence of meteoritic origin of the Tunguska cosmic body". Planet. Space Sci. 84: 131–140, 2013

CHAPTER 18

1. Milbrath, Susan. Star Gods of the Maya, University of Texas, 1999, p.266

2. Schele, Linda. Code of Kings, Scribner, New York, 1998, p.37

3. David, op. cit, p.28

4. Waters, op. cit, p.149

5. Silva. The Lost Art of Resurrection, op cit

6. Titiev, Mischa. Old Oraibi: A Study of the Hopi Indians of Third Mesa, University of New Mexico Press, Albuquerque, 1992, p.135

7. Budge, Egyptian Hieroglyphic Dictionary, vol. II; and Fell, Barry. America BC, New York Times Book Co, New York, 1976, p.174-7; David, op cit, p.247

8. Bauval and Gilbert, op cit, p.57

9. Breasted, James Henry. The Dawn of Conscience, Charles Scribner & Sons,

New York, 1944, p.69

10. The Ancient Egyptian Pyramid Texts, lines 882-3

11. Utterances 310 and 669

12. Budge, Osiris and Egyptian Resurrection, vol. II, op cit, p.307

13. Mitchener, John, Traditions of the Seven Rishis, Montilal Banarsidass, Delhi, 1982, p.253

14. Knight and Lomas, op cit, p.12

15. Makere and Te Porohau Ruka Te Korako, comp. Brailsford, Barry, Whispers of the Waitaha, op cit, p.29-30

16. ibid, p.199-200

17. ibid

18. ibid

19. ibid

20. Book of Enoch

CHAPTER 19

1. Waters, op cit, p.21

2. Prescott, William. History of the Conquest of Mexico, Modern Library edition, New York, p.49

3. Ahmad, B.M., Qur'an with English translation and Commentary, Islam International Publications Ltd, Tilford, 1988, Vol. III, p.1068

4. Silva, Freddy. The Divine Blueprint, Invisible Temple, Portland, 2012; Broadhurst. Paul, and Miller, Hamish. Dance of the Dragon, Penwith Press, Launceston, 1986, et al

5. Jahn, Robert G., et al; Acoustical Resonances of Assorted Ancient Structures, Technical Report, PEAR 95002, Princeton University, March 1995; Devereux, Paul, et al. Acoustical Properties of Ancient Ceremonial Sites, Journal of Scientific Exploration, 9:438, 1995; et al

6. Waters, op. cit, p.21

7. Silva, Freddy. Secrets In The Fields,

Invisible Temple, Portland, 2012

8. ibid, p.272-75

9. ibid, p.273

10. ibid, p.A11

11. Clube and Napier, op cit, p.150

12. ibid, p.153

13. Spedicato, Emilio. Galactic Encounters, Apollo Objects, Atlantis and Other Tales, Universita degli Studi di Bergamo, 1997, p.12-13

14. Schoch, Robert, and McNally, Robert. Voyages of the Pyramid Builders: The True Origins of the Pyramids from Lost Egypt to Ancient America, Tarcher/Penguin, New York, 2003

15. Stewart, 1861; Schoch, Robert. Forgotten Civilizations: The Role of Solar Outbursts in our Past and Future, Inner Traditions, Rochester, 2012, p.95-100

16. Nation, 2002; and Schoch, op cit, p.173-77

17. Lange, H.O. Der Magische Papyrus Harris, Det. Klg Danske Videnskabernes Selskab, Copenhagen, 1927, p.58; Lange, C, (tans.). Papyrus Ipwer 2:8, Siyzungsberichte d. Preuss, Akademie der Wissenschaften, 1903, p.601-10

18. Nature, vol. 234, Dec 1971, p.173-4

19. Harwood, J.M., and Malin, S.C.R., Nature, February 12, 1976

20. Annals of Coauhtitlan

21. Dixon, R.B. Oceanic Mythology, Vol. IX, Marshall Jones Co., Boston, 1916, p.15

22. Murray, H. An Historical and Descriptive Account of China, 1836, I, p.40

23. Mueller, Max, ed., The Sacred Books of the East, XXXVIII, Clarendon Press, London, 1892, p.33

24. Mueller, op. cit, part I, 1880, p.17; Tilak, op cit, p.350

25. Waters, op. cit, p.1-6

26. ibid, p.21

27. www.overshootday.org

28. Viravong, Maha Sila. Khun Bulomrajathirat, Ministry of Education, 2002; compare with Mollerup, Asger. Phu Tai World Day presentation, Renu Nakhon, 2012

29. Silva. Secrets In The Fields, op. cit

30. Benson, H., et al. "Body temperature changes during the practice of G Tum-mo (heat) yoga," Nature 1982, 295:234-6

31. McTaggart, Lynne. The Intention Experiment, Free Press, New York, 2007, p.177-89; Nelson, R.D. et al. "Field Anomalies in group situations," Journal of Scientific Exploration, 1998, 12(3):425-54

32. Nelson, Roger, et al. Field REG II: Consciousness Field Effects: Replications and Explorations, Journal of Scientific Exploration 12:3, 1998

33. Eneix, op cit

34. McTaggart, op cit, p.189-93

35. Dunne, B.J. "Co-operator experiments with an REG device," PEAR Technical Note 91005, Princeton Engineering Anomalies Research, New Jersey, Dec 1991; Dean Radin and Roger Nelson, Evidence for consciousness-related anomalies; and 'When immovable objections meet irresistible evidence, Behavioral and Brain Sciences, 1987, 10: 600-1

36. "Strong rains fall on fire-ravaged Amazon state," "http://edition.cnn.com/EARTH/9803/31/brazil.fires.update/, March 31, 1998

37. Dillbeck, M.C. et al. "The Transcendental Meditation program and crime rate change in a sample of 48 cities," Journal of Crime and Justice, 1981; 4:25-45

38. McTaggart, op cit p.185

39. The Book of the Secrets of Enoch, Charles, R.Hop cit, XXIV-1

ADDITIONAL BIBLIOGRAPHY

Annon. Ophiolatrea, Private Printing, 1889

Annus, Amar. On The Origins of the Watchers, University of Tartu, Ulikooli, 2010

Baty, John. The Book of Enoch the Prophet, Samuel Jefferson, Carlile, 1839

Beaglehole, J.C. The Exploration of the Pacific, Stanford University Press, Palo Alto, 1934

Best, Elsdon, Tuhoe: The Children of the Mist,

Birrell, Anne, Chinese Mythology: An Introduction, Johns Hopkins University Press, Baltimore, 1993

Bolton, Kerry R., ENIGMA OF THE NGATI HOTU, Antrocom Online Journal of Anthropology, vol. 6, n. 2, 2010

Bourney, Charles, and Asher, Teryl, The Peoples of the Hills: Ancient Ararat and the Caucasus, Phoenix Press, London 1971

Brown, John Macmillan. The Riddle of the Pacific, London, 1924

Burstein, S.M., The Babylonica of Berossus, Undena Pubs., Malibu, 1978

Casanova, E., Dos Yacimentos Arqueologicos en la Peninsula de Copacabana, Antropologia, Etnografia y Arqueologia, Pub. 82, Vol. XL, Buenos Aires, 1942

Cook, Gary, and Brown, Thomas. The Secret Land, Stoneprint Press, Canterbury, 1999

Cooke, C. Wythe. Carolina BAys and the Shapes of Eddies, United States Government Printing Office, 1954

Cowan James, 1930. The Maori: Yesterday and Today, Whitcombe and Tombs, Wellington, New Zealand.

Cowan James, The Patupaiarehe, Part 2, Journal of the Polynesian Society, vol. 30, Auckland, New Zealand.

Davis, Edward, The Mythology and Rites of the British Druids, J. Booth, London, 1809

Dietrich, O., et al. Establishing a Radiocarbon Sequence for Gobekli Tepe, State of Research and New Data, Neo-Lithics, 1/2013, p.36-41

Dillehay, Tom, et al. Chronology, mound-building and environment at Huaca Prieta, coastal Peru, from 13,700 to 4000 years ago, Antiquity Publications, 86: 48-70, 2012

Doutre, Martin, Ancient Celtic New Zealand, De Danann Pub, 1999

Dowson, John, A Classical Dictionary of Hindu Mythology & Religion,

Emery, Walter, Archaic Egypt, Penguin Books, Harmondsworth, 1972

Fewkes, J. Walter. Dolls of the Tusayan Indians, E.J. Brill, Leiden, 1894

Fleming, Daniel, and Milstein, Sara. The Buried Foundation of the Gilgamesh Epic: The Akkadian Huwana Narrative, SBL Press, Atlanta, Leiden, 2010

Frazer, James George. Folklore in the Old Testament, MacMillan and Co., London, 1919

Grace John Te Herekiekie, 1992. Tuwharetoa: a history of the Maori people of the Taupo district, Reed Books, Auckland, New Zealand.

Griffiths, J. Gwynn. Origins of Osiris, Berlin, 1966

Heyerdahl, Thor. American Indians In The Paific, Gyldendal Norsk Forlag, Oslo, 1952

Joesting, Edward Kaua'i, The Separate Kingdom. Honolulu, Hawaii: University of Hawaii Press and Kaua'i Museum Association. 1987

Kiss, Edmund. Das Sonnentor von Tihuanaku und Hörbigers Welteislehre, Verlegt bei Koehler & Amelang, Leipzig, 1937

Lewis, Mark Edward, The Flood Myths of

Early China, State University of New York Press, Albany, 2006

Linton, Ralph. Archaeology of the Marquesas, Bayard Dominick Expedition Pub. No. 10, Honolulu, 1925

Lodolo, Emanuel, and Avraham, ZviBen, A submerged monolith in the Sicilian Channel: Evidence for Mesolithic human activity, Journal of Archaeological Science: Reports, Vol. 3, Sept. 2015

Metreux, Alfred, Ethnology of Easter Island, B.P. Bishop Museum Bulletin, Honolulu, 1940

Nunn, Patrick, and Reid, Nicholas. Aboriginal Memories of Inundation of the Australian Coast Dating from More than 7000 Years Ago, Australian Geographer, 47:1, p.11-47, 2016

Oliver. How old is it" Gobekli Tepe, The Tepe Telegrams, academia.com, June 22, 2016

Papakura, Ma kereti, 1938. The Old-time Maori, Victor Gollancz Ltd, London.

Patton, Henry, et al. Deglaciation of the Eurasian ice sheet complex, Quaternary Science News, 169, 2017

Phillips, John, ed.. From the Beginning: The Archaeology of the Maori, Penguin Books, Auckland, 1987

Reed, A.W., and Hames, Inez, Myths &Legends of Fiji and Rotuma

Riesenfeld, Alphonse. The Megalithic Culture of Melanesia, E.J. Brill, Leiden, 1950

Routledge, C.S., The Mystery of Easter Island, London, 1919

Schmidt, Klaus. Gobekli Tepe, Southern Turkey. A Preliminary Report on the 1995-1999 Excavations, Paleorient, vol. 26, no. 1, 2000Sellers, Jane. The Death of Gods in Ancient Egypt

Sharp, Andrew. Discovery of the Pacific Islands, Oxford University Press, Oxford, 1960.

Skinner, H.D., Journal of the Polynesian Society, Auckland, Vol. 35, 1926

Spurny, P., et al. Discovery of a new branch of the Taurid meteoroid stream as a real source of potentially hazardous bodies, Astronomy & Astrophysics, May 20, 2017

Stein, M. Aurel. Ruins of Desert Cathay, MacMillan and Co., London, 1912

Stubel, A and Uhle, M., Die Ruinestaette von Tiahuanaca im Hochlande des Alten Peru, Verlag von Karl Hiersemann, Leipzig, 1892

Thomas, Cyrus. A Study of the Manuscript Troano, Washibgton Gov. Printing Office, 1882

Thomson, William, J., Te Pito Te Henua, or Easter Island, Rept. US NAt. Mus. for the year ending June 30, 1889, Washington D.C., 1889

Vaidya, C.V., ed., Mahabharata, Ramchandra Govind & Son, Bombay, 1921

Vogel, J., Indian Serpent Lore or The Nagas in Hindu Legend and Art, Kessinger, 2010

Wilson, John, ed. From The Beginning: The Archaeology of the Maori, Penguin Books, Auckland, 1987

Images

All images by the author, except pages 9, 10. G.W. Smythe, 1832; 19. Mohammad Fadii, Wikipedia Commons; 40. Louis Auguste Marie Le Breton; 63. Arthur Posnanski, 1945; 64. A. Stubel and M. Uhle, 1892; 68. (top and lower right) Edmund Kiss; 84, Urbina, Wikipedia Commons; 98. Mykeljon Winckel, with permission www.elocal.co.nz; 101. Edward Curtis; 106-7. Clockwise from top left: James Wilson, 1797; Frier Library; Byron 1926; 114. Louis Claude de Freycinert, 1819; 118. Willem van de Poll 1950; 122. Beeyan, Wikipedia Commons; 125. John Ware; 126. Tancrède Dumas, 1860; 132. Edward Naville; 164. Teobert Maler, c.1939; 183. University of Brest; 188. Jebrebben, Wikipedia Commons; 190; Kai Hoffman; 194. Ashok666, Wikipedia Commons; 199. Kobayashi Eitaku, 1885; 205. Philipp Franz Siebold; 222. anonymous, 8th century; 262. Athanasius Kircher; 265. Phillipe Bouache; 266. Ibn ben Zara; 272. (top) Zhangzhugang, Wikipewdia Commons; 279. Library of Congress; 283. Walter Fewkes, 1864; 287. annonymous; 296. Thomas Muir; 303. Cintos, Wikipedia Commons; 305. Charles Phelpps Cushing, 1897; 306. Ansel Adams; 372, Irena Stenner.

6:5 ratio 66, 152
360-day year 260

aanu, meaning 280
aanu-nàa-kii 280
Aaru 231
Aboriginal tribal lore 299
Abu Dhabi 103
Abydos 133
Academy of the Gods 193
Açores 182, 184
Adad 240
Adapa 236
adse 37
aerial vehicles 204
Age of Cancer 147
agricultural revolution 143
ahu 79, 81, 104
Ahu Vinapu 79
Airyana Vaejo 328
Akapana 67
akh 140
Akhenaten 208, 307
Aku Shemsu Hor 199, 200, 206, 250, 315
Al Ayin 104
Alfred Metreux 80
Al-Ma'mum 290, 263
Amenhotep III 208
Amma 232
a-nan-na 241
Anasazi, Hisat-Sinom 8, 94, 222,
   255, 282, 309, 310, 360
Anatolia 51
Andean flood myths 28
Andes 74
An-Enlil-da 239
angels 242
Angkor 153, 226, 227
An-Hel 219
Ankaa 151
An-nasz-al-waki 140
Annunage 236
Annunagi 229
Antarctica 264
Antu 224
Anu 92, 224, 237, 244, 245, 259, 334
Anunaki 100, 102, 103, 140,
   229, 232, 241

Anu-Sinom 281, 309
Aotearoa 16, 38, 42
Apis 148
Apkallu 95, 96, 103, 206, 232,
   240, 267, 280, 294
Apkallu figurines 246
Apsû 267
Arabian Peninsula 231, 235
Araucnaia 30
Architects of the Sky 161
ark 110, 208
Armen 245
Armenia 245, 254
Arunachela 192
asar 85
Ashunarsipal 96
Ashurbanipal 236
assumed human form 227
asteroid 8, 20, 257, 301, 304, 322, 326
At-Hyr festival 299
Atitlán 159, 163, 164, 185, 279
Atlantis 32, 156, 263
Atrakhasis 238
Aymara 16, 59, 74, 77
Aztec sacrifices 319

Baal 129
Baalbek 128, 129
Bahrain 233
Balam wisdom keepers 219
Bamboo Books 260
banduddû 96
bãrûs 240
basalt 105, 148, 190, 206
beard 73, 77, 79, 83, 164, 165, 232, 236
Bena 109
Bent Pyramid 152
Berekhat Ram 18
Betatakin 222
Bhogavati 227, 309
Birthplace of the Gods 17, 43, 55
bja throne 312
Black Elk 286
Black Mesa 255
Black Sea 117
blonde hair 41, 45, 101, 114, 115
blue eyes 41, 99, 101, 109, 115, 236
Book of Giants 206, 246

Books of Adam and Eve 243
Breath of God 94
Buache map 264
Buddhist monk meditation 331
Building of Knowledge 241
building periods, Andes 69
Building Texts 142, 143, 199,
   206, 267, 270
Bundaba of Australia 30
Burrangie 113
Buryat 25
Buto 207

Cainan 92
calendar stone 50
Canaanites 130
Canaria 30
Carolina Bays 8, 302, 303
Caroline Islands 108
Carrington Event 326
cart ruts 177, 185
Caspian Sea 117, 245, 254
Castle Hill 43
Caucasian 78, 83, 114, 164, 208
caves 51, 281
caves, submerged 168
Celtic 39
Chaco Canyon 94, 167
Chaldeans 32
Cham people 226
Chewong 30
Chibca 30
Chichen Itzá 164, 165, 219, 274
Chickasaw 30
Chiglit 24
Chilam Balam 163
childbirth, issues 207, 249
China 32
Chinese dragon lords 222
Chinese dynasties 203
Chocktaw 23
Cholulans 78
City of Bali the Giant 192
Clifford Mahooty 277, 287, 353, 354
closing of Great Ages 261
Codex Cortesianus 275
Comet Encke 304, 355
comet, impact 253

comets 5, 8, 30, 252, 300, 305, 323, 330
comets, fear of 28
Cook Islands 100
Copan 165
Cosmas Indicopleustes 241
cranial deformation 116
Critias 185
crop glyphs, circles 321
Crucible of the World 43
Cuba 186
Cuzco 50, 58, 72, 134
Cygnus 89, 138
Czech Republic 18

Daghda Mor 210
Dalai Lama 43
Dashur pyramids 151
David Rankin 38
Davis Island 172
day of the dead 297, 300
deluge 23, 26, 40, 45, 101, 141, 147, 192,
   193, 194, 245, 258, 299, 308
Deneb 138
denser body 243
Deucalion 27
Dhake 109
Dilmun 232, 234
Diocleciano Silva 182
DNA 38, 115, 117
Dogon 232
Dol Hareubang 206
dolmen 111, 206
domestication of animals, crops 248
Dooy 108
Draco 153, 226
dragons 222, 224
Dreamtime 113
Druid 217, 250

earlier industrial civilization 58
Early Primeval Age of the Gods 268
Earth Shaker 52
Earth's rotation 16, 32, 52,
   157, 223, 257, 264
earth turned upside down 327
Easter Island 17, 39, 40, 51, 52,
   74, 79, 84, 114, 172

Easter Island, as group 314
Easter Island flood myth 80
Edfu temple 270
egregoroi 242
Egypt 74
Egyptian King List 156, 201
Ek Balam 219
El Mirador 165
Elohim 243
elongated skulls 116, 181, 206, 243, 250
Emperor Yao 31
Enki 26, 235, 237
Enlil 197, 229, 237, 241, 242
Enmed-uranna 240
Enoch 7, 27, 147, 240-49, 294, 302,
    303, 307, 312, 313, 317, 334,
    349-57, 360-1
Enoch flood account 27
Epic of Gilgamesh 237
Era of Overturning 273
Eridu 235, 237
Eridug 202
Erra Epic 259
Essenes 242

fair skin 39, 41, 73, 79, 99, 101, 110,
    113, 114, 165, 211, 218, 243
Fiji 104, 110, 225
Fiji flood myth 225
Fiji petroglyphs 111
Finns 30
Firebird 52
fire serpents 293
Fire-Water 29
First Mesa 222
First Occasion 146, 200
fish symbolism 198, 232
Flock Hill 43, 46
flood 24-29, 33, 36, 39, 47, 50-54, 62,
    65, 72, 74, 78, 80, 82, 84, 88, 92, 100,
    102, 108, 113, 115, 123, 124, 128, 129,
    133, 147, 153, 158, 163, 164, 191, 193,
    197, 198, 200, 202, 204, 206, 219, 220,
    223, 225, 229, 232, 236, 239, 241,
    248, 250, 255, 259, 267, 268, 273,
    275, 278, 280, 281, 287, 294
Flores, city 162
Flores island 108

Flores island, flood myth 109
flying device 242
flying rock boats 203
flying shields 278
Folklore 31
Followers of Horus 199, 202, 206,
    236, 268
Fourth Sun 25
Frigge 309
Fritz Popp 333
Fu Hsi 29, 164, 197, 223

Gabri-el 244
Gadre-el 244
gamma rays 140
Gandzasar 94
Gar-sag 7, 229, 241, 243, 244, 247, 249
Geb 289
Ggantija 174, 176
giants, tall people 36, 73, 83, 84, 109,
    110, 113, 127, 174, 192, 206, 219, 247
Gilgamesh 206
Giza 115, 143, 150, 152, 176
Giza pyramids 91
Göbekli Tepe 18, 85, 88, 91
god, definition 102
golden rod 72
great celestial inundation 301
great kiva, Chaco Canyon 287
Great Mother Serpent of Heaven 229
Great Pyramid numbers 291
Great Pyramid of Giza 148, 161, 263, 291
Great Salt Lake 24
green eyes 99, 101, 109
Gunung Padang 18, 124

Ha'amonga a Maui 105
haawi 105
Hagar Qim 175
Hanaunakou 79
Harran, Harranu 92
Harris papyrus 327
Hasmonean Tunnel 128
Havai'iki 108, 273
Hawaii 273
Hawaii folklore 211
Hayhuaypanti 73, 140, 211

H-blocks 59, 65, 94
Heart of the Sky 259, 285, 308
heated megaliths 70
Heiltsuk 31
Hera 224
Hiawatha Glacier 302
Hieraconpolis 207
hieroglyphs. 108
high altitude temples 255
Himalaya flood myth 30
Hiti of Samoa 113
Hiva 81, 273
Hiva Oa 81, 104
Hoahoamaitru 274
Homeland of the Primeval
        Ones 199, 267, 268
Homer Cooyama Kykotamovi 273
Hopi 16, 220, 249, 272, 298
Hopi First World 278
Hopi Second World 278
Hopi Third World 255, 278
Hopi prophecy 328
Hor, Horus 130, 199, 207, 268
Horseshoe Canyon 277
Horus of the Horizon 130, 146
Hotòmqam 310
Hotu Matu'a 41, 81, 84, 197
House of Taga 113
H symbol 85, 93
Huaca Prieta 73
huari 73
Hua Shan 223
Huillcacoto 28
husen-gal 242
Hyades cluster 152
Hypogeum of Hal Salflieni 180

ice cores 33
I-groove 65
Indestructibles 139
Inka 58
intention experiment 8, 109, 331, 333
Inventory Stela 146
I-Pu 208
Ipuwer papyrus 327
Isatabu 110
Ishi-no-högen 203
Isis 139, 146, 197, 201, 209

island of creation 108
Island of Fire 269
Island of Primordial Waters 142
Island of the Egg 142
Island of the Sun 143
Island of Trampling 143
Išum 259
Itzá, Itz 162, 164, 165, 279, 300
Itzamna 164, 217, 218
Iwnw, iw nw 141, 142, 202
iw swht 142
iw titi 143
Iyefune 204
Izanagi 164, 197, 225
Izanami 164, 197

Jacques Cousteau 79
James Churchward 274
Japan dynasty 203
Japanese Dragon King 224
Java 123
Jeju island 206
Jericho 127
Jomon 203
Jordan valley 127

kacsina 222
Kaimanawa wall 119
Kainga Nuinui 79
kaka 54
Kalasasaya 60, 67
Kalevala 30
Kaliyuga 195
Kamilaroi flood myth 141
Kapatapuram 192
Karen 30
Karsag Dilmun 233
Kâsdejâ 229
Kásskara 279
katcina 232, 281, 282, 283, 284, 316
katsina, meaning 282
kete 40, 52, 95
Khafre pyramid 130, 144
Khufu pyramid 91, 130
K'iche' 157
K'iche flood myth 25, 158
Kiharoa 36

Kircher map 263
Kiribati 104
Kiri-puwheru 36
Kiwa 41, 112, 197
knobs 134, 191
Kom Ombu 65
Kon-Tiki expedition 79
Korea 111, 205
Kujiki 203, 225
K'uKuulKaan 164, 198, 218
Kumari Kandam 192, 194
Kupe 38
Kura Tawhiti 43, 44, 50
Kyushu, island 203

Lake Atitlán 158
Lake Peten Itzá 162, 298
Lake Taupo 51, 119
Lake Titicaca 28, 54, 61, 101,
      115, 143, 254
Lakota 285
Lamech 243, 250
langi 105
language of light 161
Laos naga kings 226
Last Glacial Maximum 260
Laurentide Ice Sheet 256
Lemuria 78, 193
levitating megaliths 73, 80
LIDAR 162
linguistics 18
Lolos 208
longevity 54, 225, 233, 237,
      238, 244, 250
Long-Tailed Heavenly Climbing Star 301
Lookers 8, 276, 278, 280, 281,
      282, 288, 289, 295, 322
Lords of Anu 241
Loretto Street 71
Louis Agassiz 264
Lua-nu'u 273
Luiseno 30
Lu-Nann 206
Lupakije 78
Lusitannii 213
Luxor 88
Lyra 90, 147

Madagascar 115
Madurai 192
magician 72, 80, 130, 160, 161, 206, 209,
      217, 229, 239, 241, 307, 308
magnetic field 264
magnetic tubes 313
Mahabalipuram 192
Mahabharata 204
Mkereti Papakura 40
Malden Island 104, 108
Malta 175, 176
Mandan 99
Mandan flood myth 100
Manu 27, 197
Manu'a archipelago 108
Maori 35, 38, 101, 113, 119
maps, ancient 263
Marduk 259, 267
Marianas 113
Marotini 44, 45
Marquesas 81, 104, 274
Marrapan 18
Marshall Islands 112
Masau'u 8, 255, 280, 299, 310
massarê 246
mass coronal ejection 32, 51, 281, 326
Mâsu 280
Māui 41, 52, 105
mawi 105
Maya 157
Ma'ya'ab 163
Maya calendars 157
Mayadana 100
Maya Fifth Sun 319
Maya flood myth 24
Maya Fourth World 158
Maya Kaanul dynasty 203, 217, 220, 308
Maya long count calendar 158
Mayan ball court 94
Mechoacanesec 30
Menehune 211
Menfer 172
Menkaure pyramid 91, 144,
      150, 175, 200, 291
Mesopotamia 102, 117, 229
meteor 8, 20, 224, 248, 255, 258,
      301, 304, 326, 334, 355
Meteor Crater 301

meteorite 8, 32, 75, 88, 147, 253, 254, 268, 301, 302, 303, 305, 326
meteorite impacts 326
Metonic Cycle 62
mica 291
mid-Atlantic Ridge 184
Milky Way 50, 137, 139
Miyoi 225
Mnajdra 176
moai 81, 82, 84, 114
Mogao caves 271
Monica Matamua 115
Mordad 299
mosque Ibn Tulum 144
Motu Taiko 101
Mount Ararat 26, 280
Mount Ardis 241
Mount Hermon 244
Mount Karioi 37
Mount Miwa 204
Mount Nisir 238
Mount Tomaros 27
Mu, Muia, Mu'ul 16, 78, 220, 272, 273, 275
Musandam 236
myrrh 243
myth 31

Naacal 274
nàaki, meaning 280
naakwatsim, meaning 280
Naga 225, 226, 229
Naga-Maya 274
Naga, Nages 108
Naga Sadhu 229
Nama 25
nanodiamonds 8, 256, 302
NASA 19, 57, 140, 313
Naupa Huaca 191
Ñaupaq Machula 73
navel of the earth 41, 85, 130, 183, 203
navel stone 50, 72, 80
Nebuchadnezzar 250
Nekhen 207
nemalah 281
nephilâ, nephilim 241, 247, 249, 313
Neterw 7, 199, 200, 202, 236, 242, 267, 269, 289, 309

Net of the World 41
Nevali Cori 93
New Britain 105
New Guinea 105
New Hanover 105
New Ireland 105
newt 217
New Zealand 16, 35, 74, 82, 110
Ngapuhi Maori 38
Ngati Hotu 113, 114
Nikharsag 241
Ninlil 197, 229, 241
Noah 26, 92, 110, 240, 241
Noel Hilliam 38
Nommos 232
November 298, 310
Nuku Hiva 81
Nü Kwa 164, 197, 223
Nurrumbunguttias 313

Oahi Caves 39
oaro 73
obliquity of the ecliptic 61
Oklahoma 125
Older Dryas 11, 16, 278
Oldest Dryas 11, 112, 184, 207
Olijato 323
Ollantaytambo 46, 59, 75
Oraibi 284
Orance Fine 264
orbits 32
Orion 5, 8, 47, 48, 91, 92, 93, 112, 137, 143, 144, 145, 152, 226, 280, 283, 284, 299, 304, 306, 308, 309, 310, 311, 312, 313, 314, 315, 316, 317, 340, 341, 344, 353
Orion and hurricane 308
Osirion 18, 134, 137, 140
Osiris 85, 91, 134, 139, 146, 197, 201, 209, 309
Ouaraa 239

paatuwvota 284
Pachacamac 46, 62
Pacific Ocean inundation 189
paeri-disa 241
Palenque 165, 219

pale skin 45
Palaeolithic cave art 181
Panoias 213
papyrus 1115 235
Papyrus of Nu 269
Paracas 116
Patalaloka 227
Patalpuri 229
Patowahkacheh 220
Patupaiarehe 38
Paul Schliemann 273
Pawnee 260
PEAR experiments 332
Pedro de Quierós 187
People of Anu 100, 232, 239
People of Light 213
People of Mu 78
People of the Serpent 216, 225, 236
Persian Gulf 102, 231, 235
Petra 130
petroleum 32
Philo 32
Phnom Bakheng 226
Pierre Laplante 258
Pillar 43 90, 95
Piri Reis map 265
Pisac 58
Pizzaro 78
Place of Emergence 279
Place of the Satisfied Falcon 153
Place of the Watchers. 284
plasma 32
platinum 302
Plato 32, 156, 185
Pleiades 8, 158, 219, 285, 298,
          299, 300, 304
Pohnpei 189
Po Nagar, empress 226
Popol Vuh 161, 211, 219, 259
Portasar 85, 91
Posnansky, Arthur 60
pralayas 33
Prebble Hill 43
precession of the equinoxes 61,
          88, 91, 131, 184, 260
Puma Punku 15, 58, 65, 152
Puqara 115
Puquina 16
Pyramid of Sekhemkhet 290

pyramid of Unas 311
pyramids, protective devices 290
Pyramid Texts 311
pyramid, underwater 182

Qatar 234
Qorikancha 71, 78, 211
Quetzalcoatl 78, 165, 198, 201, 218, 308
Quillarumyioc 213
Q'uq'umatz 158
Qur'an 240, 320, 356, 362

Ra 201, 225, 269
radiocarbon dating, C-14 86, 124
Raglan 37
Ra-latea 114
Ra-Mu 273
rebuild the former world of
          the gods. 267
re-crystallization of stone 70
Red Ant People 280, 283
red hair 39, 41, 45, 73, 79, 99, 101,
          109, 113, 114, 211, 223
Red Man of Anu 309
relief carvings 93
resonant frequency 181
reversal of the poles 260-63, 327
robe 77
rock of ages 46
Rotuma 110
Rshis 33
Running Star 30

Sabeans 92
sacbe 167
Sacred Birthing Cord of the World 41
Sacred Fish Trap of Outer Space 315
Sacred Nest 43
Sahu 310, 313
Samoan flood myth 26
Sangam 192
Sao Pa 190
Saqqara 66, 148
Saqsayhuaman 15, 58, 70, 153, 213
Sarah Ann Island 172
Saupewa 102

Sawailau cave 112
Sayil 167
Schoyen Tablet 236
Scythian 18
Sea of Reeds 231
sea water lakes 254
secret knowledge 246
Sego Canyon 281
Serapeum. 148
serpent 77
serpent boats 218, 219, 225
serpent cities 219
Seti I 133
Setnau 293
seven circumpolar stars 139
seven sages 73, 81, 95, 103, 198,
        210, 219, 224, 227, 231,
        239, 259, 268, 280, 294
Seventh Haven 242
Shamash 240
shamu 241
Shebtiw 268
Shemhazah 247
Shining Ones 73, 74, 103, 140, 143,
        199, 200, 210, 214, 236
shipwrecked sailor, story 235
Shitkut 25
Shokomish 24
shooting star 52
Shu 201
Shuruppak 237
Silustani 65, 93, 104
Sintra 214
Sioux 30
Sipapuni 255
Sippar 237
Sirius 41, 62, 143, 145, 148, 202, 232
sky-ground dualism 88
Sky-Rock-Boat 203
smoking mirror 293
Snake Clan 220
snake venom 225
snegle-das 29
Sohu, Orion intermediary 311
Solomon Islands 80, 110
Solon 156, 290
Sons of Light 250
Sothic Cycle 202
Sótuknang 8, 16, 285, 308, 319,

        321, 329, 330, 331
Southern Cross 46, 50
Soyal cceremony 310
sphynx 130, 146
Sphynx Temple 136
spring equinox 47, 50, 91, 112, 202
Sri Lanka flood myths 193
Star Fires 51
Star People 285
Starwalkers 40, 46, 83
Stennis 190
Steppes 115
Stonehenge 18
Stone People 45, 82
stones, levitating 59
straight roads 79, 108, 167
St. Vincent Islands 171
sudden civilization 248
Sumba 15
Sumer 234
Sumeria flood myth 236
Sumerian King List 202
Sumerian language 239
Sun 32
Sundaland 123

Tabââ'êt 229
Tahiti 104, 108, 114
Taiowa 285, 310
Taiwan flood myth 190
Takaofo flood myth 26
Talawaitichqua 279
Tamiara 225
Ta Neterw 199, 200, 267, 269
taonga 94
Tapaniu craters 305
Taranaki 35, 39
Tartars 25
Tarxien 39, 180
tattooing 39
Ta-Ur 269
Taurids 8, 299, 301, 303, 304, 305,
        323, 326, 337, 355, 359
Tayi 94
taypikala 74
Te Kahui Tipua 36
Te Kohanga, 45
Tell El Fara'in 207

Tell Idris 240
telluric currents 217, 320
Teokotai Andrew 101
Teotihuacan 291, 308
Te Pitaka 103, 267
Te-Pito-Kura 80
Te Pito O Te Henua 41
Te Piupiu o Nahari Kiokura 103
Thaen 330
The Land That Moved Off 273
thesauros 94
Thor Heyerdahl 79, 114
Thoth, Twt 92, 146, 148, 199,
    240, 263, 268
Three Stones of the Hearth 308
Throne of Supreme Harmony 224
Thuban 145
Tibet 273
tidal waves, tsunami 30, 75,
    166, 176, 254
Tides of Chaos 40
Tikal 159, 165, 219
Timaeus 156
Timaru 36
time of darknes 31
Tinian 104, 113
titi 54, 101
tiwa naku 74
Tiwanaku 28, 39, 55, 58, 62,
    74, 77, 93, 101, 103
Toba 329
Tolkappiyam 192
Tollan 159
Toloa as Orion 308
Tonga 104, 298, 308
Tongareva 100, 102
Tongatapu 104
toxodon 62
T-pillars 89, 92, 93, 97
Transcendental Meditation 333
treaty brides 117
Tree of Knowledge 244
Troano Manuscript 203, 275
Tse-gu-dzih 209
Tsukushi 203
Tuanaki island 172
tufan 26
Tula 293
Tulan 190

Tu Mata Kokiri 45
Tunguska 305, 326
tunupa 45
Tupenaki 102
Tupinamba 30
Turehu 38
Turin Papyrus 156, 201
Tuuwalaqa 285
two-third Apkallu 250
Twt 201, 209

Uannadapa 239
U-annu, Ou-anna 96, 231, 238, 239, 309
Ugrians 25
Ukko 30, 81
Ulutini 111
underwater menhirs 172, 173, 186
Unea 108
Uoke 80
Urashtu 254
Urshu 242, 254
Urukehu 17, 40, 41, 46, 54, 74,
    83, 102, 114, 140, 315
Utah 24
Ute 24
Utnapishtim 26
Uvea 105
Uxmal 6, 160, 161, 165, 274, 307, 308

Valley Temple 136, 146, 200
Vara 110
Vedas 31
Vega 90, 140, 152
Venerables of Memfer 201
Venus 62, 157
Viet Nam 226
Viet Nam flood myth 330
Viking knarr 116
Vimanna 204
Viracocha 73, 77, 83, 103,
    143, 197, 198, 210
Vishnu 197, 313
Visvakarma 204
Visvamitra 313
Viti Levu 225
vitrified stonework 326
vizier 209

Voguls 29

Wairaka River 36
Waitaha 17, 36, 38, 39, 41,
      45, 88, 268, 314
Waitangi Ki Roto 39
Wales 38
Walpi 222
Watchers 7, 8, 92, 229, 232, 240, 241,
      242, 243, 244, 245, 246, 247,
      248, 249, 250, 269, 280, 284,
      285, 287, 288, 294, 295, 307,
      313, 316, 317, 320, 321, 322,
      323, 331, 333, 350, 354, 357
Watchers, renegade 247
Wayna Picchu 191
Weld-Blundell Prism 202
Westcar Papyrus 146
White-skinned People of Ra 114
Wichita 23, 249
Wilburton coal mine 127
winter solstice 47, 50, 91, 151
Wise Old Ones 73
Wise Ones 209, 241
Wúwutcim 298, 310

xiuhcoatl 293

Yaghan 249
Yakima 24
Yasawa cave 111
Yehudi Ibn Ben Zara map 267
Yih King 29
Yim, Yima 72, 110, 293
Yonaguni 191
Younger Dryas 7, 11, 20, 21, 31, 33, 43,
      73, 88, 102, 112, 123, 124, 140,
      142, 143, 167, 173, 176, 177,
      178, 200, 206, 225, 235, 239,
      256, 257, 267, 270, 275, 278,
      289, 302, 305, 329, 351, 352
yryn 246
Yucatan 159, 166
Yuga 226
Yunggalya 30

Zarathustra 210
Zep Tepi 142, 256, 269
Zeus 224
Zin-Suddu 26, 237, 241
Zuni 8, 94, 249, 277, 281, 283,
      285, 288, 316, 351
Zuni language 281

OTHER WORKS BY FREDDY SILVA

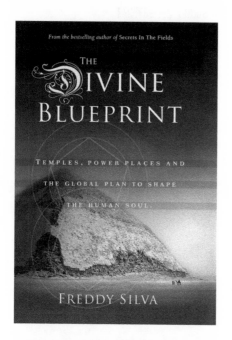

An in-depth account of the origin of temples, and the role they play in shaping consciousness. An indespensible sourcebook for lovers of sacred places and ancient systems of knowledge.

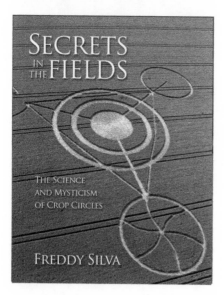

Published in five languages, this critically-acclaimed international bestseller is still the only full investigation into this most mysterious and misundestood phenomenon. One hint: people are not behind it.

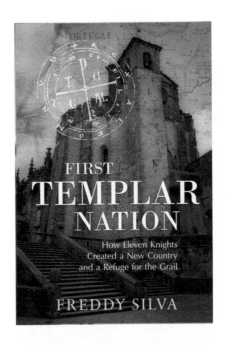
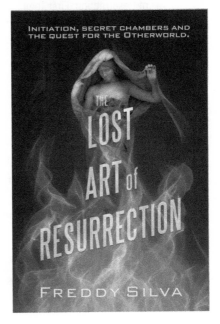

Freddy Silva is a best-selling author, and one of the world's leading researchers of ancient civilizations and systems of knowledge, and the interaction between temples and consciousness.

His published works include The Divine Blueprint; The Lost Art of Resurrection; First Templar Nation; Secrets in the Fields; and Chartres Cathedral: the Missing or Heretic Guide. He has produced a plethora of documentaries, and is also a fine art photographer.

Described as "perhaps the best metaphysical speaker," he has lectured worldwide for nearly two decades, with notable keynote presentations at the International Science and Consciousness Conference, and the International Society For The Study Of Subtle Energies & Energy Medicine, in addition to numerous appearances on GAIA TV and radio shows.

He leads sell-out tours to sacred sites in England, Scotland, France, Portugal, Malta, Yucatan, Guatemala, Peru and Egypt.

When not living inside an airplane, he is in England, New Zealand or America.

ancient wisdom for modern lives™

www.invisibletemple.com

CPSIA information can be obtained
at www.ICGtesting.com
Printed in the USA
FSHW021248300419
57715FS

9 780578 482195